J24

F/F

61443

TRAVEL, TRADE AND POWER IN THE ATLANTIC 1765–1884

CAMDEN MISCELLANY
Volume XXXV

TRAVEL, TRADE AND POWER IN THE ATLANTIC 1765–1884

CAMDEN MISCELLANY
Volume XXXV

CAMDEN FIFTH SERIES
Volume 19

CAMBRIDGE
UNIVERSITY PRESS

For the Royal Historical Society
University College London, Queen Street, London WC1 6BT
2002

Published by the Press Syndicate of the University of Cambridge
The Edinburgh Building, Cambridge CB2 2RU, United Kingdom
40 West 20th Street, New York, NY 10011–4211, USA
477 Williamstown Road, Port Melbourne, VIC 3207, Australia

First published 2002

A catalogue record for this book is available from the British Library

Library of Congress Cataloging-in-Publication Data applied for

ISBN 0 521 82312 9 hardback

SUBSCRIPTIONS. The serial publications of the Royal Historical Society, *Royal Historical Society Transactions* (ISSN 0080–4401) and Camden Fifth Series (ISSN 0960–1163), volumes may be purchased together on annual subscription. The 2002 subscription price (which includes postage but not VAT is £63 (US$102 in the USA, Canada and Mexico) and includes Camden Fifth Series, volumes 19, 20 and 21 (published in July and December) and Transactions Sixth Series, volume 12 (published in December). Japanese prices are available from Kinokuniya Company Ltd, P.O. Box 55, Chitose, Tokyo 156, Japan. EU subscribers (outside the UK) who are not registered for VAT should add VAT at their country's rate. VAT registered subscribers should provide their VAT registration number. Prices include delivery by air.

Subscription orders, which must be accompanied by payment, may be sent to a bookseller, subscription agent or direct to the publisher: Cambridge University Press, The Edinburgh Building, Shaftesbury Road, Cambridge CB2 2RU, UK; or in the USA, Canada and Mexico; Cambridge University Press, Journals Fulfillment Department, 110 Midland Avenue, Port Chester, NY 10573–4930, USA.

SINGLE VOLUMES AND BACK VOLUMES. A list of Royal Historical Society volumes available from Cambridge University Press may be obtained from the Humanities Marketing Department at the address above.

Cover illustration: 'Scene of Port Royal and Kingston, Jamaica', by James Hakewill. © National Maritime Museum, London.

Printed and bound in the United Kingdom by Butler & Tanner Ltd, Frome and London

CONTENTS

CONTENTS

I

THE LETTERS OF SIMON TAYLOR OF JAMAICA TO CHALONER ARCEDEKNE, 1765–1775

Edited by Betty Wood
with the assistance of T.R. Clayton and W.A. Speck

CONTENTS

ACKNOWLEDGEMENTS

The editor is deeply indebted to Dr T.R. Clayton and Professor W.A. Speck for their invaluable assistance in the preparation of this volume. Dr Clayton helped with the transcription of several of Taylor's letters and both he and Professor Speck provided the editor with material for inclusion in the footnotes to this text.

EDITORIAL NOTE

This collection includes all the letters written by Simon Taylor to Chaloner Arcedekne and his brother-in-law, Benjamin Cowell, between 1765 and 1775. It does not include the periodic enumeration and description of the enslaved people on Golden Grove Estate and Batchelors Hall Pen. The letters are published in their entirety and no attempt has been made to 'modernize' Taylor's often-inconsistent spelling. Wherever appropriate, however, punctuation marks and paragraph breaks have been inserted in the text to assist the reader.

INTRODUCTION

Between 1765 and 1801 Simon Taylor, one of the most important landowners in Jamaica, wrote regularly to Chaloner Arcedekne, an absentee proprietor who lived in Heveningham Hall in Suffolk. There is a gap in the correspondence between 1775 and 1781, so that the first decade's letters can be presented, as they are here, on their own.

According to Richard Sheridan, one of the leading modern historians of the eighteenth-century Caribbean, Taylor 'may have exercised greater influence in Jamaica, and for a longer period, than any other individual'.[1] Born in Jamaica in 1740, but educated like Arcedekne at Eton, Taylor served as a member of the Jamaican Assembly continuously from 1768 to 1781 and again from 1784 to 1810. Chaloner Arcedekne, born about 1743, also entered politics, being a Member of Parliament for Wallingford from 1780 to 1784 and for Westbury from 1784 to 1786. He was associated with Lord Shelburne and voted with the opposition in the years 1780 to 1782. He supported the Rockingham and Shelburne ministries, but opposed the Fox–North coalition, voting against Fox's India Bill. He was returned in 1784 as a Pittite, but left politics two years later for reasons that can only be surmised. Perhaps he was sensitive about the growing commitment to the abolition of the slave trade among his associates. For as owner of Golden Grove plantation on Jamaica he was one of the more prominent slave-owning MPs. Taylor looked after his interests on the island as his letters reveal. Whilst writing to him concerning the management of his Jamaican estates, Taylor frequently commented to him about the current state of domestic politics in the island and issues involving the imperial connection with Britain. These detailed and often highly picturesque letters form without question the most important collection of private correspondence appertaining to the political history of Jamaica in the period they cover. They clearly confirm Sheridan's insistence on the significance of Simon Taylor, though he was unaware of their existence. They have come to light in recent years among the Heveningham Hall manuscripts now preserved in Cambridge University Library where they are catalogued as the Vanneck papers.

The editors are grateful to the Trustees of the Heveningham Hall manuscripts for granting permission to transcribe and publish these letters.

[1] Richard Sheridan, 'Simon Taylor, sugar tycoon of Jamaica, 1740–1813', *Agricultural History*, 45 (1971), p. 286.

THE LETTERS

1. To Chaloner Arcedekne, Kingston, 26 March 1765

I hope this will find you safe arrived in England after a speedy and agreeable passage and that you will find all your friends is well in your part of the World [*torn*]. Came from Leeward last Sunday Evening & have not as yett had an Opportunity of seeing your Mother & aunt[1] but am inform'd they are very well. This serves also to acquaint you that have sent to Messrs. Hilton & Biscoe[2] p. this Convoy an Invoice of the Weights of fifty Hdds.[3] of Sugar ship'd on Board the *Morant* Capt. Raffles[4] and fifty Hdds. ship'd on board the *Brilliant* Capt. Millar. I have also sent them the Bills of Lading you will be pleased to order the necessary Insurance on them. Mr. Graham[5] and I have advised them also.

[1] Elizabeth Kearsey (or Kersey) (d. 1778) was a widow when, probably in the mid-1730s, Andrew Arcedekne hired her as his housekeeper. Andrew Arcedekne, who was born in 1681, was admitted to Gray's Inn in 1710 but there is no record of his having been called to the Bar. If, as seems likely, he was a Roman Catholic this would have been an avenue denied him. In 1716 Arcedekne emigrated to Jamaica where he patented land in St Thomas in the East. In the same year he became the Island's Attorney-General, a post he held for a year. Arcedekne's political career began in 1718 when he was elected as a Member of the House of Assembly for St Catherine. He finally relinquished his seat in the Assembly in 1757. Two children were born to Andrew Arcedekne and Elizabeth Kersey, Anne, born in 1738 or 1739, and Chaloner, born in 1743 or 1744. Elizabeth remained in Jamaica after Andrew's death in 1763 until her own death fifteen years later. Vere Langford Oliver, *CARIBBEANA; Being Miscellaneous Papers Relating to the History, Genealogy, Topography and Antiquities of the British West Indies*, 6 vols (London, 1910–), II, p. 175; 'English commemorative sculpture in Jamaica', *The Jamaican Historical Review*, 9 (1972), p. 46; Land Patents, XVI, fo. 98, Island Record Office, Spanish Town. The aunt referred to here was Elizabeth Kearsey's widowed sister, Frances Harris. The two women shared a house in Spanish Town.

[2] A merchant house based in London.

[3] A common abbreviation for a hogshead, which was a barrel or cask used for the transportation of liquids, such as rum, and dry goods, such as sugar. A hogshead might contain anywhere from 50 to 140 gallons. There were similar variations in the weight of the dry goods that could be packed into any particular hogshead. This was why bills of lading, which were necessary for securing insurance from English-based firms as well as for ascertaining the value of particular cargoes, always included the volume or weight of every hogshead transported.

[4] Benjamin Raffles was the father of Sir Thomas Stamford Raffles. The latter was born on the merchant ship *Ann*, captained by his father, off Port Morant, on 7 July 1781. In June 1797 the death was reported in Falmouth, Jamaica, of 'Captain Raffles of the ship *Sebastina*'. Oliver, *CARIBBEANA*, IV, p. 270.

[5] Robert Graham (1735–1797) was born in Scotland and emigrated to Jamaica in 1752. Despite his youth he was appointed Receiver General of the island as the deputy for his

You will I hope by my next receive the [*torn*] hdds. ship'd on board the *Kingston* Capt. Ellis on which you will be pleased to order also the necessary Insurance in case You Chuse to Insure all they are all three very good ships. I am inform'd Ellis seems unwilling to send up to the Rivers Mouth for Sugars but will endeavor to oblige all the ships that gett any Sugars to fetch them as I apprehend it will be more for your advantage to ship them at the Rivers mouth than at Port Morant as it saves Carriage.

I have heard several times lately from Mr. Kelly.[6] He acquaints me every thing is very well at Golden Grove.[7] The weather very good and that he is making Sugar very fast & very good. Intend going up the beginning of the next Month and seeing how every thing is and will acquaint you.

Mr. Kelly writes me you ordered him to Ship two hundred casks which you may depend shall be done by the very first ships. I am in hopes from the favourableness of the Weather for your Estate that we I mean your Attorneys will be able with the greatest Conveniency to your affairs to assist you [*torn*] for this will certainly be a heavy year on you for you for Expences in the prosecuting the grand Matter which I really think there cannot be the least doubt of your happily accomplishing.

Mr. Laing[8] is at present at Leeward at his Estate. He sent you the Negroes I think twelve Women.

---

absentee relation, Thomas Graham, a post he held until 1764. In 1763 Graham married Simon Taylor's sister Anne, and either in 1764 or 1765 the brothers-in-law formed a mercantile business that lasted until 1770 or 1771 when Graham returned to Scotland. Between 1766 and 1768 Graham sat as a Member of the House of Assembly for St David's. In 1770 or 1771 he inherited the estate of Ardoch, in Scotland, from his kinsman Nicol Bontine and changed his name to Robert Bontine of Ardoch. Back in Scotland he secured something of a reputation as a poet; his most famous work being entitled 'Doughty Deeds'. Graham corresponded regularly with Simon Taylor and also forged a close relationship with Simon's brother, Sir John Taylor (see note 109 below). Towards the end of his life, Graham was elected as a Member of Parliament for Stirlingshire (1795–1796). For more details see R.B. Cunninghame Graham, *Doughty Deeds: An Account of the Life of Robert Graham of Gartmore, Poet and Politician, 1735–1797 Drawn from his Letter-Books and Correspondence* (London, 1925).

[6] John Kelly, who also owned a jobbing gang, was the main overseer on Golden Grove. He held this position until the 1780s. The will of a John Kelly was proved in Jamaica in 1805, but it cannot be conclusively established that this was the same John Kelly. Oliver, *CARIBBEANA*, III, p. 117.

[7] The sugar plantation in St Thomas in the East that, despite the doubts raised about his legitimacy, Chaloner finally inherited from his father in the mid-1760s.

[8] Malcolm Laing (1718–1781) was born in Britain and educated at Trinity College, Cambridge. The exact date of his emigration to Jamaica is uncertain but once there he established himself as a successful merchant. In the early 1770s Laing sat as a Member of the Assembly for St Thomas in the Vale. Oliver, *CARIBBEANA*, II, p. 176; III, p. 577.

Your Cosin Robin Arcedekne[9] is at present very ill with the Gout in his Stomach.

The Assembly met the nineteenth Agreeable to the proclamation. Our Friend young Mr. Price[10] was Unanimously Chosen Speaker and demanded the priviledges which the Governor[11] Granted. The Assembly next desired that he should cancel the decree as they could not proceed to business while under such a Stigma on which he has prorogued it to the sixteen of September I apprehend to gett advices from Britain to know how he shall proceed. The Country is all this time without taxes. Where it will End God knows. The Number for the Governor was four against thirty two Exclusive of the Speaker. Will send you p. Miller the proceedings [torn]. I was not at the Contest myself and came from North side the day after the prorogation.

All your friends here are very well and ardently wish you Success. You may depend on my doing every thing that I think can be conducive to Your Interest which I will take as much care of as my own you may be assured will Render you every Service in my power [torn]. Sincerest wishes for your prosperity and success and beg our Compliments to your Brother and Sister[12] and shall at all times be excessive proud to serve you and them to the utmost of our Abilities and if any thing occurs that you can profitably want from hence be kind enough to acquaint me.

---

[9] It is unclear whether Robin Arcedekne had been born in Jamaica or had emigrated to the island.

[10] Charles Price Jr, who succeeded his father as second Baronet, was one of the most influential figures in mid-eighteenth-century Jamaican politics. For many years he represented St Catherine's in the Assembly and in the 1760s served as its Speaker. He was centrally involved in the 'privilege controversy' of the mid 1760s. (See note 11 below.) The Price family was listed among Jamaica's largest landowners and their main plantation, Worthy Park, was one of the island's premier sugar estates. For more details see Michael Craton, *A Jamaican Plantation: The History of Worthy Park, 1670–1970* (London, 1970).

[11] William Henry Lyttelton (1724–1808), subsequently Baron Lyttelton of Frankley, was educated at Eton College and St Mary's Hall, Oxford and called to the Bar at the Middle Temple in 1744. Between 1744 and 1755 he served as the Member of Parliament for Bewdley in Worcestershire. He was appointed Governor of South Carolina in 1755, a post he held until his relocation to Jamaica in 1762. Lyttelton served in Jamaica until 1766, when he was named as Britain's ambassador to Portugal. He was the author of *An Historical Account of the Constitution of Jamaica* (1764). For more details of the 'privilege controversy' referred to by Taylor, see George Metcalf, *Royal Government and Political Conflict in Jamaica, 1729–1783* (London, 1965), pp. 160–167; T.R. Clayton, 'Sophistry, security and socio-political struggles in the American Revolution; or, why Jamaica did not rebel', *The Historical Journal*, 29 (1986), pp. 319–344; and Jack P. Greene, 'The Jamaican privilege controversy, 1764–1766: an episode in the process of constitutional definition in the early modern British Empire', *Journal of Imperial and Commonwealth History*, 22 (1994), pp. 16–52.

[12] Malcolm Cowell was married to Chaloner Arcedekne's sister, Anne.

2. To Chaloner Arcedekne, Yallahs Bay, 16 April 1765

On my way down to Town I mett Mr. Allpress,[13] Who acquaints me that Capt. Millar is coming up this afternoon to sail tomorrow which occasions this Short letter to you to acquaint you have sent a Bill of Lading of 50 Hdds. of Sugar to Messrs. Hilton & Biscoe shipt on Board the *Friendship* Capt. Thompson who will sail the 22 Instant. I will certainly send you the Invoice p. the very first Vessell that sails not having time to make it now.

Was up at Golden Grove for three days and have the pleasure to acquaint you, you are making as fine Sugars there as it is possible for Sugar to be and you will make a very fine Crop in case the dry weather continues. You have not lost a Mule or Steer yet since the Crop began and every thing in my opinion is in very good order and your Negroes happy.

Shall send you 50 Hdds. p. the *America* Capt. Lauchlan McLean and 50 p. the *Kingston* Capt. Ellis. You will give your orders to Messrs. Hilton & Biscoe in case you chuse to Insure them.

I desired Mr. Kelly to Distill two puncheons[14] of Rum for your own use and to ship them on Board Capt. Raffles shall also send you a Turtle by him and one by Capt. Thompson and shall make an agreement with all the Capts. that gett sugar from me to carry you home one as they are allways an agreeable present to make to your Friends. Am in hopes we shall send you home a great deal of Sugar and whenever gett some more Negroes hope your Estate will Nett you as much as your most sanguine Expectations can amount to at least it shall not be my fault if it does not.

Reed was with me a few days ago about O'Brian's Negroes.[15] I shall be at Spanish Town on Wednesday and see your Mother and Mr. Laing about it and will acquaint you the Result as also every thing we can find reguarding it in the office and the people at Windward will follow your directions.

---

[13] A highly successful planter, Samuel Allpress sat in the Jamaican Assembly as one of the members for Vere. Subsequently he would secure a seat on the island's Royal Council. Jamaican Assembly (1765) Public Record Office, Kew, CO 140/44, ff. nn.; Jamaican Assembly, Minutes, CO 140/46, p. 265.

[14] A puncheon was a cask, or barrel, that was used for the shipping of both liquids and dry goods. Usually it contained eighty-four gallons.

[15] No further information about either person has been located.

3. To Chaloner Arcedekne, Kingston, 18 April 1765

Inclosed one Copy of 2 off mine to you one of March 26 and the other of 14 Instant and Copy of the Invoices of 50 Hdds. of Sugar on the *Morant* Capt. Benjamin Raffles 50 Hdds. on Board the *Brilliant* Frigate Capt. Millar 50 Hdds. on board the *Friendship* Capt. Thomson. I had not time to send you weights of those on board the *Friendship* by Millar but have sent them now Annex'd. I sincerely wish them safe to hand and that they will fetch a good price I am sure they would here.

[Notes that he has delivered the turtles mentioned in the previous letter to Thompson and Raffles.]

Have not been able yett to go to Spanish Town on Acct. of the Rainy weather we have had these three days past which am afraid will putt you back at Golden Grove. When was there Mr. Kelly told me that the Crop would be very late being able to keep only one mill about by which he was afraid in Case the Rains fell heavily in May he would destroy some of the Stock in taking it off and reduce the Rest low which would putt us back with the Materials for the Still House and advised the Hiring of some Negroes so as to keep all the Coppers about. I was of the same opinion myself especially as there are a great many Canes still to cut and in case we are very late this year it will infallibly occasion a very great loss in the plant or make us very late in putting about in the year 1767 which may make a very great difference both in the quantity and quality of your goods. I am sure for my own part have been a very great sufferer by being allways backward with my plants and Oxford Estate having turned out so well for many years past is in my opinion owing to nothing but their being allways very early but did not chuse to do it without consulting Mr. Laing who agreed that we should hire some Negroes. I wrote Mr. Kelly accordingly to hire some if he could gett any and at the most moderate price. I assure were your Estate my own I would do it for am certain it will be an advantage to you.

I have engaged fifty more Hdds. to send you on Board the *Susanna* Capt. John Baird who loads at Manchioneal and have sent up a stock of Herrings (Rice for your new Negroes) and several little things which altho they were not instantly wanted yett would be in the course of a Month or 5 weeks on board her as she carried them up without Freight.

I wrote Mr. Laing has sent you up twelve women but find he sent up twenty four. They were well looking but about 4 of them a little weak but will do very well. You could not have got the like from any of the factors here under £52 apiece.

Mr. Kelly sent us down about 14 days ago ten Hdds. of your Sugar

which sold here for 33/- p. ct.[16] I apprehend also that Sugar will rise
with you as we hear here the Crops in the Windward Islands are fallen
very short and I am certain this Island falls from 15 to 20,000 Hdds.
short indeed if was to say more believe I should be right. All your
friends here are well and desire to be remembered to you. Mr. Graham
likewise sends you a few lines Inclosed. I have not heard whether Kelly
has as yett ship'd the two puncheons of Rum on Board Raffles but am
pretty sure he will not forgett it.

PS Mr. Kelly when was up askt for some Ale as he says your Friends
who sometimes come like it. I have therefore sent him a Cask but told
him could make no Custom of it as it was a thing Seldom Askt but I
am hopefull it will not be thrown away as he is usually very industrious
and draws [*illegible*]. Am persuaded the Crop will please you.

4. To Chaloner Arcedekne, Lyssons,[17] 23 April 1765

I wrote you a long letter a few days ago by the Vessell that carries this
which hope you will receive safe. I am extreamly sorry to inform you
of the Dismal flood of Rain we had in this parish Thursday night last
the 16 Inst. which has play'd the Devil with almost all the Estates in
this parish. The following Acct. I had from Mr. Kelly the day before
yesterday from Golden Grove. That five of the Bridges a Wain the
flood gate little House were carried away and the Dam very much hurt
the whole Estate was under water except 2 Hills next to Stokes Hall,[18]
2 Steers all the small stock on the Estate drown'd, a White man of
Carters[19] was near drownding asleep below stairs that they miss 2
Mules & 7 head of Cattle from the Pen on the Estate. He had not
heard from Batchelors Hall[20] when he wrote. All the salt provisions on

---

[16] A common abbreviation for a hundredweight, or 120 pounds.

[17] Lyssons Plantation, in St Thomas in the East, belonged to Simon Taylor. It was
named for Nicholas Lycence, one of Jamaica's earliest settlers. Frank Cundall, *Historic
Jamaica* (London, 1913), p. 250.

[18] Stokes Hall, an estate of just over 800 acres, was in St Thomas in the East. B.W.
Higman, *Jamaica Surveyed: Plantation Maps and Plans of the Eighteenth and Nineteenth Centuries*,
designed by Dennis Ranston (Jamaica: Institute of Jamaica Publications, 1988), pp. 231–
232.

[19] Ambrose Carter, who owned a plantation in St Thomas in the East.

[20] Chaloner Arcedekne owned Batchelors Hall, a cattle pen in St Thomas in the East
that supplied Golden Grove. For a discussion of Jamaican pens and pen-keepers see
Verene A. Shepherd, 'Pens and pen-keepers in a plantation society: aspects of Jamaican
social and economic history, 1740–1845', (unpublished Ph.D. dissertation, University of
Cambridge, 1988).

the Estate spoilt the same is the Case with Every Estate in the River the Roads are allmost impassable.

I am so far in my way to your Estate and will give you a more distinct acct. by Raffles who sails in a few days. Tom Cussans[21] has lost £500 of Cattle from Winchester pen[22] there are three large River Courses through Rossell every water Work in the parish has mett with some damadge great part of Amity Hall[23] Guttering is carried away & Stanton's Estate allmost ruin'd. It is inconceivable what devastations it has made. All my Cane pieces on my Lower Estate were under water. Scott[24] has suffred greatly indeed there is not an Estate in the parish but is very much injured. It is a very great loss to you for you had the appearance a fortnight ago of making the largest Crop that was made from one Estate in this Island. It was not so violent at Yallahs but they had a great Rain there.

Your Overseer Kelly has a Touch of the Fever. I shall be up in the Morning and will do every thing in my power to gett your Mill about again as soon as possible for fear we should have such another Salution in May. All your Staves Copperwood & Empty Puncheons on the Estate were carried away & the Trash Houses very much hurt.

I heard tonight from your Mother who was very well as also your Aunt.

[*Notes that he has* 'sent on board with this a very fine young Turtle'.]

5. To Chaloner Arcedekne, Lyssons, 30 April 1765

I wrote you the 23 p. Thompson acquainting you of a prodigious flood of Rain that has been in this parish 16 Instant. The following is a copy of what I wrote

[*Repeats account in previous letter.*]

Since the above was at Golden Grove and find the flood has been very

[21] Thomas Cussans, the son of Thomas and Mary Cussans, was born in Jamaica in 1739. He matriculated at Trinity College, Oxford, in the spring of 1755. Upon his return to Jamaica he soon became one of the island's most eminent sugar planters. Oliver, *CARIBBEANA*, III, p. 265.

[22] Cussans inherited Winchester Pen, in St Thomas in the East, from his father; *ibid.* Chaloner Arcedekne bought it from him in 1773. (See Letter 61).

[23] The Cussans family owned Amity Hall plantation, in the valley of Plantain Garden River. Higman, *Jamaica Surveyed*, pp. 233–234.

[24] George Scott, the owner of Hordley Plantation. He married the daughter of John Cussans, Thomas Cussans's brother. Oliver, *CARIBBEANA*, III, p. 265.

great there. We were well advanced in the Crop or it would have hurt you excessively. What is very extraordinary there was very little Rain with the flood at your Estate and it Rained so hard at Port Morant and Morant Bay as to sink all the Ships boats in less than two hours. It has tore up the Canes from their Roots and in some places heaped up the Trash three or four feet high over the Standing Canes and on many places where they had been cutt carried it intirely off. The Timber for the Still house was carried away most part and is now lying in yours and Duckingfield Hall[25] Cane pieces. It is Surprising you did not meet with more loss of Cattle and Negroes the latter being obliged to gett upon the Tops of their houses to save themselves. I think that Duckingfield Hall has suffred more than you for being Lower down. Your Trash lodged in their Canes whereas on the other side Holland[26] lies so low Amity Hall Trash went clear over their Canes.

We have thank God gott the Mill about again and are making tolerable good Sugar. I was obliged to hire 30 Negroes to gett the Canes off for by Lying tore up by their Roots they will not by and by make Rum. I would indeed if possible have hired more Negroes to keep all the Coppers flush but could not gett them to hire for the Canes are so entangled they take double the quantity of Cutters than if they were standing. I hope after all we shall make a pretty good Crop.

The Smallpox is among your Negroes 7 or 8 lying now down. They are at Lewis's penn and very good care is taken of them and the pock is favourable so hope they will do well. You buried a very fine fellow a Driver named Humphrey within a few days ago. If you think proper intend purchasing 24 Men about Christmas for it will be impossible to keep up the Estate at such great Crops as it ought to make without it except by pushing your Negroes too much and killing them which am sure will not be for your advantage.

I have sent to Hilton and Biscoe a bill of Lading for 2 Puncheons of Rum shipt on Board Raffles. They did not gauge them at the Estate so can not tell you the Quantity of Gallons, distilled on purpose for yourself marked CA N1 & 2 which wish safe to your hands.

[*Notes that he has sent a turtle to Hilton and Biscoe.*]

I forgott to tell you, you lost only one Steer at Batchelors Hall your

---

[25] Duckenfield Hall consisted of roughly 2,400 acres. The estate, which was owned by the absentee planter Nathaniel Phillips, was located in the valley of Plantain Garden River, across from Holland and Golden Grove.

[26] At this time John Kennion owned Holland Plantation. Simon Taylor purchased the estate from him in 1771. (See Letter 54).

Carpenter that built the Roofs of your Curing and Boiling House was [*illegible*].

6. To Chaloner Arcedekne, Kingston, 15 June 1765

Inclosed send you the Copys of my several letters to you of 10 April 23 & 30 do. and hope to hear soon from you that those several ships are safe arrived and that the quality of the Goods answers your Expectation. The reason you did not hear since that time from me is because I was obliged to go down to Savannah La Mar to take care of Mr. Richards[27] Estates. Mr. Graham wrote to Messrs. Hilton and Biscoe and sent them the Bills of Loading of fifty Hhds. of Sugar on the *America* Captain Lauchlan Mclean. I herewith send you the invoice of them. He will certainly sail before the 25 of next Month. To save the double Insurance Mr. Laing also acquaints me he sent you advice to insure fifty Hhds. on board the *Charming Nancy* Captain William Foster who could only take 20 on board. Inclosed is also an Invoice of the Goods on board him. I likewise send you inclosed the Invoice of fifty Hhds. on board the *Kingston* Capt. Ellis both which ships sail the 1 of next Month at furthest. We shall also putt on board the *Susanna* Capt. Baird about thirty Hhds. I hope she will be able to sail before the 25 of next Month. We shall not be able to send you any Rum by her for the flood and Rainy weather has hurt your Estate Exceedingly in so much that upwards of two hundred and twenty acres which were to cut when the flood came on have made no more than fifty Hhds. of Sugar and your Crop is now done having made about three hundred and seventy Hhds.

It was excessively lucky you had so much made when the flood came on. All your neighbours are much worse off than you. I assure you it has not been owing to any neglect but by reasons which is out of our power to prevent. You have a very good appearance of a Crop next year and we will endeavour to put about as soon as we did this to gett it off.

Your Sugars that came to this Markett sold very well at 33 & 33.6.9 & 34/-. I hope they will turn out as well with you. I would advise you not to be in a hurry in selling them for this Island falls 20000 Hhds. short this year. In St Marys where they had the greatest appearance of a Crop the Rainy weather prevents their going about and Zachary

---

[27] Probably George Richards, a merchant and planter, who was brother-in-law to Thomas and John Cussans. J.H. Lawrence-Archer, *Monumental Inscriptions of the British West Indies from the Earliest Date* (London, 1875), p. 97.

Bayly[28] told me two or three days ago that he Expected to have made at his Estate there 1000 Hhds. but would now compound for 600.

I have paid Mr. Laing for the 24 Women you had from him so he will not draw on you as you Expected.

Your Old Correspondent John Burke[29] has sent out a power of Attorney to Reisset, Jeffray & Yelloly[30] against your Father's Estate and you for a Ballance due by the Old Gentleman and by you for two pipes[31] of Wine. I apprehend he will call on you. If they call on me will pay it to prevent their being able to say any ill natured thing which they may be very inclinable to do.

I had a very long talk two days ago with Robert Arcedekne[32] who advised me in reguard about Obrians Negroes which was to putt the proof on Reed in every particular and not to let the Marshall Come on the Estate which I told Kelly off. He told me if Dawkins[33] brought an ejectment for the Land at the Riversmouth to plead the Law for quieting possession which is a Law of this Country for that he himself can prove 20 odd years possession and also told me he did not believe they could ever recover it from you.

There was a Gentleman from Ireland one Squire Burke[34] came over

---

[28] Zachary Bayly (1721–1769) was one of the richest and most influential planter-politicians in mid-eighteenth century Jamaica. His landholdings included around 1,100 acres in St Thomas in the East and 300 acres in St Andrew Parish. At his death he also owned six plantations in St Mary Parish (Trinity, Tryal, Bayly's Vale, Brimmer, Nonsuch, and Unity) as well as roughly 3,000 acres in pens. He bequeathed Nonsuch and Unity plantations to his nephew, Bryan Edwards. Oliver, *CARIBBEANA*, III, pp. 42, 378.

[29] One of the Irish branch of the family still contesting the validity of Andrew Arcedekne's will.

[30] Merchants based in Kingston.

[31] A measure of liquid capacity equal to approximately 126 gallons.

[32] Robert Arcedekne was Chaloner Arcedekne's cousin. In the mid-1760s he sat in the House of Assembly as one of the members for St Ann. Arcedekne's main residence was in St Mary's Parish, where he owned a plantation worked by 212 slaves. He also held another property in St Catherine's that was worked by six slaves. When he died in 1768 he left bequests to his brother Nicholas and his sister Margaret Foster, both of whom lived in Ireland; the bulk of his estate went to his cousin, Nicholas Bourke. Jamaican Assembly (1765) Public Record Office, Kew, CO 140/44, ff. nn.; Inventory of Robert Arcedekne, 1 June 1769, 8 June 1769, Inventories, Island Record Office, Spanish Town, XLVI (1769), fos 216–218, 224; Will of Robert Arcedekne, 8 December 1768. Island Record Office, Spanish Town, Wills, XXXVIII, fo. 39.

[33] Born in 1728, Henry Dawkins was a member of one of Jamaica's oldest immigrant families. His grandfather, who had settled there in the 1660s, established the basis of the family's fortune. By the time he was in his thirties, Henry Dawkins was one of the island's wealthiest planters. He owned seven sugar plantations and, together with his two younger brothers, claimed around 25,000 acres of land in the Parishes of Clarendon, Vere, St Catherine, and St Thomas in the Vale. Dawkins subsequently settled in England. Oliver, *CARIBBEANA*, III, pp. 42, 95; Higman, *Jamaica Surveyed*, pp. 92–95; Richard B. Sheridan, 'The wealth of Jamaica in the eighteenth century', *The Economic History Review*, 2nd series, 18 (1965), pp. 292–311.

[34] It is unclear precisely which member of the Bourke family Taylor was referring to here.

about three weeks ago as some people say to take possession of Golden Grove. I caution'd Kelly about him but since that time they say he came to take possession of Robin's Estate.[35] They have since smuggled him out of the Island I am inform'd.

Manning your Brothers Overseer at the Swamps died about 8 days ago. Watson who was your Bookkeeper at GG succeeds him.[36] Jack Hibbert[37] went up with Kelly two days ago there. I am told they make near 100 Hhds. there this year which am very glad of for nothing can give me greater pleasure than hearing of the prosperity of you or any of your relations.

I saw your Mother and Aunt two days ago who were both very well.

A Boy that lived with Sir Henry Moore[38] came over here and told me and others that he mett your Man Ned who it seems is an old acquaintance of his in London and says he saw you very well for which am extreamly glad.

I hope you had an agreeable passage as well as so speedy a one and that you and all your affairs go on as you would wish. God grant you success.

Neither McGlashen,[39] nor the old woman of the Ferry have spoken to me since you went off but their claim on Fontanbell in all probability they will forgett.[40] I saw Dr. Gregory[41] two days ago who desired his compliments to you. All your Friends here are well and should be very glad to hear from you.

My Sister [42] lost her little girl about six weeks ago.

---

[35] Robin Arcedekne.

[36] Swamps Plantation was in St David's. Inventory of Andrew Arcedekne of Parish St Cat. Esq., Inventories of Estates, Island Record Office, Spanish Town, XLV (1765), fos 58–63. No further information has been located about either Manning or Watson.

[37] Jack, or John, Hibbert was the younger brother of the eminently successful merchant, Thomas Hibbert (see note 53 below). He emigrated to Jamaica from England in 1754.

[38] Sir Henry Moore (1713–1769), a native of Jamaica, served as the island's Governor between 1755 and 1762. In 1762 he was appointed to the Governorship of New York, a post he filled until his death seven years later. For more details see Sidney Lee (ed.), *Dictionary of National Biography* (London, 1909), XII, pp. 801–802.

[39] Probably Duncan Charles MacGlashen, who owned the Rhine Plantation in St Thomas in the East. In 1774 he also purchased Blackheath Plantation in Westmoreland. Oliver, *CARIBBEANA*, III, pp. 296–297. The 'old woman' referred to by Taylor was a Mrs Wyllie. (See note 119 below.)

[40] It is unclear precisely what claim Taylor was referring to here.

[41] Matthew Gregory (1693–1779) was elected to the Jamaican House of Assembly as one of the Members for St James in 1718 and 1722. In 1726 he sat as a Member for St Ann. In addition to his activities as a medical practitioner, he also pursued a career as a planter on his Swansey estate. In 1765 he was involved in assessing the inventory of Andrew Arcedekne's Jamaican property. Lawrence-Archer, *Monumental Inscriptions*, p. 46; Inventories of Estates, Island Record Office, Spanish Town, XLV (1765), fos 58–63.

[42] His sister Ann, who had married Robert Graham in 1763.

7. To Chaloner Arcedekne, Kingston, 11 July 1765

Inclosed is a Copy of mine to you p. the *Lady Juliana* who I hope is safe arrived.

I a few days ago had a letter from my Friend Mr. John Hope[43] who acquaints me he saw you very well. Mr. Laing being very desirous to see how your Rum would turn out in England told me he had given orders to Kelly to ship you thirty Puncheons on Board the *Susanna* Capt. Baird who is now lying at Manchioneal. I apprehend he has wrote you p. this same conveyance and concerning it he also told me he had wrote to you as the Crop fell short off all our Expectations he had sent you the Bill of parcells of the 24 Negroe Women I wrote you by the *Juliana* I had paid for you if it was convenient to pay it to his Correspondent Chandler.[44]

I had made the agreement with Beans & Cuthbert[45] who Mr. Laing bought the Negroes to pay them by a discount of my money they had in their Hands but Mr. Laing chose this way as he has wrote to you about it. I was afraid it would push you but he on that told me he had wrote you to pay it over to Chandler provided you could spare it without putting yourself to any inconvenience.

I shall go up in about fourteen [days] to Windward to see your Estate and my own we have had very rainy weather there for some time past.

We are in the midst of politicks here the Governor having dissolved the Assembly. McCullock[46] went to your Mother with Ben White[47] and told her they intended putting you up as a Candidate for Spanish Town and went so far as to advertise you standing. A few days after they went again to her and told her old Dr. Brodbelt[48] intended standing who would deliver up his seat in your favour whenever you came over on which she wrote to me. I went over and she told me as they had advertised you as a candidate. She thought you ought to stand as it would look silly that if you had only five or six Votes it was

---

[43] A member of Jamaica's eminent Hope family.

[44] It is unclear whether Chandler was a Jamaican or a British-based correspondent of Laing's.

[45] A partnership based in Kingston that was heavily involved in the slave, sugar, and rum trades.

[46] A lawyer based in Kingston.

[47] No further information about White has been located, except that at this time he was not listed as being a member of either the Assembly or the Royal Council.

[48] Dr Francis Rigby Brodbelt (1746–1795) was a medical practitioner in Spanish Town. In 1795 he was awarded the silver medal of the Medical Society of London. Edward Brathwaite, *The Development of Creole Society in Jamaica, 1770–1820* (Oxford, 1978), p. 247; Oliver, *CARIBBEANA*, III (supplement), p. 38; Frank Cundall, *Lady Nugent's Journal* (London, 1934), p. lx.

sufficient and she should be content. On which I told her I would do every thing I could and went out and wrote letters to all the Freeholders and sent them about the next morning. I found old Brodbelt had told every one he intended to resign as soon as ever you came to the Country in your favour which was the thing that carried his Election. There were also Candidates for Spanish Town Mr. Price Mr. Long[49] & James Lewis[50] who was the Clerk of the Assembly against them Mr. Harvie[51] Mr. Brodbelt and Councillor Jones.[52] Messrs. Price Harvie and Brodbelt were Returned and inclosed is a letter from your Mother who will I apprehend give you the whole story.

There was also a very Strong opposition in this Town. Old Hibbert[53] Charles Hall[54] and David Milner[55] opposed Tom French,[56] Jasper Hall[57] and me. Poor Tom French lost it after a great struggle Jasper Hall had 102, I 99, Old Hibbert 92 Dr. Milner 82 Tom French 79 & Charles Hall 64 votes. Hibbert is so angry to find himself the lowest of the list

[49] Edward Long (1734–1813) was born in England but his family had owned lands in Jamaica since the 1660s. Following his father's death in 1757, Long moved to Jamaica and the next year he married Mary Ballard Beckford, the wealthy heiress of Thomas Beckford and the widow of John Palmer. Long's brother Robert gave him a share in the family estate of Longville in Clarendon Parish. Long had influential family connections in London. His uncle was Beeston Long (1710–1785), the founder of Long, Drake and Long, one of the premier sugar factors in mid-eighteenth century London. Oliver, *CARIBBEANA*, III, p. 54. (See note 186 below.) Edward Long served as a judge in the Vice-Admiralty Court until 1769 when he was forced to return to England because of ill-health. He is best known for his *History of Jamaica*, 3 vols (London, 1774).

[50] During the 1760s and 1770s Lewis sat in the Assembly as one of the Members for St Catherine's. He died in England in 1800 and was buried at Westbury-on-Trym, near Clifton. Oliver, *CARIBBEANA*, II, p. 309.

[51] Probably William Harvie, of St Dorothy, who subsequently sat as a Member of the Assembly for St Dorothy. Lawrence-Archer, *Monumental Inscriptions*, p. 339.

[52] It is unclear to whom Taylor was referring because at this date no one named Jones was listed as a being a member of the Royal Council.

[53] Thomas Hibbert (1710–1780) was the son of Robert Hibbert, a Manchester merchant, and his wife Margaret. He emigrated to Jamaica in 1734, where he quickly established himself as one of the wealthiest merchants in Kingston. In 1760 Hibbert purchased Agualta Vale, an estate of some 3,000 acres. He was elected as a Member of the Assembly for the Parishes of St George and Portland, and during the mid-1750s he filled the position of Speaker. Oliver, *CARIBBEANA*, IV, pp. 193, 194, 325.

[54] Little is known of Hall, other than that he was an eminent planter whose estates included a pen at Mount Prospect, Liguanea. Possibly he was a kinsman of Jasper Hall (see note 57 below). Charles Hall died at Mount Prospect in 1795. *Ibid.*, I, p. 320.

[55] Milner owned Wheelersfield, a sugar plantation in St Thomas in the East.

[56] During the 1760s and early 1770s French sat as a Member of the Assembly for Kingston. His landholdings included 640 acres in St Andrew Parish, which he used mainly as a pen. Records of St. Andrew Parish, 1754; Public Record Office, Kew, CO 137/28, pp. 191–196.

[57] Between 1764 and 1770 Jasper Hall sat as a Member of the Assembly for Kingston. He also served as the Receiver General of Jamaica and at the time of his death, in 1778, was the Speaker of Assembly. Oliver, *CARIBBEANA*, V, p. 326.

that out of pique he talks of resigning as soon as the Assembly meets.

Zachary Bailly promised to return 20 Members but has been very much disappointed. There is a Contest in almost all the parishes but the Old members will gain the Majority. Old Price[58] stands for St. Mary's Bayly says he will spend one of his Estates to oppose him talks of quitting his seat to be in the Assembly himself he is much affronted at the inclosed advertisement.[59] I hope to God there may be some way found out to settle matters when the new Assembly meets. The Governor himself goes about pretending to show Instructions he has received from home which approve of his conduct tho people hear apprehend he has other orders or he would not be so anxious to exclude the old members to gett an Assembly to his mind. Numberless are the papers printed both for and against the Conduct of the Assembly.

All your Friends are well & desire to be kindly remembered to you.

[*Notes that he will send Arcedekne a turtle* 'by McLean who sails in a few days'.]

Mr. Graham & my Sister are at Northside.

8. To Chaloner Arcedekne, Kingston, 23 July 1765

Inclosed is a Copy of mine to you p. the *Jamaica* Capt. Hamilton.

Mr. Bullock[60] shewed me a Letter from you to him by which I find you are well which gives me infinite Pleasure Inclosed I send you the Power which you wanted from Dr. Gregory & Foster March. I was obliged to go up to Amity Hall with it to witness it having only got in the Twentieth. I hope you will suffer no manner of inconvenience by not having it before. Mr. Bullock did not receive your Letter untill the Seventeenth Instant so it was out of my Power to dispatch it soon. I hope you meet with all the Success you can wish. I am sorry to see by a Letter from Mr. Way[61] they have got the Attorney General from you.

I was at your Estate where everything is very well & great preparations making to build the Still house, great part of the Timber is ready & Carter[62] is very busy quarriing Stones. I do not believe it will be entirely

---

[58] Charles Price, Sr, the owner of Worthy Park and one of Jamaica's wealthiest sugar planters. (See note 10 above.)

[59] The advertisement is not included in the bundle of correspondence for 1765.

[60] Edward Bullock, a Kingston lawyer. Oliver, *CARIBBEANA*, III, pp. 38, 54.

[61] It has proved impossible to identify Way.

[62] Apparently a self-employed white artisan who was frequently employed by Taylor.

finished for the next Crop but will be able to get the Fermenting part
up & distill in the old house but you may depend if possible will get
the whole done.

Your Rum falls also short by the flood having destroyed all the
Liquor in the Cisterns of the Stillhouse & the Molasses given to the
Norrward man from whom you had your Staves. I am in hopes we
shall have a few puncheons more as your Negroes are Holling & Mr.
Kelly intends planting with the Tops very early so he will grind of the
Canes for Rum. He also intends as the Land he is holling is excessive
rich to cut the Plants while very young & bring them in next year as
Rattoons. I do apprehend you will have a great deal more & much
better Sugar from them You have a very great quantity of Canes to
cut this ensuing year & provided we meet with no accident will make
a very large Crop.

I hope you will be kind enough to let us buy 24 good able Negro
men about Christmas. Am certain they will pay for themselves by the
greater quantity of Sugar you will make for if we get them shall be
almost able to keep both the Mills about all night & one all day & be
able to take off the Crop in a reasonable time. It was excessive lucky
that your Mill went about so early last year for if you had not put
about untill the middle of January as the other Estates in your
neighbourhood did you would have been a hundred & odd Hhds.
shorter than you are now. Am very creditably informed Amity Hall
where there are upwards of 420 Negroes will not ship upwards of 280
hhds. & Duckingfield Hall not so much. Capt. McLean by whom this
goes has only received 49 Hdds. instead of the fifty he signed Bills of
Lading for, by some mistake of the Wharfinger at Portmorant 1 hhd.
for Mclean was shipt. on board Capt. Forster & tho' I have repeatedly
spoken to the different Masters of the Droggers who use Port Morant
have not been able to get it down for him.

I have since the above been favoured with yours p. Mr. James
Pinnock[63] of 23d May. I have not yet got the Watches from him as
soon as get them will carry them to your Mother & also a Letter for
her & the other for Mr. Thomas.[64]

I by this Conveyance send Messrs. Hilton & Biscoe Bills of Lading
for 28 hhds. of Sugar & nine puncheons of Rum shipt on board the
Susanna Capt. Baird who sails tomorrow. I but this very instant received
them so cannot send the Weights of the Sugar or the Gage of the Rum
but you will certainly receive it by my next which will be shortly.

[63] A member of the prestigious sugar planting family. (See note 86 below.)
[64] It has proved impossible to identify Thomas.

9. To Chaloner Arcedekne, Kingston, 2 September 1765

Annex'd is a Copy of my last to you of 23 July p. the *America* Capt. Lauchlan McLean since which was last week favoured with yours of 10 & 20 June acquainting me you had receiv'd mine of 26 March and that you had allready made Insurance on the Sugars on board the *Brilliant* and *Morant.*

I received a letter from Messrs. Hilton and Biscoe that Thompson was arrived about ten days before I received yours. I intirely agree with you in making insurance it being so low and not worth running the Risk of £1000 or 1500 for the sake of 3 p. ct.

I have a real pleasure in acquainting you your Overseer Kelly continues his diligence and Industry and behaves extreamly well indeed I see no one whatsoever goes on better.

You will see by the weights that the Sugars gone home to you averages above 1600 Nett after deducting the Fare of the Hhds. and they were all made of Philadelphia staves which are reckoned to be the best here and were purchased out of a Brigg that came to Mr. Richards[65] to Manchioneal; Amity Hall Duckingfield Hall & Wheelersfield.[66] Hdds. and Puncheons were made of the same Lumber and there was none of this Country staves mixed with them.

You may depend will gett in a large quantity of Ground Provisions on your Estate as I know the great service of it in case of high winds or hurricanes. I am very sure you have a large quantity in having long ago recommended it to Mr. Kelly and he told me he had both putt in himself and made all the Negroes putt in a large quantity. I am extreamly glad that you seem to intend putting on some more Negroes and in Expectation of them we have allready made a plantain walk to have plenty whenever they come for nothing encourages Negroes more than great plenty of provisions and it is an utter impossibility for negroes to work without a Belly full.

You will find there are 297 Hdds. shipt you and 11 Puncheons of Rum and we had at one time very great Expectations of Shipping you near 200 More and should have done it but for the flood for you had 330 Hdds. made and 200 Acres of Cane to Cutt when it came on which made only 48 Hdds. the receiver in the Boiling house every Six hours had notwithstanding all the [*illegible*] between 4 and 5 inches of Mudd.

I saw Carter five or six days ago. He told me the foundation of the Cattle Mill was done and three or four Courses above You may depend will do every thing in my power to gett it Compleated if possible before Christmas. You may depend that the Fermenting part which is the most wanted shall be done altho the weather has been very bad and

[65] George Richards.
[66] Wheelersfield was the plantation owned by David Milner.

still continues so We have had more Rain since the Month of May last than we had 3 years before.

I do not apprehend that your Antagonists will go on with their Appeal as they have not filed it yett. I hope you have Received your Power of Attorney which I sent you from Dr. Gregory and March.[67] I hope you will go on with your usual prudence in reguard to the Compromising it so that they may not be able to make any manner of handle of any thing you do as they may want to intrap you. I am sure you have had very great experience of their deceit and dark designs and if they apprehended they had any Chance they would not desire a Compromise but strip you of every thing.

The Assembly was dissolved in July last and a new one Called the 13 of August. They also were not able to proceed to business. Our Friend young Charles Price was again Chose Speaker who when presented to the Governor would not demand the usual Privilidges on which the assembly was adjourned for a day, and the day they mett the Governor sent the Provost Marshall ordering the Attendance of the House who accordingly waited on him and he again demanded of the Speaker if he would make application for the usual privilidges and on his Refusal the Assembly was dissolved. Inclosed I send you Copys of the Speeches the Governor made. It really is very unhappy that the Assembly and Governor do not agree the dammed Original Breach being for so infamous a thing.

I hope we shall have a more favourable Administration for America than the last has been for if they go on in the same Methods as the last Ministry did we shall be utterly ruin'd. The Stamp Master is not yett arrived tho daily expected. There is law come out and in favour of the Publick officers.

Your Cousin Bourke[68] absolutely declares he will never intermeddle in any Publick affairs. The Chief Justice had his Quictus sent him about a fortnight ago. Bourke on that sent the Governor his Commission as an

---

[67] Matthew Gregory (see note 41 above) and Foster March. Andrew Arcedekne had appointed them as his executors. Inventory of Andrew Arcedekne of Parish of St Cat. Esq., Inventories of Estates, Island Record Office, Spanish Town, XLV (1765), fos 58–63.

[68] Nicholas Bourke, who emigrated to Jamaica around 1740, was also Robert Arcedekne's cousin. In 1748 he married Elizabeth, the daughter of Thomas Fearon (see note 145 below). Bourke's political career began in 1754 when he was elected to the Assembly as a Member for Kingston, a seat he held until 1756. In 1757, 1768, and 1770 he was elected one of the Members for Clarendon, and in 1761 for Portland. Bourke was closely involved in the constitutional crisis of the mid-1760s, and almost certainly was the author of *The Privileges of the Island of Jamaica Vindicated: With an Impartial Narrative of the Late Dispute between the Governor and House of Representatives, Upon the Case of Mr. Olyphant, A Member of that House* (Jamaica, 1765, London, repr. 1766). In 1770 Bourke served briefly as the Speaker of the Assembly. When he died the following year his estate, which was valued at around £34,000, included two sugar plantations, two cattle pens, a house in Spanish Town, and 497 slaves. Oliver, *CARIBBEANA*, III, p. 261; V, pp. 260, 261; Greene, 'The Jamaican privilege controversy', pp. 31–32.

Assistant Judge, as did also Prevost[69] May[70] and Will James Hall.[71] Beach[72] is now Chief Justice & Iredell [73] Will Harvey[74] Seymour Gwyn[75] and Zachary Bayly Judges in the Room of those who have resigned. I likewise hear the Governor has issued two Noli Prosequi on two Different Actions brought by Samuel Jebb[76] against Douglas[77] the Collector.

As you say it is very dangerous for young fellows to think of Matrimony when Hansons case is so very recent and fresh in our memories, but still people will not take any warning. There is now an Action of the very same Nature depending between young Archbould[78] Mr. Price's Nephew and one Miss Newton.[79] It was my opinion a very bad sentence on Hanson and may open the way to a great many iniquitous Suits. As I am writing of marriage I cannot forgett to acquaint you there is a Report that on friday last a Licence was taken out for our friend Rose Price[80] and one Miss Patrick[81] a Writing Master's Daughter at Spanish [Town] and without a

[69] In the mid 1760s and early 1770s Prevost sat in the Assembly as one of the Members for St Dorothy. Jamaican Assembly (1765), Public Record Office, Kew, CO 140/44, ff. nn.

[70] Rose Herring May (1736/37–1791), an eminent planter, was a long-serving member of Jamaica's Royal Council. His local political responsibilities included acting as the Custos of Vere and Clarendon Parishes. Oliver, *CARIBBEANA*, I, p. 261; Lawrence-Archer, *Monumental Inscriptions*, p. 103. Originally a Custos Rotulorum was a magistrate placed in charge of the petty sessions records of an English county. In Jamaica the office was more akin to that of the Lord Lieutenant of a county. The Custos was the head of the magistracy in his parish and all new Justices of the Peace were appointed either on his recommendation or with his consent.

[71] During the 1760s and early 1770s Hall sat in the Assembly as one of the Members for St Andrew. Jamaican Assembly (1765), Public Record Office, Kew, CO 140/44, ff. nn. Jamaican Assembly, Minutes, April 1770, *ibid.*, 140/46, 265.

[72] Thomas Beach, who died in 1774. Oliver, *CARIBBEANA*, V, p. 277.

[73] In 1766 Thomas Iredell became Attorney General of Jamaica. He was also appointed to the Royal Council and served as its President between 1775 and his death, at the age of seventy-six, in 1796. He was described by Governor Lyttelton as 'a Gentleman of very fair Character and Good Fortune in this Island'. Governor Lyttelton to LsT 12 September 1765, Public Record Office, Kew, CO 137/33.

[74] Harvie, whose main residence was in St Dorothy, subsequently sat in the House of Assembly as one of the Members for St Elizabeth. Lawrence-Archer, *Monumental Inscriptions*, p. 339.

[75] It has proved impossible to locate any further information about Gwyn.

[76] It has proved impossible to locate any further information about Jebb.

[77] In 1767 Governor Elletson sought to remove James Charles Sholto Douglas from his post as Collector of Customs for Jamaica on the grounds of maladmininstration. (See Letter 13.)

[78] Probably Henry Archbould (1742–1805), who owned Constant Spring Plantation in St Andrew. By 1770 he had moved to England, where he died in 1805 and was buried in Bath. Oliver, *CARIBBEANA*, II, pp. 230, 338, 340.

[79] No further information has been discovered about Miss Newton.

[80] Charles Price's brother. In the 1760s he sat as a member of the Assembly for St Thomas in the Vale. Jamaican Assembly (1765) Public Record Office, Kew, CO 140/44, ff. nn. In 1788 he succeeded his brother as third and last baronet. Lawrence-Archer, *Monumental Inscriptions*, p. 65.

[81] No further information has been discovered about Miss Patrick.

Shilling but that Rose sett out the next day for the Red Hills with his Black wife. I should be very sorry he should play the fool so egrigiously as there has been some coolness between his father and him for some time past about other matters and in all probability this will so much incense the Old man that he will disinherit him for when he takes a thing into his head he is absolutely inflexible.

Your friend Capt. Lee[82] is very well. I told him you expected he would write to you and that you desired me to give him a Puncheon of Rum. He desired I would get one distilled for him which I promised him to do.

In reguard to Tradesmen on the Estate will be very easy to find a place to putt them untill they can Run up a Comfortable House for themselves & your Bookkeepers for it has no occasion to be very large and then they will be able you build you a House for yourself according to your own liking for you can gett Carpenter and Mason Negroes to hire just as well as the Tradesmen can and if they can make money still it certainly will be worth your while to save yourself.

I am now building a Sett of works in that Manner and would have built your Still House so too had it not been from the Scarcity of Negroes and the difficulty of getting the Stones an absolute impossibility of getting it done before Christmas. You have occasion to send only a Carpenter and a Mason as they will save difficiency. It will be a very small expence to you. It would be the best way to write to any Acquaintance in Scotland to send them from thence.

There has been three Bills in Chancery filed since you went in Which you are a party one by Chovett vs. Furnell[83] in order to gett a Sale of some land in St. Elizabeth this is an Amicable one and is of no manner of Consequence the other by Furnell & next Friend vs. Gregory & March this is on Acct. of Maverley's[84] Estate for which your father was a Trustee. I spoke to Bob Lee[85] who is the Sollicitor on the other side and he has promised to Lend us his bill to take a Copy of it to putt in the Answer. I do not apprehend it can hurt you at all as Pinnock[86] and Chovett came to a Compromise and

---

[82] *Ibid.*

[83] Possibly Peter Furnell, who in the mid-1750s was recorded as owning land in St Andrew. Records of St Andrew Parish 1754, CO 137/28, pp. 191–196.

[84] Possibly John Maverly, who in 1754 was recorded as being a landowner in St Andrew. Records of St Andrew Parish, 1754, Public Record Office, Kew, CO 137/28, pp. 191–196

[85] Robert Cooper Lee was one of mid-eighteenth-century Jamaica's most eminent lawyers. By 1782 he had moved to London, where he died in the early 1790s. His will was proved in 1794. Oliver, *CARIBBEANA*, II, p. 276; V, p. 220.

[86] Probably Philip Pinnock, the Speaker of the Jamaica House of Assembly from 1774 to 1778 and Custos of St Andrew Parish. Pinnock owned over 2,500 acres of land in St Andrew and was one of Jamaica's most eminent sugar planters. He squandered most of the wealth he made from sugar and was virtually a pauper when he died. *Ibid.*, p. 155; Lawrence-Archer, *Monumental Inscriptions*, p. 239.

Paplay[87] has been in the possession of the Estate ever since Mrs. Chovetts death and whatever is recovered Paplay must certainly in my Opinion be accountable for. The other is filed by Buckly[88] and you are a party by your Father having been a guardian to Miss Stoaks.[89] This also I do not apprehend can affect you but will fall upon Stokes Hall.

Our Mutual Friend Malcolm Laing has a Brother named Chisholm who was Master of a Ship. He has been making Interest among his Friends to gett him another Ship & to be station'd at Morant Bay. I have agreed to take 1/8. He desir'd me to acquaint you he would be very glad if you would also hold a part and also your Brother in Law. He has also wrote to your Friend Mr. Perrin[90] to be concerned. She would always be able to bring out all our Provisions and perhaps some other Freight which would Load her out and she could allways be dispatch'd to sail from hence the beginning of May. I do not think you can lose any thing by it and our friend Malcolm would esteem it a very particular act of Friendship. I know Capt. Chisholm he having this year loaded at Savanna La Mar and Mr. Laing Chartred him out but as his present owners have no acquaintance nor Consignment from this Island they are not fond of Sending out a Ship on a Venture for freight.

Your Mother sent me 4 days ago a small cask of Old Rum for you and desired me if possible to putt it on board the Man of Warr which I have done Capt. Gower having been kind enough to take it on board. I likewise had the pleasure of seeing both her and your Aunt on Saturday who were both very well. Mr. Graham & his wife are both very well and desire their compliments to you and sincerely wish you may be able to settle all your Affairs to your Satisfaction. By yours of 2[d] June I find you have received the acct. of the flood that happned at Windward.

I had a letter from Mr. Kelly the day before yesterday who writes me the Estate is in very good order but he wants me up so intend setting out on the 6th instant. You have no Negroes run away but a Raskal named Philip who run away the night of the flood. Mr. Kelly tells me he is a very old Offender so if you approve of it whenever we catch him we will bring him to a triall. He commonly stays for a year or two at a time out when he takes it in his head to walk and therefore I think he should be made an Example of.

[87] Probably George Paplay, a merchant-planter who in 1764 and 1765 was a Member of the Assembly for St Thomas in the East. Richard B. Sheridan, *Sugar and Slavery: An Economic History of the British West Indies, 1623–1775* (Aylesbury, 1974), p. 294.

[88] No further information has been discovered about Buckly.

[89] It is unclear which Miss Stoaks (or Stokes) Taylor was referring to.

[90] William Perrin, the owner of Retrieve Plantation in St Andrew Parish.

10. To Chaloner Arcedekne, Kingston, 11 November 1765

The inclosed is a copy of my last to you p. the *Africa* Man of war since which have been deprived of any from you altho the day before yesterday I Received a Letter from Messrs. Hilton and Biscoe and am sorry to find neither Ellis nor the *Charming Nancy* are arrived tho I hope long before this they will. Also the *America* and *Susanna* are come to port. They complain of the sugars and say there is near 1/3 foot in every Hhd. occasioned by their being shipt too green. It I must own surprises me much for of the Sugars from your Estate that were sold her we had not the least complaint from any one and did not reduce one single Cask. I apprehend that as you will chuse that the first sugars of your ensuing crop should go home we will keep them six weeks on the Rangers before we send them down to be shipt and then I hope it will not be in their powers to complain as in that time they must be thoroughly cured.

The weather at your Estate has been very bad from the beginning of Sept. untill now. I was there about the 10 of that month and never saw an Estate in finer order. I recommended much to Mr. Kelly to putt in a good store of Ground provisions but he told me without more Negroes it really was impossible to putt in much considering the many different things he was obliged to do together having about twenty of the best hands constantly carrying lime and sand and filling the wains with Stones etc.

I went also to Batchelors Hall penn and assure you the old Man there surprised me much with quantity of fine pasture you have there with so few Negroes. Mr. Kelly told me you had ordered all the Cows to be sold off but seventy as you did not apprehend you had pastures for more there. There was a few old Mares which he told me you have ordered to be sold. They are very little worth and we can gett no one to buy them. In all there were 217 Head of Cattle etc of all sorts. I told them not to sell any Cattle except it might be an old Cow that is past breeding untill they gott to the length of 300 Head of Horned Cattle and then to sell only some of those marked AGA for I apprehend there is a full sufficiency of Pasture to keep 150 Breeding cows there provided there should be 10 or fifteen more New Negroes putt on and then you will find that that place will ease the Contingencies of your Estate greatly as you will allways be able when you have that number not only to supply Golden Grove but also to sell 1200 or 1500£ worth annually from thence.

We had a Brig arrived here some time about three or four weeks ago from Guinea and as you were in excessive want of Negroes I thought you never could have a better opportunity of getting them than out of her especially as it was in our power to give you a Choice &

to let you have all Men. I consulted your Mother and Mr. Laing about it and on letting them know in what manner I should manage it they redely came in to my sentiments by which you will in reality have a twelve Months credit for them without interest and the work of them during that time. The great thing besides that induced me to do it also was that directly on their going to the Estate they should sett about putting in a very large Coco piece by which in case of a Hurricane you will next year have provisions on the Estate to supply every Negroe you have even if there should not be a plantain tree left standing. And the next Consideration was that of having hands to Ram the Cisterns of the Stillhouse which would prevent drawing any of the Seasoned hands off from the keeping the Plantation in order and at any Rate before the Crop could be taken off to any advantage and in time you would be obliged to putt on some more. I am confident they will be the means of making more sugar this ensuing Crop than will amount to the prime cost of them. The way I took to get you the best on board was, I desired four different Gentlemen and also Kelly to go on board and chuse each of them as many fine Men as they each could and on calling them together for to chuse the best out of them. Am very confident there could not have been a better choice made out of any Ship that has been these three years in this Island. The terms of payment which I made with the Capt. for ourselves were one third down on the sailing of the Vessell, one third in the Month of Aprill, and one third in Bills at 8 months sight on the sailing of the Ship which being the easiest payment shall include yours in that payment which will be payable as the Ship will sail in about the beginning of January & in all probability have 2 Months passage home they will not become due before October or November & in case we had bought Negroes from any one whatsoever they must have been paid for in May & interest after a Month. I really assure you I never bought Negroes on so advantageous terms for myself & you may depend on my doing every thing for you with as great a regard for your Interest as I would for my own.

Your Mother and Aunt whom I had the pleasure of seeing about three weeks ago were very well. Tom Cussans came over a little while ago he told me you was very well and that people in England seem'd to look on your relations there in the same light as they did here and that your affair would be as happily settled there as it was here. For my part I think it impossible to go against you. I hope November will be as favourable to you in England as it was in Jamaica.

I am just now inform'd that all the Vessels your Sugar went by are arrived you will then have received by the *America* the power from March & Gregory to you.

Sam Allpress was this moment with me he desires his Compliments to you and received your letter. He says will answer it soon. The Governor has not yett called an Assembly. We hear from N. America nothing but resignations of the Stamp Officers and declarations that they will not submit to it. God knows how it will end.

Mr. & Mrs. Graham have been both ill but are now gott better and gone to the North side for a change of Air. You must have heard that at the Windward Islands they have burnt all the Stamps.

N B You will begin your Crop at Golden Grove about the 15 of next month. I saw Carter 3 days ago. He told me he expected the Walls of your Fermenting part of your Still House were finished the 8 and Stevens[91] the Carpenter was with him. He tells me every thing is framed and he will go forward, that the Estate will not wait a moment on this.

11. To Chaloner Arcedekne, Kingston, 9 December 1765

Annexed is my last to you of 11 November by way of Bristol since which have been favoured with yours of 8th August and am sorry to find that Messrs. Hilton and Biscoe have sold your sugars at such a low price. The Sugars we sold here were not better in quality and sold from 33/- 33/6 and 34/- p. Ct., which makes a very great difference. I think they might have waited especially as Sugars were on the rise.

We about a fortnight ago had an Alarm of a Rebellion in St. Marys when Matt. Byndloss[92] and my Overseer were both murdered by a parcell of new Negroes belonging to the Overseer of Whitehall and Ballards Valley, who about two o' Clock in the morning on the 25 of last November sat fire to the Trash houses of Whitehall on which the Overseer ran down there in his Shirt to endeavour to putt out the fire and ordered a Boy to bring him his horse. Matt. Byndloss and Ballard Beckfords[93] widow who were in the House gott both up on the alarm of fire soon as which fourteen or 15 Coromantees broke into the House and killed Byndloss. Mrs. Beckford saved herself by running down to the works from whence she gott among the canes and was carried to Nonsuch[94] where Bayly happened to be.

My Overseer gott up on the Alarm of fire and went to Whitehall just after the Negroes had gott the Arms that were in the House and

[91] It seems probable that Stevens was a self-employed carpenter.

[92] Matthew Byndloss was born in 1721, the son of Paulniss and Catherine Byndloss. During the mid-1750s he served as a Member of the Assembly for St Ann. Oliver, *CARIBBEANA*, III, pp. 261, 263.

[93] Ballard Beckford (1709–1764) was a member of the wealthy and influential Beckford family. He held extensive estates – in 1750 they totaled just over 6,000 acres – principally in St Mary's Parish.

[94] Zachary Bayly owned Nonsuch Plantation.

in alighting from his Horse received a large parcell of Shott from one of the rebells in his side and fell dead on the ground. They then cutt off his Head and marched down to the Valley as the Overseer and White people were going unarmed to help extinguish the fire but the rebells making a great noise singing their Warr song in the Intervall made them imagine it was a rebellion and that it was best to return back to the House for arms which they did and in a few minutes after were attackt there. The Negroes endeavoured to sett fire to the House but could not and having their head man killed went to the trash Houses and sett them on fire and march'd back to Whitehall and from there into the woods. There were instantly parties sent after them who came up with eight that day & found five of the rebells had killed themselves and the party killed the other three another party took one prisoner who impeached many old Negroes among the rest one Blackwall[95] head Boiler on Whitehall who was burnt. Another of them was taken up in this Town who has impeached all the Coromantees on Albion[96] Trinity[97] and the Frontier[98] and that their design was to have broke out a Month after Christmas and to have attackt the fort at Port Maria to gett arms and powder and from thence to go to Sixteen mile walk where there were many of their Countrymen and that the Negroes at Scots Hall were to have joined them. That it broke out was occasioned by the New Negroes declaring that they would wait no [longer]. There is a report that there was to have been some disturbances at Westmoreland. I do not find that any of the Negroes at Windward had any knowledge of it.

I shall go up in a fortnight to spend Xmas at Lyssons and will be over at Golden Grove. I had a letter from Mr. Kelly who writes three weeks ago they had very bad weather there which has lodged most of your Canes and that he should go about as this day that the bad weather has hindered the Still House going on. I will endeavour to have it of service to you this year if I send up my own Carpenter to do it for you was a great sufferer by the old one last year. Indeed there has not been such a wett year as this has been for many years past & still I am in hopes for a fine Crop for you as the Canes were old before they lodged.

[95] Blackwall had been tried and acquitted for complicity in the Jamaican slave rebellion of 1760. W.J. Gardner, *History of Jamaica to 1872* (London, 1909), p. 141.

[96] Sir Alexander Grant, an eminent London-based merchant, owned Albion plantation. David Hancock, *Citizens of the World: London Merchants and the Integration of the British Atlantic Community, 1735–1785* (Cambridge, 1995), pp. 11, 151.

[97] Trinity Plantation was another of Zachary Bayly's estates; Higman, *Jamaica Surveyed*, pp. 116–118.

[98] Robert Stirling, a Scottish immigrant, acquired Frontier Plantation in 1742. Alan L. Karras, *Sojourners in the Sun: Scottish Migrants in Jamaica and the Chesapeake, 1740–1800* (Ithaca, NY, 1992), p. 72.

Kelly also writes me that he had turned away the Doctor and when I come up will let you know the reasons. The case is, I believe, that Kelly is rather haughty to the white people and overbearing but to give him his due he takes great care of the Negroes and manages your Estate excessive well insomuch as it is in as fine order as any Estate in the West Indies and is very capable and Industrious and I really believe has your Interest intirely at heart and I really do not know a person in the Island so capable of managing it as he is. Therefore it is better to let him have Doctor of his own choosing to reside on the Estate provided he is capable.[99]

Inclosed is a letter from your Mother. I saw both her & your Aunt a few days ago. They were very well. She sent me a Small Box of papers for you which I have given to Capt. Davis to send to you and gott him to promise to take great care of it.

Thwaites arrived yesterday and Ford[100] with him. We have no Assembly yett. I do apprehend the North American Affairs make a great noise at home and from the disposition there seems to be there they are absolutely resolved not to submit to the Stamp law. We have a report that Mr. Lyttelton[101] has desired to be recalled and that Coll. How [102] will succeed him here.

My next will bring you your Accts. made up to the 9th of this month. I shall show all the Vouchers to your Mother. Fagan[103] is very importunate for his money. He makes a very large Ballance due him for taxt Bill in Chancery. What he wants is to have the Acct. settled and he would let it be provided it was on Interest. I shall go to Spanish Town tomorrow and Consult your Mother and Mr. Laing about settling it for any Chancery day he could apply to the Chancellor to order payment when we would be obliged to pay it and it may be not intirely convenient to you to raise so large a Sum at once for you have been

---

[99] The replacement doctor, who stayed on Golden Grove for several years, was a Dr Hayward.

[100] The Hon. Gilbert Ford. Ford, who came of a Bristol family, served as Jamaica's Attorney-General and in 1764 secured a seat on the island's Royal Council. He died in 1767. Report of Governor Lyttelton of the State of Jamaica, Public Record Office, Kew, CO 137/33, fos 55–56; Oliver, *CARIBBEANA*, III, p. 43.

[101] See note 11 above.

[102] It is unclear which Col. How Taylor was referring to, but given his distinguished military career it might have been William Howe (1729–1814), fifth Viscount Howe. For more details see Lee (ed.), *Dictionary of National Biography*, X, pp. 102–105.

[103] John Fagan who during the 1750s and early 1760s, and possibly even earlier, had acted as an attorney for Andrew Arcedekne. Case: Arcedekne vs T.[homas] Hall with appeal affidavit and authentication by C. Knowles, Governor of Jamaica, 11 April 1755. National Library of Jamaica, Kingston, Ms. 1035. Clearly Fagan was close to the Andrew's branch of the Arcedekne family because in 1768 Robert Arcedekne left a bequest of £500 CMJ to his 'special friend John Fagan'. Will of Robert Arcedekne, 8 December 1768, Island Record Office, Spanish Town, Wills, XXXVIII, fo. 39.

at large Expences with one thing or another this year and ought to have a full sufficiency of cash to carry on the appeal as they would be very glad if possible to distress you.

PS I hope to be able to send you 100 Hdds. of Sugar in the beginning of March.

12. To Chaloner Arcedekne, Kingston, 29 November 1766

The foregoing is a Copy of my last to you since which have not received any from you neither indeed did I expect any as you were in Germany. I hope this will meet you returned & that your health is perfectly establisht and that you will have no more sickness at least for many years to come.

I was since my last at Golden Grove and have now the pleasure to congratulate you on your works being intirely finisht except hanging the Stills which they were about then and am pretty positive that by this time that Jobb is also finisht. I assure you you have now a sett of the best works in the West Indies and capable of making you 800 Hdds.

The windy weather in August & October has lodged a great many of your canes but you have a great many to cutt, and I really believe that you will make more Sugar this coming Crop than ever you made before.

Kelly tells me he wants a Dozen Mules which I am now looking out to purchase for you. If I can gett Creole ones the difference in price will not exceed 50/- more than the Spanish ones and one can know they are young. Kelly and the Dr. agree perfectly well and seem to be very good friends He also acquaints me that he takes very good care of the Negroes. In short there are no Complaints from thence and every thing seems to go on very well.

Your Neighbour there Mr. James McQueen[104] of Duckingfield Hall did 4 days ago in this Town [file] the Bill in Chancery that I wrote you Robin advised me to file to perpetuate the Testimony that your Father was 20 years in possession before Dawkins's Attorneys claimed the Land is going on with him and I have found out a very material Evidence for you, one Mr. Pickersgill[105] who acquaints me your father had a penn at [*illegible*] Savanna [*illegible*] & Negroes on the land, that

---

[104] It appears that McQueen was either a manager of Duckenfield or one of the attorneys for its absentee owner, Nathaniel Philips.

[105] It has proved impossible to identify the Mr Pickersgill referred to here.

he himself gave in for it at the Vestry in the year 1754. I shall gett his
deposition as soon as possible as he is an Old Man.

Your Friend Ford[106] your Mother acquaints me is against you and
has been one of those that pusht Dawkins on to Contest the Matter.
John Morse[107] of Monument yard has also been very industrious and
has given Dawkins a Sett of Instructions how to carry on the Suit. The
way I came to knowledge of this is these Instructions were sent to
Zachary Bayly by Dawkins who carried them to little Peters the Old
man that lives at Mrs. Reynolds[108] to know if he knew any thing of the
matter, who desired them to lett them stay with him and he would
endeavour to Recollect what he had ever known of the Matter but as
soon as ever Bayly was gone brought them to your Mother for her to
gett a Copy made out to arm you against your Title. You may assure
your self no time shall be lost to gett the Bill filed and have every step
taken to defeat them.

Young Charles Price vacated his Seat in the Assembly on the meeting
which was the 10th Instant. My Brother Jack[109] and Hampson Thomas[110]
were the Candidates but Thomas carried it by a Motion of Old Price
to inquire into the Effects of the Law for dividing the Island into 3
Counties which alarmed the People in this Town much and united all
the small Voters in Spanish Town against any Kingston man as they
termed him. Every thing goes on very smooth now but am very certain
Stephen Fuller[111] will be dismist as agent every body being very angry
at his Conduct which they think wrong and perfidious this by the bye
a few days will make it publick. There is now a Committee on foot to
inquire into his Conduct. There is nothing now stirring, business very
dull and no money.

I am afraid I shall be obliged to draw on you for about £800 this
Currency in about three weeks. You may depend if I can any way in

[106] Presumably Gilbert Ford.

[107] Like Simon Taylor, Morse combined planting and mercantile interests. In 1750 he
was recorded as having 8,526 acres of land in Jamaica and by 1763 was Register in the
Jamaican Court of Vice-Admiralty. Morse's business partnerships included one with
Zachary Bayly, and by the mid-1770s, another in London with Thomas Smith. Morse
died in England in 1780 or 1781. Oliver, *CARIBBEANA*, I, p. 231; III, pp. 95, 122.

[108] It has proved impossible to further identify either Peters or Mrs Reynolds.

[109] John Taylor (1745–1786) created first Baronet in 1778. His wife Elizabeth was the
daughter and heiress of Philip Haughton of Orange Grove in Hanover Parish. Although
Taylor lived principally in London, he owned lands in Jamaica and it was whilst on a
visit to his Jamaican estates in 1786 that he died in Kingston. He was buried at
Lyssons Plantation and subsequently his brother was interred alongside him. Oliver,
CARIBBEANA, III, p. 63; Cundall, *Historic Jamaica*, p. 250.

[110] Hampson Thomas was a Member of the House of Assembly for St Catherine.

[111] Fuller, a merchant and the brother of Rose Fuller, had been appointed as Jamaica's
Agent in London in 1764 and he continued to serve in that capacity until 1794; L.M.
Penson, *The Colonial Agents of the British West Indies* (London, 1924), pp. 164, 228.

the world possibly avoid it I will, and nothing but the greatest necessity will make me do it as I know you cannot have a great deal at home from the Weight of the £5000 to Your Cousin and the Supplies you have sent out.

In case you do not come out before I hope we shall be able after the Crop to sett about your House which we have not been able yett to do and most of the Bricks you sent out have been used in hanging the Still making the Tanks and windows of the Still House except you chuse the House to be of Brick we can very easily get Stone on the Spott for it which will save the Expence of Bricks and last longer.

Your Mother & Aunt are very well. I saw them yesterday. Both my Brothers Jack & Graham are very well as is also my Sister.

13. To Chaloner Arcedekne, Kingston, 24 January 1767

The Annext is a Copy of my last to you since which have been favoured with yours of 20 October and 12 November wherein you acquaint me that you received a letter from me your Accts. desiring me to pay myself out of any of your effects and not to buy any more Negroes untill you are out of debt.

I hope you found the accounts right for if there is any mistake or any thing you do not rightly apprehend be kind enough to lett me know it and I will endeavor to putt it in a Clearer light. As to paying myself out of any of your Effects do not lett any matters between you and me give you the least concern for I shall allways be happy in endeavouring to serve you and you may assure yourself you can att all times command me to utmost extent of my Creditt or Fortune.

In Reguard to buying Negroes I must acquaint you that your Mother some time ago told me that she heard John Kelly your Overseer had sold twenty Negroes that were seasoned in plantain Garden River to Tom Cussans that she wisht they had been bought for Golden Grove. I told her you had given orders not to buy any more Negroes before you came over. She on that told me that Kelly had some more to sell that I must buy them that she should have a great deal of money to pay for she did not chuse to pay Interest by which I apprehend the Old Lady is to make you a present of them. They are about thirty and I am to go up the fifth of next month and then to gett them valued. I shall see the Old Lady before I go and lett you know what she says.

In reguard to the orders for Clothes for the Negroes and Cork Provisions I desired John Kelly to send me down a list of what he should want on which he told me he would send to you a list for as he had received so many things last year he should want very few things this year and some time afterwards he acquainted me that he had wrote to you and on asking him at Christmas he told me he had wrote to you by Capt. Ellis. It is not of any Great signification as Provisions are in Generall as Cheap here as in Ireland and you have as much Iron work as will serve you for the year.

Am glad you have taken a share in Chisholms ship as our Friend Malcolm takes it excessive kind and we shall allways be able to dispatch him the second ship so that there is not great danger of our losing much by it.

I assure I you I am heartily glad Mr. Littelton did not chuse to Come back to this Country. I think he has done much wiser in going to Portugall Am sorry that Mr. Elletsons[112] conduct is not much approved of in Erasing the Record. It is very certain that he never would have gott an Assembly to do business with him had he not done it so it was rather a matter of force on him than his own Choice. Indeed some of our Resolutions are rather too Sanguine but they certainly are our Constitution, but it seems as if the Parlia. are determined to suppress all Liberty in America. Coll. Clarke[113] if he goes on in Litteltons arbitrary schemes will have but a very indifferent time of it here.

Mr. Elletson and his Councill of state have lately thought they had a mighty power lodged in them and took it in their Heads to take up Douglas for refusing to deliver up to their appointment all the Collectors Books papers cash etc. but he applyed for a Habeas Corpus which was heard in open Court and he released from his imprisonment.

By your second letter of 12 November I received the agreeable News of your papers being Executed and that you hope in a very short time to send them out either to Mr. Laing or me to gett old Robin[114] to sign them and then to Record them. I believe he will make no manner of difficulty.

I am very glad to find that the Parliament has putt a Stop to the Corn distillery it will certainly enhance to Value of our dark Sugars and raise also the price of Rum both which articles has been at very wretched prices these two or three years last past.

I was at Windward the whole Christmas and was twice at Golden

[112] Roger Hope Elletson (1727–1775) was born in Jamaica, the son of Richard Elletson, owner of Hope Estate. He was educated at Eton College and at Trinity College, Cambridge, where he matriculated in 1746. Upon his return to Jamaica, Elletson was elected as a Member of the Assembly for Port Royal and in 1757 appointed to the Royal Council. In 1767, upon Governor Lyttelton's departure from Jamaica, Elletson was promoted to the office of Lieutenant Governor, a position he held until 1768. In 1754 his younger brother Thomas married Simon Taylor's sister Susan, or Susannah. Thomas died in 1760, Susan died on an unknown date before 1760. Roger Hope Elletson died whilst on a visit to England in 1775. Oliver, *CARIBBEANA*, III, p. 42.

[113] It has proved impossible to locate any further information about Clarke.

[114] Robin Arcedekne.

Grove where every thing is going on as well as any thing can possibly do altho the very great rains we have had these two years putt us back so we could not go about untill after Christmas. There are about 70 Hdds. made of exceeding good Sugar indeed preferable to any I ever saw at this time of the year before You will make I am pretty certain a great deal more than last year provided there is no weather to take the Canes off. I intend sending you about 100 in Thompson who will be the first ship, about the same quantity in Chisholm who will sail before the first of May and in the whole about 400 Hdds. If the Crop answers my Expectations you will gett 50 or 60 more for I hope the Rum will do a great deal more this year than it has done these many years before, indeed if it does not it will be the distillers fault for there is every thing now convenient for making it.

Your Penn is also in very good order and your Cattle increase fast. I had some thought of selling some off the Steers but the fear of a Wett Crop has made me alter that Resolution for fear of any Accidents having so many Canes to cutt. Indeed I hope after this year that your Rum and the Penn will pay all your Contingencies so you will gett your Sugars clear. The Reason it will not this year is because the tradesmans Bills must be paid and there has been a great deal of work done to your Stills which Guy[115] could not do and we were obliged to employ Taylor[116] from Port Morant.

I shall send you your accts. made out to the 31 of December by the very first London ship that sails from this place. You will find you have been lucky in Reguard to your Negroes having a Decrease of only 4. It is true 14 have died but then you have saved ten children. They are all in High Spiritts.

We must soon as possible sett about a sort of House for the White people otherwise we shall lose them all, for was obliged to take down the old Cattle Mill where they slept for the Stones and since they have slept again below one has died and the other two been near it. Kelly and the Doctor who sleep above stairs are in perfect health and still agree. I assure you the Negroes thrive under his care.

I have been absolutely forced to Draw on you a Bill of Exchange dated 2 February for £500 stg. to the order of Reisset, Jaffray & Yelloly which hope you will be kind enough to Honor. You may assure yourself that no thing could have induced me to do it but my Friend and Relation Doctor Taylor[117] was sued and it was to stop the Rendition

---

[115] One of the slave artisans on Golden Grove.

[116] Taylor has proved impossible to identify, but the context in which his name is mentioned suggests that he was not related to Simon Taylor.

[117] Possibly John Taylor, a beneficiary of Simon Taylor's will. Will of Simon Taylor, Late of the Parish of St Andrew, Esq., made 2 December 1808, codicils made, 18 October 1811, proved 27 April 1813. Wills, Island Record Office, Spanish Town, LXXXVII, fos 1–34.

and prevent his Negroes being taken up and sold that made me do it for He would take nothing but money down or Bill. It gives me the greatest uneasiness that I was obliged to draw it on you for I could not borrow it here or would not have troubled you, indeed as it is at 90 days Sight. I hope some of your Sugars will be att home before the Bill becomes due. You may depend I shall draw no more for the Crop coming in will make Sugars a little Brisk again.

14. To Chaloner Arcedekne, Kingston, 2 March 1767

Annext is my last to you of 24 January which I now confirm since which have been favour'd with yours of 26 November and hope that Capt. Furnell is arrived as I sent by him a Duplicate of the letter desiring Insurance if you thought proper on 42 Hdds. of Sugar p. the *Sally*, Capt. Cummings (and also acquainting you of the safe arrivall of your Man Nedd) and also to lett you know that I had sent you 2 Puncheons of Rum distilled for your own use on board Cummings. I hope he is safe arrived long ere this. I am afraid poor Ellis is drowned as we have no manner of Acct. of him here but whatever is his Fate I hope your goods on board him are insured.

I received a letter and an Invoice from Perry & Co.[118] of Cork p. the *Munificence* Capt. Falconer who brought your Irish Provisions and delivered them all safe at my Estate which I sent up from there to the Rivers mouth and Mr. Kelly since acquaints me that he has received by one Capt. Tarbutt your goods from London but I cannot find that either Kelly or I have any letter or Invoice of them.

I hope that you never will again have any Occasion to build another Sett of works at the old Land of Golden Grove as I am confident these unless some very unlucky Accident should happen will take off 800 or 900 Hdds.

In my last I wrote you about a Conversation between your Mother and me about Kellys Negroes. I waited on her again when she told me to buy them. I shewed her your letter ordering that I should not buy any more on your account, on which the Old Lady by your Aunts and my persuasion did at last agree to purchase twenty and make you a present of them on which I went up and bought them for £1200 hundred pounds. They were markt with your mark and tolled to you, and the Old Lady has paid the money and wishes they may turn out well. I hope you will not think I acted wrong in this. I bought before I received your letter 12 fine Creole Mules and sent them up. I do not apprehend you will want any these three years to come.

---

[118] No further information has been located about the partners in this company.

You must undoubtedly by the immense Expences you have been putt to on so many Accts. have made but little nett Profitts, but as most are now at an end I hope for the future you will find the Sweets of your Estate. Be confident I will not putt you to the least Expence I can avoid consistent with the Wellfare of the Estate. As for triffles for the Overseer as Keggs of Bisquits now & then Tea & single Refined Sugar they in the Whole amount in a manner to nothing and you know Kelly he would not be pleased if they were not sent when he writes for them and he goes on so very well and has kept your Stock and in Short every thing on the Estate in fine order and you will find at the same time it is thriving. I hope you have no manner of objection at their having been sent.

I hope this year that you will be able to lay up something as when I was up Viz. 11 of Febry. you had near 100 Hdds. made better Sugar than I ever before saw on the Estate and by a letter from Kelly of 23 Feby. he acquaints me that he had very fine weather and was taking the advantage of it.

You will Please give orders if you chuse to Insure 100 Hdd. p. the *Friendship* Thompson who will sail about the 8th or 10th of next month for 100 Hdds. on board the *Nancy* Capt. Chisholm who will sail about the 25 of next month also. I intend sending also 50 Hdd. p. the *Prince George* Capt. Taylor 50 p. the *Morant*, Capt. Raffles, and hope in about a month hence to write you of many more besides as by this time I shall be better able to inform you how the canes yield for to make the Calculation of what the Crop will be. The Cisterns did not work at all cleanly & when was up occasioned by their being new but as they are now seasoned hope they have mended for the man that is your distiller is reckoned as good a one as is in the Island and is very sober which very few are.

I have not seen Clarke since I received yours. I spoke to your Mother who knows nothing about his land. I shall be at Spanish Town this week and will search the Office and consult of old Robin also. The Old Mulatto Woman Mrs. Wyllie[119] at the Ferry by her Son in Law Dr. McGlashen has brought an Action on your Father's Administration Bond against you. Dr. Gregory sent it to your Mother who sent it to Robert Cooper Lee as your Sollicitor. I think she was very right in applying to Lee in Preference to McCulloch & Wootton[120] for he is infinitely cleverer than they who told me he would gett it putt off this Court and then we might see what can be done. We have all the Proceedings in Chancery and as Old Fagan is alive who tells me he knows every thing of the matter and that there is no manner of danger

---

[119] No further information has been located about Mrs Wyllie.

[120] A partnership based either in Spanish Town or, more likely, in Kingston.

of its affecting you I think it better to have it brought on than to be by. I shall also take an Abstract of the Whole Proceedings and send you which you may lay before Council in England and lett us know their Opinions.

I have all your Accts. made out and shall send them to you p. the *Standlinch* Capt. Barnett sat which time I shall write concerning them, his Bag is advertised to be taken down the day after tomorrow.

15. To Chaloner Arcedekne, Kingston, 9 March 1767

The above is a Copy of my last to you p. the *Jenny* Cpt. McKeevia Liverpoole since which I have not had the pleasure of hearing from you. This serves to acquaint you that I have sent you enclosed your Accounts, viz. Golden Grove Accot. your Accot. Current & the different Accots. regarding Golden Grove that you may know on what accounts the sundry matters were paid to whom & for what, for the way I took that every thing might fully appear so as to be plainly understood & that you might know how your affairs stood & what wages were due.

I gave Kelly orders to pay off all the White People to the 31 December to draw on me for the money & to take their Receipts & send me which I have gott & shall leave in Spanish town with your Mother as I did last. You will please to peruse the Accounts & if there is any thing that you do not rightly understand you will please let me know. I will endeavour to explain them. Am sorry that the Contingencies are so high but you will plainly see that it is the Workmen's Bills that swell it & that there is very near 18 months wages on most of the White Peoples' Accots. There is also a Pipe of Wine for as I expected you out last year I kept both the Pipes that you might on your arrival here have Old Wine for yourself. I intend sending one of them to Kelly as you are not come out. A misfortune happened to the other on the wharfe where it was spoiled by the Negroes on which I acquainted the Wharfenger that I would not take it but that he must give me either £60 for it or procure another of the very best quality in the room. I also sent a Cooper & had a survey on the Cask by which it plainly appeared that it had been spoil'd. The man agreed to give a Pipe in the room which he has since refused but as the Cooper & my Clerk are Evidence on the survey I have sued him for £60 & make no doubt of recovering that Sum.

You will also please to remark that Dr. Troupe's[121] Accot. of £34.2.6

---

[121] There is no record of the medical services performed by Dr Troupe.

is included in the Disbursements made by John Kelly & also Nevill's[122] Accot. Of £36.13.4, which last on examining a second time I found that you had been charged £20 thereof last year & the remainder this, therefore I have made a remark that in your next Account Current the £36.13.4 shall be carryed to your Credit. I did not find it out untill it was wrote & fixed & I had not time as the Ships Bagg is to be taken away this Afternoon to alter it.

I have not been able to go to Spanish Town yet but propose going the 10th or 11th & as there is a Ship to sail in a fortnight I shall by her write you with regard to your affair with Mrs. Wyllie.

Kelly was in town two or three days ago. He informed me the weather was very well when he came down He is gone up again He tells me he has made about 180 hhds.

There is no news here every thing is very dull & no appearance of any thing of a price for Sugars & Rum I apprehend will be a very dull commodity here this year.

PS You will please to observe in the Accot. of Cattle you will see 16 Heifers sent to Swamps, they were sent by order of your Mother in payment as she told me of 40 Spanish Steers she bot. For GG in 1760 or 1761.

16. To Chaloner Arcedekne, Kingston, 19 March 1767

Annexed is a Copy of my last to you of 9th Instant p. the *Standlinch* Capt. Burnett. This serves chiefly to cover the Copy of your Accots. that I sent you p. him, since when I have seen Robin[123] & Bourke[124] who last Saturday executed the deed from N Arcedekne[125] in presence of Malcolm Laing & myself. It could not be recorded as it was not proved by the Clerk that saw N.A. sign it, therefore it must go home again, which it is to do tomorrow by this same conveyance. They tell me they shall also send the Duplicate over by the *Nautilus*. They do not like it. One of their Understrappers where I happened to dine the same day, told me that you had not got Robin's[126] Tittle to his reversion & that John Bourke at home had no orders from Robin to offer it for the £1500 Stg. & that Robin will not sell it under ten thousand Sterl. now. I told them you did not want it nor would do any

---

[122] No further information has been located about Nevill or the services he performed on or for Golden Grove.
[123] Robin Arcedekne.
[124] Luke Bourke
[125] Nicholas Arcedekne.
[126] Robin Arcedekne.

such thing. What I thought if he would sell it for £500 stg. or so it would then be a matter of so small indifference to you that you might perhaps give that sum, besides that I intended to send you home this year so much Sugar as that you might make any Settlement you pleased on any Lady marry & then you would not give a single ryal for Robin's Reversion. I knew it would be carried back to him therefore spoke in that light manner altho I hope before now you have concluded the matter for the £1500 stg. I wrote you what the consequences of the refusal would be. Bourke I am certain has orders from Robin to offer it to you for that & now he is piqued at your refusal.

I have not been able to go to Spanish Town yet for Graham is out of town & this Ships sailing has obliged me to be constantly in town.

[*Notes that he has sent Arcedekne a turtle* 'p. the *Adventure* Capt. James Sewell'.]

I have not heard since my last from the Estate but afraid the weather is bad there as it is very wett this way. The price of Sugars is not yet broke here the factors wanting 32/- & the purchasers want to beat down the price to 30/- p. cent, so there is an intire stagnation of all business untill this matter is settled.

Your Mother & Aunt are very well. I heard from them two days ago.

17. To Chaloner Arcedekne, Kingston, 8 April 1767

Annext is a Copy of my last to you since which no thing material has happened. This is chiefly to advise you that Capt. Thompson has gott on board only ninety Hdds. of your Sugar in place of 100 that I acquainted you I intended to ship on board him. I hope that it will make no very material difference. Capt. Chisholm has now gott on board about seventy Hdds. more of your Sugars as I am informed by a Master of a Vessell that putt some on board him, he will sail this month. You will also please to order insurance on 50 Hdds. on board the *Prince George* Capt. Fryer and 50 on board the *Morant* Raffles. Fryer will sail the beginning of May and Raffles about the 20 of that month.

I am informed your Canes do nott yield at all neither do any in the Parish as they did last year occasioned by the Continuall Rains we have had there. I hope soon to advise you of more Sugar for the market is broke here so very low that I believe it will answer much better to send home Sugar than to sell here this year. Neither have we any advices how the marketts are with you as there has not been any Vessell from Europe here these two months.

I have sent a Bill of Lading of the 90 Hdds. of Sugar to your Brother in Law Mr. Cowell by this Ship and shall send another by the first Ship that sails and shall also write you more particularly by the *Nancy* Capt. Chisholm of a Scheme that I have for the new Ship that we are to be concerned in which I dare say you and all the Parties concerned in will agree to and by which it will be impossible but that she must make us Money.

I heard yesterday from your Mother and Aunt who are both very well.

18. [Taylor & Graham] to Benjamin Cowell, Kingston, 2 May 1767

Annext is a Copy of our last to you. This serves chiefly to inclose you the weights of ninety Hdds. of Sugar shipt on board the *Friendship* by Capt. Charles Thompson who has been saild a fortnight from Morant Bay and who we hope is already arrived. We were in hopes also to have sent you the Bill of Lading for 100 Hdds. on board of Capt. Chisholm but have not yett received them from the Estate but that ship will sail in a Week at furthest. We shall begin to putt goods on board both Fryer and Raffles & hope also to dispatch them both this month.

Our ST[127] goes up tomorrow to Windward and when returns we shall acquaint you on what other ships we shall send the Remainder of the Sugar, & lett you know how the Estate goes on for our mutual Friend Mr. Arcedekne has acquainted our ST that he intends to return to the South of France and has left you his attorney in his absence. Therefore think it but our duty to inform you of every thing about his affairs here.

Our ST also drew a Bill on him for £500 Stg. on Acct. of what he was due us and as he is apprehensive that Mr. Arcedekne may be gone abroad before it arrives. Hopes it may meet with due Honor. It is in favor of Mr. David Reisset at 90 days sight. We shall also be obliged to draw on you for £500 stg. more this year as there is a demand of £1000 to be paid to one Mr. Fagan due this month for the Ballance of his Acct. who will take nothing but money or bills & Sugars are here in a manner unsaleable except of the very best quality and the price also very low which has made us take the Resolution of Shipping all the Sugars that are now or will be made home as we expect they will turn out better than by selling them here, except we can pass them off for any demand against Mr. Arcedekne.

---

[127] Simon Taylor.

[*Notes that a turtle for Arcedekne was* 'putt on board Capt. Chisholm'.]

19. To Chaloner Arcedekne, Kingston, 2 May 1767

The above is a Copy of my last to you p. the *Friendship* Capt. Thompson since which I have received your several favors of 10th Decer. & 3^d & 10th January. That of the 10th Decr. acquaints me that by that opportunity I should receive the papers relative to your Composition which you desire me to see Robin Arcedekne execute & that you suppose he will have no manner of Objection to have it enrolled. In regard to that matter I refer you to my letter to you of 19th March last wherein I acquaint you that both Laing & myself have seen both Robin & Bourke execute the papers but that it could not be enrolled because the Clerk who saw Nicholas Arcedekne sign it had not proved it & therefore that it must be sent home again, which it was one Copy p. the *Active* & the other is to go by the *Nautilus* who sails the 20th Instant. I did not receive any other papers by that Vessell & those came by some Ship that came to this port directed to Robin whereas your letter I did not receive above 6 days ago from Montego Bay.

Your next of 3^d Jany. acquaints me that you had received several of my Letters & a Bill of Lading for the Sugars on board the *Sally* & that mine by the *Dreadnought* arrived first tho' the last in date for which I am very sorry on account of your Insurance but hear she is put in to Carolina so she is not lost & in all probability the Sugars on board her will come to a good market As for Ellis we shall I am afraid never have any more accounts of him. I am glad you got £10 sterling p. Cask insured on him, it is better than a total loss, which I apprehended.

I am very glad you find the Golden Grove Accots. right & are contented with them. I intend before the next Crop since I find it agreeable to you to sell off some of the Steers as that is the best time for selling and I did give orders to keep up some of the Old Cows marked AA to fatten & sell off to the Butchers.

I find you intend to return to the South of France from whence you came to execute your Deeds since you found so much benefit the last time you was there from that Air & that whatever Bills are designed for Europe & Supplies for the Estate are to be sent to your Brother who is to be your Attorney & that the Accounts are to be directed to you & the Bills of Lading to him. You may depend on my punctually executing your Orders & letting him know every thing that occurs.

I shall speak to John Archer[128] to get made out an Office Copy of

---

[128] Archer was the Island Secretary, the chief official in the Office of Enrolments. All deeds had to be recorded in the Office within three months of their execution. Oliver, *CARIBBEANA*, III, p. 135.

all the Deeds & other Papers your father has been concerned in which was prevented by Robin. It is a very necessary thing & may be of very great service in many respects. Do you think it necessary to have the Titles of the Lands which your father bought & has again sold? I will also set about making out according to your desire a Sett of Books of all your father's Accounts & his Answers to all Bills in Chancery that he was concerned in on his own account & every other paper of consequence.

All our Politicks are now at an end as if there never had been any such thing. The impeachment against Lyttelton dropt & no more mention of him here than if there never had been any such person. I entirely agree with you in opinion against settling any Salary on any Governor for more than a year. I was against a stated Salary to Elletson. I shall certainly be against it for Monckton[129] who I hear is to be certainly our Governor & as these Animals come over here only to suck our Blood, after their turns are served they care not what becomes of us. Lyttelton's friends give out here also that he has carried nothing home with him, which is true for because he remitted all before that he could lay his hands on & the Country now owes him £4000 which he was very near losing & nothing but the injustice of not complying with a Law of the Assembly's own making & the apprehension of the shock it would give to all publick Faith & honor saved him.

Your Gardner arrived safe here. I sent him over to Spanish Town, he ought to be very good for the price you give.

Your next is of 10th January & I shall give you in my next or I will send to your Brot. in law all that I can get or learn of the affairs of Compere.[130] I shall also if it is agreeable to you communicate every thing concerning your affairs to him for I understand by a Letter from him to Mr. Laing that this will meet you abroad where you are already gone. Laing shew'd me your letter to him in regard to the purchasing Robins annuity & the getting your mother to purchase. I believe she will do it for she told me she would lend you money to do it. I put Laing on the Scheme to propose to her if she consents whether it may not be of service to pretend to hear that you are going to be married soon to a lady of family & fortune which may make the Old boy Robin more inclinable to sell, for if he does not sell he certainly will leave it to Bourke's Children who are under age, and he would disinherit any

---

[129] Lieutenant General Robert Monckton (1726-1782). In 1761 Monckton had commanded the land forces that captured Port Royal in Martinique, which led to the surrender of Martinique, Grenada, St Lucia, and St Vincent to the English. Despite the hopes of Taylor and other eminent Jamaicans, Monckton was never appointed to the Governorship of Jamaica. For more details see Lee (ed.), *Dictionary of National Biography*, XIII, pp. 612-614.

[130] It has proved impossible to identify this member of the Compere family.

of them did he even think or imagine any of them would ever sell it to you. We could not put about tho' any such report without speaking first to the Old Lady about it & see how she will relish it as a matter of Nicety & what a person would not chuse to do without getting some advantage for you by it.

I go tomorrow up to Golden Grove & shall then see what is made & write to your Brother in regard to the rest of the Sugars to come home tho' I believe shall ship the whole home as the Price here is low & no buyers tho' if I can get your Tradesmen to take out their Accounts in Produce will do it. I am afraid must draw £500 stg. more on you to pay off Old Fagan for there is no money in the Country & will not take goods on any account, if can avoid I will. This year will pay off all your debts that I know of except your mother's demands who will not receive either principal or Interest.

Kennion[131] who has been here near three months has not as yet made his appearance. We are informed he came here in a hurry & left another Ship to bring out his Cloaths.

20. To Benjamin Cowell, Lyssons, 9 May 1767

Taylor & Graham wrote you a few days ago from Kingston p. the *Dawkins* since which time I have been up at Golden Grove and on my arrivall here find Capt. Fryers Ship underway therefore have only time to inclose you the Bill of Lading of 20 Hdds. of sugar Shipt on board him. I intended to putt 50 Hdds. on board him and 50 on board Raffles but the canes have yielded so very bad this year that we have fallen short both in quantity & every thing etc. Shall write you more fully p. Capt. Chisholm who sails in 4 or five days. We have been able to put but 20 Hdds. on board Raffles.

21. [Taylor and Graham] To Benjamin Cowell, Kingston, 11 May 1767

[*Repeats information in previous letter about the amounts of sugar shipped.*]

We enclose you the Bill of Lading for the 94 hhds. on board the *Nancy* Capt. Chisholm & a second Bill of Lading of the 20 on board Fryer. Capt. Chisholm could take only 94 on board tho' we sent down the other 6 to him, so were obliged to put them on board the *Brilliant* Capt. Myall.

---

[131] John Kennion had been appointed to the Royal Council in 1761.

We are very sorry to inform you that the Canes at Golden Grove have turn'd out excessive ill this Year for notwithstanding we had 100 acres to cutt more this year than last we shall make near 100 hhdds. less & but little Rum for as the Cisterns were all new they wasted a great deal of Molasses in the seasoning them & did not then turn out the quantity of Rum.

We were in hopes of writing to you to order more insurances, but there are only 20 hdds. now on the Estate which we are to pay some tradesmen with for demands they have for building the works, and we are anxious to pay all the demands against Mr. Arcedekne this year except our own. There will be about 60 or 70 more hdds. to come home this year.

Our ST has also been Obliged to drawn on Mr. Arcedekne a Bill for £176.6.9¼ Stg. dated the 4th Instant in favor of Mr. John Archer at 90 days & a Bill for £130.11.8 Stg. dated the 11th Instant in favor of Mr. David Reisset also at 90 days. They are addressed to Mr. Arcedekne in his absence to you. Agreeable to Mr. Arcedekne's Instructions, there will be nothing more drawn this year for nothing but the excessive scarcity of money in this Country & every body being very pressing could have induced us to have drawn a shilling. We hope they will meet with due honor & as they are at a long sight hope they will put you to no inconvenience.

22. To Benjamin Cowell, Kingston, 3 October 1767

This serves chiefly to beg the favor of you to forward the Inclosed letter to Mr. Arcedekne, and acquaint you, that I have received your favour of 21 of July wherein you let me know that you had communicated the contents of mine to you p. Capt. Chisholm to Mr. Arcedekne.

In reguard to Golden Grove when was up last, which was about five weeks ago, the Negroes had been very sickly, but were then on the mending hand but even then there were 36 in the Hott House[132] & 21 in the Yaws which is a very great drawback on the Estate especially as there had been a very great flood in May which had laid allmost every part of the Estate under Water and the Caterpillars had very much hurt the young rattoons near the Riverside. They had then begun holling and had holed near 20 Acres. I hope we shall be able to gett in a plant from about 150 to 170 Acres, for a great deal of the Estate wants new planting, occasioned by building the Works which continually took a great many Negroes out of the field to bring stones & lime

---

[132] The plantation hospital.

having ever since Mr. Arcedekne left the Island, untill the beginning of the last Crop, had 6 Wains dayly at work, & 8 & 10 Mules to bring those materialls & sand & last year Especially all the Negroes were six weeks employed in bringing Clay & ramming the Cisterns, which putt the Plantation work a good deal out of order in reguard to putting in the Annual Plant & the new Negroes bought since Mr. Arcedeknes going off have been a good deal troubled with Yaws & some, as is allways the case in wett parts of this Island by which means we have had very little assistance from them.

We have not yett begun upon the House, tho have gott all the timber fallen on the Spott & the Lime burnt. The reason is because I want much to gett the plant in & putt in as much as possible to bring the Estate up & gett it in proper order again. In the meantime the Carpenters are squaring the timber & the Cattle employ'd in bringing bricks for the House, for from the plan & directions sent out, I do not apprehend any tradesman in this Country can build it of Stone.

Mr. Arcedekne wrote to me that Mr. Fisher[133] intended to sue the joint Bond that Mr. A. Arcedekne & Mr. Robert Delap[134] entered into in the Secretary's office, when said Cooke[135] administred on the Estate of Isaac Gale[136] & desired me to take Mr. Bullocks opinion on the Case & send it to you. I have not been yett able to do it for Mr. Cooke lives in St. Elizabeth untill I know what effects of Mr. Gales he has in his hand unaccounted for. I have wrote him a letter & he will be obliged to come up to attend the Councill, when the Assembly meets, which will be the 20 Instant & will then taken Mr. Bullocks opinion on the matter & send it to you.

In reguard to the Claim Mrs. Wylie setts up against the Estate of Old Mr. Arcedekne for a Legacy left her by one Stapleton[137] & for

[133] The bond referred to here may have been one for £1,896 1s 10d that was dated 8 September 1749 and mentioned in the inventory of Patrick Taylor's estate that was drawn up in 1759. Patrick Taylor was Simon Taylor's father. 8 March 1759, Inventory of all and singular the Bonds Securities and Debts due to Patrick Taylor late of the Parish of Assembly Kingston, as they were sworn unto us by Andrew Arcedekne, Charles Mitchell & Matthew Gregory Esqs And the Honble Sir Simon Clark. Inventories of Estates, Island Record Office, Spanish Town, XXXIX, fo. 64. It has proved impossible to further identify Fisher.

[134] During the 1760s Delap represented St Elizabeth in the Jamaican House of Assembly.

[135] Francis Cooke, one of the Royal Councillors suspended by Governor Elletson, owned close to 2,000 acres of land in St Elizabeth.

[136] The Gales were one of Jamaica's most eminent families. Their wealth and prestige originated in the early 1670s, when Jonathan Gale patented 533 acres of land in St Elizabeth Parish. When he died in 1750 Isaac Gale owned 11,838 acres of land in Jamaica. His will, which was recorded in 1748, was proved two years later. Oliver, *CARIBBEANA*, II, pp. 58, 121, 308; IV, p. 95.

[137] No further information has been located about Stapleton.

which the Administration Bond was sued, there has as yett nothing been done in it, the Plaintiffs not having made any motion to come to tryall. I believe it will be dropt and end soon for Mr. Arcedekne has no money of that Estate in his Hands but one Mr. James is accountable for it, the Father of the Present Mr. Haughton James[138] in London & whose Estate is Lyable for it. It is a Sort of Litigious suit for there has allready been 2 Bills in Chancery about it, in the old Gentlemans lifetime & also an injunction in Chancery.

The next matter is in reguard to the Land at Plantain Garden River mouth claimed by Mr. Dawkins. We have the Bill drawn ready to file & nothing prevents it but Mr. Robert Arcedekne wants to have a Conference with one Mr. Pickersgill, who is the principall evidence in Mr. Arcedeknes behalf he being the only man in Jamaica except Mr. R. Arcedekne that can prove a 20 Years quiet possession. As soon as that is over shall file it without delay & take out the Foreign Commission for one Mr. Burke,[139] who also knows the Land & send it to you to gett his evidence. When that is gott am hopefull we shall have no more Disputation on that Account and the only reason why Dawkins has delay'd filing his Bill, or bringing an ejectment, is because he knows these Evidences will be against him, and as they are old People they will in a few years drop off. This Bill is intirely to perpetuate these peoples Evidences.

Mr. Kelly the Overseer on Golden Grove, acquainted me that he had wrote home to you for the Supplies for the Estate, so they will arrive in good time. I intend going there next week when return will acquaint you how every thing is there.

23. To Chaloner Arcedekne, Kingston, 3 October 1767

I received both your letters the first dated the 20 Aprill from France the other the 23 of May, wherein you acquaint me that you was but a short time in England as you thought it was not desirable to depart from Europe before the returns of your papers you employ'd your time

---

[138] The James family had held properties in Westmoreland and Hanover parishes ever since the first English settlement of Jamaica. The family became connected with the equally eminent Haughton family of Barbados through the marriage of the Hon. Richard James (b. 1655) to Ann Haughton. Haughton James was born in Jamaica in 1738 and matriculated from St Mary Hall in 1755. He died in Spanish Town in 1797. Oliver, *CARIBBEANA*, II, p. 1; III, p. 51; IV, p. 209; Hugh Paget, 'The early history of the family of James of Jamaica', *The Jamaica Historical Review*, 1 (1948), pp. 260–273.

[139] Luke Bourke, a member of the family that challenged the legitimacy of Andrew Arcedekne's will.

in moving from place to place. I am heartily glad you found so much advantage by it.

The Lawyers on your side for the Bill to perpetuate the Evidence in reguard to the land at the River's mouth are Gordon,[140] Bullock, Webley[141] and by Robin's advice one Mr. Brown.[142] It is ready and waits for nothing but Robins coming to town to have a conversation with Pickersgill to file. I believe he will be the only Evidence in this Country that can prove the quiet possession 20 years before any suit commenced. I agree intirely with you wishing all this matter was at an end but from what Robin says I believe you need not be very apprehensive of the event.

In reguard to your Dwelling House the Timber is all fallen & the lime burnt and intend putting it on the Hill Matt Wallen[143] told you of. There is a very good Chaise road to it. Intended to have built it of stone but from the plan come out do not believe it will be possible. It is not yett begun for the great rains that brought down the River again as high to the full as in 1765 and the bad weather both before and after it together with the Negroes being very sickly after it the Estate run a good deal back and I thought it was better to bring things again into order & gett in a good plant before begun on it for can assure you though tradesmen are to find materialls they never the less are a very great disadvantage to an Estate by employing Wains & mules they must of course have Negroes to look after & follow them. You may rest satisfied it shall soon be sett about and every direction follow'd

[140] Thomas Gordon who, during the 1760s, sat as a member of the Jamaican Assembly for Port Royal and also served as the island's Attorney General. He had close ties with the Hibbert brothers by virtue of his sister Janet's marriage to John Hibbert (1732–1769) in 1760. Gordon died in 1780 or 1781, and his will was proved in the latter year. Jamaican Assembly (1765) Public Record Office, Kew, CO 140/44, ff. nn.; Oliver, *CARIBBEANA*, II, p. 175; III, p. 193

[141] Probably Edward Webley, who during the 1760s sat in the Assembly as one of the members for St David's. In 1765, together with Scudamore Wynde (or Winde) (see note 198 below), Webley confirmed the contents of the inventory of Andrew Arcedekne's estate. Inventory of Andrew Arcedekne of Parish St Cat. Esq. by Edward Webley & Scudamore Wynde of Parish St Catherine as shown by executors Matthew Gregory & Foster March, 30 April 1765. Inventories of Estates, Island Record Office, Spanish Town, XXXXV (1765), fos 58–63.

[142] Possibly William Patrick Brown, in the mid 1760s a member of the Assembly for St John. Jamaica Assembly, 19 March 1765–22 March 1765, Public Record Office, Kew, CO 140/44, ff., nn.

[143] For several years between 1750 and his death in 1797 Wallen represented the Parish of Port Royal in the Assembly. His properties included Mount Pleasant, an eighty-five-acre estate in St Andrew Parish. Wallen is best remembered not so much for his political career as for his botanical experiments. Oliver, *CARIBBEANA*, IV, p. 208; Douglas Hall, 'Planters, farmers and gardeners in eighteenth century Jamaica', The Elsa Goveia Memorial Lecture, 1987 (Kingston, Department of History, University of the West Indies, Mona, 1988), p. 4.

that is laid down in the plan except raising the foundation higher for it says 1 foot 8½.

In yours of 23 May you acquaint me of having received my severall letters of 24 Jany. & 19 March inclosing your Accots. & that you have nothing to object to them excepting that you wish the Ballance was on neither side. I beg you will not make yourself uneasy about it. It is what I am glad I have it in my power to do. Am obliged to you for accepting my Bill on you. I did acquaint your Brother of 2 more small bills I was obliged to draw on you.

I am sorry you are obliged to return to the Spa from your disorder again threatning to attack you but hope you have received as much advantage by it as you did last year.

Your papers are again arrived here and recorded. Your Mother sent to Robin about purchasing the Reversion. He sent her word the Lowest price for you was £10000 Stg. for any one else £20000. You see you will be by & by obliged to marry to save so much.

In reguard to Cookes administering on Jonathan Gale[144] & that your Father & Robt. Delap were the Securities it is butt too true. Cooke is also insolvent. That he did receive into his possession £80000 or £90000 is also true but the greatest part was in Negroes stock & the amount of his Inventory. From what I can learn he has made away with 8 or ten thousand pounds this Currency before Thos. Fearon[145] gott the Administration on a power of Attorney. Fisher has often times as also Zachary Bayly threatened to sue. If they do I have both Bullocks Beachs Tom Gordons & Fords opinion that the Heirs at Law can recover on the King's Bond against an Executor more Especially an Administration of my own. I am heartily glad you have so good an Estate to recover half of whatever be recover'd to do with as Robin Delaps.

I am informed that Jonathan Gale died in 1748. If so it blows over untill the end of next year you need not have the least anxiety after wards on that Account as you will then come within the Law which prevents any suits on which no judgment has been taken nor money received for 20 years. In the mean time do not say any thing of it to them. Cooke is to be up this month being one of the Council. I shall talk the whole matter over with him and let him know I expect that if he has any thing belonging to that Estate in his hands I shall Expect

---

[144] Jonathan Gale's will was recorded in 1740. He was a member of the influential family that traced its Jamaican roots back to the early 1670s. Oliver, *CARIBBEANA*, II, p. 120. (See note 136 above.)

[145] Between 1756 and 1764 the Hon. Thomas Fearon served as the Chief Justice of Jamaica. He also acted as the Custos of the Parishes of Clarendon and Vere. During the mid-1760s and early 1770s his elective offices included sitting as a Member of the Assembly for Clarendon. Jamaican Assembly (1765), Public Record Office, Kew, CO 140/44, ff. nn.

that he will indemnify you & go over the matters with him & send you a state of what he has not accounted for. He is a very worthless fellow & has taken in many people.

Your Mother did make you a present of twenty seasoned Negroes. I can assure you that you did want them for the Negroes all over the River have been very sickly all the year & a great many of the New Negroes have been a very long time in the Yaws. You have had at times this year 50 in the Hott House & 27 and upwards in the Yaws at one time which has putt the Estate back a good deal. It will be impossible to sett about building a plantation house immediately & your House too. After one is built we can easily begin upon another for the White people.

I am really sorry you have made so poor a Crop this year. I assure you we cutt upwards of 100 Acres more Canes this year than last & have not made so much by a Hundred & odd Hdds. owing to the Canes not yielding from the Immense quantitys of rain that fell last year and am afraid we shall make less by a good deal next year for after the flood the Catterpillars eat up all the young rattoons near the river side and they have come up but poorly since. Be assured I do every thing in my power for the advancing of your interest & shall be up once in 6 weeks to see that things are well carried on as they ought to be and intend if possible to putt in a plant from 150 to 170 Acres this year in order to bring up matters. Thank God I do not know of any debt now outstanding against your Father's Estate having taken up Fagan's debt & got a release in form & have recorded it. I have also paid all your tradesmen & for the future all your sugar will be shipt home unless you give orders to the contrary.

In reguard to Mrs. Willyes matter there is nothing done in it. I believe it will intirely drop for McGlashen who kept her Daughter & was the moving person in it, has been Courting one Miss Ablett[146] a Niece of Robin Delaps on which the Mulatto Lady was so offended she withdrew to her Mother & there has since been no Connection between them.

As you desire it shall get Bullocks opinion on Cookes matter & send it to your Brother. Your Gardner Robin Taylor[147] was sent up by your Mother to Golden Grove some time ago where the poor fellow died in a few days of a fever.

Since my last letter to you I have been up to Hispaniola to see how they make Sugar there and what sort of Country it was. I had a tolerable pleasant trip but found nothing could be learned from them but the art of watering their Lands.

---

[146] It has proved impossible to identify Miss Ablett.

[147] It has proved impossible to identify Taylor, but given his occupation it seems evident

You must know long before this that Jack Cussans[148] is married & sail'd for England in the *Phoenix* Man of Warr. Tom Cussans is gone to North America with Billy Gale.[149] Every thing is quiet at present but the Assembly meets the 20 Instant. There will be a contest about the Agent. Your friend Way will not be forgott. Malcolm takes his Snuff & I believe will gett Mr. Price on his side.

All your Friends here are well. I saw your Mother & Aunt 4 or 5 days ago, they were then very well.

PS I had forgott to tell you that I have made enquiry into the Connection your father had with Compere. They intirely relate to the Swamps & I am persuaded Mr. Laing has wrote to your Brother about them.

I shall sett about the Book of your Fathers accounts as soon as the Assembly setts that may overlook them myself & have gott a very capable man to do it. Your mother tells me one part is already entered in a Book so will continue it.

[*Notes that he will show* 'every Civility in my Power' *to one of Arcedekne's friends who is about to visit Jamaica.*]

24. To Benjamin Cowell, Kingston, 21 November 1767

The above is a Copy of my last to you since which have been up at Golden Grove when the Weather was excessive bad there and indeed was obliged to Swim my horse over every little Gully in the way & places where I never before saw the least stream of water and which continued untill about three weeks ago but since that have the pleasure to inform you that have received a letter from Mr. Kelly the Overseer that he will have finisht planting by the 10 of next month & that it will be a very fine plant notwithstanding the very severe weather we have had, that there is still a great deal to do before the Mill goes about as the Cuttway of the best mill is intirely undermined which was at first built on piles drove down to make a foundation which are now intirely decay'd and the trench that brings the water to the mill has

---

that he was not related to Simon Taylor.

[148] John, or Jack, Cussans (1742–1789), was the younger brother of Thomas Cussans. (See note 21 above.) He lived at Amity Hall and also owned property in Hanover. In 1767 he married Euphine Macqueen. Oliver, *CARIBBEANA*, III, p. 266; III (supplement), p. 40.

[149] Little is known of William Gale other than that he was a member of the pre-eminent Gale family (see note 136 above). His main residence was in Hanover and he served as a Member of Assembly for that Parish. *Ibid.*, III (supplement), p. 44.

been very much injured these things will take up a good deal of time to repair.

When was up Mr. Kelly & myself thought it would be for the benefitt of the Estate to putt in a Spring plant of 30 or 40 Acres in order to bring the Estate up again. We must hire Negroes to do it for the Plantation Negroes will not be able to do it and at the same time keep the Canes clean & the Mill about. I have also deferred yett getting about the House Mr. Arcedekne ordered to be built as was determined to gett in a Plant so as to make the Estate profitable & had I pusht both for a large plant & to build the House at the same time I should certainly have killed a good number of the Negroes which leaving Humanity aside never could have been for the advantage of that Gentleman but shall sett about it as soon as the good weather setts in.

I have seen Mr. Cooke who informs me that there is not above £1000 of any money that he received on Acct. of his administration on the Estate of Isaac Gale in his hands that the most they demand of him is £6000 of which he has paid £5000 due from that Estate to Henry Gale.[150] He has also promised to give me a State of his Accounts with that Estate & that he will allways be ready to settle with the Heirs of Gale and pay them. This I am apprehensive is out of his power as he is really insolvent but think the best way will be to lett the matter sleep and say nothing of it untill the administration Bond runs out of date which will be in three years. He tells me also that Messrs. Fisher & Hankey[151] in London & Mr. Bayly here have often threatned to sue the said Bond but have never been able yett to ascertain any thing due them. I shall loose no Opportunity of pressing him to gett a sight of the Accounts and compare them with the Inventory he he returned into the Secretary's office.

In reguard to Mrs. Wylles affair I believe it is intirely over for the person who has the Assignment was with me a few days ago and finding that he had no manner of chance of getting any thing from us without a great deal of trouble told me he was resolved to drop the Suit against Mr. Arcedekne's Estate and seek his money from James where it is really due provided that Dr. Gregory would give up the Administration of Stapleton under whose will he claims and Dr. Gregory by the will is Stapleton's Executor under Mr. Arcedekne. I told him that provided that no ill consequences could arise to Mr. Arcedeknes Estate by the Doctors giving up the administration I had no objection to the giving it up but before would consent to it would have the

---

[150] Henry Gale (1737–1767] was a member of the prestigious Gale family (see note 136 above). In 1750, whilst still a minor, he owned just over 10,065 acres of land. During the early 1760s he sat as one of the Members of the Assembly for St Elizabeth and also served as the Custos of that parish. Lawrence-Archer, *Monumental Inscriptions*, p. 306.

[151] A merchant house.

opinion of Councill. I have not yett gott it having been obliged to go over to the Northside & returned but this morning. Neither can I inform you of the Bill in reguard to the Plantain Garden River land claimed by Mr. Dawkins but that as last Thursday Mr. Robert Arcedekne & Mr. Pickersgill went to have a meeting on it. I shall write to you by the next Vessell and give you a particular acct. of it.

25. To Benjamin Cowell, Kingston, 24 March 1768

The foregoing is a Copy of my last to you p. the *Nautilus* Man of War. I should have wrote you ere this but was attacked with a Slight fever and went to Windward a few days afterwards where was again confined so that could not come to Town for seven weeks, since which this is the first opportunity that has offered for your Port.

Before I sett out I gave all the necessary orders in reguard to filing the Bill in reguard for the Plantain Garden River land & settling the Interrogatories and to put it in a Master in Chancery's hands to take the depositions of Mr. Pickersgill & then to get the Foreign Commission out, but have not since my return seen the Attorney having been in Spanish Town only about an hour.

Cooke never performed his promise of letting me see the State of the Accts. regarding the Administration on Gale, neither do I believe I shall gett a sight of them for he is suspended from the Councill. Do not believe he will chuse to Venture his Person this way as the Governor has also refused any protecting from the Court of Chancery unless it appears that a person has real business in that Court, which Mr. Cooke cannot make well appear and is greatly incumbered with debt.

I received a letter containing Bill of Lading & Invoice of Goods shipt from London by Messrs. Hilton & Biscoe & the *Friendship* Capt. Thompson which arrived here safe also the Provisions from Ireland from Mr. James Kelly[152] these excepting the Herrings which are not yett arrived.

I was at Golden Grove just after Christmas when the Weather was again terribly bad so that could not putt the Mill about. On that planted about 8 Acres of canes more. Before I came down they did putt about but were obliged to Stop again on Acct. of the Weather which has been really dismall in that part of the Country for 3 years last past and such as has never been known for 20 years before which together with the damage the flood in May last did & the short plant putt in by ramming the Cisterns for the Still house will make this Crop

---

[152] It has proved impossible to identify Kelly, although he may have been a kinsman of John Kelly, the overseer at Golden Grove.

be very short as every Estate's that way. The weather has been so bad as to destroy a great number of Cattle on Batchelors Hall, the continued rains giving the grass such a Spring as purges the Cattle to death. I could hardly believe it was not all the other penns near it in the same situation and circumstances.

Mr. Kelly again spoke to me about the Spring plant and I desired him to hire negroes to putt it in but whether he has as yett begun I cannot say from not having heard from him these three weeks.

In reguard to the House we have not even yett begun on it neither are the Window and door frames yett come out. It will be a very laborious work and am informed by the tradesmen to do it with Bricks that it would take 300,000 which would kill all the Cattle on the Estate to carry to the place where the House is to stand and we have no workmen in this Country that can build with stone to the dimensions that the plan requires, that is to make the Cornishes and raised work about the Doors & windows, but shall sett about the foundation and wait your orders. If we may build it a plain front we can do it well enough.

Inclosed I send you the Golden Grove Account Current with Taylor & Graham. I shall send you the list of Negroes & other Papers p. the *Friendship* Capt. Thompson who sails about the 15 of next month for as this goes by the man of war it makes a great addition of postage.

You will please to observe that we have shipt 50 Hhds. of Sugar on board said Ship from Golden Grove and shall ship thirty on board of the *Trent* Capt. Gillies and as I sett out for Golden Grove the 2^d of next month shall advise you further for making Insurance as I intend to ship every hhd. that the Estate makes this year to you, for now we have got the better of the Works which has been a most laborious and expensive Jobb and paid off what was due here.

I hope for the future to make the Rum pay for the Contingencies provided we do not buy negroes for the Estate, but as Mr. Arcedekne order'd none to be bought untill his arrival here I do not think myself at liberty to buy any without orders from him or you. I assure you they are excessively wanted for to carry on the Estate as it ought to be it will require upwards of 100 more working Negroes for there are a great number of old Superannuated Negroes and Young Children there, and the whole of Plantain Garden River is deem'd unhealthy even in this Country. At the same time the Estate would yield much better for them as we could take care of the Rattoons and trench the land we putt in for a plant much better. The Person who made the greatest fortune that ever was made in this Country in the planting way, Viz. old Mr. Dawkins held it for a maxim allways to have three Negroes to do the work of two, and am confident from my own Experience that is the Cheapest way to make Sugar in the long term.

By the Account Current you will see that there are four hdds. of Sugar remaining to be accounted for. They were sent alongside of Capt. Raffles's ship last year and by the negligence of the Sailors they did not chock the Hdds, so on taking out one the others ran to Leeward and oversatt the boat by which they were excessively damaged. The Capt. was with me two days ago and we are to settle the matter on my going to Windward as it is well known there & he himself is convinced that he must pay for them.

I shall be obliged in the Course of the Crop to draw on you for about £1000 Stg. to reimburse myself for what is in part is due T & G, but will put it off as long as possible but at any rate will not draw untill I ship Sugars and not then if I can avoid it.

This Minute received a letter from Mr. Kelly with the Weights of 50 hdds. of Sugar shipt on board the *Friendship* Capt. Thomson which I have enclosed herein and also the bills of Lading for them he also acquaints me that the 30 for Capt. Gillies are now ready.

26. To Chaloner Arcedekne, Kingston, 25 March 1768

Since my last to you have not had the pleasure of hearing from you which indeed I did not expect, & as am uncertain where this will meet you, write chiefly to shew you that am still in the land of the living.

I referr you to your brother in Law in matters relating to your affairs & to let you know that they are brought to this conclusion that I do not know of any debt now whatsoever that is due from your father's Estate in the world or by you but what is due to us.

We made a most miserable Crop last year occasioned by the vast quantity of rain & the flood in May. We shall also make very bad Crop this year occasioned by that & the time it took up to ram the Cisterns, but have got in a plant of 186 Acres & think of getting a spring Plant also in, so there is a good appearance if the rain & bad weather do not hurt us in the latter end of the year, which I hope it will not. I think I can insure you a good Crop next year & the year after, but I do assure you you want a great many Negroes, & am confident you would find your advantage in it was it only 20 p. ann. & them to be bought in two or three parcels you would not feel the expence putting them on in that manner. It would greatly hearten the rest & it will be impossible keeping the Estate up to great Crops without you do it. I advise you as I do myself on my own Estate & did I not think it was for your advantage would not say so.

All our Politics here are turnd upside down. Mr. Elletson has suspended Bayly, Pinnock, French, Scott,[153] Cooke, Sinclair[154] & Kennion from the Councill & all honors, Civil & Military, & has appointed young Charles Price, Welsh[155] & May[156] in their room as Councellors.

Every thing is very dull here & an excessive scarcity of money. Laing has been indisposed but got well again. I have been a good deal out of order but am much better. Your Mother & Aunt are very well. I shall go to Golden Grove in a few days.

In regard to your house am sorry to acquaint you I have not begun upon it, first from the bad weather & flood in May which hurt the Canes & Estate so much that it was necessary to put in a longer Plant to bring the Estate up again as that is the Primum mobile of everything, and secondly am informed it will take 300m Bricks & that it would kill all your Cattle carrying them there, & there is no one man in this Country can build it of Stone to answer the Plan as sent out, therefore think of building it plain & keeping as much to your Plan as possible, & carry it up as far as we can untill the Window frames come out.

27. To Benjamin Cowell, Kingston, 18 April 1768

The above is a Copy of may last since which I have been favoured with yours of 23 Jany. I assure you that you have heard nothing of the flood in May last but what was very true and that it will greatly hurt this Crop. Neither could we gett the Negroes to put in the Spring plant as we designed but have notwithstanding a very fine plant in the ground and there is a good appearance for a good Crop for the ensuing year if we should not be again pestored with Rains as we have been these three years past.

[153] John Scott owned upwards of 5,000 acres of land and his main residence was at Trelawny. Oliver, *CARIBBEANA*, III, p. 95.

[154] In 1763 Archibald Sinclair was serving as Clerk of the Markets and in that same year was recommended for membership of Jamaica's Royal Council by Governor Lyttelton. He also sat in the Assembly during the 1760s as a Member for St Catherine. Greene, 'The Jamaican privilege controversy', p. 26.

[155] Richard Welch (or Welsh) had trained as a lawyer and in 1768 was Jamaica's Attorney General. He was still a member of Jamaica's Royal Council in 1776 and by 1770 was the island's Chief Justice. In 1769 he married Lucretia Favell Dehany, who belonged to of one of Jamaica's wealthiest planting families. In 1768 Chaloner's cousin, Robert Arcedekne, left a bequest of £50 sterling to his 'special friend Richard Welch', whom he also named as one of his executors. Welch died in Bath, England, in 1782 at the age of forty-nine. Oliver, *CARIBBEANA*, III, pp. 220, 289; IV, p. 289; Will of Robert Arcedekne, 8 December 1768, Island Record Office, Spanish Town, Wills, XXXVIII, fo. 39.

[156] Rose Herring May.

I was at G Grove about 10 days ago they had then fair weather which I believe still continues and were making the best Sugar I ever saw there and the Negroes were pretty healthy. I really believe Dr. Hayward[157] takes all the care he can possibly of them. The thing that carrys off the Negroes there is the Yaws which throws them into Dropsys. I desired that for the future that when any of them gett the Yaws that they might be sent to Batchelors Hall Penn which is a dryer situation than the Estate & to be there kept cleaning the pastures as exercise is reckoned good for that disorder and it is the lightest work that Negroes can be put to.

Capt. Chisholm is not yett arrived. I gave orders to gett the Stones for the House which is sett about and as we are to have the frame we shall soon finish it. I shall also ship 100 Hdds. of Sugar on board of Capt. Chisholm if he has occasion for so many, but would not have you insure on that quantity untill you hear again from me for I would not willingly put so many on board of one Vessell without he was pusht which I hope will not be the Case. Neither can I before he arrives give any promises to the other Capts. to ship on them for as Mr. Arcedekne is concern'd in that Ship I would not by any means let her sail otherwise than full as the Parish will fall short in the quantity of Sugars and there are more Ships this year at the Bay and Harbour than ever were before.

[*Thanks Cowell for a gift of cheese.*]

I shall send you p. Capt. Stuport the Papers you mention, Mr. Bullocks Opinion on Fishers demand & the Commission for Examining Mr. Burke in reguard to Dawkins's claim. In reguard to Mrs. Wyllies affair the matter is dropt neither do I believe it will ever be again revived against Mr. A. Arcedekne's Estate. Doctor McGlashen who has the Assignment of the claim having told me he intended to endeavour to gett it from James's Estate.

All the Supplies are arrived safe and we have shipt 30 hdds. on Board the *Friendship* Capt. Gillies who will sail about the beginning of May. We received a letter from Mess. Scott Pringle and Cheap of Madeira with a Bill of Lading for 3 pipes of Wine on Board the *Augustus Caesar* Capt. Dufill on Act. of Mr. Arcedekne which is arrived but not yett landed.

Enclosed is a list of the Negroes on Golden Grove. I have not yett gott the list of the Batchelors Hall Negroes. I find that we have had a tolerable Increase of Calves there last Quarter having near 30 dropt.

---

[157] Apparently hired by John Kelly with Taylor and Arcedekne's approval, Hayward continued to work on Golden Grove until the 1780s.

28. To Benjamin Cowell, Kingston, 14 May 1768

Since the above p. Capt. Thompson I have been favored with yours of 10 Febry p. the *Golden Grove* Capt. Chisholm and am very sorry to find that you was unwell. I hope long before this you have recovered your health.

I also received the letter from Mr. Arcedekne and shall agreeable to his order consign the Sugars to you as I did last year by which means you can send the Bills of Lading to any House you please. I also received the bill of Lading for the frame of the House, you may depend on it I shall forward it as much as possible.

[*Repeats his thanks for the gift of cheese which* 'was very good and came in good order'.]

Inclosed I send you the Bill of Lading for 30 Hdds. of Sugar shipt on board the *Trent* Capt. Gillies & annex'd are the Weights of them. There are also 360 Hdds. gone from the Estate to be put on board the *Golden Grove* Capt. Chisholm. We shall ship 80 hhds. on board her and beg you may Insure on that quantity as I believe she will not want any more. If she does shall give you timely notice to insure. I think, but not untill I hear from Capt. Chisholm, to put 20 Hdds. on board the *Prince George* Capt. Fryer but would not have you insure untill you hear again from me.

By a letter of 9 Febry from Mr. Biscoe he advises me of the 3 Pipes of Wine p. the *Augustus Caesar* Capt. Duffill and desires they may not be meddled with as they are for some Friends in England and that the necessary orders will be sent out about them. As I have not yet received any orders yet concerning them am at a Loss what to do. I therefore beg your orders concerning them.

I have under this Cover sent you Mr. Bullock's opinion on Fishers demand against Cooke who was displaced from the Councill some time ago by the Present Governor and was a few weeks ago thrown into Gaol by his Creditors. He is a very worthless & insolvent Subject.

I also send you the Commission for Examining Mr. Luke Burke in Ireland. If you can gett any one who is acquainted with the Gentlemen it is directed to it will be proper to gett a letter to them. They were recommended to me by the present Attorney General here Mr. Richard Welch. If can get no other letter it will be proper to make use of his name which he has given me a liberty to do. Dawkins's Attorney here is excessively enraged at the Bill we filed for this purpose and has secretly been Caballing with Mr. Archer who is tenant in common with Mrs. Kearsey during life for 90 Acres of said land and offred if he would make no opposition to the Ejectment he is determined to bring to give him a Conveyance for his life to the half of said land which was refused, and Mr. Archer himself told me this, but there is I believe not the least risque of loosing it begin when they will, for Pickersgills Evidence is returned into the Chancery office and am informed from good Authority it is very full as to the matter in dispute. I could not see it these matters being allways returned seal'd into the Office and not opened until Publication passes before the Chancellor.

This morning saw Capt. Fryer who acquaints me that he will not be able to take any more Sugar for us this Year but there are plenty of good ships and can putt more on board of Chisholm if there is occasion.

Mr. Bullock is gone out of town without sending me his opinion but from what he told me am confident it is against us. Inclosed is a letter from our Sollicitor in reguard of what is to be done at home about the matter.

I have put on board Capt. Stupart a box of Cashew Nutts which Mrs. Kearsey sent me for Mrs. Cowell, both she and Mrs. Harris are well, I had the pleasure of seeing them a few days ago.

29. To Benjamin Cowell, Kingston, 6 July 1768

Since my last to you have been favoured with yours of 19 Aprill inclosing a letter from Mr. Arcedekne to me and two to Mrs. Kearsey and find that Messrs. Beeston Long & Co have now the consignment of his Sugars.

We have shipt on Board Capt. Chisholm 120 Hdds. and 80 on board of the *Morant Planter* Capt. Power of which we advise you in order to make Insurance. Capt. Chisholm will sail next week the very strong Sea Breezes for these three weeks past have kept him back. I intend going to Windward in three or 4 days and shall write to you about the Estate & Chisholm and also to Mr. Arcedekne and shall advise you for further Insurance as shall give the most forward Ship the Sugars as the advanced Premium is coming on and would chuse to save it.

I have been obliged to draw a Bill on you on Acct. of Mr. Arcedekne for 500 Stg. favor of Messrs. Bean & Cuthbert at 90 days sight and shall be obliged to draw on you by Chisholms sailing for £500 more for shall ship every hdd. the Estate makes this year. I beg the favor you will please to Honor them with your acceptance.

I have not as yett gott Mr. Bullocks opinion in Writing on Mr. Cookes matter but he told me a few days ago that the Estate of Mr. A Arcedekne would certainly be liable for his difficiencies. Cooke is miraculously gott out of Gaol by no other writts being at the time of the Action lodged against him by his wives giving a Mortgage on her property as a Security for the debts on which he was apprehended.

30. To Benjamin Cowell, Lyssons, 25 July 1768

Since my last to you p. Capt. Brett I have been here in my way to Golden Grove tho have not as yett been able to gett there occasioned by a hurt tho shall be there the End of the week.

Inclosed I send you the Bills of Lading for 120 hdds. of Sugar shipt on board the *Golden Grove* Capt. Charles Chisholm and for 20 hdds. shipt on board the *Morant Planter* Capt. Power. I was in hopes of having been able to have shipt thirty hhds. more on board the *Morant* but was prevented by three weeks excessive blowing weather so that no vessell could go in or come out of Plantain Garden River and when that ceased there was no vessell to be gott on any Acct. Indeed I was obliged to order the last forty hdds. to fill up the *Golden Grove* to be wained to Port Morant.

You will be pleased to order Insurance on thirty hdds. of Sugar to be shipt on board the *Prince George* Capt. Scrymsoure who will sail about the middle of next month which is the remainder of the Crop not having disposed of a Single Cask in this Country of that Estates Sugar. Indeed it is a most miserable one but greatly and must say wholly to be attributed to the Excessive wett year last and the flood with many other little Accidents.

Mr. Kelly was here three days ago he informs me that he has all the Canes in very good order and clean that the weather was very fine and that he had as yett none of the Canes lodged. If the weather continues good he is in hopes of a good crop next year to make up the badness of this of which he hath need. He also informs me that he is getting home timber to make a new floodgate for the Dam the old one being rotten. It is a very troublesome jobb but nothing in comparison of that next the Garden which was built by the navy Carpenters which also begins to grow old but we shall be able to repair it pretty well. His House will be sett about directly after Christmas they having already gott a great many stones for it and two large Kilns of Lime burnt. After the Materials are gott it will be no hard matter to gett up the House. I shall take care that it is comformable to Mr. Arcedeknes orders when I return from thence I shall be able to write you fuller on this Subject.

I have been obliged to draw on you since the Bill for £500 in favor of Messrs. Bean & Cuthbert for £250 stg. favor of Alexander Littlejohn[158] dated 12 July the other for £250 stg. dated 20 July favor of Matthias Gale[159] both at ninety days sight which makes up the 1000 stg. I

---

[158] Alexander Littlejohn's properties included The Rhine Plantation in St Thomas in the East. Oliver, *CARIBBEANA*, III, p. 297. There is no record of what goods or services he provided for Golden Grove on this occasion.

[159] Matthew Gale was a member of the pre-eminent Gale family. (See note 136 above.)

acquaint you that I should be obliged to draw for on Mr. Arcedeknes Accot. I shall not draw for any more this year and indeed it would want much against me to do it but mett with severall disappointments. I beg the favor you will please to honor them with your acceptance.

[*Notes that he has sent Cowell a turtle* 'by Capt. Chisholm'.]

31. To Chaloner Arcedekne, Lyssons, 25 July 1768

I received yours of 3 March from Naples and in reguard of Cookes matter I took Bullocks opinion as you desired me and do find that your fathers Estate is jointly lyable with Robin Delaps for his difficiencies. The best way is to say nothing of the matter and in all probability it will die away of itself. As for Cooke himself he with six others was displaced or suspended by Mr. Elletson from his seat in the Councill and was arrested at the suit of Hutchinson More by his Attorneys but by his wifes joining in a Mortgage of all her property to them he was discharged as luckily for him there was at that time no other writt lodged in the office. The Fosters[160] Attorney the next day lodged writts to the amount of £5000. I really do not think you have any great Occasion to be uneasy on this matter. The older it is the more intricate it will grow and John Morse you may depend will throw every obstacle he can in the way. As for Cooke himself I do not apprehend he has either Honor or Honesty and since above mentioned misfortune is very shy and keeps close at home.

What you say is very just that Golden Grove has been a fund for paying of other peoples debts but am much afraid that the generality of those people or their representatives have nothing to refund.

In regard to making out the Sett of Books you wrote to me about I did engage a man and the only one that I know in this Country capable of such a thing, who settled Stirlings matters and introduced him to your mother to begin on those matters but she showed so much uneasiness and unwillingness that I thought it much better to stop than run any risque of giving the old Lady umbrage as she gave apparent signs of her disappointment of overhauling the old Papers. There is a Bond of Sam Gordons[161] for £300. His Son was not askd for it poor lad. He made no manner of thing here and Bayly cheated him out of all his Fathers property so he has gone back to England. He has some

---

[160] No further information has been discovered about either the Fosters or the attorney mentioned by Taylor.

[161] Samuel Gordon's will was finally proved in 1778. Oliver, *CARIBBEANA*, I, p. 175.

relations there who I believe wrote for him. He is a very worthy good man.

In reguard of what you owe me it was last Christmas about £4000 this Currency but as there are no buildings this year to pay for, it will diminish besides have been obliged to draw on Mr. Cowell for £1000 stg. occasioned by some disappointments I have mett with this year. Your mother nor Aunt have not received anything since your fathers death. Indeed they do not want any thing for they would only lock it up and it will all be yours and your Sisters at their deaths.

I saw Kelly a few days ago who informs me that there are a great many stones gott for the House and two lime Kilns burnt. The Windows and door frames all come out p. Capt. Chisholm so your house when once sett about will not take a great while finishing. The frames shall be pitched and then painted over before it is putt up and the left rest just as you ordered. You must have misunderstood me or I must have made a mistake for my objection was that 1½ feet was not high enough. I hope it will please you when you come over as I will take care that all your directions shall be followed. Both your mother and Aunt have a great objection against the House for having no piazzas and want a Jamaica house built but as you have approved of the plan sent out shall follow it as exactly as possible.

I did receive three pipes of Wine p. the *Augustus Caesar* two of which I suppose are for the Duke of Roxburgh. They shall be taken care of and putt carefully by. I do not know whether he remembers me if he does if you will give my Compliments to him I shall be obliged to you. You may depend on anything your mother or Aunt wants shall be immediately sent and shall send them at all times anything they even seem to want.

In reguard to your Crop you have made so small a one that am asham'd to mention and could hardly believe it possible did I not myself even in this dry weather past feel the Effects of the wett weather having fallen one hundred and sixty hdds. short of what I made in 1766. I have shipt you 30 hdds. by Capt. Gillies 50 p. Thompson 120 p. Chisholm 20 p. Power and there is 33 still to ship which shall put on board the *Prince George* Capt. Scyrmsoure. Indeed the Excessive blowing weather is the thing that hindred them from being shipt on Power but no Vessell could go in and out of the Rivers mouth for upwards of 3 weeks and after the weather moderated there was no vessell to be had. This is all the Sugar you have made this year and I shall ship every cask of it.

Kelly informs me that there is now the best appearance of a good crop that he has seen since he has been on the Estate and we have had very good weather for sometime past and it is too dry for this part but very good for you. I shall be up there this week and will then write to you.

You still keep of from buying negroes. I assure you I do not write from any self Interested views and I know you do not think I do but except you do push it with some Negroes the Estate will inevitably fall back and cost you a very large Sum to bring up again. Whereas if you do not chuse to push it much the best way will be to buy about 16 Negroes a year out of 4 different Ships and it will be hard if 4 good negroes cannot be gott out of each ship and a twelve months Creditt. This will be the least you can do to keep up the Estate. You will make a good Crop this ensuing year and will make a good one the year after but do assure you Except there is a very large Addition of Negroes the Estate will fall back every year. The method I propose will be the Easiest and at the Same time a very good way for to increase your strength without putting your self to Any very great expense at once and will answer your end but something is absolutely necessary.

Robin [162] is gone to New York and getting better fast tho I believe never will be better. For his Reversion £1500 Stg. was well worth your while to give him but £10000 is a very good fortune of itself.

In reguard to Matrimony I have as yett no thoughts of it. You that are in so fair a Climate must want a wife more than one who have been so long in this Hott Country and consequently excessively relaxed. Tho as I am on the Subject there has been the Devill to pay between two disbanded Councillors Viz. Bayly & Kennion about the latters having debauched the others Quadroon Girl. Bayly says he is very glad that he did not catch them in Bed together or he would have been under the necessity of putting him to death.

Kennion and Tom Cussans want to Cutt through your River land to make a Canall to the back of the Stores and told Kelly you promised to let them but he told them he could do nothing without acquainting Laing your mother & self. On that they are to ask us to let them cutt. You know I have no orders from you. You will therefore please let me know whether I am to permitt them or not as I would chuse to take on myself to give them leave without knowing your sentiments.

Rose Price died about a month ago and old Whitehorne[163] lately greatly incumbered. Capt. Peyton has also slipped off very quietly and old Boroden[164] about the same time Price died.

Your mother and Aunt were both well when I came from Town as were all my family.

---

[162] Robin Arcedekne.

[163] The Hon. Samuel Whitehorne, who had served as a member of Jamaica's Royal Council.

[164] It has proved impossible to further identify either Peyton or Boroden.

32. To Benjamin Cowell, Kingston, 2 September 1768

My last to you was from Lyssons of 25 July p. the Capts. Chisholm & Power who I hope long before this are safe arrived. Since that time I was at Golden Grove for a Week and have the pleasure to assure you I never saw the Estate in such good order and promise so fair for a good Crop and the Negroes in good health. We having had very good weather there for some time past, neither were any of the Canes lodged. There are 182 Acres of plants 367 Acres of Rattoons to be cutt this Ensuing Crop, so that if it is not a good one it will not be for want of land enough in Canes. We shall putt in 110 Acres of plant this year. We think of going about them in the very beginning of December if the weather will possibly admitt having so many canes to cutt and so weak a Gang of Negroes. Indeed the reason of going about so early is to gain as much time as possible to take the Crop off but am much afraid the Estates Negroes will not be able to do it without help. But as I wrote fully on the want of Negroes before shall say no more on that Subject. I believe in case of no Accident that the Estate will make more Sugar the Ensuing year than ever it did and will make a better Crop the year after that.

We have had 100 Negroes there inoculated by Dr. Hayward and have not lost one. Indeed we did not think of inoculating without your orders but as every Estate about did it we were absolutely obliged out of self preservation to do it.

There are a great many stones gott for the House tho the quarry has failed us and when was up were looking out for another. There is lime enough gott. We shall sett about the building directly after Christmas. I did apprehend the Roof was come out in Chisholm but find it was only Window and Door frames etc. We have also gott home the timber for the little flood Gate the old one being intirely rotten.

Inclosed I send to you the bill of Lading and Invoice of 17 Hdds. of Sugar, Capt. Scrymsour having shut out the remainder, and pretends he could not take the rest altho we offered to wain them to Port Morant for him. We must remember him for another time. I would have shipd the remainder on the *York*, but as she is an Old New England built Vessell and this the most stormy time for a Vessell to sail for Europe spoke to one Capt. Boyd and let him know if he would bring them to this town I would lett them be putt on board his Ship, which he has agreed to if he can gett a Vessell to bring them down for there never was so great a Scarcity of Sugar drogers. I should be glad to know if you would approve of my purchasing a Small Vessell for the Use of the Estate and buy Sailor Negroes for her. Altho I can not promise that she would make much money it would be a means of never being disappointed as we could bring the Sugars to the Ships and save that freight and also send up in her whatever the Estate wanted. Untill the Warr there was allways a Vessell kept by the Estate which was then taken and since that time never had one.

I heard last night from Mrs. Kersey and Mrs. Harris who are both very well.

33. To Chaloner Arcedekne, Kingston, 27 January 1769

I have yours of 2^d August from Venice now before me wherein you acquaint me that you have not received my Accounts the Packet being so large that your brother did not send it to you but that he acquainted you that the Balance was £4800 against you & that you hope that as the most considerable Buildings are now done you will receive more from the Estate than you have hitherto got. This is what I think you have the greatest right to expect, for you have been at a very great expence in your works & can assure you that nothing has been done to them more than was necessary & I thought it was the best way to pay the Tradesmen off at once for if they are not they never will work chearfully & when there is the greatest occasion for them will disappoint which is seldom the case when they are regularly paid. The Balance of £4,800 is no addition to any other Account it being the whole item due either to me or to Taylor & Graham.

Am very sorry that the £1,000 stg. Bills I drew last Year should put you to any inconvenience & the payment to be appropriated in any part of the Crop 1768. Had I known it would have straightened you in the least would have put myself to any inconvenience rather than subject you to any, for I assure you there is nothing in my power but would do to serve you at all times & at all Seasons. Am convinced never have been extravagant but if you consider the low Condition of the Estate when you got possession of it, the Expences attending your Law Suit, the building a New Sett of Works, the Demands against your Fathers Estate & the Compromise at home, you will readily conceive how the Crops have been disposed of which also from the very great & constant & uncommon severity of the Rains have been less than might be expected not to say any thing of the two great Floods which happened in that space of time. Thank God the weather has since mended & I hope there will be a tolerable Crop this year which hope will put you in good heart & Spirits & also put you in a mind of purchasing some Negroes as I hope it will do away your present Objections, but of this by & by.

Am glad to hear you intend settling for life. By that I suppose you begin to think of marrying. I think I am confident that you must for the future have a very large income coming in annually to you now the Expence of building the Works is over. Indeed had you on getting possession of the Estate been £100,000 in Debt you must either have built a Sett or thrown up the Estate. They are now built in a manner for ever provided no Accident of Fire etc, which God forbid should ever happen.

In regard to Kelly I do believe he has your Interest as much at heart & is as industrious & active as ever. It was not his fault that the Estate has not made so much Sugar as was expected it would. The whole Parish fell short these two Years. I fell short at my own Estate last year near 150 Hhds.

In regard to the Flood Gate at the Great River he assures me it was down. Neither was that the place the River broke in at but at March & Gardners. Indeed, the River overflow'd its Banks every where & covered the whole Vale. It was not Golden Grove only that was overflowe'd but every Estate in the River underwent the same fate & yours was the only Molasses Cistern in the River that was not fill'd. I have given positive orders that that Gate shall always be shutt as soon as the Rains begin to fall in April, tho' apprehend there is rather too little Water in Negro River to finish your Crop but this must be entirely regulated by the Seasons.

When he first went there he planted rather too thin but now he puts in the Clay Land 3 Canes in a hole & in the Brick mould 4. I think the Canes stand much better for the thick planting, they are not so luxuriant but they do not lodge so much. As you mention it, will plant a Piece with 5 Canes but in my opinion 4 will do equally well.

Do not make yourself at all uneasy at any thing you owe me or Taylor & Graham. It is what I will always take on myself & I again acquaint you that all the Old Balance is included in the last Balance of the £4800 which was the whole either due to me or to Taylor & Graham. You need not think of retrenching your Expences. If there was the least occasion I would inform you. You have now chiefly to reap the advantage of your Estate & am confident the Rum will pay the Contingencies of it & you can afford to live any where you chuse yourself without renting it. I believe you will be convinced this year that what I say is true. You have sold as much Cattle as last Year. You will find Kelly will make good his promise to you of a good Crop. You will make as good a one the Year after. This will be sufficient to sett you free & Money in the Bank. It will not be the Planters this Year in words only but indeed.

You had the whole quantity of Land to cutt that Kelly mentioned to you without having occasion to purchase a Mule or a Steer tho' will not be able to sell any working Steers this Year.

The 3 Pipes of Wine are here safe & I shall wait your orders for shipping them.

Mr. Laing has been much out of order but is now better. Old Price is made a Baronet, whether with or without his knowledge cannot say. John Woodcock [165] died about 3 months ago & Young Charles is married to his Widow.

Am exceeding sorry to find we have no accounts of the *Golden Grove* Capt. Chisholm whom every body here have given over for lost. I have a Letter from Mr. Cowell acquainting me that he insured 80 Hhds. of your Sugar on board her. I hope he has also insured the 40 more I acquainted him that could be put on board by my letter of 6 July p. the *Rose* Capt. Brett. If she is gone it is exceeding unlucky. Poor George Bennett[166] has 44 hhds. uninsured on board. I hope your Eighth of the Ship was insured. I relyd so much on her goodness that did not Insure mine.

Mr. Cowell also writes me that Mr. Fisher would be very glad to do any thing in regard to his claim on Cooke to whom your Father was one of his Securitys on his administration on the Estate of Isaac Gale. I have wrote him not to be in any hurry in regard to that matter & not to give up any thing but what the Law allows for the following Reasons. I have again seen Cooke who positively insists on it that there is not above £1000 Currency due by him to the heirs of Gale & that he is willing to settle the matter himself with Fisher who has for many Years threatened him with a Law Suit but thought better of it, that Bayly has also once had that matter in his hands & had there been any thing considerable he would never have overlookt it. He also again promised me he will send me a State of what moneys he has both paid & received on accot. of said Estate. Whether he will comply with his promise or no I cannot tell. I shall not fail to urge it. You yourself know what a worthless fellow he is both in Principles & fortune.

Am sorry to inform you that Robert Delap who is the other Security joined with your Father is dead, & notwithstanding in his life time reputed a man of considerable Property & pretty clear, that his Estate will hardly pay 2 Mortgages on it & Mr. Graham this morning informed me that Mr. John Morse told him that including the 2 Mortgages his Estate owes Morse & Bayly £22,000 stg. & his Inventory amounts to about £23,000 Curry. & the Widow dowerable out of the Lands etc, so that will be a total loss whatever Fisher may get. Neither indeed if there was any probability of recovering any thing against the Estate of Delap could it be done untill Fisher has recovered a Judgement jointly against your Father's Estate & his. Morse is filing a Bill in Chancery to bring the Estate to a Sale which he will effect in a few Months as I suppose it will not be litigated. It is a very unfortunate Transaction for

---

[165] It has proved impossible to further identify Woodcock.
[166] It has proved impossible to further identify Bennett.

you. Indeed, the Old Gentleman was very unlucky, almost every one he was Security for deceived him & left him to pay their Debts. It is but a melancholy consolation for doing a good natur'd Action that the man turns out a Rascal.

Mr. Cowell wrote me you was very anxious to know what the last Year's Crop was. It was only 249 Hhds. & 1 tierce[167] every part of which I sent home to him Vizt. 50 p. Thompson, 30 p. Gillies, 120 p. Chisholm, 20 p. Power, 17 p. Scrymsour, 12 & 1trs. p. Boyd. You was lucky in one particular in my not putting 13 hdds. which were reduced to 12 & tierce & shipt on board Boyd. They were left out by Scrymsour & the Captain of the *York* wanted them much but as his was an Old Norward built Ship was afraid to trust them in her, & it is well I did not for he run her ashore off Charlestown in So. Carolina to prevent her sinking & every Cask of Sugar on board her is lost.

I was at Golden Grove a fortnight ago & staid there a week. The Mill is about & there are upwards of 100 Hhds. of very good large Hhds. of Sugar made, tho' they went on very slowly on for want of Water not having got Plantain Garden River in altho' there have been 40 Negroes from your Estate & as many from Duckenfield Hall for three weeks at work on the Weir occasioned by the bottom of the Arch being at least five feet about the Surface of the River, so that they are obliged to raise it upwards of that to turn it in & every Flood in the River either damages it or carries it away intirely notwithstanding it is made of 5 or 6 Rows of Poles drove down & wattled together with River gravell etc thrown between. The Arch was originally wrong built. It should have been as low as the bottom of the bed of the River & the Trench deeper dugg & untill that is done & faced with a Brick gutter you will always be troubled for want of Water. This must be a work of time & in the meantime must do as well as we can. Whenever is done, Duckenfield Hall I believe will be glad to be at half the Expence for they will be as great gainers as you. It must tho' be well considered before it is done, so that they may not claim a right to have the Water run in that Direction which might perhaps affect the Fall you may want in case you ever think of settling another Estate.

I believe you must next year be at some Expence altering if not considerably repairing one of the Mills which does at present little or nothing. Tom Winter[168] is to be up at Duckinfield Hall to do some work for the Mill there after Crop. I intend to consult him about it & also in the matter of the Trench I mentioned before. He is very clever & will act conscientiously.

I had your Tradesmen with me & gave them a hearty scolding in

---

[167] A measure equal to a third of a pipe, or forty-two gallons.

[168] It has proved impossible to further identify Winter.

not having begun the house immediately after Christmas as they promised & they both Stevens & Carter have positively promised me that they will sett about it by the 15 of next month & will not take any of their People off untill it is finished. The reason they give is because they have now on hand several small Jobs for different Estates which must be done before they can put their Mills about & their attention is drawn different ways which will be all finished by that time when they will bring all their several Gangs together & not break off untill it is compleated.

In regard to Batchelors Hall, was there also. I am sorry to tell you you have been very unlucky there having lost a good many of the Old Cows & their Calves, & the Cattle there look both thinner & rougher than they used to do tho' the Pasture is pretty clean & Kelly tells me that Kearney[169] is very sober & diligent. Indeed had it not been for that I should have turnd him away. He is on his good behaviour & if he does not do better I shall discharge him at the end of the Quarter. He says it is a lax they have gott. I ordered him to give them herrings which is a good thing for it. I shall be up there in a fortnight for having also the managmt of two Estates in Blue Mountain Valley intend being at Windward almost the Whole Crop time & pay my greatest attention to yours & the other propertys I have the Care of there, that the Crops are taken off to the best advantage & nothing is ever hurt by being well lookt after.

I have enrolled Pickersgill's Examination in the Chancery Office & shall do the same by Mr. Bourke's when get it from your Brother. I hear nothing now about Dawkins's claim, they will never be able to get it from you & I hope by & by to see you have another Estate as Kennion's Holland is there.

Mr. Laing & Mr. Kelly both spoke to me about sparing some Mules & Cattle to your Bros. Estate from your's. I told Kelly to spare what he could & he has sent 3 Mules which could not carry Canes but would do tolerably in a Mill & a Spell of Cattle to help down the Crop. I hope you will not be against it.

I shall ship home to Mr. Cowell on your account 50 Hhds. on board the *Friendship* Thompson & 50 on board the *Duckenfield* Foster which will be the first two ships & also something in every Ship I hope, & give you timely advice for making the Insurance. These two Ships will sail in April.

I will not for fear of Accidents promise what the Estate will make but every thing wears the appearance of a very good Crop. The 2 first Pieces of Canes that were cutt contained 27 Acres. They made 57

---

[169] It has proved impossible to locate any further information about Kearney or for how long he had been employed as an overseer at Batchelor's Hall pen.

Hhds. What has been cutt afterwards when there did not do so well. You will make a very good Crop the year after that that is next year but do assure you that without an addition of Negroes it will be impossible to keep the Estate up.

I do not want you to go to any great Expence at once for Negroes, but to put on for some years to come about 16 or 20, no more than 4 or at most 5 out of one Ship & of the best Countries & who have had the Yawes if possible to be discovered. I would not urge you to it was it not your own advantage & am confident that your Crop will be satisfactory & remove your Objections. I assure your present Negroes will last much longer for it. The New will season in this manner tolerably kindly & if you will raise a good Strength in the Estate without much feeling it as in three Years time each Negro will pay for himself. For it is a pity & for after having such good Lands & Works the Estate should fall off for want of a sufficient strength of Negroes, which if not put on must infallibly be the case.

We have exerted ourselves for the Plant we are now taking off & it was late before we went about last Year. Were we to push so for a continuance the Negroes would be destroye'd which is what I am sure you neither wish or desire. Neither shall I take up your time in telling you how every other Estate in that Quarter hire jobbing Negroes etc.

Your Cousin Robin Arcedekne went to New York for the Recovery of his health & died there. He has given £10,000 Stg. in Legacies to his Sisters being the amount of the Mortgage he had on his Brother's Estate in Ireland & money in John Bourke's hands in London, £700 to Old Fagan for Services in the Law Suit against you; £70 to Welch & the Resideum of every thing including Fontabell & the Reversion of Golden Grove should you dye without Children to Nic. Bourke. I hope you will take care to disappoint both him & Bourke by marrying. All your acquaintances are about it. Welch was marry'd last Monday to Miss Dehany,[170] a Grand daughter of Dr. Gregory's. Bullock is to be married to Miss Trower.[171] Walter Murray[172] the Naval officer to one Miss Garland & Brownrigg to Widow Jones[173] and three or four more Young Fellows so that shall hardly have a Batchelor among us.

Tom Cussans & my Brother sail the week after next for North America to take a Tour of it. Jack intends for England & Tom Cussans to visit Paoli & Corsica.

[170] Welch married Lucretia Favell Dehany. (See note 155 above.)

[171] Bullock married Elizabeth Savile Trower. Oliver, *CARIBBEANA*, III, p. 38.

[172] Murray went on to become the proprietor of Latium Plantation in St James' Parish. In 1773 he was elected as a Member of the Assembly for that Parish. He subsequently returned to England where he died in 1794 at the age of fifty-four. *Ibid.*, III, p. 86.

[173] It has proved impossible to further identify Miss Garland, Brownrigg, and Widow Jones.

I have not been lately at Spanish Town but hear your mother &
aunt are both well.

The Postage of a large Packet comes to much by a Man of War that
shall Enclose your Accounts for 1768 by the Merchant man for London,
the balance is about £3680.18.9½ in our favor including all former
balances.

34. To Benjamin Cowell, Kingston, 27 January 1769

Your favor of 4th September is now before me acquainting me of having
received the 30 Hogsheads of Sugar p. Gillies & those by Thompson
safe & that you had insured 80 p. Chisholm. I advised you by mine of
6 July to make Insurance on 40 hdds. more p. Chisholm so as to make
in the whole 120 hdds. & by mine of 25 July p. the *Golden Grove* &
Duplicate p. the *Morant Planter* intended to put 30 on board Capt.
Scrymsour but he would not take any more on board but 17, the other
13 were reduced to 12 & 1 tierce which were shipt on board the *Prince
of Wales* Capt. Boyd of which Mr. Graham gave you advice.

I am excessively uneasy on account of the *Golden Grove* as we have
no manner of Accounts of him here as yet. Indeed I make no manner
of doubt but the advice came time enough to get Insurance done for
40 hdds. last shipt before he was missing for I do not ever expect to
hear of her again. I had besides shipt on board her 44 hdds. on account
of another friend & did rely so much on the goodness of the Ship &
experience of the Captain that I would not insure any thing on 1/8 of
said Ship which belonged to me. Indeed am more uneasy at the loss
my friends suffer p. said vessell than for my own. I hope Mr. Arcedekne's
1/8 was insured. We have not heard the least thing of her in these
parts but by way of London.

In regard to Mr. Fisher's Claim on Mr. Cooke of this Country for
his Transactions regarding the Estate of Isaac Gale & for whose
Administration Mr. Andrew Arcedekne & Robert Delap were Securitys,
I would not by any means have you be in any matter of hurry to settle
it with him. Let him have what the Law will give him for have again
seen Cooke who positively insists on it that there is not above £1000
this money due by him to the Heirs of Gale & that he is willing to
settle the matter himself with Mr. Fisher, that he has been many years
talking of making him account for those matters but never proceeded
in it & that it has also been in the hands of Mr. Zachary Bayly here &
that if any thing could be done he would have done it, but the
frivolousness of Mr. Fishers pretensions to any large Sum of money
due to him by Mr. Cooke prevented his prosecuting the matter. Cooke
has again promised me to let me see a State of the Account & what

Sums he has paid & received on account of said Estate. He is indeed not worth a Penny & am afraid the Estate of Robert Delap will also turn out good for little for calling not long ago on my Attorney found him drawing out an Amicable Bill in Chancery & answer to it. Curiosity made me ask him what it was & he acquainted me it was to bring the Estate of Robert Delap to a Sale for his Debts were so large that there was no saving it as there were one Mortaged on the half of said Estate amounting with the Principal & Interest in the hands of Mr. Paplay to near £12,000 & another to Mr. Morse for £6000 Stg. & the whole value of the Property of which Mr. Delap died possessed of did not exceed £23,000 & his Widow was also intitled to Dower & there were other debts besides. As there is no such thing as getting a Judgement on said Estate or indeed suing it as liable to pay one half as being a Joint Security in the Bond with Mr. Arcedekne untill the Sum due Mr. Fisher is ascertained & they have obliged his Estate to pay it as being the most solvent, I say untill this is done there will be no such thing as coming on Delap's Estate which will long before this can properly happen be intirely sunk in paying his Debts now about Establishing in the Court of Chancery & Expences & compromising the Widow's Dower, so I do not expect Mr. Arcedekne will avail himself a penny on accot of Delap's being joined in the Bond with his Father. It is a most unlucky affair but cannot now be remedied & the only thing is not to pay any more than what is justly due & cannot be avoided, as the Old Gentleman never got any thing by the Transaction & was intirely led into it through Friendship & a desire to serve Mr. Cooke.

The Crop of Golden Grove amounted to only 249 Hhds. & 1 Tierce of which the whole was shipt to you vizt. 50 p. Thompson, 30 p. Gillies, 120 p. Chisholm, 20 p. Power, 17 p. Scrymsour, & 12 hhds. p. Boyd, shall p. the first Ship send you the Estates' Accounts for 1768 which are already drawn out. The reasons of the Crop being so small I gave you before vizt. the Weather for three Years before, the ramming the Cisterns for the Still house & the Floods.

We have had tolerable good weather here for these several months past. I was up about 14 days ago & staid 7 days there. The Mill was about & have now made upwards of 100 Hdds. Believe there will be a very good Crop made this Year if we meet with no Accidents which I hope we shall not. There are Canes enough on the Ground to make a good one. The first two pieces of Plans we cutt being 27 Acres made 57 hhds. of Sugar, the pieces that they were on when there did not yield near so well but all the Sugar then made was very good. I will not take on me for fear of accidents to say what the Estate will make this Year but assure you shall be up there every fortnight or three weeks & that nothing shall be wanting on my part to make the Crop turn out satisfactory both in the quantity & quality of the Goods.

We were very scarce of Water there not having got in Plantain Garden River altho there has been 80 Negroes (between Golden Grove & Duckinfield Hall) for three weeks constantly upon it. The reason of it is the Flood Gate was originally wrong built. The Foundation of it is at least 5 feet above the Surface of the River so were obliged to raise the River so high by a Dam across it to turn it into the Trench which carried the Water to the Dam by the Works & the Trench being cutt through a rich loose Mould the whole way is continually falling in after any heavy Rain which were obliged to be continually throwing out to keep it open. Had we a sufficient strength of Negroes on the Estate to do the work of it & keep it in the Condition it ought to be kept in we would lower the Flood Gate to a Levell with the bottom of the River & face the bottom & sides of the Trench with a Brick Gutter. The Bricks could be easily made from the Mould dug out of the Trench by which means we might command at all times what quantity of Water we wanted & loose very little in the way, whereas as it is now we loose near half of it by sinking in the Gardens. We should also save the Expence we are at in raising the River every Year & which we have sometimes occasion to do two or three times a Year for the Dam or Weir is carried away or broke by almost every flood & takes a great deal of time & work to repair it. But untill there is a sufficient number of Negroes to effect this must do as well as we can.

I believe we shall be obliged almost to build a New Mill after the Crop. One of those on the Estate being very old & does almost nothing. Think of employing one Mr. Wynter to examine her. He is lookt upon to be one of the best Mechanicks in the Country & a conscientious man. He will have some work to do at Duckinfield Hall which is the next Estate to Golden Grove & will then get him to do it at the same time as his People are at that place at work.

I have been pressing & threatning the Tradesmen on their not having begun the house at Golden Grove & they assure me they will positively set about it the 15th of next month with all their People & not take them off until it is finisht. The reason they give for not beginning now is that they have severall small Jobbs on hand for several Estates that must be done before they can go about with their Mills & that their people are dispersed & their attention drawn different ways which will be finisht by that time & then they will bring their whole Gangs compleat & pay all their attention to that one matter untill finished.

In regard to Batchelors Hall I was there also & cannot conceive what is the matter with the Cattle there they being very thin & rough & a great many of the Old Cows & their Calves have died notwithstanding the Pasture is in pretty good Order & few weeds. I spoke to the Penn keeper about it who tells me that he cannot account for it & takes all the Care in his Power. I should have discharged him had not Mr. Kelly assured me he is always on the Penn & is very diligent & sober, so will try him one Quarter more & see if it goes on better if not will then send him away & endeavour to get another. I shall be there in 10 or 12 days again.

I have got Mr. Pickersgills Evidence also in regard to the Land at Plantain Garden River & when receive the Commission sent to Ireland from you will also return that into the Office. I do not hear of Mr. Dawkins's Claim now. I believe they are satisfied they can never recover it.

Mr. Laing & Mr. Kelly both spoke to me about sparing some Mules & Cattle from Golden Grove to assist at your Estate the Swamps. I told Mr. Kelly to give what assistance he could & have sent 3 Mules & a Spell of Cattle to carry the Sugars down. I shall ship p. the *Friendship* Capt. Thompson 50 Hhds. & p. the *Duckinfield* Foster 50 more Hhds. of Sugar from Golden Grove for & on account of our friend Mr. Arcedekne. They will both sail in April. I shall also give you due notice of what Ships I shall ship on board & the quantity in each Ship in order for timely Insurance.

Our Morant Ships have been unlucky this Year. Chisholm is missing. The *York* the Ship I would not put the Sugar in Scrymsour left out is lost & the whole Cargo washt away. A Bristolman lost her Mast, had her Captain washt over board & 3 men was carried into Carolina & the Vessel condemned.

Mr. Robin Arcedekne died about 4 months ago in New York.He has left half of the Reversion of Golden Grove in case Mr. Chaloner Arcedekne should die without Children to Mr. Bourke to whom he has left the Residium of the Estate.

Mr. Laing has been a good deal out of order & still is.

I have not heard lately from Spanish town but my Brother was there lately & tells me Mrs. Kersey & Mrs. Harris were both well.

[*Notes that Laing is recovering.*]

35. To Benjamin Cowell, Manchioneal, 14 April 1769

I wrote to you about 3 Weeks ago p. the Pacquet acquainting you of my Intention of Shipping 50 hdds. of Sugar on Board the *Earl of Halifax* Captain Michael Dalton at Port Morant in case you should chuse to insure. They are now all on board as also 50 hdds. on board the *Duckingfield* Capt. William Foster who will sail in about 14 Days and Dalton by the 10 May. Shall ship next week 30 hhds. on board the *Morant Bay* Capt. Farr who am in hopes will also get away by the same time as Dalton and then 50 hhds. on board the *Prince George*, Capt.

Fryer. They are all from Golden Grove and on Acct. and risque of our Mutual Friend Mr. Arcedekne. Inclosed is the Bill of Lading and Invoice of 50 hdds. of Sugar on board the *Friendship* Capt. Thompson who I hope will arrive safe. The Sugar appears to me to be very good and the hdds. heavier than Usuall.

We have made there about 320 hdds. and in case we meet with no Accidents think we shall make about 180 more. The Weather has been very fine for the Estates in the River this year being very dry.

Inclosed is Golden Grove Acct. and Mr. Arcedekne's Account Current with Taylor & Graham Ballance in their favor £3584.13.3½ which we hope you will find right. You will see an Account of Law charges on the 8th May £19 & Aug 30 £76.12.3 an Action of Lewis Grant's[174] it being for Cedar for the Water Wheels which was overcharged near 100 p. ct. and he would neither deduct it nor leave it to Arbitration on which we thought it best to contest the matter and struck off near half of his Acct. rendered in. There were also some Cattle sold from the Estate to the Amount of £400 which we have not received as yett when we do shall bring it to the Creditt of Mr. Arcedekne. The reason of not having yett received it is because we gave a Creditt on Acct. of the Price we sold them at being £3 a head more than we could have gott by insisting on an immediate payment.

I intended to have sent you a list of the Negroes and Stock and also the Acct. of what Supplies will be wanted for the Estate, but have been obliged to attend on the Governor & his Family who are in this Parish at present for these 14 days past and the list is at my Estate which is twenty miles from hence but shall send them by Capt. Foster. I hope it will make no difference.

36. To Chaloner Arcedekne, Manchioneal, 14 April 1769

Am favored with yours of 27 Novr. and 12 Decr. from Florence and sincerely congratulate you on having had £1600 St. Insurance on the *Golden Grove* tho it is far below the loss yett it is some what out of the Time it being in my opinion impossible but that she must have perisht. Am extreamly concern'd that you have mett with much bad success in your first concern in Shipping. I shall follow your directions in not shipping above 50 hdds. on board any one Vessell. This goes under Cover to Mr. Cowell which brings him the Invoice and Bill of Lading for 50 hdds. of Sugar on board the *Friendship* Capt. Charles Thompson Capt. Foster has 50 and Capt. Dalton 50 more hdds. of your Sugar now on board the first sails in about a fortnight the other about the

---

[174] It has proved impossible to further identify Lewis Grant.

10th of May the Sugars are in my opinion very good and the Hdds. large they weigh an average 1720 H wt. If you chuse to have them larger please lett me know and they shall be made so. Am sorry the Sugar was not better last year they look very well in this Country.

I have also wrote for Insurance if you please to make it on 30 hdds. to be putt on Board the *Morant Bay* Capt. Farr on 50 on the *Prince George* Capt. Fryer who will sail in May. Shall take care to give timely information on board what ships I putt your goods. You may be assured I shall allways assist Capt. Fryer or any one else you recommend. All the Ships who gett your Sugar this year Except Thompson are to fetch them at their own Expence from the Rivers mouth there being plenty of Ships this year and all the Ships I putt your Sugar on board of after Fryer are English Built.

I observe what you say in reguard to paying your Mother and Aunt their Legacies and told them it. Your Aunt desires the money may remain in your hands and says she wants to putt more in as she does not know what to do with it and she may either lose it or have it stole from her and therefore that it is much safer where it is. Your Mother says she will receive hers tho I believe she is only joking for she knows as little what to do with it as her Sister. I will offer it to her.

You have now about 320 hdds. made and have by the Plan which is not att all exact about 190 Acres to cutt. If we meet with no Accident you will make above 500 hdds. The Weather has been very favourable to you this year indeed remarkably so but plays the Devill every where else being so dry.

The Duke of Roxburghs wine is in very good order and safe, I have it often Examined by a Cooper.

Am very glad you have consented to purchase some Negroes for the Estate for it is otherwise impossible to keep it up there being Work for 200 more working negroes than are on it without putting in an Acre more of Canes and by nursing weeding trashing them and tending the land it would yield infinitely better than it does now.

I told Mr. Richards[175] who is Attorney to Tom Cussans what you mention in reguard to the trench through Riversmouth land. In reguard to Swamps shall follow your orders when receive them, am only sorry it have given your Sister so much uneasiness. Kelly tells me it will make upwards of 80 hdds. this year. I think it can be made Advantageous to you as Norris's Pen[176] will be a good place to send any of the Golden Grove Negroes that have the Yaws to mend the Fences and plant

---

[175] George Richards.
[176] Chaloner Arcedekne inherited Norris's Pen, in St David's Parish, from his father. Inventory of Andrew Arcedekne of Parish St Cat., Esq., Inventories of Estates, Island Record Office, Spanish Town, V (1765), fos 58–63.

Guinea Grass for Plantain Garden River is much too wett for that disorder.

David Milner has been talking to me on a Subject he says he mentioned to you which is that he wants to rent a piece of your land opposite to Wheelersfield and insisted on my going to see it with him which I did 2 days ago. He desired me to write to you on the Subject. I told him I should leave it intirely to yourself for that I would by no means take it on me to recommend it to you to do such a thing for altho there might not at present appear any disadvantage to you yett in time it may be found very inconvenient and any rent that can be gott may not be found an adequate Compensation for running the Risque of a bad neighbour and if at any time hereafter you should think of Extending your Estate by putting up another Sett of Works you will have occasion for more pasture and it would be disagreeable not to be able to make use of your own land on Acct. of a Lease.

Carter has dug the foundation of your new house and has now 26 hands at Work. The Weather has been so dry there has not been Water to make Mortar though it looks for Rain now. I have been up near three weeks in this Parish with the Governor and his Family who dined at Golden Grove two days ago and are mightily pleased with it. Indeed have been obliged to attend on them so constantly that cannot be so particular as intended especially as I have just heard Thompson sails on Sunday and all my papers are at Lyssons and am now at Jasper Halls in Manchioneal.

I have inclosed Golden Grove Accts. and your Acct. Current to Mr. Cowell with a list of the Negroes etc and shall if in time write him by this Conveyance for the Supplies if not shall write by Foster as I must see the Governor & his Family imbark at Manchioneal Harbour for St. Marys on a Challenge from the Ladys and a promise I made to them on Board.

37. To Chaloner Arcedekne, Kingston, 29 April 1769

The above is a Copy of my last to you from Manchioneal since which have been at your Estate and there were then 364 hdds. made and the Weather was dry and fine They indeed were rather scarce of Water altho had taken in the whole of Plantain Garden River.

Kelly showed me the list of Supplies and desired me to write for a Still of a thousand Gallons. Mr. Cowell will acquaint you what I wrote on that Subject. As your Coppers are very old and want in a manner an intire new sett for the Boiling house have wrote for 12 Iron boilers which we find to answer very well for every thing but Clarifiers it will save a great deal of money and the old Coppers will buy or go very near it to purchase the Still. In case you send out the Still it ought to come by the very first Vessell to be in time to hang time enough for next Crop otherwise it must be useless for a Year.

I have seen your Mother and Aunt who are both very well. Your Mother gives this year 10 Negroes to the Swamps which She has desired me to send there. Your old Acquaintance John Fagan died about a fortnight ago. He had not a days health since he had the Account of his Friend Robins[177] death and last week young Boscawen second Son to the late Admirall,[178] was drowned at Sir Charles Prices in the Pond before the House at the Decoy when he went to Bath.

I about six weeks ago received from the House of Long Drake and Long 5 Cases containing a Monument of your Fathers which have sent to Spanish Town to be putt up there.

I have by this sent bills of Lading to Mr. Cowell for the 50 hdds. on Board the *Duckingfield* and also for those on board the *Earl of Halifax* tho could not send the Weights having not yett gott them from the Estate. Capt. Farr has his 30 hdds. on board and we are now shipping the 50 on board the *Prince George*. When finisht shall put if possible 30 hdds. on board the *Brilliant* Capt. Myall and 30 on board the *Maria Beckford* Capt. Castle who will sail after Fryer.

38. To Chaloner Arcedekne, Kingston, 1 June 1769

My last to you was p. the *Morant Bay* Capt. Farr and the *Prince Frederick* Capt. Johnston Covering the Bill of Lading for 50 hdds. of Sugar on board the *Prince George* Capt. Fryer. Annext is the Invoice of them and inclosed is the Bill of Lading for 30 on board the *Brilliant* Capt. Myall with the Invoice also who will sail in a fortnight. Shall begin to ship on board the *Maria Beckford* Capt. Castle the *Friendship* Capt. McLeod and the *Nancy* Capt. Cleland. On board the latter shall putt 50 hdds, the two former 30 in each. Since my last Capt. Dalton is saild and I hope safe arrived before this reaches you. The dry weather still continues and they are still making Sugar at the Estate.

39. To Chaloner Arcedekne, Kingston, 2 June 1769

I this minute received yours of 20 March & Cannot help being Excessive uneasy at the Concern & uneasiness I find you are in which makes me

---

[177] Robin Arcedekne.

[178] Admiral Sir Edward Boscawen (1711–1761). For more details see Leslie Stephen and Sidney Lee (eds), *Dictionary of National Biography* (London, 1908), XI, pp. 71–81.

not delay a Single Minute in informing You, which I do with the greatest pleasure, that your apprehensions are a good deal imaginary. But to begin to the first part of your Letter you may depend on it will follow your directions intirely in regard to Swamps & believe Our joint friend Mr. Laing will still act for you there also. Am really Sorry that the Estate hitherto has not turn'd out so well for Mr. Cowell as I could have wisht.

I wrote by the *Diligince* Man of War on 27 January Last which Letter Could not possibly have reached you at the time you Wrote me, by your Uneasiness, but hope it arrived soon after. I also wrote p. the *Grenville* packet a Duplicate of it & also acquainted you of having received yours of 2^d August from Venice & of the State of your Accounts & that the Weather had become better the Latter end of Last year than it had been for three years before and that you had a good appearance of a Crop & would begin to find the Estate more profitable than it had been, that the Wet weather had prevented the Estate from rising before & had also backt every Other Estate in the same part of the Country. I also Wrote you about Cooke but as suppose you must have either received the Original or Duplicate referr you to them. I acquainted you that I had Sent home every Hdd. of the last Years Crop it being only 249 hdds. & 1 Tierce & acquainted you with the Ships they were put on board of Vizt. 50 p. Thomson, 30 p. Gillies, 120 p. Chisholm, 20 p. Power, 17 p. Scrymsour, 12 & 1 Tc p. Boyd. Chisholm was unhappily Lost & I am really Sorry that the remainder turned out so very bad as to Nett you only £1300.

As for your Accounts you will see by those I send you p. Thomson that your Debt to Taylor & Graham was lessened £1291.17.9½ the Balance due the 31 Dec 1767 being £4786.11.1 & the balance due the 31 Dec 1768 being £3584.13.3¼.

I wrote you also of 4 April Congratulating you of having had £1600 Stg Insurance on the *Golden Grove*, & that should obey your Orders in not Shipping above 50 hdds. on board of any One Vessell and acquainted you of having shipt 50 hdds. on board of Thomson, 50 on board of Dalton, & 50 on board Foster & that the hdds. weighed on an average then 1720 lbs each. I also Acquainted you of my intention of Shipping 30 hdds. on board the *Morant Bay* Capt. Farr & 50 On board the *Prince George* Capt. Fryer, all which is now on board & gone except those by Fryer who Sails on the 4th. Have now 30 hdds. on board the *Brilliant* Capt. Myall & 30 On board the *Morant Planter* Capt. Power, Shall also Send you 30 p. the *Maria Beckford* Capt. Castle, 30 p. the *Friendship* Capt. McLeod & 50 p. the *Nancy* Capt. Cleland. These Sugars I have engaged & have wrote for Insurance on them.

I shall go soon to Windward & Let you know what more shall send you. I have the happiness to think you will not be disappointed this

Year in Your Crop. We have had dry Weather which still Continues & your hdds. that are gone weight one with another 1617 lb. nett after deducting the fare. You will now See that you have not so much occasion to be frightened as you think.

I also acquaint you that your Debt will be much lighten'd to us & that there will be no Bill drawn on you this Year. I wrote you by the *Duckenfield* on 29 April Acquainting you that you had then 346 Hdds. made, that you was rather scarce of Water & that the Weather was dry, that the list of Supplies was gone home & my sentiments on a 1000 Gallon Still, a Copy of which I now Send you.

In regard to the Swamps I never was on it in my life but once & then only rode through it but that the Sugars of that & its Rum together with the Golden Grove Rum will do much more than pay the Expences of both Estates. Neither Can I Conceive how it can bring you in Debt much less so much as £500 p. annum, I know it ought not. Depend on it I shall do every thing in my power to make it profitable too. If I fail imput it not to design but Accidents.

The Weather is here very dry & every thing burnt up. Shall write you Soon again for am really uneasy to find you under so much anxiety.

Your Mother & Aunt are both well. I believe your Mother intends to make you a present of Some Negroes. She has allready bought Five & intends Seven or Eight more for Swamps.

I saw Carter Yesterday. He is at Work on the House & tells me that he will not leave it untill finisht.

40. To Benjamin Cowell, Kingston, 2 June 1769

On the other side is the Copy of a letter I wrote you yesterday p. the *Prince George* Capt. Fryer since which received yours of 8 Aprill and by it find you have not received mine to you of 27 Jany p. the *Diligence* Man of Warr wherein I acquainted you both concerning Cookes matter and the Estate. I sent a Copy of it p. the *Grenville* packett and the last year Accts. p. Capt. Thompson. I am very sorry you should imagine that you are forgott. It never having been my design to give you the least reason of Complaining for the future shall oftner write to you.

I saw the Mason who is at Work on the House yesterday and he acquaints me that he will not break of from it untill it is intirely finisht. I shall go up there as soon as I possibly can though this is the busiest time of the year here as most all the Ships are to sail on or before the 26 of July.

I sent you yesterday p. the *Prince George* Capt. Fryer the Bill of Lading and Invoice for 30 hdds. on board the *Brilliant* Myall. Mr. Kelly has putt 30 hdds.of Sugar on Board the *Morant Planter* Capt. Walter Power. I did not intend to have shipt on him so soon which made me not write for Insurance in case Mr. Arcedekne chuses to Insure. I shall also putt the other Sugars I acquainted you of on board the other Ships also and think of sending you more by other Vessells as soon as see how much the Estate makes. Shall take care when receiving Mrs. Kerseys Beer to forward it to her.

41. To Benjamin Cowell, Kingston, 20 June 1769

The above is a Copy of my last to you since which have not been favoured with any from you. Hope as I hear the *Diligence* is arrived that you have received the letter by her of 27 January. I sent you bills of Lading and the Invoices of the Sugars p. this Ship by Capt. Fryer and the *Augustus Caesar* Capt. Duffel. I have not yett got the Weights of the Sugar on board of [*torn*] nor the Bills of Lading as yett as soon as gett them shall forward. The *Friendship* Capt. McLeod has also gott his 30hdds. and Capt. Castle is taking his in, as soon as gett the Bills of Lading and Invoices shall forward them to you and sett about getting Capt. Cleland Sugar on board.

The Carpenter that was at Work on Mr. Arcedeknes house I find by a letter from Mr. Kelly died last week. I shall employ another and have wrote to Mr. Kelly on the Subject.

I am afraid we shall fall short at Golden Grove of what I expected from the appearance of the Canes. Mr. Kelly writes me it has taken 30 hdds. to repack & fill up those allready shipt but hope to send you more than have as yett wrote for Insurance for.

42. To Benjamin Cowell, Kingston, 14 July 1769

Annexed is a copy of my last to you since which have received the Cask of Beer and a Box for Mrs. Kersey which I forwared to her. Inclosed are Bills of Lading for 50 hdds. of Sugar on board the *Nancy* Capt. John Cleland 30 on Board the *Maria Beckford* Capt. Lawrence Castle 30 on Board the *Friendship* Capt. Peter McLeod. Mr. Kelly writes me he sent the Bill of Lading for the 30 on Board the *Morant Planter* Capt. Power who sail'd yesterday as am inform'd for did not see him before he sail'd.

Inclosed is the Invoice of the said parcells of Sugar I shall send also between 30 & 40 hdds. in the Capt. Thomas Edwards if he can take them in so as to sail by the 26th Instant they are fallen in the weights (which I assure you is not my fault) particularly those by Power. The reason they give me for it is as some of the Staves are longer than others they use the Long ones together and the short ones in the same manner which occasions that difference. I heartily wish them safe home and to a good markett as I shall directly after the 26th Instant go to Windward shall then write you about the condition of the Estate and how far the House is advanced for have not been able to go up for these 10 Weeks past.

Mrs. Kersey and Mrs. Harris were both well a few days ago when heard from them.

43. To Chaloner Arcedekne, Kingston, 7 October 1769

My last to you was p. the *Augustus Caesar* and the *Brilliant* Capt. Myall which I hope you have long since received. Since which have not heard from you but had a letter from your Brother in Law Mr. Cowell who acquaints me that you are very anxious to have the House finisht. You may depend on it shall use the whole of my endeavours to gett it done for you as soon as possible which I hope will be about March. Have had for these ten months past a Parcell of tradesmen at Work and Carter with his masons on that and on your Mills one of which was in excessive bad order but hope it will be done so well as to take off the Crop as it ought. Have also given orders to build up a wall before the floodgate by the garden the Wooden work being quite gone and we lost one half of the Water neither could it be repaired but by a very large expence am hopefull that this will answer. Will throw in stuff between the Wall and gate and as there is another gate to the Dam there will be no risque of damaging it.

The Estate was in very good order and a very good appearance of a Crop. We shall putt about the first week in Decr. but shall not be able to put in above 60 or 70 Acres of plant with the Plantation people so that there will be an absolute Necessity for hiring negroes to hole and plant 40 or 50 acres for a Spring plant. Without it the Estate must fall which will be a pity now it is brought up.

There has been no Negroes arrive since your orders for buying more. The first that arrive you may depend shall buy for you. It is what have all along desired and if you continue with the same mind which is to dispose of the Swamps Sugar and Rum and the Rum of Golden Grove am pretty confident that they will not only pay the Contingencies of both but supply as many Negroes on Golden Grove as it will be prudent to putt annually on or am much mistaken.

The Weather this year has been very favourable for your Estate and the others in the River but has hurt all the rest of the Island exceedingly being so excessively worse than 1767 which you remember. Your Cattle at Batchelors Hall have also recovered greatly with it.

Your Brother also acquaints that You have consented to lett Dr. Hayward have a piece of Land not to be within 150 yds. of your House. The place the Doctor wants it at is at the Corner of the Line by Duckingfield Hall and Edlynes so that the nearest part of his Land will be above a quarter of a Mile from your House. He also acquaints that you agreed to allow Philander[179] £5 p. annum as long as he behaves well which will pay him.

I did intend to have shipt thirty Hdds. more but there was no ship either at Windward or here for London. One Edwards intended to go for London but found he could not gett a load so changed his intentions to go to Bristol.

Your Brother has also wrote me that he cannott find Luke Burke. I had the direction from Capt. Crean who is his Friend. It would be better could he be found but if he cannott it will be no very great matter for the Courts here have lately adopted a Sistem from Burrouhs reports of the determination of Lord Mansfield[180] that twenty years quiet Possession is a good Title which Old Pickersgill has proved for you so cannot believe you will be further plagues with Dawkins's claim.

Your Brother also wrote me to know whether I do not think it would be better to give Fisher a Sum of money as 2, 3 or 400£ to release your Fathers Estate from any further claims on the Acct. of the Administration of Isaac Gale. I really think if it can be done for that it would be the best way for the Expences of a Law suit alone would come to much more & Cooke is not worth a Shilling and Rob. Delaps Estate will turn out Bankrupt.

Your Cousin Bourke has lately mett with a sad disappointment. Munro left his Estate to his Niece one Miss Jenkins for her life and then to her Children, if she should have any, failure of which to Bourke and his Children. He gott possession under the Will, takes care for three years to remitt her nothing and on the Ladys coming to the Estate his Overseer genterly turns her out of Doors, on which she went to Spanish Town and luckily for her brought a letter to Mr. Harrison[181] the Attorney Generrall who immediately files a Bill agt. Bourke on her behalf. Bourke finding he could not keep possession was reluctantly obliged to deliver up possession last week after having before spread a

---

[179] Philander was a slave on Golden Grove. There is no evidence of why Arcedekne agreed to make this payment to him.

[180] William Murray, (1705–1793) first Earl of Mansfield. Mansfield had served as the Lord Chief Justice of the King's Bench of Great Britain since 1756, a position he would continue to hold until 1788 when he resigned the office. For more details see Lee (ed.), *Dictionary of National Biography*, XIII, pp. 1306–1312.

[181] Thomas Harrison, who died in 1792. Lawrence-Archer, *Monumental Inscriptions*, p. 237.

report the Girl was mad and that he lookt on the Estate his own. I heartily wish he may be disappointed by her Marrying, and getting Children. All his murmurings have it you as also dying. Why do you not disappoint them at once by marrying. I would do it really to vex them. On hearing the above of your being ill I told them it was not true for Miss Jenkins was engaged to you that was the reason she would not marry in this Country.

All our Politicks are now asleep but apprehend they will be again revived as the Assembly is to meet the 24th Instant. Tom Gordon has gott a privy seal come out and young Price stands in his stead for the Walks.

My Brother and Tom Cussans have been in North America ever since Feb. last. I hear they are gone up the Lakes and to Quebeck so suppose you will see them soon as I apprehend they will return to England this winter, as Cussans will not be disappointed in his intentions of going to Corsica to see Paoli as he will have no opportunity of seeing him in England.

I saw your mother and Aunt a few days ago. They were both very well.

44. To Chaloner Arcedekne, Kingston, 25 February 1770

My last to you was p. the *Adventure* Man of War since which have received your Favor of 20 Aug. from France and Mr. Cowell's of 4 Decr 1769. Yours acknowledges the Receipt of 2 of mine with the Accts. by which you find that the Amount of your debt to us is lessened and that you earnestly wish it was possible to find out a way of diminishing the Contingencies which eat up all your produce. I assure you that I have in every particular as farr as has been in my power endeavoured to make your contingencies as low as possible. The Years 1765, 66 & 67 were very wett and in those years we had two of the largest floods ever known, which hurt your Estate excessively. Yours was not the only one that suffred, every estate about was hurt as much as yours, and you constantly made 100 hdds. more than any of your Neighbors altho inferior to them in the Strength of your Negroes.

The Negroes putt on, and given you by your Mother, have not answerd so well as I wisht or expected It arose for the Badness of the Weather and the Yaws. The Reason that Kellys negroes were employ'd was because you had not sufficient Number of your own, and had you tradesmen of your own certainly you would not then Occasion to hire but you have not gott them, and thought that as you hired them yourself before you went off you would have no objection they should be continued. The Land he has you gave him yourself.

I am really concern'd to find the Crop 1768 turned out so small a Matter as £1000 & that for 1/2 of that you was obliged to your Brother for the after Insurance on Golden Grove. I am glad you sav'd it at any Rate, and assure you [torn] Insurance, or any other had been been made, I should not have been [torn].

Mr. Cowell by my letters p. the *Friend* Capt. Gilles, and the *Dawkins* Capt. Stupart of Aprill & May that I should ship 80 hdds. on Board her, and p. mine of 6 of July by the *Rose* [torn]. I acquainted him of shipping 120 hdds. on Board her I mean the *Golden Grove* a Duplicate of Which I also sent home. You may depend on it I have allways done, and allways will do every thing in my Power to serve you, and augment your property, which I should have more improved had Negroes been putt on as I recommended.

I acquainted Mr. Milner with your Determination about the land. Your Fathers monument has been a long time up. In reguard to your House it is going on altho never had such a jobb before as to gett it heartily sett about, shall acquaint you when it is finisht.

Since the Above have been favour'd with Mr. Cowells letter 4th of Decr. acquainting me of your safe arrivall in England which gives me Real pleasure as I hope you will now marry and gett Heirs to disappoint your Cousin Bourke. The Impediment to your not marrying before must be now removed, for altho the Crop of 1768 was bad I do not suppose you can find any fault with that of 1769 and am confident will send you this year near 600 Hdds. so you will have money enough to make settlement both on your Wife and also on Younger Children.

You have got about 22 hdds. made of the best Sugar I ever saw on your Estate, and a very large quantity of Canes to cutt. I have for some years past promised you a good Crop this year, you will not be disappointed, I hope, and nothing but some unforeseen Accident can hinder it, which God Forbid. This has been the most favourable year for your Estate that ever I know but has since allmost the Rest of the Island we have not had a good rain for 10 months past no manner of negroe provisions to be had and many Estates about the Old Harbor and Withywood will not make a Cask of Sugar all the Southside is in a deplorable Condition. I have suffred exceedingly on my lower Estate. Indeed on it and every estate on the Sea Coast there is not a Cane but is tainted and Worm eat and God knows if shall make a Cask on it next year the Young plants being in a manner burnt as if they had been in an oven and am afraid if we even had rain that they are to farr gone to be recovered. On the Contrary in Plantain Garden River you have just rain enough to give plenty of water and make the Canes flourish with out so much as either to hurt your roads or prevent the Yielding of the Canes.

I have purchased for you since my last 12 Negroe men six about three months ago and 6 last week. They are really very fine people and I must purchase some more as soon as can gett them as good as what these are. There is also an Absolute necessity of hiring negroes to putt in a Spring plant as the Estate will otherwise fall away again very much. Your Mother whom I consulted on the matter agreed to it or would not have done it after what you writt of not hiring negroes. I assure you on my word and Honor the Estate now and has ever since your being of age wanted £10000 worth of Negroes to be putt on it. They are not Steel or Iron and we see neither Gudgeons nor Capooses can last in this Country and was it my Estate I would not hole an Acre for three years to come with the Estate's Negroes but hire Jobbers to do it. In your Father's time when it made the Crop of 508 Hhds. there were 540 Negroes on it. By the not regularly supplying since that time the loss of Negroes by purchasing others in the Room of the Old ones have fallen of and those on it are now workt and have been all along above their ability neither from the small number of workers can we avoid it.

The Mill went about in the Beginning of Decr. and will not stop till August. This is 8 months wherein the poor Wretches do not gett above 5 or at most 6 hours out of 24. We shall go about in Decr. again and what time is there for Cleaning and putting the Estate in order putting on a Plant holling the land and preparing Copperwood.

The first 6 that were bought were putt in the Still House and promise to Turn out very well. As soon as the Crop is over will insist on their and any other negroes that may be putt on to be sett no other work than Building houses for themselves that is a house for each of them and then to be put to making grounds for themselves and kept to it untill they have such a quantity as will prevent any possibility of their ever again wanting provisions. By this means I hope we shall be more lucky with our Negroes than we have hitherto been. There is a loss of the time taken up for their Houses and Grounds but apprehend by their being happy and contented it will be very soon be made up. It is the method am determined to proceed in for myself with all I buy, and make no doubt of its succeeding. Had the Estate a proper number of negroes on it, would exceed your most sanguine wishes. I have wrote you so often and so much on this Subject that shall say no more at present on it.

Your Mills are in the best order this year I ever saw them and we built a Wall between the Floodgate and the trench by the Garden which answers very well and do not loose half the Water we did. Shall build a wall next year on the other side of the Flood by which am in hopes we shall save the Whole.

The large still came too late to be putt up this Year as did also the Boilers and so were obliged to hang the old Coppers again but with the Old Copper shipd last year what will send you this and the old Coppers I will take up after Crop will fully pay the Amount of the Still and Boilers.

Dr. Hayward has gott his Land Run out and it is half a mile at least from your house. The House that is the Walls are about 2/3 finisht. It is a much worse jobb than building any one of the Houses of the Works the Water Lime stones sand etc being all to be brought up Hill and now the Mill is about attention must be paid to it and getting off the Crop nothing on my part shall be wanting to further it.

Mr. Laing and I were at Swamps. He will send you the Valuation he and I putt on the Negroes stock etc he on Mr. Cowells part and I on yours. He will send you a list of the Negroes and all the particulars relating to it by this conveyance and also a Copy of the Lease you wrote for and will refer you to him for the matters relating there to. Do not believe it will make above 50 or 55 hdds. this year but the Sugar is good. There is about 80 Acres of plant putt in last year but the dry weather has rather hurt it. The man on it was one of your Bookkeepers at Golden Grove and is very Industrious sober and diligent and seems to go on very well. Am in hopes that the Estate will turn out much better than it has for these some years past.

I shall send you by Capt. Thompson of the *Friendship* all your last years Accts. Ballanced up to 31 Dec. last the list of the Negroes Cattle etc as Usuall. I shall also ship you p. the *Friendship* Capt. Thompson 50 hdds. of Sugar p. the *Duckinfield* 50 [*torn*] *Morant Bay* Capt. Farr 30 hdds. and p. the *Vernon* Capt. Robert Rindall 30 hdds. he sails from Manchioneal Harbor. These ships will sail I apprehend in the first week of April next and shall send 50 Hhds. p. the *Prince George* Capt. Fryer 50 p. the *Earl of Halifax* Capt. Dalton and 30 p. the *Brilliant* Capt. Myall. These will all sail in early May in case you should chuse to Insure. Believe that Sugar will fetch a very great price at home this year. Am sure this Island will fall twenty thousand Hdds. short of what it did last year. No part of it will make tolerable Crops but Plantain Garden River and St. Marys. This I assure you is true in order that you may regulate yourself in the prices of your Sugar as I would not give you false intelligence. Am confident you will be greatly pleased with the Quallity of the Sugars as far as the first 200 hdds. which have been seen and hope the remainder will not be inferior.

The Governor has sided with the Councill agt. the Assembly in a Clause for appropriating the Surplusage of the Revenue which was putt into the Difficiency Rum and Poll Tax Bills by which means the Rum and Poll tax Bills are not passed. The Soldiers are unprovided for and he Fryday last dissolved the Assembly. Am confident his Reign here is but short. Have desired my Friend Capt. Gardiner to forward you a Newspaper containing the most Material heads, the Message of

the Councill to the Assembly Their Resolutions the Governors Speech
at the close of the last Sessions and the Remonstrance with his Answer.

All your Friends and Acquaintances here are very well. I saw your
Mother and Aunt Thursday and both well.

45. To Chaloner Arcedekne, Kingston, 14 April 1770

[*Notes that he has* 'put 20 Hhds. more Sugar on board the *Morant Bay*'
and will be 'shipping 30 hhds. by the *Amity Hall* Capt. Tarbut'.]

46. To Chaloner Arcedekne, Kingston, 16 April 1770

[*Notes the amounts of sugar* 'on board the *Morant Bay*' *and* 'the *Amity Hall*'.]

Enclosed are Bills of Lading for 50 Hhds. on board the *Friendship* & 50
on board the *Duckinfield*. Kelly told me he would send down the weights
but has not done it, but as he is to write you may very particularly
suppose he will send them to you by this Conveyance & also the Bills
of Lading for the 50 on board of Farr & 30 on board of Kendal The
Prince George Capt. Fryer apprehend has by this time almost got her
quantity being 50 Hhds. I have not received the weights of any of the
Sugars at all yet. As I doubt not but that Mr. Kelly will inform you of
every thing relating to the Estate shall leave that to him.

Enclosed I send you Golden Grove Account & your Accot. Current
with Taylor & Graham balance in their favor of £2342.9.7¼ which
hope you will find right. I made a mistake last year in reguard to a
parcell of Cattle sold from the Estate as you will find by perusing my
Letter to Mr. Cowell of 14 April 1769. I say this, 'There were also some
Cattle from the Estate to the amount of £396 which have not received
but when do shall bring it to the Credit of Mr. Arcedekne, the reason
why we have not received it is because we gave a Credit on account
of the price we sold them at being £3 more than we could have got
by insisting on a Cash payment', but you had Credit for them on 2^d
of March for £276 & 2^d Septemr. for £120 more being the amount of
£396 I acquainted you of & being the Cattle I meant. You will see
£47.10/- charged for a Horse called Swinger. Mr. Kelly acquainted
me that you had wrote him to buy 2 for you which he has done & this
is one of them. There is a plan made out for you which was to have
been sent also down to be sent to you but that also is not come so that
apprehend it will be sent from Windward.

I received yours of 16 July from London & am very sorry to hear
you have been so much out of order & are obliged to go to Bath. Hope

you have perfectly recovered your health by this time & have fixed on some Lady with an intention of marrying for your Cousins here are in very high spirits in hopes of your being very ill. You must from the Crops of this last year have as much money at home as would make a good settlement on any Lady in England & there will not be a shilling drawn on you for anything whatsoever.

I also find by your said Letter that you had sent out a fresh Power including your Aunt & John Kelly on account of your new connexion with the Swamps. I send you inclosed the List of Negroes on Golden Grove & Batchelors Hall & also the Cattle on those places.

The weather still continues as dry as ever. Am confident that I shall not put about my Mill next year at my Lower Estate the dry weather having absolutely killed all the Young Canes & it is so dry at Golden Grove that have been waiting 7 weeks to plant the Spring Plant that is holed. I never knew nor the oldest people here so dry a year. All the Springs are dry & I yesterday passed Spanish Town River at Price's farm & the Water was not over the fetlocks of my Horse.

I three or four days ago saw your Mother & Aunt who had a Letter from Swamps that Mrs. Gale[182] was running her Lines & had not given any notice of that the Overseer had taken away some of her Surveyors Instruments. I wrote him to stop the Chain provided they came on any Land that was within your Lines & also to let me know if I would come up, but have not heard any thing further on that head so I suppose they have stopt running. There is no News whatever this way, every thing very dead & People apprehensive of a Famine.

Your Mother & Aunt are well, I saw them two days ago.

47. To Chaloner Arcedekne, Kingston, 10 May 1770

I wrote you the 16th of last month p. Thompson and sent a duplicate by Foster since which have not had the pleasure of hearing from you. Inclosed I send you the Invoices of 50 Hdds. of Sugar on Board Thompson 50 on board Farr 50 on Board Foster 50 on board Fryer 30 and on Board Kendall all which ships I wrote you should ship on.

I also acquainted you that should ship 30 hdds. on Board the *Amity Hall* George Tarbut but as George Richard's child is going off in him and they want much on Acct. of the Child to send him away soon have promised 20 hdds. more to him which makes 50 that he will have. You will also please to take notice that shall ship 50 Hdds. of your Sugar on Board the *Nancy* Capt. Cleland 50 on Board the *Morant Planter*

---

[182] It is unclear whether Taylor was referring to the widow of Isaac or of Jonathan Gale. (See note 136 above.)

Capt. Power 50 on board the *Friendship* Capt. McLeod and 50 Board the *Maria Beckford* Capt. Castle. I expect all of these ships will sail before the 25 of July. I shall also send you every hdd. of Sugar you make this year at Golden Grove according to your orders. Kelly I apprehend will send you the Bills of Lading as he has only sent me one of those Sugars that are now shipt consequently there are two of each at the Estate which suppose he will send. He was in Town two days ago and tells me he had made 450 hdds. so will have the number cured to go by the 26 of July that I mention. I apprehend he will write you about the Estate.

French who is at Swamps was down a few days ago. He tells me the Crop there will not be above 50 hdds. for he has done. The Weather has been excessive dry tho they have had pretty rains at Swamps. I shall go there in about 10 days. Mrs. Gale thought proper sometime ago to run a parcell of Lines about Swamps to encroach on you without giving notice but the Negroes inform'd French of it who went and took away the Surveyors Staff and Compass. They have indited him for it as an assault, as he acted in defence of property with the Care of which he was entrusted. Have told him I would defend it for him on your Acct. and shall bring an information agt. the Surveyor for running without notice it being a parcell of Land that has been in Canes & possession of the Swamps for 30 years past and patented by one Long. I believe the only Title to it is possession and therefore must act Cautiously not to lose the possession. I have given the papers to McMillan[183] in the Secretarys office to trace the Title. I hope you may approve of what have done.

Your Mother Acquaints me there is a power of Attorney come out to Mr. Lee and Mr. Ford[184] of this Town to claim a large sum of money said to be due by Norris's Pen to some Woman of the name of Compere. It will be a troublesome matter but apprehend they will not make much of it. I shall see your Mother & Aunt a few days hence about it, they are both well.

48. To Chaloner Arcedekne, Kingston, 18 June 1770

My last to you was of the 10 of last month a duplicate of which was sent you by the *Hibbert* Capt. Burnett since which have not received any letters from you.

Capt. Tarbutt after his pressing sollicitations back'd by George Richards and his Wife has shipt you out the 20 hdds. he so ardently

---

[183] It has proved impossible to further identify McMillan.
[184] Gilbert Ford.

desired, and Capt. McLeod of the *Friendship* has left Morant Bay to go to Savannal La Marr as he could not get a Compleat load at the former place, so that he has also disappointed me.

Mr. Kelly acquainted me that both Clelands & Castles complements of Sugar was made.

Inclosed are the weights of 30 hdds. p. the *Brilliant* Capt. Myall. I send you the weights as soon as I gett them.

[*Notes he has sent turtles to Arcedekne and Cowell*].

49. To Chaloner Arcedekne, Kingston, 30 June 1770

Annext is a Copy of my last to you p. the *Eagle* since which have not heard from You. Inclosed are the weights of 50 hdds. of Sugar p. the *Morant* Power 50 p. the *Nancy* Cleland & 50 p. the *Maria Beckford* Castles. I apprehend Mr. Kelly will send you the Bills of Lading for them.

The weather at Golden Grove is very wett but Mr. Kelly writes me that he is still about and will be able to ship 50 hdds. on board the *Earl of Hallifax* Capt. Dalton from Port Morant & 50 hdds. on Board the *Two Sisters* Capt. Rogers from Manchioneal. This is as much as shall be able to send you home before the 26 of July. The remainder of the Crop shall be sent you and timely advice given if you chuse to insure. Indeed there are no more London ships now at Windward to Load for London.

50. To Chaloner Arcedekne, Kingston, 23 July 1770

My last to you was of 30th June of which a Copy went by the *Lady Juliana* since which have been favor'd with both yours dated 24 April, one of which was a Letter of recommendation of Mr. Poole[185] & very unluckily he did not deliver it till the day before he sailed for Pensacola. Be assured of my shewing him every civility in my power or any one whom you recommend. The other I now sit down to answer.

I am sorry to find you think me so dilatory in writing to you. It must be owing to the Man of War not having arrived as I wrote you of 25 February by the *Levant* Man of War & sent you a Copy p. the *Anna Teresa* Pacquet, of the state of every thing & by the *Friendship* Thomson I sent you the Accounts, & indeed have sent you advice of every thing that was to be shipt that you might if you pleased have made Insurance.

I am sorry to find you have been so ill but am glad that the Bath

---

[185] It has proved impossible to further identify Mr Poole.

has been of service to you. It is very hard that at your time of life you do not enjoy better health & are again obliged to sett out to Aix La Chapelle. I shall according to your desire send your letters & Accounts to Messrs. Long Drake & Long[186] & the Bills of Lading & Account of Supplies to Mr. Cowell.

In reguard to the Leases of Swamps, Valuations etc, Mr. Laing was to have sent them home p. the *Levant*. As that Ship is arrived you must undoubtedly have them long 'ere this. You may depend a regular & distinctive Account shall be kept of the Negroes that are bought & born in order that no confusion may arise on delivering back the Estate. The same is done at Golden Grove.

In reguard to purchasing fifteen Females to five Negroes it can by no means answer you at Golden Grove, for you want Men infinitely more than Women, for there are many things which Women cannot do, as Cutting Copperwood, Wainmen, Boilers, Distillers, Stokers, Mulemen, etc. Had you a sufficient number it would do well enough to go in that scheme. Indeed it is a sort of miracle to conceive what they have done this year & it is impossible to keep the Estate up at it. Indeed it is against your Orders but have been obliged to hire Kellys' Negroes to cutt Copperwood & clean the Canes.

The Mill has been about ever since the beginning of December & will not stop until the middle of next month which is near nine months, in which time the poor wretches of Negroes have not had above six hours of rest out of 24, & what with getting their little provisions etc. what time have they had to Sleep; the Estate is to be cleaned, Pastures bill'd, Negro houses to be repaird, Plant putt in, Copperwood cutt, & to be again about in Decr. I have laid all these matters before your Mother & Aunt and they both see the necessity of hiring Negroes to put in the whole Plant. I assure you it is an utter impossibility without murdering the Negroes to keep it up without.

I have all along promised you a great Crop this year. There will be a very great one, & was the Estate mine I assure you I would not for these four years to come Plant & hole with the Estate's Negroes. The expence will be about £600 p. annum & you will save your Negroes & make twice the value of that Expence by the Sugar & Rum. Am

[186] During the middle years of the eighteenth century Long, Drake and Long were among the premier London-based sugar factors and commission agents who dealt with Jamaica. Beeston Long, the uncle of Edward Long, and a director of the Royal Exchange Assurance Company, was a founding member of the firm. In 1760 he served as the chairman of the recently formed West Indian Merchants in London. One of his sons, Beeston Jr, was also involved in the family business and became a director of the Bank of England, while another son, Charles, became Baron Farnborough. Sheridan, *Sugar and Slavery*, p. 300. For further details see R.M. Howard, *Records and Letters of the Family of the Longs* (London, 1925).

confident that there will be no occasion to draw Bills on you. The Negroes I purchased lately are well, & if you will let me go on in my way of purchasing, which is buying of the best Negro Men of Corromantee Country out of each ship, will in time establish a Gang of fine People for the Estate, & not to take any but what have had the Yaws & Smallpox & then put them to making Houses & Grounds for themselves before they are put to other work, & by so doing will not exceed the number you yearly propose, and the Rum & Sugars of Swamps & the Rum of Golden Grove will pay the Contingencies of both Estates & purchase the Negroes, & I have expectations will also pay the Rent, that is when the Estate is put in order. There is a tolerable appearance for a Crop next year & there will be a very good one the year after.

Your Negroes will have much better Grounds by putting them in the Bottom in Lewis's Run & not so much exposed to the North winds there as about the Great house. A Hott house is much wanted but the Mills being about have not been able to gett home the Timbers for the Great House. The Walls are built & will as soon as can gett the Hothouse sett about, on Doctor Hayward's Plan it ought to be out of the place it is now in.

After the 26 of this month will write you about Fearon's Bond to Mrs. Cowell & Fothergill but assure yourself if in case of Fearon's death it is not better than Waste Paper, also concerning Orgill's[187] Bond & Peyton's,[188] tho' I believe he dyed insolvent. I applied to Jackson,[189] Mr. Hibbert's Partner but he as well as myself have been much hurried for these three weeks last past, but as soon as it is over shall be able to write to you on these matters.

I called on your Mother & Aunt & shew'd them your Letter, your Mother wanted you to come over & does not at all agree to the giving up Sam Gordon's Bond to Mr. Welch. She tells me Young Grant[190] has promised to pay it.

I have settled your Quit Rents & shall gett the Receiver General's separate Receipt, they were paid with several other ones. I shall also talk with your Mother in reguard to the St. Mary's & St. Ann's Creditors. I wish you had before mentioned taking assignments to the Demands against your deceas'd Father's Estate for as some of the

---

[187] The Orgills were a prominent Jamaican planting family. It is unclear which member of the family Taylor was referring to. The likeliest possibilities are Samuel (died 1741), William (died 1770), John (died 1779) who in 1754 was recorded as owning land in St Andrew Parish, or Thomas (born 1726). Oliver, *CARIBBEANA*, III, pp. 276–279; Records of St Andrew Parish, 1754, Public Record Office, Kew, CO 137/28, pp. 191–196.

[188] It has proved impossible to further identify Peyton.

[189] Samuel Jackson.

[190] It has proved impossible to further identify Grant.

Creditors are dead we may meet with difficulties in the matter from their Executors but will do what I can.

I have sent home the three Pipes of Madeira to the Duke of Roxburgh to the care of Messrs. Long Drake & Long p. the *Rose* Capt. Morce & advised them how they are to go. There is just now no London market Madeira Wine for Sale that is good enough to lay by & send home. As the Ships will in about two months from this time begin to arrive will purchase the two Pipes for Mr. Colmore[191] & the two to be layd by against your arrival.

I shall as I do not know whether this will meet you in England, send home the Invoice of 50 Hhds. of Sugar shipt on board the *Earl of Halifax* Capt. Dalton & of Fifty shipt on board the *Two Sisters* Capt. Rogers of which I advised you by the *Morant Planter* Capt. Power & by the *Lady Juliana* Capt. Stephenson to Mr. Cowell. Mr. Kelly seems to be apprehensive that Rogers will not sail by the 26th Instant. These make 540 Hhds. that we have now shipt & I am hopefull to send you 80 more. There is at present no ship for London at Windward, we must see & gett one.

Your Mother & Aunt are both well.

51. To Chaloner Arcedekne, Kingston, 14 September 1770

Inclosed is a Copy of my Last to you since which have been at Golden Grove and find that both Dalton & Rogers did not sail by the 26 of July. I wrote your Brother in Law Mr. Cowell about p. Capt. Cleland who Sailed the 23 of July, was oblig'd to put back having Sprung a Leak which oblig'd him to unload his Cargoe & heave down here. By good Fortune his Cargoe is not at all Damaged & this Letter goes by his Ship.

You have finished crop at Golden Grove & have made as much sugar as will fill about 90 hhds. more, so that with the 540 already shipt you will gett home good 630 hogsheads, which is more than any Estate ever yett made in this Island.

I was oblig'd to hire Kellys Negroes to cut the Copperwood & Clean the Estate. I know you do not like hireing Negroes, but without it your Estate must fall back. I consulted your mother on it & she is now made Sencible that it is for your advantage to hire Negroes to put in the plant. Indeed the Estate Cannot be kept up without it, & you have this year reapt above 100 hhds. by it, as it would otherwise have been Impossible to have taken off the Canes. I shall follow Your Orders about putting on Negroes, & hope in time that shall be able to do

---

[191] It has proved impossible to further identify Colmore.

without hireing any Negroes at all. You must plainly see by the Last & this years Crop that your Estate is not neglected. Indeed, was it my own I could not do more for it.

The Walls of your house are finished & the Carpenters are at work finishing the Roof. It would have been done before, but could not while the Mill was about get home the Timber.

You will go about again by the Beginning of December & I do again if no unforeseen Accident happens, promise you a good Crop [torn] as much as this, for had we choose the Weather Could not have had it more favourable for your Estate It is now in good Order & hope you will now find it profitable.

There is no Opportunity of Sending home your Sugars as there is no Ship at windward nor any Ship in Town for London [torn] wait for an Opportunity.

I will give Mr. Cowell timely notice for Insurance & shall send you them all home having been in the Country and Sam Jackson who does all the Business at Hibbert's house being also out of Town, have not been able to get the Account of the Papers you want, but as he is Soon Expected will write to Mr. Cowell about them.

Every thing is very dull here, but Expect we shall have warm work when the Assembly meets, as the Requisition of the money advanced by the Treasury in Litteltons time Comes again on the Carpet, & People do not Seem to Like the giving it up. The present Majority are much afraid of Dissolution. The Parish of Saint James have also a Petition to have the Assize Court held alternately at Savannah LaMar & at Montego Bay, which will also cause Some Bustle.

There is nothing else new here, no Vessel having arrived from Europe for some time. We have at Last got Some Rains at Windward after having been Excessive dry which hurt our Canes at the far Side very much.

I shall see your Mother & Aunt tomorrow. I believe they are very Well.

I have had as yett no Opportunity of Getting Mr. Colmore wine, but as the Ships will in November & December fall in from Madeira Shall not neglect it.

52. To Chaloner Arcedekne, Kingston, 20 October 1770

My last to you was of 14 Sept. Since which I have been favour'd with yours of 7 July and am glad you have received your Accots. P. Thompson and are pleased at the Prospect of your Crop. I have all along made it my business to consult your Mother on every piece of business concerning your affairs.

In reguard to your being more in debt more than you expected I can say nothing to it but only know I have done every thing in my power to bring you out of it and the Charges you mention of £90 in 1768 and money in 1769 for freight of Sugar In Thompson and other Ships is what other people did pay for Thompson is allways the first ship and I never could apprehend but that you chose to gett your goods as soon to markett as possible, but indeed the Charge has this year been done away, every ship have brought the goods round in their own Boats. It is very true that Cussans and Dr. Gregory do ship from a Wharf at the River's mouth and Kelly has since Crop been building one for you and I have sent up the plank for it as they will undoubtedly charge wharfinger for what has been shipt.

I am very glad to hear you are gott so much better and wish to hear you was married. One of your young Cussins Jenny Burke[192] was married last week to Charles Palmer.[193]

I have seen Mr. Phillips[194] and he tells me that he does not know he is in possession of any part of your land, that he will employ a Surveyor and if it shall appear he is, he will willingly pay a Consideration for the use of it and we have referred the matter until we both go up after Christmas.

I shall ask your mother relating to the land about Black Morass and lett you know. The land in St. Johns is still in being. You hold it as Mortgagees in possession. White[195] has never mentioned renting it to me. The land he bought in Spanish Town was a lott of Land Mortgaged to your Father together with 2 Negroes. Ben White agreed with the proprietors to sell his Equity of Redemption and then to compromise the matter with us by giving what it might be valued at which is the land sold [torn] I apprehend gives him good Title.

I have seen Mr. Jackson who acquaints me that the Judgement on Fearon's Bond to Mr. Cowell and Fothergill is an Old one but that Fearon is really in such Situation that I do not know if were it will be good. In regard to Orgills Bond this is a deed of Trust of His Estate to secure payment of about £27,000 to the Hibberts which comes in prior to the demand of Mr. Cowell so that very little can be expected from that. The next is Peytons. His whole estate was sold some years ago by a Decree in Chancery and did not pay his debts consequently the demand is good for nothing.

We have been sickly for some time past. George Richards Tom Cussan's Brother in Law is dead, Young Vallette[196] is also dead & John

---

[192] Possibly Nicholas Bourke's daughter.
[193] It has proved impossible to further identify Palmer.
[194] Almost certainly Nathaniel Philips, the owner of Duckenfield Hall.
[195] Benjamin White.
[196] Probably the son of Augustus Vallette, who owned land in St Thomas in the East. The Vallettes were a family of French Huguenot extraction. Vallette Sr had been one of

McLeods Son.[197] They went of in the space of about 10 days of one another.

The Assembly is to meet the 23 Jan.

You have 90 odd Casks of Sugar at your Estate which I really do not know how to gett to you there being no ship at Windward and only one here the *William Beckford* Capt. Foot. I offered him 50 hdds. if he would fetch them and run the risque which he refuses and on asking your mother she thinks it more Eligible to lett them stay than run the risque for the Estate.

Winde[198] tells me he expects a small Snow in. If so she is to take 50 and run down to Annatto Bay to fill up. I will be very particular to give Mr. Cowell proper notice to make the Insurance and how it is to be made as she is to go to two different Ports so that there may be no difficulty in settling it if an Accident happens.

I was last week at Swamps, there are 45 Acres holed and planted and the Overseer was to begin holing last Monday. Shall gett in 20 Acres more. The Estate is in very good order and the Canes look very well so that it will make a tolerable Crop the Ensuing year and then I think after that it may be kept up at about 100 Hdds. annually.

I saw your Mother and Aunt two days ago your Mother seems to break fare, your Aunt is very well.

53. To Chaloner Arcedekne, Kingston, 26 March 1771

I wrote you by the *Kingston* Pacquett Capt. Mattocks since which I have not had the pleasure of hearing from you.

I have by this conveyance remitted to Mr. Cowell your Account for Golden Grove and Swamps and a small Acct. for Sundries supplies etc. to your Mother and also your Acct. Current up to the 31 of Decr. last with Taylor & Graham Balance in their favor the sum of £4037.14.8½, which hope when you have perused you will find right.

You will find also the contingencies for the Swamps high, but then

the witnesses to Patrick Taylor's will. Oliver, *CARIBBEANA*, III, p. 296; Cundall, *Lady Nugent's Journal*, p. 89; Will of Patrick Taylor, made 3 September 1754, proved 12 September 1754. Wills, Island Record Office, Spanish Town, XXIX, fo. 206.

[197] It has proved impossible to ascertain either the name of the age of John McLeod's son.

[198] Probably Scudamore Winde, whose main residence was in St Catherine's Parish. In 1765 he was involved in assessing the inventory of Andrew Arcedekne's Jamaican property. Inventory of Andrew Arcedekne of Parish St Cat. Esq., Inventories of Estates, Island Record Office, Spanish Town, XLV (1765), fos 58–63. In the 1760s he acted as the Attorney for Duckenfield Estate and was also a close friend of Thomas Cussans. The exact date of Winde's death is uncertain, but his will was proved in 1776. Oliver, *CARIBBEANA*, II, p. 175.

you will please to consider that no less a Sum than £805 of it is for Mules and the still house which was almost intirely demolisht by the Earthquake and that we shall not have occasion to bear that Expense this year as the Estate is now well supplied with stock, and that in the Contingencies for Golden Grove there is the Sum of £1677.19.6½ for Mules Negroes and Jobbing, which last is an Expense that I could wish you freed from would the Situation of the Estate allow it. But I assure you had it not been for that the Estate would have fallen back in spite of everything we could have done, and must be continued for some time longer untill we have more Negroes on the property. I have purchased 16 and drawn on you for the Amount of them at 90 days a Bill for £680 stg. in Currency £952 favor of Thomas Hibberts Snr. & Jnr. Your Aunt & Mother being at Spanish Town and Kelly at Windward I could gett the Bill only signed by Mr. Laing and myself, but I have sent Mr. Cowell a duplicate receipt for the money from the Hibberts which I hope will answer the same and as all your Attorneys signing it and that it will meet with due Honor.

[*Notes that he has* 'drawn on you' *three bills totalling £1,000 sterling* 'in favor of Hercules Ross',[199] *each* 'at ninety days sight', *and* 'directed them to Messrs. Long Drake & Long'.]

And be assured we will get every thing we can as cheap as possible and draw in the way directed by you, when we can, and when no more than one or two of your Attorneys are present send home duplicate receipts and mention on the Bill what it is drawn.

I intend buying 14 more new Negroes for Golden Grove out of a Ship now in the Harbour who opens sale in two or three days, for I do really want to do away with the Hiring of Negroes, and this is the best time of the year to buy new Negroes to be a little accustomed to the Country before the bad weather setts in in Sept. & Octr.

I really can not inform you of the quantity of Sugars you have made at Golden Grove and Swamps not having been at Windward for some short time past, but shall soon and then be able to lett you know how much is made at both Estates and how be shipt. Thompson has 50 hdds. of Golden Grove Sugar and 25 Puncheons of Rum, and Brankston, in the ship belonging to Messrs. Long & Co., 50 hhds. & 25 Puncheons of Golden Grove produce and 20 hdds. and ten puncheons of Swamps, of which I have acquainted Mr. Cowell and shall by Thompson send him the Foreign Commission to examine Luke Bourke in the Case of the Riversmouth land.

Your Mother & Aunt are both very well.

---

[199] It has proved impossible to further identify Ross.

[*Notes that he has* 'drawn on you of this day's Date' *three bills totalling £900 sterling each* 'in favor of Christopher Stephenson'[200] *and* 'directed them to Messrs. Long Drake & Long'.]

54. To Chaloner Arcedekne, Kingston, 13 April 1771

My last to you was p. the *Grantham* packett & *Seaford* Man of war since which have been favor'd with yours of 4 Decer. and I cannot conceive what should make you apprehensive that the lease of the Swamps ever can be a troublesome thing to you. I am confident that it will clear a large sum of money every year if properly managed. It has the last year making only 50 hhds. cleared money What will it do when in order.

Mr. Kelly will send you home the list of the Negroes on it & on Golden Grove. The Accts of both these Estates I enclose by this Conveyance to your Brother Mr. Cowell. The Ballance is large in our favor but it is swelle'd by the House and hir'd Negroes work, which am sure will doubly pay you both in Sugar & Rum and saving your Negroes.

Capt. Thompson has the remainder of your last year's Crop on board. I cannot justly say the Number of Casks but believe it to be forty, which with the fifty that went in the *New Shoreham* Capt. Graham makes the quantity last year about 630 hdds. He has as much new Sugar on board as makes up 50 hdds. Capt. Tarbut has 30, and believe by this time Capt. Fraser has his 50. We are now shipping on board Fryer Power and Myall 50 hdds. on each. Then will come on the *Jamaica* Capt. Taylor, the *John Gally* Capt. Watt and the *Vernon* Capt. Kendall, and am hopefull to send you home 500 hdds. of new Sugar by the 25 of July.

I forgott to acquaint you, as you that some years ago wrote me to assist Capt. Stupart of the *Dawkins,* and Sugars from the dry Seasons being exceeding scarce this way, have agreed to lett him have 20 hhds. from GG on condition that he brings them down at his own Expence and risque. He has accordingly sent a Vessell for them. He will sail about the 10 of May, Farr and Tarbutt about the end of this month, Power, Fryer and Myall all in May.

I have bought 13 New Negroes for the Estate, and the first ship that comes in will buy as many more as to make up the number 30, in order to prevent as much as is in my power hiring any people whatsoever. I assure you I do not like it, but there was an absolute necessity of either doing it, or letting the Estate fall back again. Was

[200] It has proved impossible to further identify Stephenson.

there an opportunity of purchasing a larger gang of real good Negroes, seasoned in Plantain Garden River and accustomed to works, it would be a very great object to you, as it would remedy that Inconvenience at once, & then to putt on New Negroes to keep up the Number there would be little risque in the Seasoning as there then would not be too many new ones at once.

I again repeat my Assertion that I am clear in my Opinion that the Rum and Sugar of Swamps, and the Rum of GG will pay every Contingency and putt on the Number of Negroes that will be yearly requisite. Because Swamps has for some years past done nothing, owing I am sure to mismanagement, that is no reason why it never should do any thing. They have now made about 60 hdds. and believe we will make 80, and if we meet with no Accident will next year come near 100, and the Contingencies will not I hope be much larger than when it made 33 only.

You may depend on my allways consulting your mother, and that I will not spare any pains to enable you to purchase the Small Estate that you want of £100 p. Annum & marry. I wish you would think a little Serious on that matter and do it as soon as possible, for I assure you I should be very sorry to see Robin Arcedeknes Heirs in possession of any part or parcell of what they wanted to defraud you off.

I am glad the Duke received the Wine and the Turtle. I have bought two pipes of Wine for Mr. Colmore, one of which I have shipt on board the *Judith* Capt. Brett, the other I have in my Store to be kept, untill I receive your or his directions. I have also bought two pipes for you.

I heartily congratulate you on the Birth of another Nephew it is what was not expected, and should like to see some of those that you mean also to have.

As I allways wanted to be in your Neighbourhood in Plantain Garden River that we might be near one another, and not to have far to go to smoak a pipe together, have bought Holland Estate from Mr. Kennion and the Moro Penn.[201] I have given an Amazing Sum of money for it, no less than £100,000 Stg., payable in the following manner, the first 6 years I pay £10,000 each year without Interest, and pay the remaining 40,000 in 8 years more at the Rate of £5000 Stg. p. annum with Interest 5 p. ct. It is to be delivered me on the 2 October with 2 Water & 1 Windmill in order, the Works in repair, 400 Negroes, 100 Mules, and 100 head of Cattle. I shall cutt on it the ensuing Crop 430 Acres of Canes. I hope it will make then near 500 hdds.

I have also taken the lease of the 90 Acres of Land given by your

---

[201] Moro pen, or pasture as it was sometimes known, was also in St Thomas in the East and formed part of Hordley Estate. Cundall, *Lady Nugent's Journal*, p. 94.

Father to your Mother, and Creighton & Archer which is now rented at £300 this money p. ann., as it is detacht from Golden Grove and you have great plenty of Land there, more than sufficient to answer every purpose of the present, or indeed if you were ever to settle another Estate there by & by. Will be exceedingly obliged to you if you will grant me a lease of it for your life, in case of the deaths of your Mother & Archer, and I will willingly pay you the same consideration for it, for even if that event was to happen the land would be nor could be of any Use to any one but myself, Duckingfield Hall having now more cane land than they for many years will be able to occupy, and it is very remote from their works, and there is no settlement near it, could it be of any material Service to you I am sure I would be the best person to ask it, and what I want it for, is to keep it in Canes which is improving the land greatly in its value. If you would also lett me have a little more of it, I should be glad to take it, and will not cutt any Timber from it, but putt it into a Plantain walk, being so near the Negroe Houses, for altho I have great plenty of Land at the Moro fitt for provisions, yett it is rather too farr for a Negroe to go to a noon time to cutt a fee Plantains. I hope you will oblige me in this, and will when I know your determination either send you home a lease to sign (provided you consent to it) or gett it from your Attorneys here just as you may think proper.

Your Mother & Aunt are both well.

55. To Chaloner Arcedekne, Kingston, 5 May 1771

Above is a Copy of my last to you, since which I have been up at Golden Grove and find you have now about 400 hdds. made, and believe you will make about 550 hhds. there this year.

Kelly has fenced off a large Parcell of Lewis's Run for Negroe Grounds, with which the Negroes are highly pleased, and seem to be well satisfied at. He wanted to hire Negroes to putt in about 70 Acres of Provisions for the new Negroes that are to come, but as I did not know your Mothers determination referred him to her. I believe when she sees Kelly who is every day expected in Town to give Evidence in a Suit in Chancery, that she will consent.

When I was up I heard that the Court had issued a Writt of Possession for some land recovered from Edlyne's[202] Estate by Mrs. Inglis,[203] and that the Surveyor intended giving part of your land to that Lady, as the land recovered from Edlyne. On that I sent one of

---

[202] Possibly Thomas Hope Edlyne.
[203] It has proved impossible to further identify Mrs Inglis.

the Bookkeepers to hinder them from running on your land, as there was no Action or Suit against you, and the Court had no right to dispose of your property without an Ejectment. The Bookkeeper stopt the Chain, and I have not since heard anything about the matter.

About a week ago being in Company with Dr. Gordon[204] one of Dawkins's Attorneys, he told me that he had orders to prosecute his Claim to the land at the River's mouth, and should Send us an Ejectment this Court for the land, that he had received from Dawkins, the Opinion of Wedderburn,[205] Dunning,[206] and someone else that he should recover it. Since that I have as well as your Mother, Aunt, & Laing been served with a demand to deliver it to Dawkins's Attorneys, and as we have refused to do it suppose we shall have an Ejectment this Court.

I have putt Dawkins's Title into the hand of Mr. East[207]who has been my Attorney for many years to search the Office, and see if we cannot find any flaw in it. I am not Lawyer enough to judge, but do not think he ever can be able to make it out. Zachary Bayly had a Power out from Dawkins some years ago to recover this land, and Instructions from John Morse how to do it, with his own remarks & the Title traced to 1764 from the Patentees. Bayly gave it to one David Peters[208] who was a Sort of Relation to the Penhallons[209] the Patentees of said land. To endeavour to gett some intelligence from him about the family, he gave the papers to your Mother, and she to me, by which it means we are able to know on what grounds they go. Pickersgill is dead but his Evidence is in the Court of Chancery. It will be highly necessary to

[204] Probably Dr John Gordon, a medical practitioner whose main place of residence was St Mary's Parish.

[205] Alexander Wedderburn (1733–1805) was appointed Solicitor General in January 1771. He went on to become Attorney General in 1778, Lord Chief Justice of the Court of Common Pleas in 1780, when he was ennobled as Baron Lougborough, First Commissioner of the Great Seal in 1783, and Lord Chancellor in 1793, a post he had long coveted and which he held until 1801. Lee (ed.), *Dictionary of National Biography*, XX, pp. 1943–1945.

[206] John Dunning (1731–1783), first Baron Ashburton, a client of Lord Shelburne, served as Solicitor General between 1768 and 1770. His greatest claim to fame was the resolution he moved in the House of Commons in 1780 that 'the influence of the Crown has increased, is increasing, and ought to be diminished'. Stephen and Lee (eds), *Dictionary of National Biography*, VI, pp. 213–215.

[207] Hinton East was a creole of English parentage who at one time owned The Rhine Plantation in St Thomas in the East. At various times during the middle years of the eighteenth century he served as the Judge Advocate General and the Receiver General of Jamaica. He was also elected as a Member of the Assembly for Kingston. East, who died in 1792, is better known for his botanical experiments, and the botanic garden he established at Spring Garden, than he is for either his legal or his political career. Oliver, *CARIBBEANA*, III, p. 296; Hall, 'Planters, farmers and gardeners', p. 4.

[208] It has proved impossible to further identify Peters.

[209] It has proved impossible to locate any further information about the Penhallons.

gett Luke Bourke's Evidence from Ireland sent out to be lodged in the Court of Chancery, & to lett one know if he is still alive, for if he is, we must Examine him viva voce, and a Foreign Commission for that purpose sent home. Be kind enough to lett us have an immediate answer to this part as the land is much too valuable not to make a Vigorous Defence. Indeed I think it will be impossible ever to recover it by Law, and shall leave no stone unturned to prevent them getting it. At the same time we must not neglect any necessary part of the defence.

Capt. Farr will bring you 50 hdds. I have not received the weights of the Sugars on board him, nor on board Thompson, nor the Bill of Lading. I wrote Kelly for them. Tarbut who has 30 hdds. of your Sugar on board him, will sail in a few days, as will also Capt. Fryer. Stupart has the 20 on board. I wrote by my last I should ship 20 hdds. on Board him. He will sail in about 10 days. Power and Myall will also sail in the Course of this month. I shall ship fifty Hhds. of Sugar on board the *Jamaica* Capt. Richard Taylor 80 p. *Port Morant* and also 50 more on board the *John Gally*, Capt. David Watt the Same places. They will both sail the beginning of next month. When they gett their Sugar will write you for more Insurance, being still hopefull I shall send you 500 hdds. of new Sugar by the 25 July.

Nothing else new Occurs to me at Present but that you will soon see Mr. & Mrs. Graham in England, they are going in the *Lady Juliana* Capt. Stephenson.

Your mother & Aunt are both well I saw them about four days ago.

56. To Chaloner Arcedekne, Kingston, 18 May 1771

On the otherside is a Copy of my last to you by Capt. Farr, who I hope is safe arrived. I have by this Conveyance sent to your Brother Mr. Cowell the Bills of Lading and Weights of the Sugars p. Thompson, Farr, Fryer, Tarbutt & Stupart who Sail in Company with this Ship.

I have nothing new to acquaint you of, but that we have had very heavy rains at windward and the Rivers have been very high. I am afraid they have done mischief tho have not yet heard of any, as I have not heard from Plantain Garden River last week.

Mr. Dawkins has brought his Ejectment for the land at the Rivers-mouth. I shall when the Court meets pray for a foreign Commission to Examine Luke Burke in Ireland. I am not very apprehensive of what he can do. I think there are flaws in his Title which he will not be able to gett over, and Pickersgills Evidence will cart him if he can even make out his title.

[*Notes that he has sent Arcedekne a turtle*].

There is a Guinea Man come in, but as the Slaves rose on the Coast of Guinea and murdered the Capt. many were drove over board and drowned I did not think it prudent to buy any for you out of her as they might be troublesome and think it better to wait a little till we can get some not quite so mutinous.

Your Mother and Aunt are very well your Mother has wrote you by Mr. Graham and proposed him to recommend Matrimony to you.

57. To Chaloner Arcedekne, Kingston, 24 July 1771

I wrote you by the *Lady Juliana*, and sent a Copy by the *Prince George*, Capt. Fryer, since which I had the Letter wrote me p. Capt. Curtis.

[*Notes that he has* 'received the 3 Cases of Wine and Garden seeds sent from Leghorn'.]

Your Crop has fallen 50 hdds. short of my Expectation owing to the very heavy rains in the latter end of it, which putt a great spring in the Canes.

The following is the Acct. of it and how shipt, 20 on board Thompson, 50 on Farr, 50 on Fryer, 30 in Tarbut, 20 on Stupart, 50 on Myall, 50 on Taylor, 50 on Watt, 50 on Bower, 30 on Kendall, 10 on Raffles, 40 on Foster, and 50 on McLeod, which makes 500 hdds. Am sorry it is not better, but hope the ensuing one will be better than that of last year At least the Estate had never such an appearance of making a large Crop as at present.

Swamps has done pretty well. It will ship 80 Hdds. and Rum pretty well in proportion, and hope to turn 100 the ensuing Crop. It can allways be kept thereabouts.

Doubtless Mr. Cowell has informed you about the Ejectment Dawkins's Attorneys have brought. I have many things to lay before your Council but have not yett been able to procure a Consultation, as they have been some, at Leeward, some busy others at Spanish Town, but as our assize begins next Tuesday shall then all meet, and will send their opinions to Mr. Cowell. Depend on it I will spare no pains to keep the Land for you.

There has not been a Guinea man in since my last. We are now putting in by the Consent of your Mother 70 acres into provisions for new Negroes, as it would be a pity not to have plenty for them when putt on. The wett weather and the Catterpillars by eating up all the grass has made the Cattle rather low, but as the Crop is finishd I hope they will soon pick up. We are now att work putting every thing in order for the next Crop but as Mr. Kelly will no doubt write you every thing reguarding the Estate anything I say will only be a repetition of what he says.

I shall go to Spanish Town in a day or two to see your Mother & Aunt who are both very well.

There is nothing new stirring here we have very heavy rains at Windward which sett in about two months ago and have continued hitherto which promises us all the prospect of a good Crop after having been three years burnt up.

58. To Chaloner Arcedekne, Kingston, 4 September 1771

I wrote to you by the *Eagle* & the *Grantham* Pacquet since which have only to observe to you that have been at Windward & went as much over the Land at the River's mouth that is in dispute with Mr. Dawkins as I could, & find that the part rented at present to Holland Estate is the only valuable part of it, the rest being a mere Morrass & Quagmire.

I have not been able to get a Consultation of the Lawyers occasion'd by the death of Tom Gordon & was up yesterday to get one, but was prevented by the death of Tom Bullock on which his Brother immediately set out for this town to attend his funeral.

As the Land is not of that great value I always supposed it to be, & if Mr. Dawkins would give up his pretensions for a trifle, I would advise you to settle it with him, as the Law Suit will be very expensive on all sides, & if he should recover he would only get the half of 90 acres of good Land as either Capt. Willer or Wallen, who says he has bought from Waller the other moiety would sett aside immediately the division made in 1728 & get a new one, for their part is only Morass. For this reason I think it would be Dawkins's Interest to give it up, for a trifle, the original purchase from Pearce[210] being only £150 this Currency.

I am very sorry to inform you that I think your presence would be very necessary here soon for the following reason, Your Mother seems to break fast & is very old. She has lately made her Will & has appointed Charles Kellsal,[211] Samuel Smith,[212] & James Fraser[213] her Executors. Smith is honest but gives himself no trouble about his owner

[210] It has proved impossible to further identify Pearce.

[211] Little is known about Kelsall, a planter-merchant, other than at the time of his death in 1780 he owned at least one plantation, Hermon Hill, in St Mary and a moiety of the *Union*. He was also £3,000 in debt to Thomas, Stephen, and Rose Fuller of London, merchants. It is unclear why Elizabeth Kearsey placed so much faith in someone who was so despised by Simon Taylor. Oliver, *CARIBBEANA*, III, p. 123

[212] It has proved impossible to further identify Smith.

[213] Probably James Fraser, a partner in the Kingston-based mercantile house of Fraser and McQueen.

matters, Fraser is honest but greatly involved; & Kelsal, who would be the only acting person as great a Villain as ever was hang'd. What a situation do you imagine matters would be in his hands. You know the advantage it was to you to have been present at the death of your Father. It will be, comparing small matters with great, as necessary for you to be here on the death of your mother as the Will now stands. Was you to come over & stay never so short a time would be able to get her to do as you please in the matter & put it in other persons who would do you justice in case of her death, & I believe you know that she is very well worth your while to look after. Excuse this, it was by mere accident I learned the names of her Executors & my friendship for you is the Occasion of my acquainting you of it.

59. To Chaloner Arcedekne, Kingston, 3 December 1771

My last to you was p. the *Duncanon* Pacquet Copy p. the *Dunkirk* Man of Warr, since which I have not received any from you & my Brother in law Mr. Graham writes me that you are still at Florence.

I had a letter from Messrs. Long Drake & Long acquainting me that they had received the Pipe of Wine I sent them by your desire for Mr. Colemore. I hope he likes it. It was not long enough in the Country but believe it will turn out very good.

I have at last after long sollicitations got Webley & Browns Opinions on the Plantain Garden River mouth Land, & sent them to Mr. Cowell. I have not yett gott Mr. Bullocks owing to a very severe illness, & he still continues in the greatest danger with the Belly ache; as soon as he is better & able to attend business will get it & forward it to you.

You will observe there is a Question more put to Webley than to Brown for this reason. Wallen who pretends Capt. Weller has sold him his quarter part of that Land, was talking of sending a Writt of Division to Dawkins provided he recover'd the Land from you. Browne is Wallen's Son in Law & I would not state that Question to him to give him any alarm, but put it in your Power to have quietly purchased from Weller, but Webley's Opinion you see is that the Judgement in partition will stand valid. I really think if you could Compromise for a Trifle with Dawkins, it would be the best way, & the cheapest for you in the long run. I dare say Mr. Cowell whom I have wrote to on the subject, will send you the Opinions of the Lawyers here, & also of those at home on the matter.

John Archer is lately dead at New York, & has by his Will mentioned a Matter which is this. One Dr. Collins[214] who I believe formerly livd

---

[214] It has proved impossible to further identify Dr Collins or establish the dates when he was employed on Golden Grove.

at Golden Grove kept a Wench belonging to you named Catharine, & had by her three Sons whose names are, Johny Chapplin Edward Kidvallede Collins & Isaac Collins. He left Archer his Executor & money in his hands to buy the Freedom of these people, he gave himself no trouble about it in his life time but by his Will he mentioned it, & desires they may be bought. Your Mother acquaints me that she wrote to you for a power to sell them, but your answer was that you could give no Title but for your Life. It is true, but as the Old Lady seems anxious about the matter for the Children to be free, I am pretty confident that if you can get Mr. & Mrs. Cowell to join in a power of attorney to relinquish their Reversion in them, Bourke would readily do it on his part.

I should be myself much obliged to you to let me know if you will still lett me continue your Tenant on the 90 Acres of Land I at present rent from your Mother at the River's mouth. It would be a great loss to me to be deprived of it, & no immediate advantage to you. I wrote to you about it in April by Capt. Thompson, but have as yet had no answer to it.

Winde who is attorney for Duckinfield Hall Estate, spoke to me 3 or 4 days ago to give him leave to Cutt a Canal through your land at the Rivers mouth, to carry Duckinfield Sugars to the Stores at the Bay. I told him I had no power to grant any such leave, & did not suppose you would be against it provided the Proprietors of Duckinfield Hall permitted you, if you pleased, to carry your Sugars from Golden Grove to Duckinfield Hall, & ship them in Canoes on Duckinfield Canal but not otherways. He seem'd miff'd at it, but I would by no means was I in your place permitt them to dig through that Land without granting you the previledge of the Canal. I mention this to you to be on your guard, as this matter will certainly be askt of you & you will know what answer to give to it.

We went about yesterday at Golden Grove, & I hope you will gett the best Crop you ever yet had from it. There is a fine show of Canes. I hope also to be able to send you home some Sugars by the 15 of next month, for as Sugars are so high at home I would choose that you should reap the advantage of the good prices. I am in treaty with a small Ship to go up to load & am hopefull to be able to prevail.

Your Mother and Aunt are very well. I saw them both to day.

60. To Chaloner Arcedekne Kingston, 9 January 1773

Above is a Copy of my last to you via Liverpool since which I have been favoured with yours of 17 October acquainting me of your being at Suffolk where you intend to reside untill after the Christmas Holyday if the weather is good. I shall according to your desire record the Conveyance.

I am obliged to you for your orders to Mr. Long to accept Bills when drawn by me on you. You may depend on it, I shall only draw as there is occasion for money on your Account.

I heard you intended sending another Shallop[215] out. I apprehend she will be a good one for the builder is generally lookt upon as the best man that sends out Shallops here they being both strong and fast sailors.

I am sorry to find you will not be at allowed for buildings on Golden Grove, works being as necessary as any articles in the world. You may depend upon it I shall send the Sugars home consigned to you.

In reguard to Swamps I will make every thing as clear as I can. It wants negroes and I think a water work could be erected there at a very small Expence but as you intend to give up the lease it will not be worthwhile for you to do it but would erect one on it was it my Estate.

I have sent by Span of Spanish Town the Foreign Commissions & Robert Arcedeknes will in a Small Box with some papers of my own to the Care of Mr. Robert Cooper Lee and have desired the favor of him to forward it to you which make no doubt of his doing. You will be pleased to send out the Commission executed as soon as possible in order to be in time to produce in Evidence.

Your Mother and Aunt were both well about 10 days ago I saw them.

You have made about 80 hdds. of Sugar at Golden Grove. I shall endeavour to gett a Small Ship to go up to carry those that are cured home together with some of my own and to sail if possible by the 10th February before the Glutt comes in.

61. To Chaloner Arcedekne, Holland Park, 25 January 1773

I am favoured with yours of 20, & 27 August, 3 Sept, & 8 October, by the first of which I find that you are arrived in England in high health and Spiritts for which I am very glad.

I return you thanks for having honoured all the Bills I drew on you, but sorry that I drew you for the Balance of Taylor & Grahams last years Acct. as you did not mean that I should, but I thought you wanted all the Accts. settled & had it not been for that, I would not have done it.

[215] A shallop might be a two-masted ship with lugsails or a small open boat propelled by oars or sails. Both types of shallop were used chiefly in shallow waters.

In reguard to the Land at the River mouth I return you many thanks for your kindness, and be assured I will not take any part that will in the least injure your property. Mr. Dawkins must have misinformed you, when he said I had wrote to him to buy the land of him. I never wrote a letter to him in my life. I wrote to my Brother to endeavour to gett it for me that I might be certain of it untill I could bring in my own Land at Holland. And I now send you a Copy of what I wrote to my Brother, and what I received in answer from him.

In reguard of his designing it for an Estate for a younger Son, I am very sure it would take an Elder Sons Fortune, to make an Estate of it, for before they could do any thing they must drain 1200 acres of a Morass, the Whole of the land being under water but about 90 Acres which I now rent and 30 Acres by the River side, and 20 Acres of what I do rent is not above 6 Inches above the Water and the additional land what I shall gett from you is intirely for the Mangoes to gett firewood as I shall in two years more have finishd my wood at Holland. At any rate, I hope Mr. Dawkins never will gett it. If the matter can be settled in the manner I proposed in my last letters to you, I apprehend it will be for the Advantage of both of you, and Mr. Dawkins, & a very great disappointment to the Lawyers. I am very sure that Kelly and I shall agree on the land that I want, and will get a lease executed and send you a Scheme of it.

I observe what you write about your Mothers Will, and the Uneasiness you feel at her leaving Kelsall one of her Executors, as he might on her decease, possess himself of your house, papers, & effects which she has of yours under the Power of Attorney from you to her. And in order to frustrate Kelsalls design, you inclosed me a power of Attorney directed to Welch, to be made use of at my discretion. I have received it but have not spoke to Welch about it, as the power is defective, and not valid, not being attested before the Lord Mayor, and under the City seal, or having one of the Subscribing witnesses here to prove it before a Judge. In regard to Kelsall I do believe him to be as damned a raskall as ever lived, and I do not believe there is any connexion between Welch and him, further than that they are of one Country.

What I have done is this. I have desired one Mr. Allen[216] a Lawyer & Man of Honor & Integrity and who lives now in Spanish Town, in case your Mother should be taken ill to send me an express to Kingston, which will be instantly forwarded to me from there And I will immediately go there and in case of her death take possession of the House, and every thing in and about it, as your Attorney turn Mr. Kellsall out of Doors, and when we have gott her papers together deliver them over to Smith or keep them untill I am well advised by

---

[216] Almost certainly John Allen, who also acted as an attorney for Thomas Cussans.

the Lawyers what to do, at any rate not to lett Mr. Kelsall touch them. As the Power is not Valid I never mentioned it to any one but Mr. East my Lawyer, to ask his Opinion, on the Validity of the Probate of it, and he informed me that it was defective. I shall be soon in Spanish Town and will gett an opportunity of speaking to your Aunt on this subject, and will freely lay before her as from myself the consequences that may arise from your Mothers not leaving you one of her Executors, and hint at Kellsalls Character, and the danger of trusting such a man, and also tell her that I mention it to her out of my reguard to the Family, and purposely for her to mention it to her Sister. I will do it with all the delicacy I possibly can and which such a Subject requires.

I am confident was the Old Lady to go any where out but to Church, she must have heard of Kelsalls character, but as she seldom sees any body she thinks him one of the best men in the World, because he is officious about her in the Killing a Sheep or Goat, and collecting her wainage, and now and then borrowing money from her. If I have at any time the Acct. of your Mothers being sick, and gett to Town before she dies, I defy him to hurt you.

The Person who informed me of the Will is now at Bristol. His name is Jacob Rudhall.[217] If you inquire for him at Mr. Robert Cooper Lees it is 10 to one but he can inform you where he lives now, or the most likely place to hear of him. Depend in case of the Old Ladys death I will do every thing for you as if I was acting for my self.

I shall buy some more new Negroes for you as soon as those that were putt on the Estate last year are well of the Yaws which 16 or 17 of them have. Indeed, Mr. Kelly and myself have agreed to send them down to that place that was Whittles at Yallahs, to plant Guinea Grass there, and that being a Warm dry air is infinitely better for them than this Wett part. I shall also follow your orders in putting 5 Annually on Swamps.

I am much obliged to Mr. Cowell and the Duke of Roxburgh for mentioning me.

[*Notes that he will send Arcedekne* 'some Turtle as soon as the Season comes in and also the 2 pipes of Madeira Wine I have of yours'.]

Your second letter of 27 August acquaints me that you had not as yett gott the Sollicitor Generalls [218]opinion relative to Dawkins business, and that the Barr is so low at present at home that you do now know whose opinion to take, as Dunning is failed so much. I will not give up any point in that matter you may be assured of. In reguard to a Compromise

---

[217] It has proved impossible to further identify Rudhall.
[218] Alexander Wedderburn (see note 205 above).

I do not see it in the light you do as you will find by my late letter.

In reguard to Cussans's Title (it is the Quitt Rent Act) and I have been pushing your Attorney and do hourly expect from him your Title which will send you home, and I also desired him to take out the Proceedings in the Chancery Court & your Fathers Answer regarding the Water. I shall also endeavour to keep the tryall off for this Court and if possible the next, so as to have your Answer.

I was really glad to read that part of your letter wherein you mentioned purchasing Winchester Penn. Cussans fixes the price at 15,000 payable in 10 years in annual payments. Had you left it to me and not contradicted it by your subsequent letter, I would have through some third person have agreed with him for it, at those terms provided it was without Interest and he recovered the land from you which he pretends to, as you would then secure that land, secure the water from Marchs, and have room for a very fine Estate which would be to whomever you chose to leave it to.

Indeed from your last Letters I am exceedingly glad to find that you do intend to marry. I think you excessively in the right and hope you will have Heirs enough of your own to inheritt your Estate for the Children of Bourke, and Bourke himself lookt on Golden Grove as a matter that would of course be theirs.

Yours of 3 Sept. brought me the Sollicitor Generalls opinion, which I agree with you is full to the Point. In case it is not compromised at home, if it is Given in your favor they are instantly to appeal, as they say they are sure of carrying it at home. Indeed the Cheapest way is to gett it settled between yourselfs, if that cannot be done we must defend it inch by Inch, and follow the Lawyers' directions.

In reguard to Mr. Nisbetts [219] letter it is evasive and nothing to the Purpose, and those trenches they stopped, were made by James McQueen[220] when he was Overseer on Duckinfield Hall, to prevent their trash houses being over flown. We cannot as yett bring any action of damages untill we find how the land that was over flown turns out. In reguard to letting Duckinfield Hall cutt a trench through your River mouth land, if they give you free Navigation through Duckinfield to carry your goods to markett, you need not mind which way the trench goes it cannot affect your land, or the land I am to gett, any further than the size of the trench, and the Navigation would be worth more to you than that. What I mentioned it to you for was not to allow them a great conveniency without they accommodate you also, which I am confident they can do without the least prejudice to themselves. But I know they will rather forego the water carriage of their Estate, than give you a right to go through it.

---

[219] Possibly an attorney for Duckenfield Hall.
[220] It has proved impossible to ascertain the dates of McQueen's service on Duckenfield.

Indeed I am afraid you are mistaken in one matter, which is this, of the water that turns their Mills. I am sure they claim a Property in the water and do not reckon they hold it by Sufferance only, but as their Right. They certainly were at some part of the Expence in digging the trench jointly with your Father from the River, and I wish you would take an Opinion whether the free and uninterrupted enjoyment of the water, the helping to digg the Canall, and the annually assistance of building up the Weir, all which they have had and done for them 14 years, does not give them a property in the water, for if it does not and we have a right to direct the water from them at our pleasure, we can easily force them to dance to our pipe, and make them good neighbours in spight of their teeth by taking an opportunity of diverting the water from their Mills when they have a quantity of canes there.

You mention you wish your Mother would putt a new Roof on the House in Spanish Town. It is already done in three Roofs, the flatt Roof before the door is made into a Common one the same over the Hall and the back Hall is raised so you would hardly know the House, it is so much altered for the better.

I have wrote to Westmoreland to inquire about the Mountain belonging to Black Morass but have not heard from thence. Yett what you ask is so very moderate that no Gentleman can refuse to pay a reasonable rent and acknowledge your right.

In reguard to your Man at Northside that owes you the Money Mrs. Murphy[221] mentions, his Name is Jennings,[222] and he is not worth a Bitt. His whole property is Mortgaged and will be sold under a decree of the Court of Chancery. You have neither mortgage, nor Judgement, and may give up the money for lost indeed. I never saw the state of the Act. as all those papers are in Spanish Town, & your mother keeps them lock'd up as old Gold.

Your next of 8 October wherein you Surprise me by complaining of Poverty and desire me not to Purchase Winchester Penn, as both the letters came to hand the same day, I had consequently done nothing on it.

In reguard to your Mothers and Aunts Annuity, I mentioned to them what you wrote to me. They both desired me to tell you you need not be in the least uneasy about it, for neither they nor any whom come after them shall be able to distress you for it. Indeed they have more money than they know what to do with, and if they will take it it is well, if not I shall tell them they ought then to make you a present of it, and not keep it hanging over your head.

Suppose that Winde would sworn what he had done, as he told me

---

[221] It has proved impossible to further identify Mrs Murphy.
[222] It has proved impossible to further identify Jennings.

he would. We have dug a trench which I believe they will feel the inconveniency of, whenever the wett weather setts in, and when we come to the Pieces that were over flown, we shall be better able to fix matters for bringing an Action of damages.

I shall send your Books home by some of the London ships. I assure you they are all in very good order. Your Aunt has taken great care of them.

We have had in October, Novr. & Dec. the Heaviest rains that ever have been known in these parts, which has prevented our going about so soon as we intended, and consequently are backward in the Crop, and sorry I am to inform you, there is not a Cane piece in Plantain Garden River that is not covered with the Black blast, a thing never before known here about. It will affect this Crop exceedingly and God knows if we shall any of us make Sugar next year, the Canes being as black as soot, and a Sort of Soot comes off them when you touch them. I have it in a most terrible manner at Holland, which hurts me much, both in the goodness & yielding of the Sugars.

62. To Chaloner Arcedekne, Kingston, 19 March 1773

I found you inclosed a duplicate of my last to you since which I have not had the Pleasure of hearing from you. I also send you inclosed an Office Copy of the Release of Tredway to your Father of the land patented by Penhallon at Plantain Garden River mouth and which Mr. Dawkins had brought his Ejectment for. I send you the office Copy to show Mr. Dawkins that you will be able to prevent his Sons being at the trouble of draining Morasses & settling an Estate at Plantain Garden River mouth and that Mr. Tredway did execute a Release to your Father as well as a lease.

I sincerely congratulate you on the discovery. It was found out by chance by a man who employs a great part of his time in hunting after old and obscure Titles and is recorded in the Clerk of the Courts office in Lib. 35. p. 427. It was not mentioned in the Margin what deed it was nor was it in the Alphabet which is the thing that has prevented the discovery so long.

I was obliged to pay for the Discovery two hundred Pistoles and at the same time promise to recommend it to you to add something more to it which I assured him I would recommend it to you it being a matter of so much consequence and I am confident will putt a final end to the Ejectment and consequently to Writts of Error Bills in Chancery Attorneys Bills & Lawyers fees. It will at the same time make him be in Honor bound to discover to you any defects he may find in any of Your Titles. No Gentleman would ask any thing to have discovered such a matter but the man that discovered this release makes a living by it therefor do recommend it to you to give him something further.

I do also send you a State of both yours and Mr. Cussans's Title to the land in dispute between you. You will find it to be intirely a matter of Boundary, both your Titles being very short and clear. A few days before the Court Cussans came to me and told me that he found the Ejectment very expensive and if I chose it he would write to you himself on the Subject and see if you could settle it together. I told him that I thought considering your acquaintance together that he should have fallen on that Method before he brought the Ejectment.

What has brought him to this is an action he brought against Kennion which he finds much more expensive and contested than he imagined and after having spent a very large sum of money he finds that he is not one single step advanced and will in all probability not recover anything and be £1000 or 1500 out of pockett. How to advise you in the matter I cannot tell for if he should recover it would be a very great loss from the water.

I have been wanting Cunliffe[223] much to go up with me to go over the land. He has surveyed it for your Father and was the person that first advised the Ejectment against him when the land was recovered but he acquainted me that he could not possibly come up but would do it before the next Court and would lett me know when he would come to Spanish Town and I have told him that I would have a Carriage ready to bring him up and intend to go over all the land with him and gett him to make out a platt & Scheme to send to you. In the meantime will endeavour to keep the matter off until can hear your determination in reguard to Cussans.

I think of setting the same man at work who found the release to search and endeavor to find out some flaw so as to give him such another Check as Mr. Dawkins will gett. I do apprehend you will meet with no further molestation from him and that the Release will putt an end to his claim. Should he pretend that there is a flaw in the Release that it is not enrolled in the Secretarys office you will find on examining the Laws of Jamaica that the Law for enrolling deeds in that office was not made untill the year 1731 & this Release is enrolled in the Clerk of the Courts office in 1725, six years before. By stating it with the Opinion I sent you home you will find that it is the record we want.

Mr. John Morse desires your thanks for having taken the pains to arrange Dawkins Title to take away your land.

[223] It has proved impossible to further identify Cunliffe or to ascertain for how long he had worked as a surveyor.

In reguard to the Mountain which did belong to Black Morass I wrote to you in my former letter that I had wrote to Westmoreland to inquire of it from Dr. Wedderburn. He informs me that it was not worth the Quitt Rents. That one Bossleys Estate joined to it who covered the greater part by a prior platt but that it was actually not worth any thing at all. He is a Man of veracity whose word I am sure is to be relyed on.

Mr. Angus McBean[224] wrote to Mr. Cowell the first Instant for the following Insurance 80 hdds. & 25 Punch. on the *Standlinch* Brankston from Golden Grove & for 20 hdds. & 10 Puncheons from Swamps on board the said Ship. I wish them same home and to a good Markett. I have closed all the Golden Grove & Swamps accts. which will go home by the *Standlinch* who I expect will sail in 8 or 10 days at farthest and have drawn on you the Several Bills undermentioned: which make not the least doubt but will meet with due honor

[*Notes that all the Bills are dated 4 March 1773 and all are* 'at 90 days sight'. '2 Setts favor of John Kelly being for Sallary & Negroe hire' *totalling £866.19.7 stg.;* '1 Sett favor of Angus McBean for Wages due to the Doct. & white people on Golden Grove, £312.13.0.; 1 Sett for Balance of John Meigham's Acct. for Carpenter's work done on Golden Grove, £78.11.5; 1 Sett favor of Angus McBean for Supplies & Moneys paid for him on Actt. of Golden Grove, £338.4.8; 1 Sett favor of Angus McBean for Supplies & Moneys paid by him for Supplies & Moneys paid by him for Swamps Estate, £159.2.2; 1 Sett favor of Angus McBean for Wages due and paid by him to the White people on Swamps, £58.13.8; 1 Sett each to John Kelly, Malcom Laing, Mrs. Eliza. Kersey, and Mrs. Frances Harris for [their] 1/5 Commission on your Estate £167.15. 3½; 1 Sett favor Simon Taylor for disbursements by him & his Commission on your Estate, £511.13.9.']

The Acts. are to bulky to send by the Pacquet but shall send them by Capt. Brankston who I expect will sail next week when will also send you the duplicates of the Receipts and also your Title and Cussans's to the land in dispute shall go by the other Pacquett that sails in the next Week.

63. To Chaloner Arcedekne, Kingston, 25 March 1773

I wrote to you the 19 Instant and send you a Copy by this Vessell, and have been untill the Mail is Closing waiting for to send you the

---

[224] A merchant based in Kingston.

Title between you and Cussans, but by some mistake they have not Compleated them, but am Confident everything will go by the *Standlynch*.

Have Jointly with your Mother, Aunt, and Mr. Laing drawn on you of 19 Instant for £169.12.10 Sterling, being the Sum of £237 10/- Currency Paid to Brodie for the Discovery of Tredways Title to your Father, which was the Occasion of that wanting a Compromise, if you have entered into any. I believe the inclosed will putt it out of doubt that they must have intended a Fraud. The Gentleman is one of Dawkins's attorneys, and am sure he would not tell an untruth.

64. To Chaloner Arcedekne, Holland Park, 9 April 1773

I Inclose you a Copy of my last to you which I now confirm and do now send you home a State of the Accts. both of Golden Grove & Swamps and your Act. Current which you will find clos'd. I have also sent you duplicate receipts of the moneys paid you will also please to observe that the Articles marked before with X I have only one Voucher or receipt for and I send you home the duplicate copy of those marked / thus.

I am really sorry not to have it in my power to send you your Title by this Ship to the land in dispute with Cussans which I hardly could doubt of having been able to accomplish but the forms of Lawyers are hardly to be altered or their motions quickened but as ships will be going every week now shall not want Opportunities. I however send you Cussans's Title. The only thing that keeps your Title is looking for the Title of 1/2 of Lewis's run. All the others were out of the Office before I left town.

Capt. Brankston has 80 hdds. of Sugar and 25 Puncheons of Rum from Golden Grove & 20 hdds. of Sugar and 10 Puncheons of Rum from Swamps on board. Capt. Watt in the *Jamaica* will bring you 80 hdds. of Sugar and 25 Puncheons of Rum, and I doubt not but Mr. Kelly will inform you of the quantity he intends for Thompson, Farr, Fryer, & Tarbut.

[*Notes that wine for Arcedekne and Colemore has been shipped to Benjamin Cowell*].

65. To Chaloner Arcedekne, Kingston, 1 May 1773

I wrote to you on the 25 March & 9 April Copys of which I now Send to you Since which I have been favored with your much Esteemed favor of 1 Febry.

I am very well convinced that you will not at this time conceive yourself to be so much obliged to Mr. Dawkins as you apprehended yourself to be, he having in my Opinion acted a very dirty part as you will find by Doct. Gordon's[225] Letter I sent You. He knows that we had found out your Title & should have non suited him, & therefore he offers to make you a Title to what he has not. His Prevarication in this is equally infamous as is his Lye that I wrote to him to buy the Land from him.

You will long before this have received my answers to your Letters in August & Sept. p. the *Grantham* & *Grenville* Pacquets. Since which I have Sought & have only Yesterday found an opportunity of Speaking to your Aunt apart from your Mother in regard to her will & the nominating you Executor. I laid before her every reason the Badness of Kelsal's Character, the Injury she might do, the Violence of the Persecution formerly carried on by people who called themselves your Father & her friends, the lucky Escape you had by being in the Country your Self, & the ingratitude of every one of them to your Mother. She seemed to be much Struck at the mentioning of your knowledge of Kelsal's being an Executor. She told me she did not know the purport of Your Mother's Will, that there were other Executors & She believed you was named; that she would ask your Mother & that she also saw very Clearly the Necessity of your being named one of the Executors & that She should strongly recommend it.

This will be delivered to you by my Particular Friend Mr. Hinton East. Some little matters call him home. He has a Small Account against you for £136.2.3 Currency making Stg. £97.4.5½. I told him that as it was so small that it was not worth while drawing a Bill for it but that you would give him an Order on your Correspondent. He also brings you home the proceedings in Chancery between Cussans & Gregory & your Father which you wrote for & I do now Send you home annext the different Titles to the Land Cussans brings his Ejectment for, as you will see by the Inclosed Abstract.

As I am Confident you will not give up Land to Cussans we must next Court move for a foreign Commission to Examine Witnesses in Cornwall where the Penhallons come from as you will See in the Sale from Peters to Lewis & also in Lewis's to your Father. Mr. East will be able to Explain to any Councill the whole matter & referr You to him he & his Partner being Concernd for you in this Case.

Your Mother & Aunt are both very well & desire my Compliments to Mr. Cowells Family.

I forgot to mention to you that Mr. Kelly Informed me that he wanted to Sell you his Negroes & would give you the preference. They have their Houses & Grounds on your Land & Consequently would

225 Dr John Gordon.

Suit you better than any Person in the West Indies. They have all had
the Yaws & are really as fine a parcell of negroes as are in the Island &
being Seasoned in plantain Garden river makes them much more
Valuable. They are 140 of them which I am sure With the Strength
that is on the Estate & the blast does not Injure us, would keep the
Estate up at about 700 hhds. besides save £1,000 a year you now pay
for Jobbing. On my almost Moral Certainty of your Agreeing to Kellys
proposal, I have not nor will not buy any new negroes for the Estate
untill I hear further from You on this Subject. He offers them also at
a Valuation one person to be chose by Your Attorney the Other by
him & he further Says he is in no immediate want of the money.

66. To Chaloner Arcedekne, Kingston, 21 May 1773

I am favoured with yours of 26 Febry. and you will see by my former
letters to you that I have received your letter reguarding the River
mouth land and that you are not quite so much obliged to Mr. Dawkins
as you thought you was.

I am really sorry to see from the content of your letters that you
have given up all hopes or thoughts of marrying. I have urged it so
often that shall for the future say nothing more on the subject.

In reguard to the debts of the Estate that you have paid becoming
your property I shall speak to Frazer [226] the Surviving Copartner of
McQueen, [227] and Frazer to see their Books and what you have paid
but I do not recollect any thing but a Bond that you took up your self.
In reguard to mine all that I have paid is a debt to John Burke[228] of
London of about £550 which was remitted or ought to have been by
Reisset Jaffray & Yelloly about two thousand pounds to Fagan, and I
question much if I shall be able to gett his Representative to assign to
you having had a release from Fagan to your Father's Estate of all
debts dues & demands whatsoever.

Pray lett me know if the Building a new sett of works at Golden
Grove will come in as there was £4000 paid to Carter the Mason
besides Stevens acct. of Carpenter's work is about £2000 and there
was an absolute necessity of either building a new sett of works or
throwing up the Estate.

In reguard of the Cattle they all bear your mark, the mules do not

[226] Probably James Fraser (see note 213 above.)
[227] Daniel McQueen was a merchant based in Kingston. In 1754 Patrick Taylor,
Simon's father, named McQueen as a beneficiary of his will. Will of Patrick Taylor,
made 3 September 1754, proved 12 September 1754. Wills, Island Record Office, Spanish
Town, XXIX, fo. 206.
[228] Possibly one of Arcedekne's Anglo-Irish relations.

breed consequently are all yours and the names of the Negroes putt on by you shall allways be putt annually in the Secretary's office as you desire it but it will be of no consequence putting it there as it will be of no record.

In reguard to your paying 25 Guineas p. ct. Premium for your first Sugars I am very sorry for it being excessive high. Indeed am glad the Vessell with the last parcell arrived safe and that you sav'd the Insurance on her.

You must undoubtedly have received my letters to you in answer to those in Septr. and I am heartily glad to see you are so well and God Grant you a long continuance of it.

I am much obliged to you for your kind intention of recommending me to your Friend Lord Charles Montague[229] if he had been appointed Governor. We hear that Sir Basil Keith[230] is appointed. He is very well acquainted here and well liked in Generall.

[*Notes that he is sorry not to have sent Arcedekne a turtle but* 'they are this year scarcer here than in England'.]

67. To Chaloner Arcedekne, Holland Park, 14 July 1773

My last letter to you was of the 21 May pr. the *Holland* Capt. Taylor copy p. the *John McCartin* via Liverpool since which I have been favoured with your ever esteemed favor of 2 Aprill and am very glad to find by it that you have received my letter of 25 Janry.

You will see by my letters that I have received yours relative to Mr. Dawkins & your settlements and did receive by Capt. Carr in the *Clarendon* Mr. Dawkins's Title. He should have thrown off the Grievance and not pretended to have given what he very well knew he had no right to give away. I shall when go to Kingston for have not been since my last consult a Lawyer whether it is proper to record it or not and shall also see your Aunt and gett an answer from her relative the Executorship. I am sure if gett to Town time enough that Kelsall will never be able to do so much mischief as he intends if it is in his power he being worthless enough.

I am sorry to find that I am right with reguard to Duckingfield Hall having a right in the Water. They seem to be tolerable peacable just now. I believe Winde had a conversation with Mr. Nisbett about it.

---

[229] Lord Charles Greville Montague (1741–1784) served as the Governor of South Carolina between 1766 and 1773. During the American War of Independence he saw active military service as the commander of the Duke of Cumberland's Regiment.

[230] Keith served as Governor of Jamaica until his death in 1777.

The Papers brought sure enough the Accot. of the Barronette having stopt and Kennion writes me that they find he values his 1/3 of Duckingfield at £60,000 Stg. or £180,000 for the whole Estate. They have not made 200 hdds. of Sugar on it and what is made is excessive bad tho the blast is leaving it and the Estate is in better order than it has been in for some time past. It has play'd the very Devill with it and Holland this year and hurt Amity Holland Hordley a little this year and I am much mistaken if they do not feel it very severely next year.

You have hitherto escaped tolerably well. God Grant you may continue so to do. I am not quite free from it but not afflicted with it to any degree of comparison to what I was last year. It is particularly hard upon me to be so checkt in the first setting out and having such amazing heavy matters on my hands. I should have been able to have gone through all matters very well had it staid away but as it is I must putt my Shoulders to the Wheel and do everything in my power to gett the better of it as I cannot help it and it is too late to retract. It certainly would have been for the Benefit of the Public if proper means had been taken at first to have destroyed the Canes that were first infected by it but at Duckinfield Hall they are keeping the most easterly piece of canes in their Whole Estate which will not make a quarter of a hdd. an Acre and has the blast in it and consequently are keeping it for ever in their Estate as it is to windward of every cane piece they have. The Same they are also doing at Amity Hall keeping a ruinate in a manner to destroy both themselves & their Neighbours. What can be the reasons for it I cannot say.

Kelly tells me he has regularly wrote to you about Insurance and I think he told me he would ship about 460 or 70 hdds. of Sugar besides Rum from Golden Grove. I shall write to you again soon when have seen your Mother & Aunt which shall in a few days.

PS I am exceeding sorry to inform you of the untimely end of your Shallop which was wrecked on the Pitch of the East end the 2^d Instant being drove a Shore in a Calm and Bildged. She luckily was coming up light having just delivered a load at Port Morant on board the *Friendship* Capt. Watt. The Rigging and Sails are saved. If you chuse to send out another you had better gett one built by one Wood. Indeed this was the most Scandalous piece of Work ever seen and the Ugliest thing, being as broad as long and would not go any more than a hay stack. After she was putt up I was obliged to send her to Kingston to have beams put into her to strengthen her. You also need neither send out sails Mast Boom Rigging nor Anchors & Cables as the Shallops were saved.

68. To Chaloner Arcedekne, Kingston, 25 July 1773

I wrote to you the 14 Instant p. the *Friendship* Capt. Watt and sent you
a Duplicate p. the *St. Thomas in the East* Capt. Holbrook via Bristol
Since which am Come to this Town but this being a very Busy time I
have not been able to go as yet to Spanish Town. When I do which I
suppose will be within these three or four days I shall have a long
Conversation with your Aunt on the Matter I before wrote to you
about. The Event of which I will Acquaint you with by the *Great Marlow*
Capt. Kitchen who does not sail before the 1st of August.

You have 29 hhds. of Sugar and 12 Puncheons of Rum more to go
from Golden Grove and 11 hhds. and 1 Trcs. of Sugar and 20 Puncheons
of Rum from the Swamps which I intend to send in a Ship which
is at Port Morant called the *Lovely Betsy* Capt. Marshall. I Could not
get them away before the 26th as we had lost the Shallop and the
Current went so strong to Leeward that the Boats Could not go up to
Windward.

I have drawn on you jointly with you other Attornies the following
Bills.

[*Notes that all are dated* '24 July 1773 *at* 90 *days sight.* 1 sett in favor of
Angus McBean for £50.8.10; 1 Sett in favor of Simon Taylor for
£313.10.2; 1 Sett in favor of Thomas Gray[231] for £315.2.10½'. *Taylor has
sent* 'the Duplicate Receipts by the *Great Marlow*'.]

69. To Chaloner Arcedekne, Holland Park, 17 September 1773

I wrote to you by the 25 July and should have wrote by the *Great
Marlow* but on my going to Spanish Town I had no opportunity of
asking your Aunt any Questions about the Will. Indeed it is only
about 10 days ago I had any opportunity when she told me she had
asked her and was informed that you, Mr. Cowell, Sam Smith James
Fraser & Charles Kelsall were her Executors but could gett no more
out of her.

She also desired me to tell you that you must excuse her not writing
to you for if she did which she willingly would some of the Negroes
etc about the House would tell your Mother of it who she says would
be jealous and begs you will excuse her as she would not have the
least uneasiness if possible between her & her Sister but if anything
extraordinary happens she will lett me know to write to you of it.

[231] A merchant house based in Kingston.

I am favoured with your two letters first of 6 May the other of 31 of said month. By the first tho they both came in the same ship you advised of your having made the Insurance on the *Standlinch* and sent a letter to Cussans in answer to one he wrote to you about the land in dispute and first to show it to your Mother before I delivered it to him.

I shewed it to her and she insists the land should not be given up by any reason. Indeed his method is so very vague of the water that it is nothing. He should also first gett the land before he pretends to give away the water. I wish you would take a sound opinion on this point whether since Cussans should recover the land he could stop the Course of that water which has turned your Mills so many years and when you had before recovered the land from him.

I have not delivered your letter to him nor shall not as I am in hopes to hear very soon from you the opinions of the English Lawyers on it for Mr. East who has been now some time in England carried all the papers reguarding the Title to you and I have applied to the Council for a Commission to examine Elizabeth Walters[232] in Cornwall whom Mr. Dawkins Examined and can prove the descent of the Penhallons mentioned in the Sale of Peters to Lewis which should have gott last Court but for the sickness of John Allen Mr. Cussans's attorney which shall send you home as soon as possible which pray gett Executed as soon as you can for the Old woman is upwards of 80 if alive and no other person can prove the Family that I know of.

By Yours of 31 of May I find the *Standlinch* is arrived and brought you your Accts. Sugar etc. I find that there was a vessell missing which brought you the deed of Tredway to your Father and the Bill for £165.12.10 was the Amount of 200 pistoles I gave for the discovery of that deed. I received the Release and do not think there is the least occasion of recording it the deed from Tredway to your Father being better from the Originall than the descendant.

In reguard to Cussans giving you the water he writes to you he would give you the Use of the water. In the letter he writes to me he says he will give you the use of the water for your life paying a pepper Corn p. ann. As he and I are not at present very gracious I send you a Copy of a letter he sent me for John Kellys telling him I had a letter from you for the Settlement. As I had not seen your Mother at that time I sent answer to his letter I had not heard from you on the subject. As I would not by any means be a fomentor of disputes between Neighbours or misrepresent any thing whatever you chuse to be done in the matter I am ready to follow your Instructions.

In reguard to the discovery of Tredways Title to your Father it is

---

[232] It has proved impossible to further identify Elizabeth Walters.

this. John Sheckle[233] Mr. Dawkins's attorney and one Rome[234] his Surveyor were searching for a writt of division of some lands belonging to Mr. Dawkins & another person in the Clerk of the Courts office when they stumbled on the deed from Tredway to your Father. Sheckle mentioned it to Dr. Gordon. This was last October or November. They said nothing of it to any one but wrote an account of it to Mr. Dawkins but not giving Rome a Sop he agreed to go halves with one Broady who offered to cutt it out of the Book for 1000 Pistole. But Dr. Gordon to whom he made the proposall would have nothing to say to him on which he came to me and on getting the 200 Pistoles in which Rome went halves they shewed it to me. Had Dr. Gordon mentioned it, it would have saved that money.

Mr. Dawkins not knowing that this matter was found out pretends to do you a favor by granting you a Title to it and confirming an Obligation on you when he really actually and Bonafide knew he had no Title and that the Title was vested in you and whenever the Cause came on he would be nonsuited. What Dr. Gordon mentions in his letter that every thing that was fair & Honourable had been mentioned to Mr. Dawkins he means Mr. Dawkins was Acquainted with the discovery made by Sheckle & Rome.

The next part of your letter seems again to want to settle the dispute at Winchester Penn by Arbitration. If the lines are clear they will be by and by as clear as they are now and I want to gett two men out of the way who pretend to know something of the matter tho in fact they know nothing of it. What I mean by out of the way is that they will die off. Delay found out Dawkins's Title to be bad delay may make Cussans tired of Law and a Jury is as good an arbitration as any other people. Indeed was it mine it should be tryed in England where people can gett good Lawyers for Judges and I am convinced Mr. Cussans will have at any event a platt of 100 Acres thrown out.

Kelly I suppose has wrote to you on the Subject of his Negroes. I am very happy to hear we are not likely to have a war soon. It must do a great Injury to us Planters and can do no good. Taxes must be raised on our goods, freights & Insurance will be high and probably the price of Sugar low. In case of war on the Contrary tho the price

[233] John Sheckle (1712–1782) emigrated from Britain to Jamaica in the late 1720s. In addition to his legal work he served as the Custos of Clarendon and Vere and was also appointed Brigadier General of the local militia. Lawrence-Archer, *Monumental Inscriptions*, p. 305.

[234] John Rome was one of the most important land surveyors in eighteenth-century Jamaica. Much of his work during the middle years of the century was undertaken for the Dawkins family. (See note 33 above.) By the 1790s Rome appears to have abandoned surveying in favour of coffee planting in Clarendon parish. Upon his death in 1797 his estate, which was valued at £3,080, included forty-one slaves. Higman, *Jamaica Surveyed*, p. 31.

of Sugar and rum may be low freight and Insurance are also low as well as staves & hoops.

In reguard of your talking about Matrimony I wish you would resolve seriously upon you who are in the land of Beauties. For my part, there are none my way but Mauritanians & their issue being in a manner a constant accident in the Country and have no opportunity of seeing of but seldom indeed.

I have the pleasure to acquaint you your Estate is free of blast and I am much clearer than I was. Indeed should have been intirely so had not Duckingfield Hall kept a piece of canes to windward of one that will not make them a hdd. of Sugar and which at the same time is to Windward of all their own Estate and has again infected my canes as well as their own. It seems as if they did it on purpose never to gett rid of that Virman tho' they have suffered allready so much by it.

70. To Chaloner Arcedekne, Kingston, 8 December 1773

I am favoured with yours of 11 July acquainting me of your having received my letter acquainting you how the release was discovered and that you had accepted the Bill in favor of Ross for the use of Brodie. He has never ask'd any thing more and therefore have not given him any thing. He is a damned worthless fellow and will I suppose be one day or another hanged but he was in this matter of Service to us was it only to have shown Dawkins's underhand dealing and think you did right thing in Shewing Mr. Long Dr. Gordons letter which I suppose had he not seen Dawkins would have denied. Whatever gloss they may putt over it you may depend he would not have given up land or at least the Claim could he possibly have expected to have succeeded in it. You are right not to take the costs they being a trifle. They have not offered them to me nor shall I take them.

I am glad to hear that you have made a purchase of a freehold Farm at £100 a year as I hope it will induce you to marry and stay at home.

I have agreed with Kelly for his Negroes to be valued by one person chose by him another by you in case of dispute a third person to be called in. The money to be paid in 4 equall payments in 1774, 1775, 1776, 1777 with Interest. Your mother and Aunt were present when I agreed and were satisfied with it which I also hope you will approve off. You have been allways complaining of Poverty. I hope the addition of these negroes will give you larger Crops. I assure you it is out of my power to manage for you with more frugality than I do.

In reguard to the Capts. Of Ships not taking the quantity they engaged there are reasons such as Sugars not being made and they cannot then be shipt and the boats are obliged to go back empty. Some time disappointments will happen. If you will plan to direct how and in what Ships you chuse your Sugars shipt they shall be sent. I assure you I have no interest or share or part of any Ship that Sails the Sea and therefore they are all intirely indifferent to me, and Brankston shipt me last year 28 hdds. out that he might take 20 of yours in as he presented to me that he would be obliged to ship one or other of us out and I agreed that he should ship me out rather than you. I have according to your desire shown your letter to Kelly.

I shall by the Man of war send you a Commission to examine Eliza. Walters of Philleigh in Cornwall. I beg you will return it as soon as possible for Cussans seems to be very impatient to bring it to a tryal and a Copy of Rob. Arcedekne's will shall be sent with it.

Your Mother and Aunt are both very well.

I saw Kelly about a fortnight ago. He said he should go about the 1 of this month. I have not since heard from him but I know the weather has been very bad at Windward.

71. To Chaloner Arcedekne, Kingston, 12 March 1774

My not having heard from you lately makes me have a little more to say than just to acquaint you of a few matters that have happened since my last to you when I acquainted you that we had begun Crop at Golden Grove and it is with very great pleasure I can acquaint you that I saw Mr. Kelly yesterday who informed me that by this night you will have about 360 hdds. made there.

We have also bought from Mr. Kelly for your account 120 Negroes. They were valued by Mr. Joseph Orr[235] on Mr. Kelly's part and by Mr. Robert McDermet[236] on yours and amount to the Sum of £8714, for which Your Mother, Aunt, Mr. Laing & self have given four Bonds to Mr. Kelly for the Sum £2178.10 each payable in 1775, 1776, 1777 & 1778. There was also a further charge on them which was their houses and grounds and which those Gentlemen putt valuation of 3 p. Ct. on the Value of the Negroes but Mr. Kelly gave up the half viz. £130.14.2¼ and your Mother paid that and also the Sum of £248.10 which last Sum is wrote off the Bond payable in 1776 being the Amount of two Bonds she had in her hands of Mr. Kellys. Indeed I would not have allowed the 130.12.2¼ the one & half p. Ct. on the Negroe Grounds but that Kelly by selling the Negroes gave up a profit of near 1500 p. ann. he made by them for the Interest on the purchase money. I do assure you I think them a prodigious acquisition to your Estate and

---

[235] An eminent planter-merchant.
[236] Like Orr, a planter-merchant.

that you will not feel the purchase as you will by this means be enabled to enlarge your Crop and save your Capital and there will be no occasion of pushing so hard as we were formerly Obliged to on the Estate.

Lett me recommend it also to you to give orders for the purchase of 20 young Negroes annually to be bought for the use of the Estate and by that means they will become as good as any Creoles and very little risque in the seasoning of them and the Yaws which is the most distructive thing in a wett Country does not make half the impression on them as it does on grown people and make no doubt but that you will find your income yearly increasing more than sufficient to pay for them.

Your and my Antagonist Mr. Cussans pushed exceeding hard to bring on the Ejectment of the land at your Dam but I got it starved off this Court. As am in daily expectation of hearing from you the opinions of the English Lawyers on the titles I sent you by Mr. East I hope there may not be the least delay in the Commission to examine Elizabeth Walter of Philleigh in Cornwall her Evidence being exceeding material.

[*Notes that he has* 'drawn on you the following Bills' *all at* '90 days sight. 1 Sett drawn by Eliza. Kersey, Frances Harris, Simon Taylor in favor of John Kelly for £1617.7.7½; 1 Sett drawn by Eliza. Kersey, Frances Harris, Simon Taylor in favor of John Kelly for £160; 5 Setts drawn in favor of Angus McBean' *totalling* '£1196.5.9¾; 1 Sett each to Eliza Kersey, Frances Harris, Malcom Laing, John Kelly for £154. 4. 8½'. *Adds that* 'Mr. Laing was out of Town or he would also have signed them. I have also given Messrs. Long Drake and Long advice of them'.]

Mr. Kelly acquaints me that he has wrote for insurance on the Sugars and will write to you p. Brankston.

72. To Chaloner Arcedekne, Holland Park, 10 April 1774

I wrote to you the 12 of March acquainting you of my having drawn on you for the Ballance of Golden Grove and Swamps Estate and that I should send those Accounts by the *Standlinch* or the *Friendship* which ever sailed first. I do now therefore annex them and hope on your perusing them that you will find them right.

There has nothing has occurred since my last to acquaint you off but that Mr. Cussans is again going to revive the Lawsuit against Golden Grove Acct. of the water. We must do our best to oppose him. He is extreamly fond of Law and I do firmly believe he is pushed on in this matter by Dr. Gregory. This is my surmise though I cannot say positively it is so.

You have made upwards of 400 hdds. at Golden Grove and have a great many canes still to Cutt which I sincerely hope will turn out well. Kelly tells me he will write to you fully by this Ship reguarding the Estate.

Your Aunt mentioned to me a few days ago that your Mother took it unkind in you not writing to her for that she had had only two letters from you since leaving the Island and desired me to acquaint you of it.

[Notes that he has sent Arcedekne a turtle].

73. To Chaloner Arcedekne, Kingston, 23 April 1774

On the other side is a Copy of my last to you p. the *Standlinch* which ship is sailed since which I have been favoured with yours of 20 Janry. acquainting me of having received mine of 7 Sept. and that the Proceedings of the Chancery Suit I sent home are so voluminous that you have not been able as yett to gett the Opinions of the Lawyers upon it but that you will be as expeditious as you can in sending it to me as also the Commission when you secure it. I wish heartily for the Commission.

I do intend to secure an Ejectment on Philips Estate on your behalf this insuing Court for some small piece of land that your Surveyor tells me he is in possession of bordering and being part of Edward Stantons platt which piece of land Phillips claims under a Title from Mr. Phillip Pinnock and Coll. Swarton[237] being patented by them and half of said land being warranted to Phillips by Pinnock when he sold the half of the Estate to Philips. It seems Pinnock is Cussans chief Evidence. My reason for the Ejectment is to shew that Pinnock is an interested Person and not an Impartial Evidence.

The next Evidence they depend upon is Dr. Gregory to Prove Cussans's mother in Possession before her marriage with his Father. Now Dr. Gregory is in my Opinion also an interest Evidence for if Cussans gains the land they have a right to the place where your weir that takes in the water stands. Consequently even if they lett you take it up they will only give you as much as they please under pretence that the rest is wanted for his Mills and as the Water first turns Dr. Gregorys Mill he certainly will be a gainer. Therefor I shall object to his Evidence. He is the Chief promoter of the Suit they are going now to commence for the water. It is very true that they have had a scarcity

---

[237] It has proved impossible to further identify Swarton.

of water at Amity Hall this year owing chiefly to Mr. Kellys having taken in a great deal more water than usual to keep the two Mills about and having been a little wanton with it.

I shall now give you the true state of the matter as it now stands for you to be able to state the real Case to your Lawyers. Amity Hall some years ago erected and built a Water Mill on the Estate when it was a joint property between Gregory and Cussans and took up the Water to turn it from Plantain Garden River and is the oldest Mill that was turned by Plantain Garden River in the Neighbourhood. Your Father had before that Erected a Water Work on Negroe River and some time afterwards a second Water Mill. In the years of 1758 or 1759 he jointly with Duckingfield Hall took up Plantain Garden River to convey the water thereof to his and Duckinfield Hall Mills.

By this you see Amity Hall Mill is the oldest Mill by what I have allways understood had a right allways to have sufficient Water to turn it while it remained on the Construction it stood when your Father erected his Mill or turned rather the water on his Mill from Plantain Garden River. Butt on a division of the Estate of Amity Hall in 1764 or 1765 they that is Gregory and Cussans settled a new Sett of Works above the old Works of Amity Hall and Called them Hordley. In order also to have a water work on the said Estate of Hordley they divided the fall of water between the two Estates and consequently took away part of the fall from Amity Hall Mill by which means it must necessarily require a larger body of water to turn it than when they had the whole fall and not interrupted by Hordley Mill. Consequently what I mean to inferr is that the Mill of Amity Hall had a prior right to a Sufficient quantity of Water to turn it when on the Construction it was on in 1758 or 1759 but if it does it self an Injury surely I do not think it can have a right to remedy itself by injuring you.

I myself heard Dr. Gregory talk to Cussans to bring the Bill but that his Dr. Gregorys name must not be mentioned in it. As you have all the papers at home your Lawyers can inform you whether such Bill can be brought without making Dr. Gregory a party whose Mill is one of the great causes of their Scarcity of water by taking away the fall from Amity Hall Mill. I hope I have explained myself so that you may understand me. I shall act for you in the matter as if it were my own concern and shall defend the Ejectment in the manner you mention.

I was heartily sorry to hear your Sister had been so ill but glad to hear she had gott better.

I sent to Spanish Town the receipt of your letters to your Mother and mentioned to her that you was very well but that your Sister had been very ill but was better but in a poor way in reguard to her Health.

In reguard to Kellys negroes you have allready bought them as you will find by his and my letters and have 4 years in place of two for the payment. Kelly assures me that he will make near 600 hdds. this year. He is Attorney for Duckingfield Hall for which I am very glad as he will be a good neighbour which I cannot say was quite the Case of his Predecessor for had he destroyed the piece of 3^d Rattoons I mentioned to you he would have freed all that part of the River from the Blast. You have a good deal of it about Golden Grove but it has not yett done much mischief there. We have some of it still at Holland where thank God it has not done near the mischief it did last year. It begins to turn out better than it did and looks towards 450 hhds. this year.

In reguard to Sir George[238] I really pity him. It must be exceeding grating to a Man who inheritted so very great a property to find himself reduced to so low an Ebb as to sollicit for a Clerkship. Had they the least Spark of Gratitude they never ought to have lett him come so low but have before provided him some sinecure Government or Employ to have maintained him. I do not though think he ought to have been trusted with the Key of the Money Chest having taken so little care of what he had of his own.

They will make near 400 hdds. at Duckingfield Hall.

In reguard to your Rum I shall write to Mr. Kelly to make it to your proof tho it will be a loss for being so strong a great deal of the Spirit must evaporate in the running off the Spirit but as you desire it it must be done. I am sorry to hear that that article is at so low an ebb. I hope the Elections will give it a start which it seems much to require.

74. To Chaloner Arcedekne, Holland Park, 2 July 1774

My last to you was of 23 Aprill p. the *Standlinch* Capt. Brankston and a Copy of it went p. the *Jamaica* Capt. Watts since which our antagonist in the last May Court pushed us to a tryal of the Ejectment for the Land at the Dam. And notwithstanding that we mentioned that the Foreign Commissions was not arrived the Court forced us on to a tryall when after the swearing two Witnesses and objecting to two more one of the Jurors was taken ill in the Box and obliged to go out of Court which I am informed by our Lawyers makes a discontinuance. Our Friend Cussans was so very angry that he mentioned that he believed that the Man was bribed to fall sick. His disappointment was exceeding great having got his Friend Winde who has lately been made an Assistant Judge to sitt that day which and the times that the matter was expected to come one was the only time that he thought to propose or could spare time to sitt.

---

[238] It is unclear to whom Taylor is referring.

They also brought Dr. Gregory as an Evidence but I objected to his Evidence for severall reasons. First as he was a trustee for that land under both the deed and will of your Father. Secondly that he was a party concerned and had filed a Bill jointly with Mr. Cussans against your Father to take away the water and that this Ejectment was principally designed to do it and if Cussans should succeed that by taking away your Dam he would be much benefitted by the water.

I objected also against Old Philip Pinnock's Evidence also for this reason. There is a platt of 25 acres of land to the Southward of your platt of Stanton that was patented by Stanton also which Pinnock and Stanton Exheated severall years ago and which is the land you wrote me some years ago to demand of Philips which I did and Philips so wished to settle the matter before he went home but did not. I therefore thought it best to bring an Ejectment for it as Pinnock sold it that is a moiety of it to Philips when he sold the half of pleasant Hill to him in 1761 and warranted it now by fixing your platts as they were fixed the Judgement in 1756.

Your prior platt covers near half of the platt of the 25 acres and consequently if you recover that from Philips he will have recourse on Mr. Pinnock his warrantee but by fixing the platt as they want it now you would not touch the platt of 25 acres and consequently no recourse could be necessary for Philips. This was my motive for bringing the Ejectment for if Pinnock's Evidence was admitted he would be against you in order to save himself from the Warrant.

If I have done right and according to your sentiments I shall be glad if not I assure you I did it for the best and intirely with a view for your advantage and to have the Evidence of the Surveyors who will be employed on the Writt of view to prove that Pinnock was intrusted. But the Gentleman who is the most busy and most angry in the whole matter is Matthus Wallen who really knows nothing of the matter but to appear as a man of consequence speaks it in all Companies the ill usage Mr. Cussans received from your Father in taking away [*illegible*] and that he sat on the tryall as a judge and gave his voice against the recovery but it turns from what the other Judges who sat on the tryall table tells me as does also the surveyor [*illegible*] stops his lips upon the subject then I am very sure that he will give a very [*illegible*] for was it a matter of his own he could not seem to be more anxious than he is now to injure you.

I was I must own very glad of the accident of the man being taken sick as it was such a disappointment to them and putt them so much back indeed. I did imagine that Cussans would have been found dangling in a Garter the next morning but he has mett with such disappointment in all his Law matters that he is determined to leave the Country and his Law suits to be carried on by some more able Generall than himself. He goes home in the *Portland* Man of War Admiral Rodney[239] and I suppose will come out with a whole budgett of my Oppressions and litigiousness and Quirks of Law but will not say a word that he has brought the whole thing on himself and begun them every one.

And a man certainly has a right to defend himself when attackt and if he is so very eager and earnest to gett what he imagines his property could be but affect that would think that other people has just as great a reguard for what they conceive to be theirs and will defend as obstinately as they are attackt.

From the scope of their Lawyers arguments I could find in the small part that came out they wanted to prove Cussans's mother in the possession of the disputed land in 1753 and that it continued in her and her Husband and the present Cussans's possession by his Guardians untill the year 1756 when it was recovered by your Father. And tho they want to fix as a quiet possession of 20 years under a deed whether that possession of 20 years will stand good against your possession from 56 to 74 is a point the Lawyers must give their opinion on tho I do not believe they can prove it for I am pretty certain that Dr. Gregory cannot give any Evidence for the reasons Cussans stated and I do as well as your Councill here imagine that the Ejectment against Philips will be a Counter to Mr. Pinnock's Evidence.

I have wrote to Mr. East on the subject so if you see him you will know what point I want to have the opinions of the Gentlemen at home in case we should be obliged to appeal home in the course of the Case. I am hopefull he has his hearts content of Law for I find that Old Doctor Gregory has told Mr. Kelly that if he will only take in from Plantain Garden River as much water as will turn our Mill he will not go on with the Bill in Chancery they have been preparing but I told Mr. Kelly to do no such thing without your Express order for lett them do what they can except they take away the [*torn*] where your Dam stands and where the trench now is they can do neither [*torn*] they putt Amity Hall Mills in the Situation they were in when your Father took in Plantain Garden River. They have no right to complain for want of water and which they cannot now without taking away Hordley Mills altogether for in year 1759 when your Father took in Plantain Garden River they had 12 feet fall on the Mill of Amity Hall and it continued so during the whole lawsuit with your Father but in the year 1765 or 1766 they agreed to settle a new Estate and give its

---

[239] Admiral George Brydges Rodney (1719–1792), first Baron Rodney, who would go on to play a critical role in some of the most significant naval actions of the American War of Independence. For more details see Lee (ed.), *Dictionary of National Biography*, 17, pp. 81–87.

Mills half the fall of Amity Hall Mills which is that thing that makes them at times be a little scarce but surely if they injure themselves you are not accountable for it.

You have finished a most notable Crop at Golden Grove and will get the whole of the Sugars home by the ships that will sail on or before the 26 of July. I think it is 636 hdds. Kelly told me that he would be able to ship and you have 60 odd acres of cane more to cutt next year than this. Thank God Holland has turned out pretty well this year. I have turned four hundred hdds. and have fifty acres still to cutt. If it does but continue at it and rise a little every year it will do tolerably well.

My Overseer at Lyssons who has lived a great many years with me has lately bought a wharf at Morant Bay which is near or by half a mile very deep sandy road nearer to Blue mountain Valley than the Old Wharf where they used to ship and does the business there much cheaper than they do it at Old Wharf and I will venture to say every bitt as well. I shall therefore Esteem it a very great favor if you would appeal to your Friend and acquaintance Mr. Perrin to order his Attorneys for his Estate of Blue Mountain to send the Sugars etc from and the Supplies to said Estate to Patersons wharf at Morant Bay instead of the Old Wharf for he has been a very faithfull Servant to me for many years and I would be glad to assist him.

Your Mother whom I saw about 14 days ago was very weak and seems to be falling off fast & your Aunt was very well.

As Kelly acquaints me he is to write to you I shall leave him to give you an acct. of your Estate.

75. To Chaloner Arcedekne, Kingston, 25 July 1774

I wrote to you on the 22 of June last and sent the Originall p. the *Trecothick* and copy p. the *Cyrus* via Bristol since which I have had the Pleasure of hearing from you.

I have little more to say than that the Surveyors are to go on the land in dispute between Mr. Philips and you and then I am pretty confident their Evidence will stop Mr. Pinnocks.

Cussans went home in the Man of Warr that Admiral Rodney went with and as I am informed out of Chagrin but gives out to settle the matter of the Land in dispute between you and him. If you come to any conversation I give you this Caution that he has a very convenient memory adapted to forgett or remember just as his Interest sways and also if you agree to leave any thing to the decision of the man of the Law you must find him very close he having argued in a dispute to leave it to the Opinion of Lawyers. When four out of six gave it against him he flew off as he said it was a matter of too great consequence to leave to the decision of Lawyers any where but in Court. He is very angry.

I produced the letter you received from him and sent to me and to show there was a compromise going on that we waited to see the Effect of it before we send out the Foreign Commission. All that I advise You is to act Cautious with him for I look on him to be a man of weak Head but very bad Heart but if you agree what ever you direct me to do I will.

I am informed Malcolm Laing & John Sheckle are his attorneys. He allways resided at the Formers house when in this Town but whether he was his Law adviser or not I cannot tell but he seems also to be angry at my not communicating to him the nature of your Lawsuit and the defence for I did not think it prudent that a Man should know too much of a very contested Lawsuit when the person who was carrying it on with the greatest rancor was his Bosom Friend and lived in the same house as his Guest not that I do accuse Laing of having done it but then a Man that knows nothing can tell nothing. It is a very disagreeable Subject to dwell on therefore shall drop it.

I was mistaken when I told you you had made 636 hhds. It is 628 tho that is a very great thing. Your Estate is going on very well and thriving and I make no manner of doubt of its continuing so. There will be a great deal to do to one of your Mills this year and also to the Still house over the Rum Store where the Beam broke last year but will Endeavour to gett every thing done in time.

[*Notes that he has* 'drawn on you the following setts of Bills' *all* 'at 90 days sight 5 in favor of Angus McBean' *totalling* '£720.9.7½ 1 in favor of Simon Taylor for £141.4.1½'.]

Your Mother and Aunt are pretty well. I hope your Sister is gott better.

76. To Chaloner Arcedekne, Kingston, 19 November 1774

I have before me your much esteemed favors of 15 June and 6 July by the former of which you acquaint me that you had received mine of 12 March and that you had not received the Commission for examining the Old Woman in Cornwall till within a month owing to some unaccountable delay. Bob Lee by a letter I received from him yesterday tells me that it was occasioned by the neglect at the Inn where the Falmouth Waggon putts up and I am very sorry for it more especially as the Old Woman is dead.

I return you thanks for having honoured all the Bills I drew and that had been or would be presented. I am very happy that you are pleased

at the Purchase of Kellys negroes and the mode of payment for them
and also that you come into the proposall of putting on 20 negroes
annually and when a good Cargo comes in I shall buy that number
for you.

In reguard to what Kelly writes you of my offering him £122 for
work done at Golden Grove I do not clearly recollect this matter, and
what that you might have heard said of his doing work for Golden
Grove tho he did not charge may be very true but has he ever given
you any rent for 100 Acres of Your land that he occupies exclusive of
the 50 Acres you gave him for life. Take my word for it he has been
exceeding well paid for any work he ever did for you and did not
charge in reguard of the annotation of its being a common practice in
this Parish to give from 10d to 1.10½[240] p. day for each negroe hired
on the different Estates tho Mr. Kelly charges but 1/3.[241] The case is
that he could better afford to work at Golden Grove for 1/3 than three
mile further for 18d or 1.10½ for when working at Golden Grove his
people slept in their own houses every night and Were at home whereas
being at a distance they lost time in going home to their houses in the
Evening and coming to their work in the morning.

I am sorry that you have no account of the Produce altho I had
wrote that there was an appearance of a fine crop and am very well
pleased that you saved the Insurance on the goods by Brankston and
Farr tho you ought certainly to have had advice of the Shipments to
have left it to your choice to have insured or not.

I suppose you must have seen Cussans long ago as he was to go to
you on his arrival. I am glad that Mr. Woodcock thinks we stand on
such firm Ground. It is Dr. Gregory who pushes him on to secure
water for Hordley Mills.

In reguard of what you mention concerning your Mother your Aunt
told it me to write to Your Mother has since told me she has heard
from you.

I am very sorry to hear that your Brother in Law has acted so very
ungenerous a part by you. He certainly should not have done it after
all you have done for him more especially in renting the Swamps at
1000 Guineas a year. I assure you I would not give above the half for
it. It is a disagreeable Subject therefore lett us drop it and think at
once seriously and marry, and gett Heirs to Inheritt your Estate yourself.
That will at once putt an end to any insinuations or expectations
whatsoever to your disadvantage and what I am sure would give your
Mother the highest pleasure of any on Earth for she is breaking very
fast being very weak and feeble without any sickness but a gentle decay.

---

[240] One shilling and tenpence halfpenny.
[241] One shilling and threepence.

I find that you are not pleased at the Nisbetts and do insist that Hayward should not act as Doctor there and at Golden Grove. I told it to Hayward who seemed very uneasy that he should have given you any offence as he did not mean or design any in taking charge as the Doctor there but told me that if you did insist on it that he would much rather sacrifice his own Interest than forfeit your Friendship. As I apprehend it that you might have been angry with the Nisbetts just at the time and wrote in a hurry I told him that he better wait the arrival of another letter when you might not be quite so angry for if you will give me leave to mention it to you you are not punishing Mr. Nisbet in this Case for his Insolence but Hayward. Was there not another Doctor to be gott for Duckingfield it would be something but there are very great Plenty. You will please to write what your determination is on this Point and I know that Dr. Hayward will rather give up Duckingfield Hall than incur your displeasure.

I observe what you say in reguard to Mr. Easts being Employ'd drawing out Papers the one being a lease of the Land I now rent from your Mother if it should revert to you and the other the lease of the land I wrote to you about. I am extreamly obliged to you for your good intentions towards me in these matters. If they will not putt on negroes on Swamps the sooner it is given up the better. I never saw the lease but every thing is so much older than it was at the Commencement of the lease and from the naturall decrease.

Your next of 6 July acquaints me that you had received my letters with the Vouchers & Accts. and also the Agrmnt. about Kellys negroes and had also received mine of 23 Aprill. I am glad you approved of my having served the Ejectment on Pleasant Hill. I very well recollect your writing to me about the matter and my applying to Mr. Philips abt. it who promised to settle it before he went off but did not. I do not think of bringing it on to a tryall untill Mr. Philips arrives and I believe that the matter will appear so clear that he will not contest it he not being fond of Expence at Law.

I have heard nothing further about the Chancery suit from Dr. Gregory but am extreamly glad to find by yours that Mr. Woodcocks opinion and mine are the same in the matter of the water and that he has made himself perfect master of the Subject. The Water is what Dr. Gregory wants and they will stick at few things to gett it.

In reguard of his Evidence I am confident he cannot give any for I can prove that he is interested in the Event of the Suit and consequently cannot be an Evidence. I should be glad to hear the Opinions of some of the very best men at the Barr on the following matter tho it must be seriously considered by them before we do it and their Opinion clear and explicit that we have a right to do it and that no Action of damage will lye against us for it, if so, I can in two years make them dance to your Pipe and they not have a drop of water to the Mills of either Amity Hall or Hordley. The case is this, the North Bank of the River where Amity Hall and Hordley take up the water for their Mill is high, the southside of the River is opposite your land and very low, and every flood encroaches on your land. What I want is to drive an Iron Barr fifteen or 16 feet down by the side of the River on your land at the High water mark, that is in a flood, and provided the river incroaches on your land, & would prevent them driving a Pile, or making a weir to stop the River if they should come within the Iron Barr, which I propose as a perpetuall testimony that the land there is yours, altho overflown by the River. *If we have a right to prevent their making a weir within the Barr which I mean as a land mark*[242] they cannot raise the River to take it in their Trench, & will be totally deprived (without your Permission) of any water whatsoever.

Mr. East wrote to me on the Subject of the lease and acquainted me that he had executed the lease to the first land which I now rent with the Limitations you mentioned. I am very well satisfied with it so it goes to my Heirs. I am pretty confident that I shall never sell or lease Holland and should not wish you to be troubled with a bad neighbor. I shall not mention it to your Mother. Indeed I do assure since I have had the Estate it has not hitherto paid the Rent owing to the Blast and being in young Canes but it is at the same time very good land. The part that is of the ninety acres is often overflowed by Duckingfield Hall back Water.

I also received the Power of Attorney for your mother to have one part of the land not included in her lease. I will rather send home the Platt to you to gett a lease than to apply to her. The use the land would be to me is for Copperwood and by clearing it it would be giving my Canes more Air but for any thing else it is absolutely useless not being 2 Inches above the Water and in the wett seasons intirely overflown. It is covered the rest with mangoes and small Mahoe which will burn and save me going further for wood. I have not taken the land or cutt a twig on it nor shall not without your approbation. Why I want a lease is to prevent any Malicious person having it in his Power to say that I was cutting Copperwood of your land and was stealing from you which I would not do was You in the Country. Therefore I shall not care how long or how short the lease is so I have one. I shall be very glad to see Mr. East and hope you approve my having Employed him in your affairs.

Indeed the North American matters give me real Concern. I wish they were settled and how it is possible for them to settle I cannot conceive. After what the Americans have done Britain cannot give up

[242] Emphasis in original.

the Point it would only be making them more arrogant than they at present are I look on them as dogs that will bark but dare not stand when opposed loud in mouth but slow to action.

I will endeavor the first good opportunity to gett up as many staves as will last you two years. I cannot conceive how your staves last year should have been sappy or bad they were the same I had, out of the same ship. I bought 100000 of them together, they arrived in June 1772 and must have been cutt in the preceding fall and I thought them the best Philadelphia staves I ever saw.

I am glad to hear that you find a profitt in making your Rum strong and that it sells so well and also to hear that you have made money by not having advice to insure. I shall endeavor farr as I am able that you shall have regular advice to insure or not as you please.

Your Friend Cussans's Lawyer tells me that he intends to bring on the Ejectment this Court for the Land at the Dam. I have issued Subpoenas for our witnesses in order to defend ourselves as well as we can. You my depend that nothing on my part shall be wanting to ingage your success.

I had a letter yesterday from Mr. Kelly at Golden Grove. He tells me every thing is going on very well there and he talks of putting about in 10 or 12 days.

77. To Chaloner Arcedekne, Kingston, 31 January 1775

My last to you was of 19 November since which I have been favoured with yours of 5 & 24 October.

I am extreamly obliged to you for having spoke to Mr. Perrin in favor of Paterson's wharf and I received his letter to you on the Subject. I am much afraid that as he has left it to Laing that Paterson will not succeed for he is a Sort of Patron to the Man that keeps there the other wharf and his Coattorney and Co Attorney Dr. Blow[243] is his particular Friend but Paterson and I are equally obliged to you as if he had succeeded.

I find that you had come up to London to see Mess. East and Woodcock[244] before the Formers coming, and that you had putt some Queries for the opinion of Councill that Mr. East would bring out. Mr. Cussans did push as hard as he could but when I come to yours of 24 Octr. I shall relate the whole in the manner it happened.

In reguard whether it is a discontinuance to the Suit the Juror being taken sick I cannot tell neither on further Consultations with our

[243] It has proved impossible to further identify Dr Blow.
[244] Hinton East's legal partnership in London.

Councill do I believe it will act as such but at any rate we will argue it, and as you rightly observe Lord Mansfield will have nothing to do with it. There shall be nothing that can be advised or devised by Councill but what shall be done to save your land. If quiet possession will do, you have had a quiet possession from March 1756 untill Cussans came out under a judgement of a Court.

Dr. Gregory is still wavering about his Bill of survivor. About 14 days ago he told me he had given over all Intentions of it, but since the Arrivall of Welch he tells me that he had intended to drop it on the Proviso that you should work only one Mill at Golden Grove and that Kelly should make a Memorandum of it in Golden Grove Plantation Books and give him a Certificate of it. Kelly did mention to me the Drs. having made such a proposal some time ago but I told him he had no right to do such a thing and not to do it but as he has refused that he will serve the Bill as he cannot be in a worse situation than he is at present in. I argued with him in the situation of his Mill but not in opinion that he has any claim on Golden Grove Mills which were turned by Plantain Garden River in 1759, and his was not built untill 1765.

I think there will be but little trouble in confuting his claim for if Amity Hall joins in the Lawsuit with him they must putt their Mill on the same footing it was in 1759 and that of itself will render Hordley Mills useless. He is intirely sensible of his Situation and I advised him not to be rash in beginning a matter that would pull down an Old House about his Ears. Indeed I do not know except from the Expence, but that it would be an advantage to you for him to file his Bill, and I will as you desire it bring it on so as that there may be at once an end putt to it as we can never have more evidence to prove what Amity Hall Mill was in 1759 and what injury the Proprietors of Amity Holland, and Hordley have done it themselves.

You acquaint me that you had received my letter to you of 24 July and that the Bills for £239.6.0 are accepted. I think that you have seen that those were the half yearly Bills.

By your last letter I am very glad You find that your Crop was large but very sorry to hear the Sugars did not fetch so good a price as they used to do. I do consider the great Expence you are at, but I assure you I do save every thing I can, and nothing is thrown away and in Consideration of Sugars not netting as much as they used and the payment that Kelly is to have, I have not purchased the negroes I mentioned to you as there was no absolute necessity for it.

I shall advise you as soon as I have made up the Accts. how much they will amount to before I draw and shall obey your orders relative to the Swamps. The Buildings and works are in much better order than when you took possession of them.

I find Mr. Cussans is arrived, and as I suppose full of Complaints, he has himself to blame acts in Every thing like a Child, crying because he has not every thing his own way and thinks that every body should give up their property to him because he fancies it to be his.

I am much obliged to you for your good wishes to me reguarding Holland and am extreamly obliged to you in Letting me have the lease it being a very great assistance to me.

Your next of 24 October was delivered to me by my worthy Friend Mr. East and I am glad by it to find that you see that the Bills you mentioned in yours were for the half year and that you was satisfied.

The stores by Brankston arrived safe. Indeed, I do not think on the good Ship there is any great necessity of Insuring on but I would on the *Catonus*, but in reguard to that I will not pretend to advise.

I am much obliged to you for sending me out two letters from the Hero of Amity Hall, and ten thousand times more obliged to you for your answers to them and your attention to my Honor, Character, and Reputation. In reguard to the first part of his first letter wherein he mentions to you that he had wrote to you about two years before but had not received an answer they was convinced you wrote one which arrived safe to my hands as well as the Originall as the Inclosed Copy. I do acknowledge that I received them, and if you recollect you desired me to advise with your Mother whether I should deliver your letter to him which I did, and she desired me not to do it.

On taking out the Commission he was to have taken one also out, and there was an agreemt. between Mr. Allen his Attorney, and Mr. Syms the Partner of Mr. East, and he Mr. Cussans himself commanded that both Commissions should go home together. Mr. Allens sickness which obliged him to go off prevented the Commission going home. I then endeavoured to gett your Commission expedited. In the mean time he was pushing to come to a tryall notwithstanding he knew that it was impossible to have a return to the Commission and the time he alludes to.

I did produce *his*[245] letter to you to prove that he had been writing to you about an amicable Settlement, and at the same time was endeavouring to hurry you on to a tryal before your Commission was arrived. The Bench forced us to a tryall it is true and most people *were hurt at it* but not in the way he mentioned *but* in this that Mr. Winde, Cussans's bosom Friend and Factor, who two or three days before the Court had been made a Judge but had never satt but one day before *and that to fix a day for your tryall should expressly come there to sitt on that tryall and not at any other time before.* That is the thing by which people were hurt and the Injustice done you in not giving you the time to have a

---

[245] All the emphasized sections in this letter are in the original.

return to your Commission and by that means precluding you of your evidence, and there was not a Man in the Court but those of his Caball but who declared, that God Almighty had given you the Justice the Court refused when one of the Jurors was taken ill.

In reguard to *the Claims in the letter being overruled*, I do not know what he means, as it was *his* letter to you I produced. I admire his clear sightedeness *in seeing your Interest sacrificed to the resentment of your Attorney besides other advantages he may have in the Contest.* What Interest I can have sacrificed to my resentment I know not, except endeavouring to protect your property may be sacrificing your Interest and what advantages I may reap from the Contest know not except I having attended the Grand Court seven or 8 times the whole Court and waiting on Lawyers may be an advantage.

Your own Surveyor gives me 50 Acres of what I claim and witnesses that 50 acres will take away the right of Carrying the Water to your Mills, and if I take away the Water you know the advantage it will be to the Mills below and your Attorneys Estate will not receive the least benefitt. It is the most Impudent and lying falsehood that ever was penned. He did in the Country say that Mr. Gordon your Surveyor did say that he had a right to the 50 Acres, which I informed Gordon of, who called on him Cussans and asked him how he could spread such a report, when he said he heard it from Matthew Wallen in a Cursory manner. I refer you to Gordons letter on the Subject to Whom I wrote in a way as if to recollect what passed at that time.

In reguard to that 50 Acres taking away your right of carrying the water to your Mills, it does not for we can dig a Gutter lower down in your land. Was you to loose the 50 Acres he talks off and if more water comes down it will certainly be a very great benefitt to my Mills which often want water and he knows very well that twelve months ago he and Dr. Gregory had widened their trench to take in more Water. On my Complaining and threatning them with a Bill in Chancery they were obliged to narrow it to the former dimensions and the Overplus of the Water that their trench cannot contain must come down the River to my Mills in spight of their teeth and he himself knows it and admitts it will come down and be of advantage to the Mills below.

He Besides to invalidate the Testimony of a Witness has sent a fresh Ejectment against Mr. Philips and has promised His Attorney that it shall not come to tryall, the Expence of which Ejectment I would not pay for 700 Guineas. I did bring an Ejectment against Mr. Philips for you, with a view to invalidate Pinnocks Evidence, on what I think I have Happily succeeded, for he would at once have Sworn to lines to mark out the Quantity of a parcel of land that Swarton and he took up on the Quitrent Law and sold to Philips, and warranted the Title. By this Ejectment I am confident that I can prove by what the Surveyors tell me, a trespass of Philips of 30 Acres of land on you and Mr. Pinnocks being the Warrantor he will not be allowed as an Evidence being a party concerned.

And in reguard to my telling His Attorney I would not come to a tryall he has left out part which was untill Mr. Philips Come to an Amicable Settlement and save the 700 Guineas he mentioned, but where he pickt up that Sum do not know, there has been no Law Expences, no Lawyers fees, nor anything done in it, but the Surveyors going on the Land to run it.

I mention these matters to shew you how far he would injure his Best Friend to satisfie his own resentment. In reguard to what he means by these matters I suppose is my producing his letter to prove he was pushing you to tryall before you had your Evidence, my denying that your Surveyor had given him the 50 Acres which he says he has, my Denying that you could not carry the water to your Mill was You ever to loose the 50 Acres, and saying that I should be benefitted by an addition of water to my Mill when I want it, and my invalidating an Evidence of an Interested person who would have sworn your land away.

If from these Facts you still think him worthy of Guarding your Interest I wish on your Acct. for Amendment In him. If I had not defended an Ejectment brought against you to take away 270 Acres of your land and the Water that turns your Mills, but had calmly submitted to it to benefitt Mr. Cussans and my Mills, if I had lett Dr. Gregory and Mr. Pinnock interested people to come to prove lines to favor their own purposes, the one to secure himself against a Warrantee, the other to benefit his Mills, I should have indeed been a very unworthy person to Guard either yours or any other persons Interest and should have stood in very great need of Amendment but as the Case is opposite I can say I am so very well satisfied with my conduct that I would just again repeat the same measures.

You will oblige me to give me a letter to him signifying your disapprobation of this affair but if you should think the Opportunity favorable to disengage you from a Man who has no Tie in Nature abstracted from Sordid Interest. I would wish to have nothing further to say to a Man so farr below my notice. I cannot think myself much obliged to him for Solliciting a letter of disapprobation of my Conduct or recommending the Opportunity favourable to disengage you from a Man with whom you have been so many years acquainted, and who flatters himself that you think he has allways had your Interest as much at Heart as his own and having a Tie in Nature abstracted from Sordid Interest.

In my not giving up to him my property which he says is worth ten thousand pounds, and that he would not lett me have it under, my Defending Mr. Kennion with whom I have been intimate these fourteen years when (through the incapacity of the people whom he left concerned for him from never having had to do with a matter of such a nature) he wanted to plunder him of three or four thousand pounds, and to make it a precedent to plunder me of as much, when by proper levillings made, I plainly shewed that what he and his Adherents Alledged was absolute impossibilities.

My not prosecuting him to the utmost when he came upon my Estate with 150 Armed Negroes and wanted me to go into the Canes where he had hid them, and where had I gone, I should in all probability have been murdered. My restraining my Negroes from destroying both himself and his Negroes while committing outrages on my Estate. My Suffering him to escape when a Bill was found by the Grand Jury against him for coming with armed negroes on my property and committing hostilities there, and for which he would have been well off to have gott off for £2000 fine and twelve months Imprisonment on his promising Amendment. My not giving him a good thrashing when he attackt myself, and I threw him into the Canes and had him down there, when the only Amendment I found in him afterwards, *was* having agreed to leave the matter to the Opinions of six Lawyers three on Each side, and it was given by them in my Favor, his flying off, saying it was a matter of too great consequence to be determined by the Opinions of Lawyers, and directly filing a Bill in Chancery against me and a Bill for an Injunction. Swearing in his Petition for the latter, that my Lock would be liable to putt his Mills in Backwater, Overflow his Lands, and hurt his Navigation which three articles he had before admitted in different Companies could not possibly happen from it, and all this to gain two feet fall on his Mills and by that means to deprive me of the water that had turned my Mills from the first Settlement of the Estate. I say when all these matters have happened and are all record on Oath I think the Imputation of Sordid Avarice lays at his own Door.

In reguard to his wish not to have any thing further to say to a man so farr below his notice, I believe he would be very glad that I would not have any thing further to say, or do with him, but that is not the Case we must have more matters still, and in reguard to his abuse all I can say to it is that I scorn the Slander as much as I dispise the Slanderer.

I have wrote a great deal more on this head than I intended when I satt down for I can thank my God for it say Nil consurri sibi mens consciasecti Neilla palescare Culpa and I have not the least doubt of convicing him to his Cost for I have not only the Opinions of the Men of the Gown here but also Messrs. Dunning, Forrester, and Wallaces. I do sincerely believe that his Mind is so agitated by Disappointments, Avarice, Revenge, and resentment, that he is at times not sensible, having been at first led on by a parcel of designing people, and mett with persons who know their own rights better than he did his own, and who would not give up their Opinions or properties to him, these with the Excessive ill management of his property some years last past, building to pull down, buying negroes to starve, making Indigo by destroying his provision Grounds have allmost drove him Frantic. His Attorneys Bill I am informed for his transactions while last here having amounted to £2700 and he not reimbursed a penny, and in all probability never will.

I am tired of the Subject but can not help again thanking you for your having reasoned with so much judgement and perspicacity on the matter, and having viewed it in so dispassionate a manner as you have done. I shall keep the Copy of the letters by me and I assure you that no person whatsoever shall see them or shall I ever communicate the Contents to any one. I do not believe he will apply to you any more. His hopes were to have carried his Matters by Surprise, and gott your hand to your Opinions. I heartily thank you for having disappointed his Views. He is not the person he pretends to be, when his Bullies are not backing him, he would much rather use his Tongue than his hands and went home from hence notwithstanding his threats and menaces like a blubbering Boy to complain to his Mammy that they would not give him a rattle.

I received by Mr. East the Dormant Power of Attorney but it is not properly proved. There should have been an Attestation of the Proof under the Seal of the Corporation, attested by the Town Clerk, or have been Witnessed by a person coming to Jamaica to have proved your Signature before a Judge of a Court of record here. But it does not signify, as I should not have putt it on record without an absolute necessity, for I would not make a man your Enemy altho he has not shown that reguard to your Interest he ought to have done. I have not yett had any time to have a Conversation with my Friend Mr. East when I have I shall write to you again but the Subject I have been on has harrassed my mind.

I cannot however conclude without informing you that the weather has been and Still continues very wet at Windward, in so much that had you not a very large Crop to take off I would have stopt your Mills, as your Cattle are weak and the roads so bad that was obliged to have a Horse to go between your House and Boiling house.

You have made about 180 hdds. of Sugar and if the weather comes fair you will have the best Crop that ever you had. The Sugars will be shipt to you in the same proportion and by the Same ships as last year, but I advise you to Insure on the *Morant Bay* Capt. Farr, as his Ship is old, tho she may be very good. I would not have putt any on board her but you some years ago recommended him to me, not that I have the least disreguard to the Man but on the Contrary a very great reguard and Esteem as being a very worthy honest good Man, but I cannot say so much for his Ship.

I saw your Mother three or four days ago she seems to be breaking fast and is very weak. Your Aunt is very well.

78. To Chaloner Arcedekne, Kingston, 27 March 1775

My last to you was of 31 Janry. since which I have not had the pleasure of hearing from you. There has been nothing material happened since my last.

I saw Mr. Kelly who tells me that every thing is going on well at Golden Grove.

[*Notes that Kelly intends to send* 'the Following Goods on the *Clarendon*, 100 hdds., 40 puncheons; the *Duckinfield*, 50 hdds., 25 puncheons, the *Morant Bay*, 40 hdds., 15 puncheons, the *Prince George*, 40 hdds., 20 puncheons, the *Port Morant*, 50 hdds., 20 puncheons, the *Holland*, 40 hdds., 15 puncheons, the *Amity Hall*, 30 hdds., 15 puncheons, the *Friendship*, 40 hdds., 20 puncheons, the *Standlinch*, 20 hdds., 10 puncheons, the *Hibberts Boyd*, 20 hdds., 10 puncheons'.]

The *Morant Bay* and *Prince George* will sail from Morant Bay the *Amity Hall* Capt. Tarbut from Manchioneal Harbour & the *Hibberts* Capt. Boyd from this Port all the rest from Port Morant. Therefore if you please to insure you may. I wish them all home safe and to a better Markett than last year. The *Morant Bay* & *Friendship* will sail the first week in Aprill the *Standlinch* and *Duckinfield* the 2^d Week.

I shall send home to you by the *Friendship* Thompson all your Accts. made up to the 31 of Dec last. They amount to for Golden Grove, and Swamps, & Acct. Current the Sum of £4099.11.6½ in which you will find included the Sum of Interest on the Bonds we gave Mr. Kelly the Amount of the Negroes bought of him. He wanted me to draw for the first Bond but as I had no orders from you I did not chuse to do it untill I heard from you. You will be pleased to lett me know whether I must draw for it and I shall follow your directions.

There was nothing done the last Court in the Ejectment between Cussans & you altho they said that they would positively come to Tryal and obliged us to issue Subpaenas and bring up our Evidences. I wish that we had the Evidence of the Old Woman before she died or any that could prove the Family of the Penhallons and that Peters married the Heir at Law.

I shall be obliged to you to giving your positive orders whether we are to putt in any more Canes at Golden Grove by Jobbing as it will not be in my power to prevent it without your orders to me to that purpose for I do apprehend that the 100 Negroes were bought to prevent it and when I have your orders I stick to them literally without I see that your Interest would materially suffer and then in that case I would do for you as I would for myself. If I understand right the Intention was also to putt on 20 Negroes a year added to those you bought of Kelly in order to enable you to keep up the Estate and do your own work. The fall in the Price of Sugars made me defer the Purchase untill I hear from you and the money saved from Jobbing will help pay for them and the negroes are your own. Please to write to me on the matter fully.

   Your Mother and Aunt are very well.

79. To Chaloner Arcedekne, Kingston, 17 April 1775

My last to you was of 27 March since which I have not been favoured with any from you.

   I have by this Ship sent home to you your last years Accts all made up and settled to the 31 of Decr. last. I hope on the perusing them you will find them right and lett me know. I have also drawn on you the Annual Bills as usual payable at Messrs. Long Drake and Long, and they are signed by your Mother, Aunt, Laing, and myself Kelly was at Windward so he could not sign them.

[*Notes that all the Bills were* 'dated 13 April' *and all* 'at 90 days sight'. *2 payable to John Kelly totalling £984.11.8½; 1 each payable to Elizabeth Kersey, Frances Harris, and Malcolm Laing for £196.10.5; 3 payable to Angus McBean totalling £984.11.78½; 3 payable to Simon Taylor totalling £737.1.3½.*]

There was an Accident happned to five hdds. of your Sugar and five of Duckinfield Halls which were on board of Brankstons Shallop who in going out stuck on the reef and sunk by which yours & the Duckingfield Halls Sugars were lost. I have wrote to Mr. Kelly to take and also agreed with the Capt. that he shall give Bills of lading for the five hdds. as well as of the other Sugars on board for to endeavour to recover it of the underwriters or if that cannot be done of the Ship and told him that I doubted not but that You and Mr. Long would be able to settle together. Indeed the Capt. was not to blame in the matter and it was a real Accident that happened from the Wind suddenly dying away when the Vessell was in the Channell between the Reefs and two boats had gone out in less than a quarter of a Hour before.

   Kelly was speaking to me again about allowing Duckenfield Hall to cutt a Canall through your land at the Rivers mouth to carry their

Sugars to the wharf by water and tells me that the Proprietors of that Estate would on that consideration give you liberty of carrying your goods through that Estate by which you would also have a water Carriage for your goods also to the Barquader.

If you are not too angry with Mr. Nisbett to allow him any advantage from the Situation of your property, I should think it for your Interest to allow it as it would be a very great ease to your Cattle there being all the Crop time two wains constantly carrying goods down and bringing up Supplies and by the water Carriage two boats and 4 negroes would do it which would be a considerable Saving to your Estate but you should on no Acct. do it without a liberty of navigation for your Estate if such a thing was agreeable and to be brought about. I should be glad to hear from you as from my thorough knowing the matter I would take care to point out what would be the necessary things to be covenanted for you to render your navigation perfect and not to be liable to interruption.

There has been nothing new here. Your Crop at Golden Grove promises fair and I believe will be the largest you ever yett had from that Estate. We were putt back at first with the wett weather but that has been made up by keeping both Mills and work and making some weeks 40 hdds. p. week.

80. To Chaloner Arcedekne, Kingston, 5 June 1775

My last to you was of 17 Aprill p. the *Friendship* Thompson and the *Clarendon* Brankston both which Ships are safe arrived long before this will reach you I hope.

I have been favoured with yours of 22 Jany. wherein you mention that you do not recollect any of my letters to you are unanswered but that you would be glad to know that you did nothing disagreeable to me in the letters that passed between Cussans and you.

By my letters to you in answer to them you will see all the High Opinion I entertain of your Conduct in that matter and I again thank you for it. I am very certain that you are no loser by the Friendship between you and him being at an end and from the terms he and I are on shall say no more.

In reguard to Mr. Nat. Philips I suppose he has been with Cussans but you need be under no apprehensions in reguard to his releasing Pinnock from the Guarantee. There are more people to be consulted before he can do it lett his inclination be ever so good as the Attorneys of Admirall Hughes[246] and the Representatives of the late Mr. Biscoe

[246] Admiral Sir Edward Hughes (1720? –1794). For more information see Lee (ed.), *Dictionary of National Biography*, X, pp. 172–175.

who have a Mortgage on his Estate and consequently the Title of Pleasant Hill is not in him to enable him to clear Pinnock lett his good Intentions for Pinnock be what they will. I see he wants to befriend Cussans that he may steal your land. He cannot avail himself of the Quiet Possession for 21 Years I having demanded it from him before he went off and should have brought an Ejectment but for his promise to settle it before he went off.

I am also sorry that he cannot forgett the Taylors Trick of lying in telling you he heard from his Attorney that I was prosecuting the Suit agt. him with great Vigour. And I spoke to his Attorney and asked him if he had done so who informed me that he had wrote no such thing to him and consequently he must have made it himself or his Friend Cussans for him. There shall be nothing left undone in my power to keep your land. They now publickly own it that it is the Water they want and it is to gett that that they have brought the Ejectment for there will be nothing done in the matter this Court but we shall certainly come to a tryal the next.

In reguard to the land patented by Penhallon belonging to you there is no part of it but the 90 Acres I have of you of any value to any one person in the World but the Proprietors of Holland and that only on Acct. of the Copperwood it being all overflown. When the Riversmouth is barred up it is full of blood wood and such stuff as is good for fewell but that can only be brought out in dry weather and is too great a Carriage for any Estate in the Island but Holland.

The 90 Acres I have is as good as any land in the Island but the lower part is allmost continually overflowed by Duckingfield Hall back water. The part of the land that joins the Bay is very valuable for wharfs Stores and the part next to the East end would make a good fattening pen by putting it in Guinea Grass it being gritty and Rocky which is the best sort of land for Guinea Grass but all aback of the Stores to the great road for carrying the Sugars to the bay is all Morass and Quagmire and in my opinion too low to drain.

The disputes between Britain and America are truly alarming and I am afraid will not be ended without a great deal of Bloodshed but in case the former keeps steady and prevent their trading any where but to Britain and her West India Colonies they must submitt. What I am certain of is that wherever there is profitt to be gott there the Americans will send Vessels. Two or three Colonies may be obstinate but if one breaks through the Agreement the rest will immediately follow the Example.

In reguard to our Situation I am in great hopes that good will arise from evil. We can do tolerable well without America. We have land enough for provisions lumber etc except white Oak staves. It is very true they will come dearer but still we can gett them but then the

Money that used to be paid to the Americans will rest among us and not be carryed to Hispaniola to purchase Sugar Molasses and Coffee there to Smuggle into America to the ruin of our Colonies and the whole of the disputes between America and Britain, whatever the Gloss the Americans and their writers may put on it are that the Several Revenue acts passed in the present reign are so many checks to their Smuggling trade with Holland Hamburgh France & the French Islands and it is a specious argument that they have laid hold of their not being represented. When there were not half the Number of Inhabitants in North America they used generally to export from this Island between 7 and 8000 hdds. of Sugar. They did not export last year above two thousand and it is known that their Consumption of Sugar is near 3000 hdds. annually.

I shall be sorry to find that Government should have any thoughts of endeavouring to fix a duty of $4\frac{1}{2}$ p.ct. on our produce. I should think that they must see the bad consequences that have arisen on the Continent and first putt out that Fire. Besides, this Country would at this present juncture be absolutely ruined by such a tax first from the low price of our produce last year and then by the Excessive great quantities of negroes that have been imported within these two last years and the number of Bills which have come back protested.

I have according to your desire purchased a Cargo of Staves for you which will be sufficient for two years at least and send the Vessell up to Port Morant to deliver them their in the whole 70m staves of which 50m are white Oak staves & Puncheon heading the rest are hdds. staves. I have gott them at £8 pm. I shall draw on you for the Amount when they are all delivered. I have also bought 8 blls. of Tar which will serve you two years. There is no lamp oil to be gott but we can plant Oil Nutts. I have wrote to Mr. Kelly not to lend any staves on any Acct. to any one.

I am very glad that you have consented to Dr. Haywards taking the Charge of Duckingfield Hall He being deservedly Esteemed and liked by every body.

81. To Chaloner Arcedekne, Kingston, 24 July 1775

My last to you was of the 5 June p. the *Holland* Taylor & I sent to you a Copy p. the *Hibbert* Capt. Boyd since which nothing has happened Material.

The Norward Man landed all the Staves etc. that is she went to Port Morant and I gott Vessels to carry them round to Plantain Garden River where they now are.

Mr. Kelly came down last night and tells me that he will be able to

Ship you from Golden Grove this year 740 hdds. of Sugar which is the most extraordinary Crop that ever was made on any one Estate in Jamaica and I am hopeful that you will be pleased with the quality of your Sugar as I think they was very good. I am sorry that you have lost severall Cattle indeed such a Crop must be hard on them.

I have with your other Attorneys, drawn on you two Bills of Exchange as follows:

1 Sett at 90 days sight favor of McBean & Bagnall[247] £465.10.7. stg.
1 Sett at 90 days sight favor of myself for   £567.6.8

the first being for the Supplies from this Town which consisted chiefly of Lumber the other being in Favor of me for the Norward Cargo I purchased for you and the Taxes for Golden Grove Estate.

You have now a provision of Staves & heading for two years to come in case that matters should not be before that time settled in America. Indeed they seem to me to be growing worse and worse there. God only knows what will be the issue.

Your Mother and Aunt are both well.

Mr. Kelly tells me that he wrote to you reguarding the Situation of the Estate by the *Bull* Capt. Jones and tells me that he wants Bills for £500 stg. on Acct. of his Negroes purchased for Golden Grove which I have promised to lett him have by the next Ships that sail.

82. To Chaloner Arcedekne, Holland Park, 10 August 1775

My last to you was by the *Great Marlow* and Copy p. the *Judith* Capt. Brett since which time I have not had the Pleasure of hearing from you.

Mr. Kelly a few weeks ago told me that he was in want of money and desired me to give him a Bill upon you in part payment of the Negroes purchased from him for you for the use of Golden Grove, I have therefore jointly with your other Attorneys drawn on you a Bill in his Favor at ninety days sight for five hundred pounds sterling which I make no doubt but will be duly honoured.

I have agreed with Capt. James Hay of the Ship *Eagle* now lying in Kingston to take 80 hhds. and 30 Puncheons of Rum to be carried from Plantain Garden River at his Cost and on the risque of the Ship so that if you please you may insure the Quantity.

---

[247] A merchant house based in Kingston.

83. To Chaloner Arcedekne, Kingston, 11 September 1775

I wrote to you about three weeks ago from Windward informing you of my having jointly with your other Attorneys drawn a Bill of Exchange on you for £500 sterling in favor of Mr. Kelly in part payment of his Negroes.

I at the same time informed you that I should Ship to you by the Ship *Eagle* from this Port 80 hdds. of Sugar & 30 Puncheons of Rum being the remainder of your Crop at Golden Grove which has been a very great one indeed tho there has been a great many of your Cattle died which could not be helped the very bad weather in the beginning of the Crop hurt them much and the great deal of work they had to do in the bringing Canes to the Mill and the Carrying goods to the Bay knocked them up. I now confirm what I wrote concerning the Bill and the Insurance on the *Eagle*.

I have been since favoured with yours of 9 June and find that you have given my Queries to Mr. Woodcock, but have not yett gott his answer. You need not give yourself any uneasiness on my Acct. of the Abuse of the other Party should the Lawyers agree to what I proposed. I despise the Malicious Madness of any one while I am conscious in my own mind of acting right. While my Conscience is clear I allways pursue one direct road without turning to the right or left and am allways prepared.

I was in a good deal of Agitation (when I wrote to you) at the Infamous letters of that Unhappy Boy. He must now be convinced of the Villainous Part he acted for from a letter I had from Bob Lee I find out that His Lawyers on a Consultation have all agreed that I have a right to erect my lock and that he cannot depress my trench by which his whole mine is blown up and he may Wistle for the money he has so idly thrown away. I cannot say that I shall extend my Compassion so farr as even to Pity him in the Choice he has made of his Wife for now what with his disappointments in this Country, His Lawsuits, the Distraction of his Affairs, his failing in his Attempt to make you a Party to his Malice by his Unfair representations and such I wish to Boot I think he has now the only Alternatives of a Pistol or a Garter. His Conduct while in this Country the last was all of a piece Alien. In reguard to the Power you mention coming out I shall keep it by me untill I hear from you again.

I find that you received mine of 5 March and made no manner of doubt but that the Bills would be honoured and am glad to hear that you gott and are pleased at my Advice for Insurance. I am glad it was done more Especially as we have an Acct. of the Totall loss of the *Port Morant* Raffles and I see by a letter from Messrs. Long Drake & Long to Mr. Kelly that you was insured which I am very glad. I had 100 hdds. of Sugar on board her and I have not yett any Acct. of my being insured but as I wrote by two Severall Ships that sailed before her I am hopeful that I am.

I should be glad of the Pedigree of the Penhallons from Charles Penhallon and his Brothers down to the Intermarriage of the Heiress with Peters that is the time we want further back is of no Service and he purchased the Lands in this Country and patented them.

In reguard to Kellys bond I will draw on you for the Amount of the first and so annually if we make good Crops and you do not give me contrary orders.

I am hopefull that the disputes between Britain and the Colonies will soon come to a Crisis God Grant that it may be a favourable one for to both Countries. We shall now have no more news from America but by way of England the Congress having ordered the Printers to Print nothing but by their orders. I apprehend that they have received a Check and dare not lett the Common people know. If they continue their non Importation or Exportation you are provided for two years to come with Lumber and need be under no Apprehensions of wanting Provisions for notwithstanding Mr. Ellis's[248] [account] before the Committee of the House of Commons this Country cannot want Provisions and you have not an Able Negroe but with working only two hours in his Grounds on a Sunday morning but by that small piece of labour will gett as much provisions as will satisfy himself and family for a Week. I shall show that part of your letter to Kelly when I see him reguarding the Hire of Negroes.

I do not think without your orders of buying the 20 Negroes annually untill we see the fate of the American disputes and what effect it will have on the Value of our Produce for altho for some years they have taken very little yett from Ellis's Acct. the people may be led to think there will be a very great quantity come home which the Americans used to take.

And as for the money he mentioned they brought here he did not tell the whole truth. That they brought money for three years is certain. The first year it was so mixed with Brass & Copper that a Doubloon that passed at £4.15 was not intrinsically worth £3 and after that money would not pass. They carried of what little good money we had that was full weight and the Spanish Milled Gold and there fabricated light doubloons which they passed here for Produce and I myself being

---

[248] Welbore Ellis (1713–1802). Elllis sat in the House of Commons between 1741 and 1802. He was the Member for Petersfield from 1768 to 1774 and for Weymouth and Melcombe Regis from 1774 until 1790. During the Stamp Act crisis Ellis had advocated that a firm stand be taken against the American colonists. For more details see Sir Lewis Namier and John Brooke (eds), *The History of Parliament: The House of Commons, 1754–1790*, 3 vols (London, 1964), II, pp. 397–400.

the then Chairman of the Committee of Accts. went by order of the House of Assembly to count and weigh the Money in the Receiver Generalls Office and found it on doing it to be 33 p. Ct. below the proper weight and that may be a further means of the Fall of Produce.

I do not believe that they intend to send any provisions to Jamaica more than any of the other Sugar Colonies and the letter you mention to have come from here is void of foundation for they rely on the Clamours of the Manufacturers at Home and the necessities of the Sugar Colonies as the great Channell through which the repeal of the Laws they Complain of will come.

I shall go to Spanish Town tomorrow, and will see both your Mother & Aunt.

The Case between you and Cussans does not come on this Court but certainly will the next.

I had a letter from Holland 4 days ago which informs me that the weather is good therefore it must be the same at Golden Grove.

85. To Chaloner Arcedekne, Kingston, 9 December 1775

The foregoing is a Copy of my letter to you by the *Mary* Capt. Smith who carried to you the advice of the Bill I drew upon you and the advice of the Insurance on the *Eagle* Capt. Hay who I hope is safe arrived. The Bills of lading were sent to you as also the Invoices by Mr. Kelly. I was not in Town when that Ship sailed or I would have wrote to you.

I have been favoured with yours of 19 June and received from Messrs. Long Drake & Long the Papers reguarding the Penhallon Family which I am sorry to inform you I am told by our Lawyers here will not be suffered to be read here in Court it not being a Bill in which either your Father or Cussans Family was concerned in.

I have also secured from Messrs. Francis and Tilghman[249] of Philadelphia 40 blls of flour and a parcell of Lumber for Golden Grove. I had as you will before this reaches you find purchased a Cargo of Lumber for you. Your Mother shall have what quantity she wants of the flour. Indeed it would spoil long before it could be used and have taken 10 blls of it for myself.

Do not be afraid of wanting Provisions for your Negroes. I have constantly resided in Jamaica near 16 years and when there has been no Hurricane know we can supply ourselves with Provisions if we will but plant them.

[249] A mercantile partnership that was formed between Tench Tilghman and his nephew Tench Francis, Jr in the early 1760s.

I find by Mr. Longs letter that you are insured on your Sugar on board Raffles but not your Rum which I am sorry for. I did not know the quantity of the Rum or would have lett you known it. Thank God I was insured.

Since my last we have had excessive heavy weather all over the Country which has lodged many canes but it is now broke up.

I am very much afraid I shall draw largely on you for have been obliged to buy a good many Cattle to take off your ensuing Crop and Kelly has done a great deal of Jobbing work on your Estate and then tells me it is done. It is certainly the way to increase the Produce but at the same time requires more Cattle more Negroes etc to take it off. Please to give positive orders whether you will have it continued or not. Was you married and had Children to reap the advantages of putting on more Negroes increasing the quantity of your Canes Cattle and pasture and your improvements to go to whom you yourself pleased it would be very well. But for you to be continually advancing and keeping your self drained for perhaps those on the one side that you have no affection or reguard for is the reason and motive of my mentioning it.

The more Sugar and Rum is made is certainly pleasing and adds both reputation and Emolument to the Agents but I leave it to you to Judge and consider whether you chuse to have more Sugar and Rum than the naturall strength of your Estate will make. It is a disagreeable theme for me to write on therefore I shall say no more. But give me if you please positive orders and they must be obeyed for if more and more land is putt in you must want 100 more Negroes 100 more Steers and 2 or 300 more acres of land opened for Pasturage at the same time.

That I mention this to you I hope you will not conceive that there is any disagreement or Jealousy whatsoever. I do it intently to know your sentiments that I may act in conformity to them and not to be liable to blame or censure.

I saw in a letter to Mr. Kelly from you a mention of Hay to be made at Batchelors Hall. I do not apprehend that you could make Hay there from the Nature of the Grass but if 100 Acres of your land of Penhallons Run was putt into Guinea Grass it would answer all the End of making Hay and saving your Cattle. But another reason of their dying last year was the quantity of work they had to go through more than usual. Putting in 100 or 200 Acres of Guinea Grass where I mention would also give you an Opportunity of fattening all your old Cows which are now lost.

I cannot tell positively whether the Ejectment with Cussans will be tryed this Court or not. I have Subpoenared all the Evidence but Cunliffe who is our Chief Evidence is not come up his Wife being dangerously ill and not Expected to live. I have made an affadavitt in hopes the Court will putt it off untill he comes up otherwise Tuesday was the day appointed for the Tryal.

As Kelly was plaguing me for the payment of the Negroes purchased of him I have drawn on you two Bills one for £613.10.9 the other for 513.10.9 being the Amount of the Principall and Interest due on the first Bond and have taken it up and the Bills are dated the 27th of Nov. I have also drawn upon you a Sett of Bills for £50.15.4 in favor of Messrs. Long Drake & Long at 90 days sight being the Freight of the flour & Lumber from Philadelphia. I would have given the Capt. the Money but he begged me to give him a Bill as those Gentlemen were the Proprietors of the Ship and at the same time your Correspondents. I have no doubt of their meeting with due Honor.

Your Mother and Aunt are both pretty well.

PS I forgott to mention to you that I had received your Power of Attorney which shall keep by me until I hear from you again. I also received the Case Mr. Woodcock sent me.

INDEX

II

JOHN LANGDON
THREE VOYAGES TO THE WEST
COAST OF AFRICA 1881–1884

Edited by Martin Lynn

II

CONTENTS

PREFACE

The typescript of John Langdon's memoirs, 'Three Voyages to the West Coast of Africa, 1881–1884' is held by Bristol City Library. It is published below virtually in its entirety. Short passages of no more than a dozen words or so in each case have been excised from the beginning and end of 'First Voyage', the beginning of 'Second Voyage' and the beginning and end of 'Third Voyage' and have been marked in the text appropriately. These passages refer to Langdon's future wife and have no bearing on the subject of the memoirs. Apart from these excisions, few other changes have been made to the text. Where corrections to spelling and such like are appropriate, these have been made in footnotes.

Thanks are due to Bristol City Library for permission to publish this edition of Langdon's memoirs. Langdon died in January 1947 and according to his will, left one child, Lilian Elizabeth Langdon, wife of Frederick George Smith of Vancouver, Canada, to whom he bequeathed his estate. Numerous attempts were made to contact Mrs Smith and her descendants, including the publishing of adverts in the Vancouver press. Efforts were also made to trace the family solicitors, Salisbury, Light & Co. of Bristol, which ceased to do business in 1971. None of these attempts bore fruit. Apologies are hereby offered to the Smith family for publishing this edition without succeeding in establishing contact; they are urged to contact the editor at Queen's University, Belfast.

Thanks are also due to Dr Freda Harcourt who first suggested that an edition of this typescript should be published, and to Dr Steven Greer, Professor Andrew Porter, Dr Nigel Rigby, Professor Lydia White, and the staff of Bristol City Library. Other debts of gratitude are acknowledged in relevant footnotes. Such errors that remain are entirely the editor's responsibility.

INTRODUCTION

John Chandler Langdon, the author of 'Three voyages to the west coast of Africa', died in Bristol in 1947 aged eighty-three.[1] In his teens Langdon had worked as a seaman on ships belonging to R. & W. King of Bristol during three trading voyages to West Africa. Following his third voyage, Langdon left the sea and became an apprentice in the bookbinding trade, finally retiring as the owner of his own firm, Langdon & Davis of Bristol. Shortly before his death, he presented the typescript of 'Three voyages' to Bristol City Library.

The memoirs were written in 1930 and are based on his recollections of his experiences during the three voyages he made to Africa in the early 1880s; for the third of these voyages Langdon kept a diary, also held by Bristol City Library, on which the latter part of his account was based. In addition Langdon wrote a paper on trading methods in West Africa, 'Barter trade from Bristol ships, west coast of Africa', also in 1930, and an account of the attack on his ship at Sassandra, 'Our bust up with the nigger of Sassandrew River, west coast of Africa, 1883–84', in 1932. Both these accounts borrow heavily from 'Three voyages'. Although the narrative of 'Three voyages' is in places fictionalized, with accounts of conversations given that can hardly have been recollected so precisely some forty years later, the overall accuracy of the memoir, its use of dates and geography, and its detail of the voyages, when confirmed against other sources, cannot be faulted.[2] For all its unsophisticated language and colourful depiction of characters, it gives the reader an accurate picture of life on board a sailing ship in the West African trade in the 1880s. Its importance is that it tells us much about the place of Bristol and its merchants in the African trade, the techniques used in that trade, and the commercial potentialities of parts of West Africa just as the scramble for the region was getting underway.[3]

---

[1] Langdon died on 8 January 1947 and his Will, a copy of which is available in Somerset House, was granted probate on 21 February 1947.

[2] For example, where possible the dates of his voyages have been confirmed against *Customs Bills of Entry* records.

[3] A more extensive consideration of these issues can be found in M. Lynn, 'Bristol, West Africa and the nineteenth century palm oil trade', *Historical Research*, 64, 155 (1991), pp. 359–374. For Bristol's broader economic history in this period see C.E. Harvey and J. Press 'Industrial change and the economic life of Bristol since 1880', in *idem* (eds), *Studies in the Business History of Bristol* (Bristol, 1988), pp. 1–32; B.W.E. Alford, 'The economic development of Bristol in the 19th century: an enigma?', in P.M. McGrath and J. Cannon (eds), *Essays in Bristol and Gloucestershire History* (Bristol, 1976), pp. 252–283; K. Morgan, 'The economic development of Bristol, 1700–1850', in M. Dresser and P. Ollerenshaw (eds), *The Making of Modern Bristol* (Tiverton, 1996), pp. 48–75.

The picture of seaboard life Langdon's narrative draws is given from the viewpoint of the ordinary seaman and herein lies its central significance. It is a long time since maritime history was conceived as being simply the history of captains and officers, yet little material exists recording the experiences of ordinary sailors.[4] In this, Langdon's memoirs are unique for the West African trade. The descriptions produced by British participants in this commerce in the nineteenth century are very much the product of relatively educated men – supercargoes, traders, ship's officers or surgeons – writing for a relatively informed audience of businessmen, geographers, and armchair commentators. Adams, Bold, Smith, and Whitford, to name but few, were attempting to speak to their own kind, and doing so largely within the accepted parameters of contemporary travel writing.[5] Even popular missionary descriptions of the trade, such as by Waddell, or the work of writers like Mary Kingsley, while differing in detail from these trading accounts, fall essentially within this remit.[6] Langdon's memoir stands in sharp contrast to these volumes. His interest lay in trying to convey what life was like for the majority of those involved on the British side of this trade: the ordinary sailors who crewed the ships to West Africa and for whom the traders – an awareness of the sharp social gulf between crewmen and traders permeates Langdon's work – had little time. The value of 'Three voyages' therefore is that it gives us, albeit in ingenuous and somewhat naive language, the recollections of an ordinary seaman concerning life on trading ships to West Africa in the late nineteenth century.

In 'Three voyages' we see the crewman's experience of the stresses and strains of the voyage to West Africa spelt out vividly. Clearly, this was a hard and dangerous career. Not only were there the usual shipboard privations concerning long absences from port, hard work, pests, rats, poor provisions, and the petty cruelties of officers – all of which Langdon describes – but there was the ever-present danger of shipwreck, as experienced by him in the North Sea on his second voyage. For many sailors some of these experiences would have been commonplace, though they rarely feature in accounts of this trade.[7] Further, in the case of the West African trade, there were the added

[4] This argument is developed in M. Rediker, *Between the Devil and the Deep Blue Sea: Merchant Seamen, Pirates and the Anglo-American Maritime World, 1700–1750* (Cambridge, 1987).

[5] J. Adams, *Remarks on the Country Extending from Cape Palmas to the River Congo* (London, 1823); E. Bold, *The Merchants' and Mariners' Guide* (London, 1822); J. Smith, *Trade and Travels in the Gulph of Guinea* (London, 1851); J. Whitford, *Trading Life in Western and Central Africa* (London, 1877).

[6] H.M. Waddell, *Twenty-Nine Years in the West Indies and Central Africa* (London, 1863); M.H. Kingsley, *Travels in West Africa* (London, 1897).

[7] An exception to this is J. Fawckner, *Narrative of Capt. James Fawckner's Travels on the Coast of Benin* (London, 1837), who describes being shipwrecked near Benin.

dangers of disease and attack from the shore. Although the discovery of quinine as a prophylactic for malaria in 1854 reduced mortality rates in the West African trade, disease remained a constant threat. Langdon reports the way numbers of his fellow crewmen fell ill whilst in the Cameroons – their lack of treatment from a drunken surgeon being all too typical of the trade – and records the death of a Bristol captain on the Ivory Coast. Equally, one of the most vivid scenes in the narrative comes with the attack on the *Edmund Richardson* at Sassandra on Langdon's third voyage. Perhaps the most striking feature of the narrative however, is the sheer tedium of the shipboard life in the West African trade, with the need for speed generating pressures that were felt by the seamen. 'Work, work, from 6 till 5 on deck or in ship's hold in an almost unbearable heat', Langdon notes of the Cameroons and 'oil, oil from morning till evening' he writes concerning the Ivory Coast.[8] Exotic encounters with Africans may characterize most narratives of commercial activity in West Africa, but the reality for the crewmen in the trade was that shipboard life was a humdrum one of cleaning and tarring the ship, fishing, loading and unloading, and maintaining watch through the night. Langdon's voice not only provides a counterpoint to the conventional picture, but deserves to be heard in its own right.

If providing the viewpoint from life 'below decks' is the chief significance of Langdon's memoirs, then its second is in reminding the reader of the continuing role of Bristol in the African trade of these years. Again, Langdon is unique as a source for this. Liverpool is – rightly – regarded as the British port with the most significant connection with Africa in these years; nineteenth-century accounts of West African trade are all based around voyages from Liverpool.[9] In contrast there are no narratives of the trade generated from Bristol. Yet Bristol was Britain's second port for much of this period and its West African trade was of considerable and continuing importance to the end of the nineteenth century.

Bristol had at one time been the leading port in Britain's slave trade with Africa. By the mid-eighteenth century this position had been lost to Liverpool and with the abolition of British slaving in 1807, Bristol's remaining African traders, such as they were, had turned to the so-called 'legitimate trade' in produce. This produce trade encompassed a wide variety of items, not least ivory, gold dust, dye-woods, and skins, though in the early decades following abolition it was timber in its various forms that was at the heart of British imports from West Africa

---

[8] See below, pp. 204 and 237.

[9] To give one example, R.M. Jackson, *Journal of a Voyage to Bonny River* (London, 1934). See also M. Lynn, 'Liverpool and Africa in the nineteenth century: the continuing connection', *Transactions of the Historic Society of Lancashire and Cheshire*, 147 (1998), pp. 27–54.

more broadly. By the 1830s palm oil – oil extracted from the fruit of the oil palm, *elaeis guineensis* – had emerged as the major commodity imported from the west coast and by the early 1850s Britain's imports of palm oil had reached an average of over 577,000 cwt per annum, worth over £1 million.[10] Palm oil's value was as a lubricant for machinery, particularly before the discovery of petroleum resources in the USA in 1859, and as a major component in the manufacture of soap and candles. In the latter part of the century, palm kernels – the kernel of the fruit, left once palm oil has been extracted from the pericarp, and hitherto ignored by British traders – became an increasingly important part of British imports from West Africa, though its use in margarine manufacture and for cattle feed was, at least until World War I, led by the German and Dutch markets.[11]

Though Liverpool remained at the centre of this commerce throughout these years, Bristol's share of the African palm products trade was not negligible, with the port accounting for some 14 per cent of British imports in the middle of the century.[12] African commodities found a ready market in Bristol. The city was a major soap manufacturing centre and the mid-nineteenth century saw this Bristol industry at its most prosperous. The city had long been a renowned centre for soap production and one of its soap firms, Christopher Thomas & Bros, was to be the major soap manufacturer of western England and was to hold, at one time, some 8 per cent of the UK market.[13] Equally, candle manufacture, usually undertaken in conjunction with soap processing, was of considerable significance in the city. Tinplate manufacture – which used palm oil as a flux in the plating process – was important to Bristol's economy, while nearby South Wales saw the largest tinplate industry in Britain.[14] The development of railways, with the Great Western opening from Paddington to Bristol in 1841, generated further demand for palm oil while also strengthening the links between the port and its hinterland.[15] As the cargoes of the ships on Langdon's first and third voyages show – being primarily composed of palm oil – there was a continuing demand in Bristol and its hinterland for palm oil.[16]

Also important in explaining Bristol's role in the nineteenth-century

[10] M. Lynn, *Commerce and Economic Change in West Africa: The Palm Oil Trade in the Nineteenth Century* (Cambridge, 1997), pp. 13–14.

[11] C. Wilson, *The History of Unilever*, 2 vols (London, 1954), II, pp. 25–27.

[12] Lynn, 'Bristol, West Africa', p. 361.

[13] T. O'Brien, 'Christopher Thomas and Brothers Ltd', *Progress* (1949), pp. 43–48; C.J. Diaper, 'Christopher Thomas and Brothers Ltd: the last Bristol soapmakers', *Transactions of the Bristol and Gloucestershire Archaeological Society*, 105 (1987), pp. 223–232.

[14] W.E. Minchinton, *The British Tinplate Industry: A History* (Oxford, 1957), pp. 55–58.

[15] Palm oil was used as a lubricant for railway carriages in the period before the discovery of mineral oil.

[16] Lynn, 'Bristol, West Africa', pp. 359–374.

West African trade was the manufacturing sector in the city. Far from being simply an entrepôt, Bristol in the early nineteenth century was a major manufacturing centre and its goods were exported across the globe.[17] It was noted for its metallurgical industries: brass and copper in particular. Both these products played a major role in the African trade. So too did glassware, alcohol, and cotton cloth, all of which were manufactured in Bristol in this period. As Langdon's account shows, particularly important in the African trade were three items of Bristol manufacture: gunpowder, lead shot, and manillas. Gunpowder was produced on a considerable scale in Bristol, and it is notable how all three of Langdon's voyages began with large quantities of gunpowder being loaded on board. Also significant in the trade was lead shot, the lead coming from the nearby Mendip hills, while manillas − horseshoe-shaped rings from an alloy of copper and lead − were of central importance as a currency in the West African trade and particularly on the Ivory Coast; Langdon rightly stresses the importance of the manillas in the trading goods his ships carried to West Africa.[18] Further, Bristol's links with its hinterland, particularly the West Midlands, provided the port with a ready source of the firearms and hardware that Langdon's ships required to trade on the coast, and that were so prominent in their cargoes, while Bristol's continuing West Indies connections provided the rum so ubiquitous in the trade.

Langdon's narrative reveals how this Bristol African trade functioned. In its structure, the trade continued to reflect the organization of the slave trade of the eighteenth century. Essentially, very little changed in the organization of Britain's African trade, both with Liverpool and Bristol, after 1807. While slaves were no longer transported in British ships − or at least not legitimately − the same mechanisms and techniques as in the slave trade continued to be utilized by British traders. The reason was that the sailing ship remained the method of transport of the African trade. In the nineteenth century, as in the slave-trade era, Bristol's trading voyage (as was Liverpool's) was organized around the despatching of a sailing ship to the coast, usually owned (or occasionally, chartered) by a trader rather than a shipper, with a cargo of manufactured goods to be exchanged for produce; these manufactured goods were then given out to local African brokers

[17] Harvey and Press, 'Industrial change', p. 2; C.M. MacInnes, *A Gateway of Empire* (Bristol, 1939), pp. 381–399; W.E. Minchinton (ed.), *The Trade of Bristol in the 18th Century* (Bristol, 1957), pp. ix–xvi; Morgan, 'Economic development of Bristol', pp. 48–75.

[18] W. Babington, 'Remarks on the general description of the trade on the West Coast of Africa', *Journal of the Society of Arts*, 23 (1875), pp. 245–257; A.H.M. Kirk-Greene, 'The major currencies in Nigerian history', *Journal of the Historical Society of Nigeria*, 2 (1960), pp. 132–150; F.J. Pedler, *The Lion and Unicorn in Africa: the United Africa Company, 1787–1931* (London, 1974), pp. 21–22.

on the basis of credit (or 'trust' as it was called).[19] The sailing vessel would then remain on the coast until the coastal brokers had collected produce from the interior and returned to redeem their trust.[20] In this system, each voyage was a discrete trading venture, funded by a trader in Bristol or Liverpool, whose capital was thus tied up on the coast for a year or more before it could be realized. The costs of this system were high and the risks, from shipwreck or from brokers defaulting on their credit, were higher still.

Bristol traders utilized two trading techniques for their trade in West Africa, both of which are aptly illustrated by Langdon's three voyages. The heart of the West African trade in these years lay in the Niger Delta and its neighbouring rivers.[21] This area was very much the preserve of the major Liverpool firms. Here these Liverpool firms, at least before the middle of the century, followed what Langdon termed the 'river trade' system, namely sending a ship direct to one river to fill its cargo at one port, the ship remaining until a full cargo was purchased. This was possible where, as in the rivers of the Niger Delta or the neighbouring Cameroons estuary, there was a natural harbour where ships could wait for their goods to be sold and produce purchased. Although Bristol traders eschewed the Niger Delta, this technique was followed by them in the Cameroons estuary, as can be seen from the description of Langdon's second voyage. The Cameroons had become an important centre for Bristol traders. These traders were to be found developing the ivory trade of the area early in the century, while by the 1850s an observer complained of how Bristol 'monopolized' the river's trade; another noted Bristol traders' particularly lawless behaviour in the Cameroons.[22] By the 1880s Bristol traders, purchasing ivory and palm products, had been operating for many decades in the Cameroons and, as Langdon's account strikingly suggests, were using this river to buy palm kernels to send direct to the German market.[23] This system, utilizing Liverpool techniques but trading with Hamburg, showed a remarkable degree of innovation by Langdon's employers; there is little evidence of other British firms, whether from Bristol or Liverpool, doing this.

[19] W.E. Minchinton, 'The voyage of the snow *Africa*', *Mariner's Mirror*, 37 (1951), pp. 188–190; Minchinton, *Trade of Bristol*, pp. xvi–xix; K. Morgan, *Bristol and the Atlantic Trade in the 18th Century* (Cambridge, 1993), pp. 128–151.

[20] C.W. Newbury, 'Credit in early nineteenth century West African trade', *Journal of African History*, 13 (1972), pp. 81–95.

[21] M. Lynn, 'Change and continuity in the British palm oil trade with West Africa', *Journal of African History*, 22 (1981), pp. 331–348.

[22] Hutchinson to Clarendon, 23 February 1857, FO 84/1030; Burton to Foreign Secretary, 14 January 1862, FO 84/1176.

[23] The development of the Hamburg market can be traced in L. Harding, 'Hamburg's West African trade in the 19th century', in G. Liesegang, H. Pasch, and A. Jones (eds),

The other trading technique used by Bristol traders, which has not received due attention in studies of the African commerce, was 'coasting'. This technique, of which no direct accounts have survived apart from Langdon's, was utilized on those other parts of the West African coast where Bristol traders were prevalent – particularly the Ivory Coast, the destination for Langdon's first and third voyages, and known in this period as the 'Bristol Coast' from the ubiquity of Bristol ships; few if any, Liverpool firms would be found here.[24] The list of Bristol ships Langdon noted during his third voyage confirms this. Here the physical geography of the littoral meant that there were few natural harbours and the 'river' technique was an impossibility. Coasting required sailing along the coast buying small quantities of produce from numerous different ports and involved trading in a variety of different produce – ivory, oil, skins, grains etc. – with a cargo containing a wide variety of different manufactured products to appeal to different tastes in different areas. This meant, as with Langdon's experience, the ship might pass along the coast three or four times on a single voyage; given that this required beating against the wind when returning westward, this was a very time-consuming activity for a trade where time meant money. Langdon's two coasting voyages to and from the Ivory Coast took around eighteen months each, while his river voyage to and from the more distant Cameroons took only five months. Coasting's advantage however, was that it enabled traders to spread their risk across a variety of produce and a variety of markets in West Africa. It clearly was a robust system and, as Langdon's narrative shows, it still thrived in the late nineteenth century.

Profitable it might have been for Langdon's employers, but as he makes clear, the coasting system was a laborious system of trading and one that generated considerable stresses among the crew. Although sailors preferred it to the river trade, seeing it as healthier and less risky than the river trade – though there is little evidence to confirm this[25] – it generated much work for the crew. 'We had to do battle with a very strong current, head winds and calms', notes Langdon of sailing back along the coast, adding that occasionally the ship ended the day further down wind than it had started.[26] His narrative is characterized throughout by the efforts required by the length of time coasting involved: 'it was nag, nag, nag, day after day'.[27]

Figuring African Trade (Berlin, 1986), pp. 363–391.

[24] Pedler, *Lion and Unicorn*, IV, p. 153. Coasting was a long established mechanism and fitted into local structures of trading on the coast; D.N. Syfert, 'The Liberian coasting trade, 1822–1900', *Journal of African History*, 18 (1977), pp. 217–235.

[25] Mortality rates among sailors were high whichever system was used, until the discovery of quinine as a prophylactic in 1854.

[26] See below, p. 209.

[27] See below, p. 208.

Whichever technique of trading was used – river or coasting – considerable quantities of goods had to be given out to coastal brokers as trust. The main goods used in this system, as Langdon's description of the cargo on his first voyage makes clear, were firearms and gunpowder, salt, cloth, or spirits; gin, rum, and Dutch schnapps were particular favourites.[28] The development of a trade direct to Hamburg no doubt enabled the loading of a cargo of schnapps for the return to West Africa.[29] In the middle of the century, textiles made up around half of British exports by value to West Africa to the east of the River Volta, spirits some 20 per cent and firearms some 16 per cent.[30] Contrary to Langdon's view, there is little evidence that shoddy or second-rate goods were acceptable to brokers on a wide scale; African brokers were skilled and perceptive purchasers in their own right. Nonetheless, adulteration – by both European and African – was a problem in the trade. Palm oil could be adulterated by the addition of water or impurities; for this reason, as Langdon describes, it was boiled on board ship before being purchased. Less prominent in Langdon's account – though certainly recognized – is the repeated adulteration of manufactured goods, particularly spirits and gunpowder, by British traders and the all-too common practice by British traders of selling short measure.[31]

The trust system took time for goods to be turned into produce, and the risks in it for Bristol traders were obvious, with brokers liable for a variety of reasons to default, and with traders, keen to increase their cargo, tempted to give out more trust than a port could ever realistically hope to redeem in produce. Such situations often degenerated into conflict, with traders calling on the nearest British authorities for help in redeeming their goods, or on occasion, taking the law into their own hands through violence.[32] In the longer term no-one benefited from this. Thus ship's captains and supercargoes had to build relationships over time through liberal use of 'dashes' (gifts) and symbolic and ceremonial ties. Langdon notes the way Captain Swan ('Pincher') had done this and shows how such relationships – and conversely their breakdown in a 'peppering' – were at the heart of the success or failure of trading voyages such as these.

[28] J.E. Inikori, 'West Africa's seaborne trade, 1750–1850: volume, structure and impli-cations', in Liesegang, Pasch and Jones, *Figuring African Trade*, pp. 49–88, examines the issue of West African seaborne imports in more detail.

[29] W.I. Ofonagoro, *Trade and Imperialism in Southern Nigeria, 1881–1929* (New York, 1979), pp. 95–96.

[30] Inikori, 'West Africa's seaborne trade', pp. 84–85.

[31] Ofonagoro, *Trade and Imperialism*, pp. 78–81, 114–120.

[32] This is the theme of K.O. Dike, *Trade and Politics in the Niger Delta, 1830–85* (Oxford, 1956).

One other way traders guaranteed themselves against brokers defaulting on their trust is startlingly revealed by Langdon. This was through the taking of pawns on board ship, whom Langdon refers to with the euphemism of 'passengers', to be redeemed once the trust was repaid. This practice was illegal under English law – and, being effectively slaving, had been so since 1807 – and its existence on British ships in the 1880s is surprising, to say the least. Langdon admits that it was a practice that had to be concealed from passing Navy vessels, yet it is also clear from his narrative that it was routine on the Ivory Coast in these years. Lack of other evidence, due to its clandestine nature, means that it is impossible to establish how widespread this practice was outside the Ivory Coast.[33]

Langdon's memoirs are also of significance in a third way. His employers on his three voyagers were R. & W. King and Langdon's narrative throws important light on the history of this firm.[34] While there were several Bristol firms that participated in the African trade, not least Lucas Bros, Edward Gwyer & Son and Francis Bruford, the leaders of it in these years were undoubtedly the King brothers.[35] Kings had their origin in the career of Thomas King (1759–1841), a Bristol trader who came to prominence in the West African and West Indies trades in the late eighteenth century. In the early 1830s his two sons, Richard (1799–1874) and William (1806–1887), took over his business and renamed it R. & W. King. The King brothers were to be of considerable prominence within Bristol life, their rise to prominence coinciding with the prosperous years of the African trade. Richard was elected a City Councillor in 1835 and remained so until his death in 1874. He was mayor between 1844 and 1845 and was regarded as, in effect, the leader of the City Council throughout these years; he led the Docks committee, was prominent in the Chamber of Commerce and in the Merchant Venturers, and was master of the latter in 1851– 1852. William King was elected councillor in 1841 and master of the Merchant Venturers in 1850–1851 and became sheriff in 1871–1872.[36]

The King brothers concentrated the activities of the King firm on West Africa and, more particularly, the Ivory Coast and Gabon areas

---

[33] See below, p. 209. The only other area for which evidence exists of this practice in this period concerns the Loango coast; P.M. Martin, *The External Trade of the Loango Coast, 1576–1870* (Oxford, 1972), p. 103.

[34] The history of this firm is outlined in M. Lynn, 'British business and the African trade: Richard & William King Ltd. of Bristol and West Africa, 1833–1918', *Business History*, 34 (1992), pp. 20–37.

[35] Lucas Brothers derived from the late eighteenth-century cooperage firm of Thomas Lucas and was developed by Edward Thomas Lucas (1824–1863) and John Frederick Lucas (1831–1893). Lucas Brothers often operated in tandem with Edward Gwyer & Son; Lynn, 'Bristol, West Africa', pp. 366–367.

[36] Lynn, 'British business and the African trade', pp. 25–26.

that their father had pioneered, while also developing important markets on the Gold Coast and Slave Coast; they specialized in palm oil but also traded extensively in other commodities, especially ivory. In following this pattern they were avoiding the areas of West Africa the big Liverpool firms concentrated on, such as the rivers of the Niger Delta. This allowed them to avoid the pressures and costs that competition with these major firms would have generated – Kings' ships were small, on average some 216 tons in 1850 compared to a Liverpool figure twice that; it should be noted that Langdon's first voyage in 1881 on board a barque of 293 tons was on a relatively small vessel for the African trade of that time.[37] Nonetheless Kings' timing was good. They focused on the West African trade just as produce prices began to rise during the 1830s and the firm correspondingly flourished. Indeed by the time Langdon sailed on their ships in the 1880s – just at the moment that William King finally retired from the business and handed it on to his son, Mervyn (1844–1934) – it was one of the ten biggest African firms in Britain. It was to survive as an independent business until it was taken over by William Lever in 1918.[38]

Langdon's experiences reveal much that lay behind Kings' long-term success. Clearly they knew the Ivory Coast market well. Here their choice of captain for their voyages would have been critical, for the African trade was a highly specialized trade, requiring detailed knowledge of a series of different markets both along the coast and in Britain, and one where, as Langdon shows, that detailed knowledge was jealously guarded by participants.[39] Repeatedly, Langdon notes, efforts were made to ensure competing traders (even from within the same firm) did not have access to the market information that was critical for success. Much indeed rode on the skill and knowledge of the individual ship's master and/or supercargo in choosing where to trade and who to give credit to. Striking in Langdon's account is the fact that Kings clearly trained younger captains in the details of the trade. Further, their willingness – unlike the other Bristol firms – to take on the Liverpool giants in the Niger Delta and its environs can be seen in Langdon's voyage to the Cameroons. In 1879 indeed they began trading in Old Calabar, one of the major entrepôts for the African trade in this region and a Liverpool centre for many decades. Moreover their willingness to employ steam in West Africa – as seen in the steam vessel that towed the *Edmund Richardson* out of the Cameroons estuary – and

---

[37] Indeed these ships were not markedly larger than Bristol ships used in the African trade in the 1790s; Morgan , *Bristol and Atlantic Trade*, p. 44; M. Lynn, 'From sail to steam: the impact of the steamship services on the British palm oil trade with West Africa, 1850–90', *Journal of African History*, 30, (1989), pp. 227–245.

[38] Pedler, *Lion and Unicorn*, pp. 8–26, 151–156.

[39] See below, p. 205.

their willingness to enter the relatively new Hamburg and Rotterdam trades, is clear evidence of the entreprise and innovation that characterized this firm up to World War I.

Langdon's narrative is of less value in a fourth area of interest, namely in the picture it gives of the West Africa he visited. In one sense at least, this might be seen as understandable; Langdon remained a seaman, whose interests remained the ship and its life and whose attitudes reflected the society he came from. Nonetheless, although he did spend time on land in West Africa, there is little here on the people of the Ivory Coast that Langdon spent so many months sailing along. Such information that he does give on the region is characterized by crude stereotyping.

The area of the Ivory Coast that Langdon visited was one of considerable complexity in terms of its political organization.[40] The western part of the coast, between modern Liberia and the Bandama river and Grand-Lahou, was an area of immense political fragmentation inhabited by Kru-speaking clans and with only limited resources for external trade. This was an area of small-scale, so-called 'stateless societies', where political authority remained diffused and where no centralized, large-scale states existed – though clearly Sassandra was of significance in its own right as a trading entrepôt.[41] To the east of the Bandama river was a region of considerable economic importance, linked to the Akan speakers of the Gold Coast and an area that had attracted European traders for centuries.[42] The Avikam brokers of Grand-Lahou had sold slaves, cloth, gold, and ivory to European traders and had established a major trading system, linked via the Bandama to interior producers like the Baule and others.[43] Bosman, writing of the early eighteenth century, stressed the commercial acumen of the traders in this area, a theme taken up by Adams a century later.[44] The closing of the Bandama and the move in trade routes to

[40] There is little detailed work in English available on the history of this area. For a general introduction see Y. Person, 'The Atlantic coast and the southern savannas, 1800–80', in J.F.A. Ajayi and M. Crowder (eds), *History of West Africa*, II (2nd edn, London, 1987), pp. 257–262; Y. Person, 'Western Africa, 1870–1886', in R. Oliver and G.N. Sanderson (eds), *Cambridge History of Africa*, VI (Cambridge, 1985), pp. 227–228.

[41] G.E. Brooks, *The Kru Mariner in the Nineteenth Century* (Newark, DL, 1972); C. Behrens, *Les Kroumen de la Côte occidentale d'Afrique* (Bordeaux, 1974); R.W. Davis, *Ethnohistorical Studies on the Kru Coast* (Newark, DL, 1976), pp. 5–9; E. Tonkin, 'Creating Kroomen: ethnic diversity, economic specialism and changing demand', in J.C. Stone (ed.), *Africa and the Sea* (Aberdeen, 1985), pp. 27–47; J. Martin, 'Krumen "down the coast": Liberian migrants on the West African coast in the 19th and early 20th centuries', *International Journal of African Historical Studies*, 18 (1985), pp. 401–423.

[42] T.C. Weiskel, *French Colonial Rule and the Baule Peoples* (Oxford, 1980), pp. 5–32.

[43] Person, 'Atlantic coast and southern savannas', pp. 262–265.

[44] W. Bosman, *A New and Accurate Description of the Coast of Guinea* (1705, repr. 1967), p. 487; J. Adams, *Remarks on the Country Extending from Cape Palmas* (London, 1823, repr. 1966), p. 3.

the east due to changes among interior producers during the late eighteenth and early nineteenth centuries, saw the relative decline of Grand-Lahou and the shift of trading power towards the Alladian brokers of Jacqueville. By the 1880s indeed, a French agent reported that Grand-Lahou was in serious decay compared to its former trading prosperity and that Half Jack and Grand Jack were now the major trading centres of this region.[45] Certainly the pattern of Langdon's two voyages to the Ivory Coast reflected these shifts in economic power towards the Alladian brokers; in each voyage, Half Jack, which Langdon notes was the largest trading town on the coast, was the final destination visited before the ship returned home. Yet, regrettably, his narrative tells the reader little of this region, beyond details of which were the major entrepôts, and predictable comments concerning conflicts between various ports such as Sassandra and Grand Drewin.

Langdon's narrative gives no more detail on the Cameroons, though admittedly Langdon was only in the river for a relatively short period. This was an area where, by the 1850s, palm oil and kernels had largely replaced the earlier trade in slaves and ivory.[46] The two main lineages of the Cameroons estuary, whose leaders were recognized as 'Kings' by Europeans – Bell and Akwa – were now facing considerable political problems, generated partly by the new trade and more particularly by the rise to prominence of Deido, the third of the three main towns of the estuary. Only following the execution of the leader of Deido in 1876 did a rough equilibrium come to be re-established and the stability necessary for trade to flourish return.[47] None of this appears in Langdon's memoirs and it is striking that no reference is made to him actually landing in the Cameroons.

The limitations of Langdon's views of West Africa would have been shaped by the society he came from. Further, as a seaman, his activities would have been tightly controlled by his captain, making it unlikely that Langdon could have undertaken the sort of examination of local customs that other visitors to West Africa were able to. Nonetheless, the lack of information on African societies in Langdon's account is striking, given that a good proportion of the crewmen he shared his shipboard work with were Kru from the Ivory Coast. They are constantly in the background of Langdon's narrative. Such Kru were regularly employed on British ships both for coasting and for the river trade for, as seen in Langdon's narrative, traders preferred to sail out

[45] Weiskel, *Baule Peoples*, pp. 30–32.

[46] M. Johnson, 'By ship or camel: the struggle for the Cameroons ivory trade in the nineteenth century', *Journal of African History*, 19 (1978), pp. 523–578; R.A. Austen and J. Derrick, *Middlemen of the Cameroons Rivers: the Duala and their Hinterland, c1600–c1960* (Cambridge, 1999), pp. 55–57.

[47] *Ibid.*, pp. 91–92.

to the coast with only sufficient men to handle the ship at sea and then recruit Kru labour to undertake the physical work of loading and storing produce.[48] On occasion, as Langdon notes, British crew would be returned home by other ships belonging to the firm. The Kru had a long history of this employment on board British ships; in addition to their maritime skills and extensive seafaring experience, they were less likely to fall ill than British sailors and most importantly, were significantly cheaper, being paid substantially less in wages.[49] Yet they remain peripheral figures to Langdon's story, the butts of jokes and figures of fun but little more. 'Koffee' is ridiculed for his pretensions, his English is caricatured (as in considering 'the grand debil'), while Langdon's creation of a kite is used to poke fun at Kru beliefs in 'witchcraft'. Kru are portrayed as prone to violence, and easily seduced with poor pay and an unseaworthy boat.

Indeed Langdon's views of the Africans he met on the coast are overtly and heavily racist. The term 'nigger' is used repeatedly to describe Africans and the 'talented' Africans he describes on one occasion are explained in terms of their European 'crossings'. Langdon loses no chance to portray those he meets in patronizing and stereotypical terms. His accidental stumble over an African woman on board is termed 'the horror', while on his first voyage he relishes the way he fools the African crewmen in his pretence of swallowing a knife, using this to highlight their supposed childishness.[50] The Africans portrayed in Langdon's narrative are either simple, easily-fooled 'children', prey to superstition and myth, or are seen as overly violent, threatening, and prone to cannibalism. The Cameroons is dismissed as in thrall to the 'witchcraft business'. Alternatively he reflects contemporary views on alleged African sexual appetites with his comments on King William's 700 wives. Similarly the contempt he expresses for the West Indian missionary – a typical 'trousered black' as they came to be stereotyped – he encountered at the Cameroons is considerable, with slighting references to his size, the number of his children, and his cupidity in 'cadging' goods from the ship. Undoubtedly, Langdon was not unusual among British sailors of his time in holding these views of Africans, and the image he portrays is quite clearly that which he brought with him from Bristol. What is difficult to establish however, is how far the

[48] G.E. Brooks, *Yankee Traders, Old Coasters and African Middlemen* (Boston, MA, 1970), pp. 224–225. Kru employment on British ships was clearly long established, according to G.A. Robertson, *Notes on Africa* (London, 1819), p. 43.

[49] Smith, writing in the 1850s, gives Kru wages on ship as 5s per month; *Trade and Travels*, p. 103; D. Frost, 'Racism, work and unemployment: West African seamen in Liverpool, 1880s–1960s', in *idem* (ed.), *Ethnic Labour and British Imperial Trade: A History of Ethnic Seafarers in the UK* (London, 1995), pp. 22–33.

[50] See below, p. 206.

racism of the narrative was shaped by the 1930s Langdon was writing in, rather than the 1880s he was writing of.[51]

Despite this limitation in Langdon's memoirs – serious though it is in restricting the picture he drew of West Africa – his account remains of value. In its description of shipboard life, of the organization of the West African trade and of the activities of R. & W. King, Langdon's narrative gives a viewpoint not revealed in any other account from this period and historians' understanding of the West African trade is the fuller for it. Moreover, there is a further dimension of Langdon's memoirs that pervades the entire narrative and that is of critical importance. Permeating 'Three voyages' is the fact that this was a trade that in the 1880s was undergoing considerable changes.

These changes were partly economic and partly political in origin. A ubiquitous motif in Langdon's narrative is the appearance of the mail steamer along the coast. On the first voyage the mail steamer carrying the King of Cape Lahou is encountered, another steamer is used to carry Captain Swan's note to Cape Coast, later still SS *Roman* is met; on the third voyage a doctor on the steamer is contacted and a sick crewman is despatched home on board. The steamship arrived in the West African trade in 1852, with the development of a steamship service from London (operating from Liverpool from 1856).[52] A government mail contract was taken up by the African Steam Ship Co. in that year, and shared with the British & African Steam Navigation Co. from 1869. In time a German line, Woermann's, operating from Hamburg, entered the west coast commerce and developed a significant German trade, particularly from the Cameroons. The mail steamers had an immense impact on the African trade, not only by shortening voyage times but also by allowing traders to operate at a wide variety of ports along the coast. Further, the steamers allowed fresh staff to be despatched to the coast, new supplies to be forwarded to traders, and information about prices and markets to be updated readily. The arrival of steam thus led to increasing specialization of function between trader and shipper, and allowed traders to reduce costs by abandoning the purchase or chartering of ships and despatching their produce as freight. Over the years, the advantages of steam drove out sail and by the early 1880s, when Langdon went to sea, only some 10 per cent of palm products were being shipped from West Africa to Britain by the old methods.[53]

[51] A useful introductory survey of British ideas about race is P.B. Rich, *Race and Empire in British Politics* (Cambridge, 1986); M. Dresser, *Slavery Obscured: The Social History of the Slave Trade in an English Provincial Port* (London, 2001) considers Bristolians' attitudes to Africans and to the slave trade. See especially pp. 53–95.

[52] P.N. Davies, *The Trade Makers: Elder Dempster in West Africa, 1852–1972* (London, 1973).

[53] Lynn, *Commerce and Economic Change*, p. 110.

In particular, the steamship services had a major impact on the river trade. Some of these changes can be seen in Langdon's second voyage. By obviating the need for traders to own their own ships and employ their own masters or supercargoes to undertake their trade, the steamer service encouraged the use of resident agents, based for a season or more in West Africa, and the use of hulks as store ships to bulk produce while waiting for the steamship to arrive. Langdon encountered one in the Cameroons, the *Lord Raglan* of Bristol, with its white clerks 'ghastly white, bloodless, dressed in immaculate white, walking corpses [...] no manual work (above it)'.[54] For all Langdon's sarcasm these white clerks were to be the future of the trade and the system represented by the *Edmund Richardson* and its crew would soon be obsolete.

Moreover, these new trading techniques, by allowing in small-scale traders who had hitherto been blocked by the high capital cost of purchasing their own ship but who could now survive on much lower profit margins, sharply increased competition in the trade and drove down prices, a problem that came to be seen acutely in these years. Langdon's account does indeed reflect the fact that he was writing of a time of considerable difficulty for the West African trade as prices fell, at least partly because of the changes generated by the steamships. Indeed Langdon picked the right moment to leave the trade – 1884 – for African produce prices were soon to slump to the lowest level of the century. With hindsight, the early 1880s marked a brief rally in a longer-term fall in prices that had begun in the early 1860s; by 1887 palm oil prices had fallen to £19 a ton, the lowest for several decades.[55] As Langdon realized, this had broader implications for the African trade and its organization; 'the barter trade was near its ebb' he noted of this period.[56]

Langdon's brief career on board Kings' ships unquestionably occurred at a moment of considerable transition in the African trade. The commerce was about to be transformed. Not only did the depression of the late 1880s drive many firms out of business – though not, it should be noted, Kings – those that survived were amalgamated into increasingly fewer hands; Kings merged their Old Calabar business into the African Association in 1889.[57] Further, the impact of the steamship lines was to make the techniques and practices outlined by Langdon largely redundant. 'Coasting' such as Langdon experienced it, no longer made economic sense in the steamship era; indeed the practice of traders owning their own ships, as Kings did, represented

[54] See below, p. 237.

[55] Lynn, *Commerce and Economic Change*, p. 111.

[56] J.C. Langdon, 'Barter trade from Bristol ships, west coast of Africa, fifty years ago', I, typescript in Bristol City Library.

[57] Pedler, *Lion and Unicorn*, p. 139.

an increasingly outmoded form of commercial organization in a trade that was moving to specialization of function between shipper and trader, resident agents, and land-based factories. The 10 per cent of the palm oil trade that had been carried in sailing ships in 1880 had fallen to around 1 per cent a decade later.[58] Kings themselves, who held out longer than most, turned to using the steamship services during the 1880s, and abandoned the type of trade that had characterized the African commerce for so long and which is described in 'Three voyages'. The trade system that Langdon had been a participant in disappeared very quickly indeed after his final voyage in 1884.

Equally striking in Langdon's narrative are signs of the political changes that were occurring in West Africa, as represented by an increased external presence. One element of this was the missionary. Missions had been present on various parts of the coast since the start of the century; missionary activity quickly followed the establishment of Freetown as a base for freed slaves in 1787.[59] The establishment by the American Colonization Society of the settlement of Liberia in the early 1820s – and in 1834 at Cape Palmas by the Maryland equivalent – had also been followed by considerable missionary endeavour in the area.[60] In the 1840s a further wave of missions had arrived in West Africa; not least among these had been the Baptist Mission Society that, prompted by West Indian churches and staffed partly by West Indian missionaries, had established itself in the Cameroons in 1841.[61] Langdon encountered several representatives of these missions during his voyages, such as the American missionary encountered at Cape Palmas and the West Indian at the Cameroons, though, like many involved in the trade, he reveals considerable cynicism concerning them, castigating their behaviour particularly towards the men below decks.

Whatever Langdon's views might have been, missions saw their function as spiritual rather than temporal. A more politically charged presence on the coast was the growing British activity in the area that is referred to repeatedly by Langdon. Although both the Ivory Coast and the Cameroons were still independent of foreign rule when Langdon visited them in the early 1880s, the British presence was growing steadily. By the 1880s the problems generated by the trust system and by low prices were increasingly involving the British authorities in the west coast trade. Striking in Langdon's narrative are the numerous references

[58] Lynn, *Commerce and Economic Change*, p. 110.
[59] A. Hastings, *The Church in Africa, 1450–1950* (Oxford, 1994), pp. 177–188, 242–247.
[60] M.B. Abasiattai, 'Sierra Leone and Liberia in the nineteenth century', in Ajayi and Crowder, *History of West Africa*, II, pp. 301–339.
[61] H.H. Johnson, *George Grenfell and the Congo*, 2 vols (London, 1908), I, pp. 19–29; J. van Slageren, *Les Origines de l'Eglise Evangélique du Cameroun* (Yaoundé, 1972), pp. 11–37.

to British officials, particularly to the Consul and to the Governor of
the Gold Coast at Cape Coast Castle. Equally important is Langdon's
reference to the Navy, as seen in the arrival of HMS *Electro* on his third
voyage; since the ending of the French wars in 1815, a Royal Navy anti-
slavery squadron had been based along the coast, though its function had
largely changed by this period and the numbers of ships involved had
been reduced.[62] British consuls had been appointed along various parts
of the coast – though not the Ivory Coast – since 1849, while British
traders had been established on the Gold Coast for centuries; in 1874 the
Gold Coast was annexed to the Crown.[63]

Although the German presence in West Africa, at least before 1884,
was largely limited to shipping and commercial interests, particularly
in the Cameroons, French activity was more extensive. The French
were present, as they had been for some time, in the colony of Senegal.
Minor French garrisons, following Bouët-Willaumez's voyages in this
area, had been established on parts of the Ivory Coast in 1843 – though
a short-lived French fort had been opened earlier at Assini in 1701 and
a factory at Grand-Lahou in 1787 – and during the 1860s and 1870s
sporadic negotiations had occurred between the British and French
authorities to exchange these for the British territory of the Gambia,
but little came of these proposals and the French garrisons were
eventually withdrawn during the 1870s.[64] Yet, as Langdon shows, by
the 1880s French traders were once again active on the Ivory Coast
and his third voyage ends with reference to growing French ambitions
in the region.

This external presence which is such a feature of Langdon's narrative,
reflects the fact that the West Africa he visited in the 1880s was
undergoing considerable political change, and particularly on the Ivory
Coast. Although Bristol traders were the main maritime traders to be
found on this coast throughout the nineteenth century, it was the
French not the British authorities that moved to assert their presence
on the Ivory Coast in the 1880s, ignoring not least in this process long-
standing Liberian claims to the western end of the littoral. In 1886,
two years after Langdon's last voyage, the French occupation of the
Ivory Coast began, and three years later was recognized by the Anglo-
French agreement of August 1889. By 1890 Grand-Lahou was occupied
by France and by 1891 the whole of the eastern end of the coast lay in

[62] C. Lloyd, *The Navy and the Slave Trade* (London, 1949).
[63] E. Reynolds, 'The Gold Coast and Asante', in Ajayi and Crowder, *History of West Africa*, II, pp. 215–249.
[64] P. Atger, *La France en Côte d'Ivoire de 1843 à 1893* (Dakar, 1962); J.D. Hargreaves, *Prelude to the Partition of West Africa* (London, 1963), pp. 125–129, 145–195. Bouët's voyages are described in E. Bouët-Willaumez, *Description Nautique des Côtes de l'Afrique Occidentale* (Paris, 1849).

French hands; in 1893 a formal declaration of a colony was made.[65] Bristol traders experienced a similar fate in the Cameroons, where a growing German trading presence made it an easy target once Germany's bid for colonies in Africa began; in July 1884, to the considerable chagrin of Bristol traders, the German flag was raised over the estuary.[66]

Not only was the system of trading represented in 'Three voyages' coming to an end, but so too was the West Africa to which Langdon travelled between 1881−1884. In November 1884, just four days before Langdon returned to Bristol from his final voyage, representatives of the European powers and America met in Berlin to discuss the political future of West Africa.[67] In July of that year, the Germans had moved into the Cameroons; in 1886 the French began their expansion on the Ivory Coast. As far as trading interests were concerned, it was those of Bristol, in particular, who were to lose out from this expansion by Germany and France into areas that the city had traded with since the start of its slave trade in the sixteenth century. Significantly, the German and French moves were accompanied by numerous protests − ineffectual in the event − from the Bristol Chamber of Commerce.[68] In more ways than a few, the picture drawn by Langdon of Bristol trade on the Ivory Coast and Cameroons in the 1880s is one that represents the end of an era.

[65] J.D. Hargreaves, *West Africa Partitioned*, I, *The Loaded Pause, 1885–89* (London, 1974), pp. 242–246; II, *The Elephants and the Grass* (London, 1985), pp. 51–60.
[66] Hargreaves, *Prelude*, pp. 316–338; Austen and Derrick, *Middlemen*, pp. 91–92.
[67] S.E. Crowe, *The Berlin West African Conference, 1884–1885* (London, 1942); S. Förster, W.J. Mommsen, and R. Robinson, *Bismarck, Europe and Africa: the Berlin Africa Conference 1884–85 and the Onset of Partition* (Oxford, 1988).
[68] Bristol Chamber of Commerce Annual Report, 1884, pp. 97–98; 1885, pp. 9–10; 1890, pp. 14, 90–92; Minutes of Bristol Chamber of Commerce, vol. 8, 27 November 1889, 22 January 1890; R. & W. King to Granville, 23 December 1884, FO 403/48, R. & W. King to Salisbury, 18 January 1892, FO 854/2240.

FIRST VOYAGE

1 March 1881 to 10 September 1882

'Hurrah! Hurrah! I've a ship at last.' Such was my inward exclamation, when the Master of the barque *Ceara*[1] of Bristol told me that I was to become ship's boy on a trading voyage to the West Coast of Africa. This occurred towards the end of February, 1881, one of the coldest winters of the 19th century. Could it be true, after months and months of sea lust, and, during my spare time walking along the quays, looking longingly and lovingly at the smart windjammers, which were to be seen in our harbour at that period. My time had not been wasted, however, for whenever a ship was laid up, and the watchman absent, I was climbing the rigging and yards, and well remember the glow of pride, which was occasioned by my first venture 'over the top' on the old barque *Look Out*. Hitherto, the lubber-hole[2] had been freely used for that purpose, being the easier way.

Was it a dream?

I was to sail in a week, and until then I had to work on the ship for which I was to receive fifteen shillings: during the voyage my wages were to be one pound per month.[3] Visions of exalted wealth rose before me, and I there and then sported ten-pence half-penny for a cheese-cutter cap with a gilt cord.

Kind folk advised me not to go: they said it was a dog's life; and my employer offered me an increase in wages. But no, I was a free lance. My mother had passed away some three years ago, and there was no one to say to me thou shall, or thou shalt not. Besides, had I not for a year fended for myself on a very small wage, and known what it was to tighten my belt towards the end of the week? Even if my new venture was to be a dog's life, it could not be worse than the one I had been living: indeed, I anticipated that it would be better. Moreover, I fully realised, even then, that for me it was either get on, or get off, and here was the means to an end.

[1] 293 tons, R. & W. King, owners, *Bristol Presentments*, 14 September 1882.
[2] The lubber-holes were holes which afforded easier access for the inexperienced sailor while climbing a mast than using the ratlines.
[3] Langdon may have been receiving the going rate for an apprentice seaman; however, his wages were low compared to ordinary seamen in the African trade; M. Lynn, 'The profitability of the early nineteenth century palm oil trade', *African Economic History*, 20 (1992), pp. 77–97.

I spent that week stowing away cabin stores, until all the lockers, store-rooms and 'lazaretto'[4] were filled to overflowing. My word! What cart-loads of tinned provisions, fruit, vegetables, rice, flour, wines, and 'bass's',[5] a huge medicine chest, with twenty-eight pounds of Epsom salts, etc.

At last signing-on day came, and even now I can hear the shipping master (Attwood) reading the ship's articles, with Thompson and Learway, the Board of Trade 'runners', standing by.[6] The articles were duly signed. Outside the pimps and parasites were waiting to fleece the sailormen of their advance notes. 'Hi, lad, I'll cash your advance note; come and have a drink.' It did not come off with me, oh no; for although young in years I had some knowledge of boarding-house runners and shanghai tricks. My note was cashed by a respectable tradesman.

Eventually, the great day arrived. 'Sailing day March 1st. Join your ship at Bathurst Basin, 6 a.m. Attwood.' Well do I remember that early morn, as [...] I [...] trudged the dear old streets of Bristol. The snow from the recent great snow-storm was piled high in the Haymarket.

On board at last. Good-bye was said. 'Bon voyage' from the shore; and away we went.

What confusion! The crew were drunk, but it did not matter, for there were runners on board to handle the gun-powder, which was to be taken in at Kingroad, where the ship swung to the tide.[7] 'Let go!' came from the pilot. What a clatter and vibration are caused by the letting go of the anchor; it was a terrific din to a green-horn.

'Fires out!'

A lighter hauled alongside and fifty tons of powder were stowed in the magazine aft. Bum-boats brought beer from Pill for the crew.[8] The skipper was absent, and the mate in charge. Both this latter and the second mate made a raid on the bass in the cabin, and, having told me to get a corkscrew, which I could not find, they gave me my first lesson in cutting off the neck of a bottle with a knife, and pouring out the liquid without making a froth.

---

[4] The lazaretto was the space between decks used as a store room or quarantine bay.

[5] Presumably Bass ale.

[6] The Board of Trade was responsible for regulating the merchant marine. Its responsibilities included administering the Merchant Shipping Acts, examining the seaworthiness of ships, checking officers' certificates and the supervision of the engagement, payment and discharge of seamen. Langdon is using 'runner' in the sense of agent.

[7] Given the dangers associated with loading gunpowder in port, it was the practice for this to be loaded at sea. Kingroad referred to the stretch of water between Portishead and the mouth of the Avon, where this could be undertaken safely.

[8] Bum boats were responsible for carrying provisions to vessels. The village of Pill lies on the left bank of the Avon near the mouth of the river.

The mate 'had the wind up'.

The second mate had a great thirst – almost 'dead-o', but still wanted more – more, until at last he was full and had to be carried to his bunk, which was over mine. Besides, he had done much hard drinking ashore. The rats were now coming on. It may be said, what did I know of these things? I got to know much from observation, and without any revelation my mind was then and is now fixed to keep to the tea-pot.

It was evening, at early tide, the barque *Cambria*,[9] bound for Cameroons, West Africa, and in charge of Captain Williams, passed us at Kingroad. One of our crew remarked 'There goes another coffin-ship, she's loaded right to the plimsoll mark.[10] Salt in bulk.[11] Her bottom will drop out. When I was in her on such and such a voyage, we spent three out of every four hours at the pumps. Nobody would take her except young Williams, and he only to get a first command. Somebody is going to get the insurance.' That night it blew great guns – the sunset and sailormen were right. The *Cambria* was never again heard of, and it was supposed that she had foundered near Lundy.[12]

The second evening. The skipper returned with the pilot, ready to sail early the next morning. At the last moment, a Mr Smith, the second mate on the barque *Mervyn*,[13] was to sail with us as a passenger. We already had a negro boy as passenger, and there were only three bunks for five sleepers. Something had to be fixed up. The skipper had a look round and there was a fuss made about the bass and the state of the second mate, who was very ill, and would not be fit for duty for some length of time. It was blowing too hard to have him sent ashore. The mate too wished to leave, but on account of the weather he had to carry on. It was arranged that Mr Smith was to act as second mate, and have my bunk. I was to be in his watch and sleep on a locker, and the negro boy was to sleep on the other. This, however, did not answer, for our second mate was kicking up a terrific shindy in his delirium, and Smith could not sleep, so he shared the first mate's shake-down.

The next morning we manned the windlass, and there was a feeble attempt at a shanty, but singing was impossible, the fumes of the drink had not worn off. The topsails were shaken out, and we sailed

[9] 231 tons.

[10] This refers to the loading line marked on ships, established by the Act of 1876 following the campaign led by Samuel Plimsoll.

[11] Bulk salt was a staple of the African trade in the nineteenth century and much in demand on the coast for trading inland in order to purchase palm oil and other produce; A.J.H. Latham, 'Palm oil exports from Calabar, 1812–1887', with a note on the formation of oil prices to 1914', in G. Liesegang, H. Pasch, and A. Jones (eds), *Figuring African Trade* (Berlin 1986), pp. 265–296.

[12] i.e. Lundy island in the Bristol channel.

[13] 288 tons, R. & W. King, owners. Presumably named after Mervyn King (1844–1934), son of William King.

before a north-easterly gale. How I itched to be with the men who were manning the yards, but I was feeling too queer. 'Well, Jerry (my ship's name), how do you feel?' 'Alright, sir.' But I didn't. For some time I had tried to hide the fact that I was feeling queer, but no, I had to go to the lee rail, and up it came. I here received my first baptism in salt water, for we shipped a lee roller, which soaked me up to the neck.

We were then off Rat Island (Lundy), and had been sailing for seven hours. I heard the skipper say, with a Yankee twang, 'Waal, Mr Pilot, I guess as your boat is not here to pick you up, I shall have to take you to sea, and land you at Madeira.' 'Waal, Mr Captain', the pilot replied, 'if the boat was here, I guess I could not board her in such a running sea. I'm going below, your course is so and so'.

I lay on my locker in my wet clothes, and to add to my discomfort, a flashlamp filled with turpentine had got adrift from its hook, and crashed down upon my head, saturating my pillow and clothes. What a night! I heard the mate calling 'Pilot, will you come on deck, there are lights all around, and land to the south?' As far as I was concerned, I did not care if she went ashore. At last morning came round and the skipper said, 'Jerry, you're in a bad way, go for'ard, get a bunk and stay there until you are better.' I found a bunk in the fore peak of the fo'c'sle, dark and smelly; just the place into which a cat would crawl to die, away from the vulgar gaze of everybody. It was heaven to me, away from the grinning face of the negro boy. I was now with the so-called common sailormen. Thank God this was not true, although, poor devils, most of their misfortunes were caused by the pimps and parasites on shore. 'Hi, lad, have a dish of tea and a bite.' That tea! How delicious! No milk in it, except the milk of human kindness. Four nationalities were represented in that crowd, and with only one exception they were real white men.

We were then three days out, and I felt better, especially after taking some food, which I had been without for thirty-six hours. During the late afternoon watch I heard a cry of 'Sail O', and went up on deck for a peep. I was spotted by the skipper, who called out, 'Jerry, come aft', and I received my first lesson in flag-wagging. The sail turned out to be the barquetine *Queen of the South*, bound for Bristol. 'Will you take a Bristol pilot?' 'Rather!' Both the ships heaved to. Getting out the gig took some time because it was inboard and filled with lumber, and the sea being very choppy, great care had to be taken in dropping her at the right moment. However, it was managed at last, and, with the mate in command, the gig, now on the crest of a wave, now in the trough, sped towards the *Queen of the South*. The return was safely accomplished without a smash. It appeared to me at the time that the boat was thought to be of more value than the men's lives. 'Square the yards!' and away we sailed southward. The skipper was elated at having saved the pilot's fare home from Madeira.

I was now getting my sea legs, was sent back to duty in the cabin, and was told to share a watch at night with the acting second mate. I got very little sleep, but I didn't mind. I was not allowed to mix with the scum for'ard, and on the whole I was happy. The black boy, 'Koffee', whose native name commenced with a big B, was bumptious. 'He was the son of a King.' We scrapped, and I came off second best, for the simple reason that I kept the rules of fair play, and he didn't. Later on we scrapped again, and that time I used his own tricks. Just as I was about to give him 'fum-fum' (native word), I was pulled off. Of course, it would not do for 'Koffee' to return home with marks on his beautiful visage. Mine did not matter. After this he was more respectful, and we were chums.

In future I shall indicate the officers and some of the crew by their nicknames, as this will greatly facilitate what I have to say with regard to their characteristics. Mine, as already stated, was Jerry.

The skipper was known as 'Pincher', and he was; just your pound and pint in rations; pompous.[14] When dealing with any transgressors he always said the same thing, 'There was a time when I could have flogged you for that', or for a more serious offence, 'I have power to shoot you for that'. It was said that on a former voyage a real old devil dare sea-dog replied, 'Shoot, Captain, shoot, but, by —— if you miss, you will never shoot again.' Of work-up Joe (punishment) he had many, the worst being that of polishing the copper on the ship's side down to the water edge, slung in a bowline. We were in shark-infested waters!

Is my pen able to describe 'Mister Mate'? A gentleman. During that long voyage I never knew him to bully anyone, not even the boy. Here I must fit in one of the many bits of philosophy heard in the fo'c'sle. This one was between the ship's boy and a dog. 'Rover, do you know that the Captain is down on the Mate, that the Mate is down on the Second Mate, the Second Mate on the men, the men on the boy, and, Rover, I'm down on you.' He then commenced to pommel the dog. The reason why 'Pincher' could not get on with 'Mister Mate' was because the men always spoke of him as 'Mister', and were always ready at his commands – out of respect, not fear. Cabin boys see and hear things while waiting at table. 'Mister Mate's' table manners were above reproach. One could easily see that he was trying to heal the breach, but it was impossible, he was a new hand to the coast, and what was happening was all in the usual programme, of which more anon. The yarns 'Mister Mate' told at table would fill a book. Just one briefly: his father was a captain in the Chinese trade, piracy was rife,

---

[14] Captain Swan.

and his mother, who sailed with him, had on several occasions been put in a barrel, given a revolver and told to shoot herself if the ship was overpowered.

The Second Mate, 'Old Shocker', was a Scotchman, and had always been in the West Coast trade: he was morose. When speaking to 'Pincher', he would take off his glengary cap and shoot his quid of tobacco into it. Nobody took any notice of him.

Then there was 'For'ard Bung', the cooper,[15] and 'Moses', the cook, a nib[16] when drunk and could not boil water without burning it.

Next, a well-educated Swede, an able seaman, sailing in English ships to gain experience. He had been away from home six years and was going back after this trip. He always did any cubic measurement which wanted doing. A splendid fellow, from whom I learnt much.

Then there was a Norwegian, a fine type of man, but he was not with me long; he was transferred to a homebounder, with two others. This was done to save expense, for on the Coast 'Kroo Boy' labour is very cheap.[17]

'Old Joe', dear Old Joe ('I owe thee much') had sailed the Coast many years, had a beard almost white and a head as smooth as a billiard ball. He was very muscular and a good all-round hand, especially expert in stowing the oil casks. He had been with 'Pincher' a number of voyages, was scrupulously clean and his clothes were always neatly mended. From 'Old Joe' I learnt splicing, knots and heaps and heaps of things useful to know on a ship; and above all he gave me sound advice. 'If, lad, I had started like you, things would have been different; now its Davy Jones' Locker or the workhouse. Beer and women have been my ruin: it's the same with most sailormen.' He told me several sordid yarns of Bristol Boarding Houses, naming several. 'There's that one on the quay, kept by old mother R——', he said, 'who used to give the gals on the street so much a week to live

---

[15] As casks were needed to store palm oil, it was the practice to convey these to West Africa in shooks of staves in order to leave space for the outward cargo. The casks were then put together by the ship's cooper once the ship had arrived on the coast.

[16] A slang term for a gentleman, meaning unclear in this context.

[17] It was usual for British ships involved in the African trade to collect crew from the Kru region of modern Liberia and Ivory Coast to undertake the hard labour on board ship, and particularly the loading of palm oil, once West Africa had been reached. The Kru had great experience in the maritime trade and had the further advantage of being cheaper than labour from Britain; G.E. Brooks, *The Kru Mariner in the 19th Century* (Newark, DL, 1972); J. Martin, 'Krumen "down the coast": Liberian migrants on the West African coast in the 19th and early 20th centuries', *International Journal of African Historical Studies*, 18 (1985), pp. 401–423; E. Tonkin, 'Creating Kroomen: ethnic diversity, economic specialism and changing demand', in J.C. Stone (ed), *Africa and the Sea* (Aberdeen, 1985), pp. 27–47; D. Frost, *Work and Community Among West African Migrant Workers since the Nineteenth Century* (Liverpool, 1999).

with us men, we were soon skinned and then chucked on an outward-bounder, drunk'.

Lastly, 'Cockney', an ordinary seaman, who served on the training ship *Formidable*, was far from being wholesome in either language or ways. He was slovenly, dirty; and because of this he had a rough time. He thought the men were down upon him. Rot! They would have treated him alright if he had acted decently.

One morning, when I turned in at 4 am, after I had been keeping mid-watch, I found 'Old Shocker' in a bad way, tossing in his bunk, and murmuring 'They've got me; let go, there's thousands of 'em'. I dropped off to sleep, but later awoke and saw him getting out of his bunk, dressed only in his vest. He went into the fore-cabin, then on to the main deck, up the companion ladder to the poop-deck. (The ship's cabin was on deck, with a low bucket rail, alley-ways on each side.) The ship well heeled over, and was rolling. The helmsman was the only person who had seen what was happening, and, not daring to leave the wheel, shouts out 'Captain, come on deck, quick'. 'Old Shocker' takes a spring, but I already had hold of his vest, and we rolled on to the deck together. 'Pincher' arrived and sat on him. 'Mister Mate, why in the —— don't you look after the ship? Another moment and they would have been overboard'. (This was the only time I ever heard 'Pincher' hold forth.) 'Sorry, sir', said 'Mr Mate', 'I was working for'ard'. 'Get a canvas jacket', said 'Pincher', 'and put him into it'. This had to be done for the poor fellow was raving. 'Pincher' was not unkind in this, indeed he had, and was doing, all he could for poor 'Old Shocker'. The same evening he said, 'Mr Mate, I'm going to give the second mate opium. It's kill or cure. You measure it out and sign the log'. 'Shocker' was given some weak brandy. 'Good', said 'Pincher', 'I'll save him yet'. And he did.

We now sailed into lovely weather. Every hour was an experience. 'Pincher' showed me how to make a reef-knot. I made some grannies and they were spotted. 'Jerry, what's this?' 'Reef-knots, Sir', I replied. 'They're not', retorted 'Pincher', 'if you made a grannie on a top sail it would jam, and somebody might lose his life. I shan't show you again. Make them properly, else you'll get no breakfast'. I made them properly.

I've done it. Hurrah! Been aloft. First day over the top, (not so easy as on the old *Look Out*), second day, the cross-trees, third, the royal yard.[18] I was sitting on the yard and looking down on the white sails, bellied out. Wasn't it glorious! The lovely blue sea and sky. It was good to be alive. The truck[19] was only five feet above me, a bare mast pole —

---

[18] i.e. the topmost part of the mast.
[19] The truck was a small block of wood through which the rigging was threaded.

no rigging. 'Pincher' was looking up. Could I do it? I must. I remembered my first lamp-post climb in Bristol. I stood on the yard. One, two, three, and I'm up. I put my arm over the truck and hung on for about a minute, and then slid back to the yard. My heart was going pit-a-pat. Finally, I returned to the deck and 'Pincher' said, 'Jerry, you've been to the royal yard. In future that sail is yours. Whenever it has to be stowed, watch on deck or below, you've got to do it. Fetch my ruler.' I thought I was going to 'cop it', but on handing him the ruler, he tied his pocket-handkerchief to it, saying, 'This is the main royal'. He then showed me how a sail was furled. (Mr Mate, when my watch below, had ignored this order on many occasions.) A few days after a squall came on and the sail had to be taken in. 'Up you go', said 'Pincher', 'and mind you don't fall overboard'. It was hard work, but I did it.

On an outward-bound West Coast trader there is much work to be done in preparation for carrying on trade. Our winter sail had already been unbent and the summer suit bent (replaced). Many lengths of canvas hose had to be made to carry the oil from the starting tub[20] amidships to each end of the ship. Heavy planks had to be nailed over the main deck to save damage from the casks. The cooperage on the port-bow had also to be planked. 'Bung' had to make oaken pegs, cut up empty tins for patches, and get everything ready for cask-making. The fore-hatch was to be opened immediately the weather could be depended upon, and the Packs (casks packed in small compass) and hoops had to be got out.[21] This, however, could not be until we had passed the Doldrums.

We saw a ship on the weather-bow without sails, and this being rather unusual we bore down. It turned out to be an American whaler, cutting in a whale. We could see the men cutting in. I could then watch the very thing which had so much delighted me to read about.

Up till then the weather had been most delightful, but, on nearing the Doldrums, it changed. What rain, lightning and thunder! It was terrific. I liked watching it nevertheless; it had always fascinated me. The sky was black with clouds, and at times very heavy squalls rose, and then a dead calm. The wind boxed the compass. While 'Pincher' was having supper, a water-spout was reported on the port-beam, and he rushed on deck at once; I, of course, following. 'There are three, and another forming', said he, 'if they come too close we'll put a shot into them'. I was expecting this, as I had read that anything passing through a water-spout would break it. (Moreover it was one of my

---

[20] The starting tub was the cask on deck into which purchases of palm oil would be poured.

[21] i.e. packs of shooks.

duties to clean and oil once a week some guns and revolvers, with orders not to touch a certain one as it was loaded. I had surmised it was for this purpose.) I watched the spout forming. At a point in the dense black cloud an inverted peak was forming downwards, and underneath the water was in great commotion. A great mass of water ascended spiral-like and branched out like a vine. At last it burst, and the great mass of water fell. Everybody, except the helmsman, who had his south-wester well down, took shelter. There was no wind. Couldn't be. Breathing was affected. We felt as though we were in a glass case looking through greenish water. For a time we could not clear the decks of the tons of water. It was up to the hatches, and the ship was deep in the water, but we gradually rose, and then came heavy rain. Our fresh water tanks and barrels were filled with rain water, for the water had begun to be tasty, since it was stored in palm-oil casks. Everybody had a family wash. I washed 'Pincher's' shirts and vests. My own were a small affair, for my wardrobe was scanty, having been bought with my advance note and a few shillings I had saved. Thanks to 'Old Joe', it was kept well mended. 'Patch upon patch and patch over all.'

All, except 'Cockney' and 'Pincher', then had a nature's shower bath in the rain. It was warm; it was jolly. 'Cockney' did not like water, and 'Pincher' had a bath in his cabin every morning, regardless of water allowance.

In a week we were again in fine weather, with Old Sol showering down his burning rays. It was a lovely blue sea, with Portuguese men of war with sails set, and flying fish skimming over the surface. Yes, I know, chased by Beneto Albicore I had my first lesson in catching these fish. I had to go out on the jib-boon[22] with 'Moses', and a fish-hook baited with white rag. Flip 'em on the surface to imitate a flying fish. Always hook 'em in the upper jaw. A bite! Haul up and mind the spines. Put your fingers, like this, up the gills, and bring them up through the mouth. 'He'll bite', I said. 'No, he won't, he can't breathe.' I then got an electric shock, and found myself handling a live ten-pounder, sprinkling blood. 'Take him aboard and bring out some rattling line. Don't mess up the sails with blood.' (It was a crime on ship to stain a sail, and when it did occur, one would hear 'There was a time when I could dock your wages for the damage done.' The elder men confirmed this.) To get back over the foot-ropes with a struggling fish in one hand and holding on with the other, was no easy job. But it had to be done, and it was. Thereafter I was a fisherman. Every after-watch below, and fish about, I was at it. Fine sport.

'Old Shocker' was convalescent, basking in the sun. The men were

---

[22] Presumably jib-boom.

very kind to him and made him very comfy, for he had been very near death. He had had his hair cut and his beard trimmed, and looked more like a human being. He had become very grey.

Night after night I kept watch with the acting second mate. The men said he was a 'Square-head, a Yaw-Yaw, a German'; he wouldn't talk, and had much side (at least, I think so). He gave me to understand that the weathered side of the ship was his, and the lee mine. I couldn't understand why there should be so much caste on shipboard. He had orders to 'keep that young beggar aft'. Couldn't be done. 'I will report you'; said the second mate. Reprimand after reprimand followed. 'There was a time, etc'. The men acted as a magnet to me. I drunk in their yarns. I wanted to know, to find out things, to ask questions. And the men willingly answered and helped me.

It was during the night watch with all the lee main deck to myself, that I found myself with little or nothing to do, and four hours in which to do it. I had to keep aft a bit until the last bust up had simmered down. 'Never had such a boy. There was a time, etc'. Was I lonely? No, far from it. I had the lovely moon, the glorious stars, the phosphorescent sea, the lapping waves and the gentle breeze. It was all music. I sat and thought. Picture after picture glided by. My first day at school. Picking linen rags for the poor wounded soldiers (1871).[23] My schoolmaster – 'Read, read, boys, it will serve you well in life'. Old King Street Free Library, eight o'clock until ten; how quickly the time went! Home through the dark narrow Marsh St, every footfall seemed startlingly loud; I had been reading *The Phantom Ship*.[24] That hell at the end of the street, the 'Ship and Castle', where boys and girls, not much older than myself, were drinking. If they only knew.

'In the Haymarket, where all flesh is grass,
But grass makes hay, 'tis human hay, alas!'

These lines seemed to fit: I read them over several times to fix them on my memory. (I had been reading, surreptitiously, a book in the cabin, called *Evils of London Life*, but it had been locked away. I had a sort of idea that 'Koffee' had narked.) That proud day, when a third standard boy whacked the whole school at geography. I loved it. The inspector made me come forward and stand on a platform. 'This boy', he said, 'has a wonderful knowledge of geography; he should be a sailor'. He didn't ask how I knew. If he had, I should have told him that I had two brothers at sea, and that I just drank in everything they said. I was the fourth now. My mother was always ill; had fits. I heard the doctor say she must not be left alone. I stayed home from play

---

[23] This must refer to the Franco-Prussian war of 1870–1871. Langdon would have been seven.

[24] Probably F. Marryat, *The Phantom Ship* (London, 1839).

many a time, but she did not know it; and I did want to play. Then my last day at school. Didn't know it was to be the last, and I only eleven years and four months to the day. At work. I've got a ship. What had I learnt since then: Heaps and heaps. 'Mr Mate' had let me have *An Epitome of Navigation*, a most wonderful book.[25] Why had not my teacher at school told me what geometry was? Perhaps he did not know. The compass was easy, except the lubber's point, and 'Old Joe' put that right. Latitude was easy, too, each being equal, but longitude was more difficult as these went off to nothing at the Poles. Everything appeared to come from circles. Almost every day I held open the chart for 'Pincher', because he would not use pins, and spot how he ruled out the course. The world is round, we were sailing south, the north star every night was sinking lower, the Southern cross was rising higher in the sky. That proved it. 'Jerry, what are you doing?' 'Nothing, sir', I replied. 'The binnacle light is out and you were asleep.' 'No, sir', I was thinking. I wondered if he would tell 'Pincher' that I was asleep on watch. Although I wasn't.

We were then sailing in lovely weather. Some days light breezes, others a dead calm. 'Pincher' would walk the poop-deck whistling for wind. It would be a crime for anyone else to whistle. It was very hot and the tar on the deck was melting. For some time past I had discarded boots, wearing only trousers and shirt. I was sure-footed aloft, coming down hand over hand, or if the sails were being hoisted on the halliards, I landed on the men's shoulders who would exclaim that the young beggar ought to have a tail.

The general work of the ship is now complete, and the work of a trading voyage will now begin.

As yet, of course, I was but an apprentice hand, and to try and describe trading on the West Coast, I must use mature knowledge and explain any subject or item, for the sake of clearness, as we proceed.

The fore, main and after hatches being lifted, cockroaches began to crawl out in scores, and a few rats were seen. These were to become a pest before we left the coast. A good supply of packs and hoops, with which 'Bung' was kept busy making casks, would be later loaned to the natives for oil. The after hold had the next attention, most of the cargo in which was hoisted on deck so as to get to the ground tier. Planks had already been laid to form the floor or deck and this was to be the 'Trade room'. Cases of each kind of merchandise were kept together. 'Pincher' superintended, and when finished it was a general store. I will try to remember what were the goods in stock, and later give a brief description of a few items. Gunpowder, guns, rum, gin,

---

[25] Mrs Janet Taylor, *An Epitome of Navigation and Nautical Astronomy with the Improved Lunar Tables* (9th edn, London, 1842).

ginger, wine, tobacco in leaf, pipes and snuff-boxes, flimsy fabrics of all shades and patterns (each had a special name), second-hand coats (unredeemed pledges), sheets, rugs, manillas[26] (native money tokens), clocks, odd pots and pans of all descriptions, fish-hooks, small needles and thick threads, neptunes, trade-boxes, odd crockery-ware, odd bed-room-ware, odd cutlery, scissors, razors, brushes, boys' tool chests (list of tools on lid, but many missing), trashy jewelry, pomade, scent, soap, salt, mirrors, glass tumblers, umbrellas, etc.[27]

The West Coast must be a happy hunting ground for dumping goods not saleable at home. Everything was most shoddy, oddments or throw-outs.[28] The guns were six feet in length, with a very short curved shoulder, painted red, flint and pan, and were packed twelve in a case.[29] The cases were sometimes used as coffins. Neptunes were thin copper discs four feet in diameter, used for the evaporation of sea water to obtain salt. Manillas were native money tokens, valued at 2½d, made in Bristol under currency rules, and were used for exchange.[30] They were used also as a bond of good faith in the settlements, the debtor and creditor each taking hold of a manilla, breaking it between

[26] Manillas (from the Latin, *manus*) were horseshoe-shaped tokens used as a currency. They were made of an alloy of copper and lead and were common on the Ivory Coast and in the Niger Delta and its hinterland. They came in various sizes, with different varieties being utilized in different areas. First used by Portuguese traders in the sixteenth century, they ceased to be legal tender in southern Nigeria in 1911. By the nineteenth century, Bristol had emerged as a major centre of production for manillas, this being linked into Bristol trade with the Ivory Coast; W. Babington, 'Remarks on the general description of the trade on the West Coast of Africa', *Journal of the Society of Arts*, 23 (1875), pp. 245–257; A.H.M. Kirk-Greene, 'The major currencies in Nigerian history', *Journal of the Historical Society of Nigeria*, 2 (1960), pp. 132–150.

[27] This is a fairly typical cargo manifest for the African trade. Customer taste varied sharply from area to area, and consequently traders needed a great variety of goods, particularly textiles, in order to trade on a long stretch of coast. Bold, in 1822, stressed how precise and particular customers were in West Africa; E. Bold, *Merchants' and Mariners' Guide* (London, 1822), p. 60.

[28] In this judgement Langdon is reflecting a later view. Contrary to the belief that Africans accepted 'throw-outs' and suchlike, in the nineteenth century at least, their choice was very particular. See Bold, above, and Laird to the 1843 Parliamentary Committee on Africa quoted in M. Johnson, 'Cloth on the banks of the Niger', *Journal of the Historical Society of Nigeria*, 6 (1973), p. 354.

[29] These flintlocks were more usually termed 'dane guns'. Firearms were a major import into West Africa in the nineteenth century, and accounted for some 12 per cent of the value of British exports to the Windward Coast in 1850, second only to textiles. At the Brussels Convention of 1890 European powers agreed not to sell firearms to Africans; J.E. Inikori, 'West Africa's seaborne trade, 1750–1850, volume, structure and implications', in Liesegang, Pasch, and Jones, *Figuring African Trade*, pp. 49–88.

[30] Hutchinson estimated the value of manillas at 3d each in the 1850s; T.J. Hutchinson, *Impressions of Western Africa* (London, 1858), pp. 255–256. According to Babington, by the 1870s they were valued at 3d each on the Ivory Coast; Babington, 'Remarks on the general description of the trade', p. 249.

them, and retaining the two halves until settlement day, when they were returned. Trade-boxes were collapsible and put together on the coast. The native must have a box. In the 'Trade-room' there was a large cask which would hold 250 gallons, and was called the 'dash-rum cask' – 'dash' means discount.[31] No matter how small the service or transaction, the native must have dash. He thought he was getting something for nothing. We'll see. On the main deck the casks of rum were hoisted from the main hatch, and from them were extracted, according to size, three, four, five, or six gallons, which were replaced with fresh or salt water. The abstracted rum was poured into the 'Dash' rum cask with a liberal supply of brackish water; a quantity of tobacco leaves were added to give it fillip. We were also kept busy making 'Dash' heads of tobacco – two or three leaves rolled at the top. Everything was now ready to start trading, and it was only a matter of time to sight the coast and reach our first trading town. It was here I had my first pleasure of a shark hunt. There were three large ones under the stern, accompanied by a pilot fish. A swivel hook was baited with salt pork for a bite, but it was of no use, for the shark took the hook on the side of the jaw and before a running bowling reached him, had broken away. Sharks should always be hooked in the top jaw.

Land ho! We bore towards it and soon saw a canoe making for us. 'Koffee' also made for the cabin sharp, and when he returned he was dressed in his native costume. Asked why he took off his trousers, he replied, pointing to the land and the canoe, 'Dem be grand debil land, and my people would say I had a witch if I had on trouser'. Such was one of the many superstitions of the coast. Two young fellows boarded us from the canoe – fishermen, and 'Koffee' received them with some dignity. I heard the salutation for the first time, 'I-U-I-U-Ka', and each snapped his fingers. 'What land is that?' we asked. 'Cape Palmas. Dash, cappy, Dash', and we gave them two rums and two 'Dash' heads. I noted that 'Koffee', before handing them the rum, sipped it himself, as a proof that it was not poisoned. This was the custom, and to omit to sip would be considered an insult. Nevertheless, there is much poison used, even though drinks are sipped beforehand.

We let go the anchor at Covally River,[32] a few miles below Cape Palmas, and ere long two white men came aboard, an American trader and a Missionary.[33] 'What's the news of the world? Got any newspapers?'

---

[31] More generally used in West Africa to mean 'present' or 'gift'; from the Portuguese, *dar* 'to give'.

[32] More usually spelt Cavally River. Robertson in 1819 spoke of 'considerable trade' at Cavally, while Babington in 1875 found very little trade along the next sixty miles of the coast; G.A. Robertson, *Notes on Africa* (London, 1819), pp. 67–81 ; Babington, 'Remarks on the general description of the trade', p. 248.

[33] American Protestant missionaries had been based at Cape Palmas since 1838.

was their greeting. 'Yes,' said 'Pincher', 'about eight to ten weeks old. Have a bass.' 'Rather!' and three bottles were opened. 'That's the first we've had for months', they said. 'Pincher' asked them to dinner, which was served in the state cabin. (I noted that 'Mr Mate' was not invited.) The best family plate was laid on a new table cloth, and I thought I should hear the missionary talk about his good work among the poor black men, but I was somewhat surprised at the way in which he mopped off the bass. But to see a real live missionary was great. I was disappointed, however, for during dinner nothing was said about his mission work, the conversation being all about trade and the Grand Debil, who was supposed to reside in a cave not far from this place, and to whom the natives made pilgrimages, bringing gifts and offerings from far and near. 'Pincher' asked whether he was ever seen. 'Of course not', said the missionary, 'deities are never seen'. 'Then what becomes of the gifts?' inquired 'Pincher'. 'Oh, we both see to that', replied the missionary.

The next day we heaved up from Covally River, and this time the men manned the windlass with a jolly rollicking shanty, well knowing that the next time she came up the Kroo boys would do it. The sails were set, and we sailed down the coast with a good sea-breeze. This wind blows from the west-south-west almost regularly every day, except during the month of November, when the Harmatton blows from the east.[34] This is a cold, dry wind and it makes the natives themselves shiver. In my spare time I tried to take in the coast scenery, much of which was low-lying land, with golden sandy shore, on which the white surf broke. There were also numerous palm trees.

It was Good Friday,[35] and I could not get the thought out of my head of 'One a penny, two a penny, all hot buns'. How jolly to earn a few pence for an extra at Easter. 'One box of paper collars, size 12½, and two fronts, please, Miss. Plain, or frilled? Plain, please. Eight-pence half-penny, please. Thank you.' None of that now, but nevertheless, you're a lucky boy, Jerry. How many Bristol boys would like your job? I remember another Good Friday, 1877 – horrible day! Shall I ever forget it? While out at play I discovered sixpence in my pocket – mother's change. I had the bright idea to buy buns and sell them, but I speck a failure: nothing doing; I ate the buns and went home. Nothing was said, but oh, my conscience! A few days after mother had her last fit. She knows all about it now. Oh, the bitter remorse!

'Man the port braces, we're heading off land.' 'What's up?' I heard one of the coast men say 'Pincher' will give Berraby[36] a wide berth, for

---

[34] Usually spelt Harmattan; this wind from the east and northeast can bring with it considerable quantities of dust.

[35] 15 April 1881.

[36] Grand-Bérébi in modern Côte d'Ivoire. Given changes in economic fortunes, not all of the towns mentioned in Langdon's narrative have easily identifiable modern

if the Berraby men catch him, he will get peppered. Peppering is a native summary justice, meted out to anyone who has incurred their displeasure, generally for over brutality or chicanery tricks in trading. It was carried out as follows. A crowd of natives would come on board in the usual way of trade, when the culprit was thrown overboard, and usually towed ashore. On reaching the shore he was peppered, i.e., every part of his body was coated with a thick solution of Chile peppers, special attention being given to the eyes and other delicate parts. He had then to run the gauntlet of the whole town armed with sticks, and lastly was given over to the women, who performed actions too disgusting to write about. He was then returned to his ship, generally to die. I heard a fully corroborated story of a man getting out of this peppering. Captain P—— when serving as mate had incurred the natives' displeasure, and was taken ashore in the usual way for peppering. He was, I know, a very tall and commanding man, who by sheer bluff and playing on their superstition, fearlessly addressed them something like this – 'Do what you like, me no care, you no savey me got witch, you no kill me; you tink so, and after, I come again your town and fita bring small-pox, crock-raw (ring-worm) and all the diseases known'. Needless to say, he so played on their imagination and superstition that he was returned to his ship uninjured.

'Man the star-board braces.' 'Pincher' had now passed his danger zone, and we were again running near the shore, and early next morning we let go the anchor at Grand Drewin,[37] our first trading town.

At dawn I had a good look at the land, and to my mind it was the prettiest I had seen, or was yet to see, on the coast. For about three miles the land rose some two hundred and fifty feet, well wooded. In fact, it reminded me of Leigh Woods.[38] I spotted a clearing near the top, which turned out to be a small village, for I could see the stockade round it, and the black people were looking at our ship. At Grand Drewin Town they swarmed through the stockade and launched large and small canoes. We watched them paddle through the surf. At times they appeared to stand almost on end. When they got into smooth water they formed up. There were six large and many small canoes.

equivalents. However, a useful map giving the position of the towns and ports of this coast in the 1840s can be found in the Appendix to the Madden report, *Parliamentary Papers* 1842, XII (551), p. 520f.

[37] Grand Drewin today refers to a beach and small hamlet close to Latéko, some six to seven miles to the west of Sassandra in Côte d'Ivoire. Adams refers to St Andrew's and Drewin together, 'the people here have a small quantity of ivory, for which they always wish an exorbitant price'; J. Adams, *Remarks on the Country Extending from Cape Palmas to the River Congo* (London, 1823), p. 3.

[38] On the left bank of the Avon on the outskirts of Bristol.

In the leading one sat King Quee and his son Atto, and all were singing a monotonous chant, and after each dip of the paddle it was swung over their heads and the stock end bumped on the gunwale of the canoe. Everything was done to rhythm. (This, I was told, was showing off.) They encircled the ship three times and then boarded. The King, his son and headmen are received at the gangway by 'Pincher'. 'Koffee's' father was there and a rubbing of noses followed. All was now excitement, for some two hundred or more natives were on our deck, and there was a lot of 'I-U-I-U-Kas' and snapping of fingers. Palm wine and fruits were plentiful. I tasted the wine for the first time and didn't think much of it. A taste for it had to be acquired, and, as Old Joe said, God help you when you have.

We will now see what was going on in 'Pincher's' state cabin. A grand palaver[39] with the King and his headmen was taking place concerning the goods we had to sell and the commodities they, too, would render in exchange – palm oil, gold dust, ivory, ebony, logwood, palm kernels, cokernuts. Rum (not 'Dash') flowed freely, and a good deal of tobacco and snuff was consumed. I heard some say that they expected to have ready within the next twelve months so many bonnys of oil.[40] Bonnys are casks made specially to fit in the surf boats, and hold about 110 gallons. 'Pincher' was now ready to accept their orders. Then came the great haggle, and, like the French onion men, the natives always asked for more than they knew they would get. The King's son acted as umpire and his decision was final. His awards were generally in 'Pincher's' favour, and his own, for he and his father drew a big commission on the transactions – via 'Dash'. Orders now came fast and furious, contracts were made and manillas were broken as a pledge of fulfilment.

It is necessary here to describe briefly how trade was carried on. In the first place our merchandise was sold on credit, and the natives having no word in their language for credit, the simple word 'trust' was used, i.e. we first of all sailed down the coast giving out 'trust'.[41] We should return several times to gather in whatever goods were ready. A very reliable headman would receive 75 per cent 'trust', others 50 per cent, and doubtful ones 25 per cent, the balance on or near completion of the contract with the return of the broken manilla. The

---

[39] The etymology of the word 'palaver' is unclear but it is may be derived from the Portuguese word *palavra* (speech), and by this period it had come to mean both a dispute and the negotiations to settle it.

[40] A bonny was a large cask for palm oil, named after the port of Bonny in the Niger Delta.

[41] i.e. credit in the form of goods. Trust was usually given out calculated according to a unit; on this part of the coast termed a 'round'; C.W. Newbury, 'Credit in early nineteenth-century West African trade', *Journal of African History*, 13 (1972), pp. 81–95.

King or headman had often to whip up the lesser men to pay. They are responsible only to a certain extent, for it sometimes happened that the harvest was at fault, and as a last resort, to save default, they would part with some of their niggers (slaves). William, King of Half Jack[42] and other well to do men were always ready to buy at a price. These poor wretches, by the way, were always carried as passengers.[43] Should a tradesman wilfully default it would mean taboo from all the other traders on that particular part of the coast.

Apart from trust trade there was what would be termed as petty cash sales. The small men and boys would bring to the ship almost every hour (save on Fetish days which occur every sixth day) small quantities of palm oil, kernels, cokernuts, etc, and these would be paid for 'on the nail' with the usual 'Dash'. These natives were so dense that they had no idea of measurement and sometimes most unfair advantage was taken.

With so many [...] crowded in the cabin it had become awfully stuffy, and having learnt much, I went out for some fresh air, if it could be got. On deck the Kroo-boys were being engaged – all Drewin boys, twenty-eight in number, thirteen to work the surf boat and the remainder for the ship. Their headman, 'Dabbery', was a fine stalwart man, prominently marked with a navel about the size of a small tea-cup, which was common – want of attention at birth. He tells them to give of their best to a good Cappy. And they will. He was a real leader, never expecting the boys to do what he would not do himself. He also had the power to flog, but this was not necessary, for the boys as a rule were a most cheerful set, always ready to work at any time. They now had a job for some twelve months or more, on very small pay and half a pint of rice per day. They were in 'Clover', as 'chop' (food) on shore was always very limited. Visions of wealth rose up, whereby they could save sufficient to buy a wife, which was to them the royal road to fortune. Wives and niggers did all the work on shore.

It had been a most exciting day, and I was glad to turn in at eight bells,[44] looking forward to the next day's work, when the trade room would be opened, and for some time I should be a shop assistant, serving out all manner of goods.

At six am I started my new duties. The Swede who had been with 'Pincher' on a former voyage was in charge, with two black assistants

---

[42] Modern Jacqueville, close to Abidjan in Côte d'Ivoire. In the early nineteenth century this was already an important source of palm oil; Robertson, *Notes*, p. 92.

[43] These 'passengers' were being used as pawns to guarantee trust; in effect this meant that Langdon's ship was being involved in a form of slaving. Given the abolition of Britain's slave trade in 1807, this was highly illegal behaviour; hence the captain's desire to avoid naval vessels.

[44] i.e. at the end of his watch, either 8 pm or midnight.

and myself. I might say in passing that these West Coast traders liked to train their own men for this particular kind of work, making them work up from cabin boy to trader. Years of special training were necessary before one was admitted inside the ring of traders. As before stated, our stock was in perfect order, and we knew just where to lay our hands on everything. We had many orders from yesterday to deal with. One will suffice to illustrate the lot. Take King Quee's order – one case of ginger wine, one hogshead of rum, two cases of guns, eight kegs of gunpowder, 200 heads of tobacco, six trade boxes, twelve neptunes, pomade, soap, scent – in short, something from almost every kind of merchandise we had in stock, including 40 pieces of cloth. Here I must explain that cloth means the flimsy fabrics, twelve yards to a piece. The natives had no word for calico or muslin, so the word cloth was used to cover every kind of fabric, except sheets and rugs. In addition to the orders the usual 'Dash' had to be made up in proportion to the size of the order. Cloth was also sold in small quantities of one fathom, which, before being wetted, was large enough to make a full-dress suit. Another class of customer had to be attended to – the petty cash dealer. Their small quantities of goods were brought to the ship and received by Mr Mate at the main deck gangway, who measured it, gave book (receipt), and took the order to 'Pincher', who shouted to the trade room to serve, say, four fathoms of cloth, heads of tobacco, rum, etc, with the usual 'Dash'. This kind of work was carried on day after day, until all the stock was sold.

The general routine on board a West Coast trader varied but little from day to day, save when sailing from place to place. For it was turn out at 5.30 am, have coffee, set to work at six, washing decks, cleaning brass, etc, 8 o'clock having breakfast, 8.30 start trade with Mr Mate at the main deck gangway to receive whatever might be brought on board, every [except?] ivory and gold dust, which 'Pincher' dealt with in the state cabin. The surf boat boys, who generally slept ashore, brought off next morning whatever oil might be ready, when it was sampled. Adulteration, at which they were adepts, had to be watched. The oil was then boiled,[45] and from the boiler it was poured into the starting tub, thence through the canvas hose to any part of the ship's hold, where 'Old Shocker' Joe and his gang filled and stowed away the casks. All small spaces were filled with cokernuts and the small breaker cask. The starting tub was one of the most trying jobs on board, what with the fierce sun and the heat from the boiling oil. At times it was almost unbearable. Oil, oil from morning till evening, and if one should get a splash of oil in the eye, it had almost the same effect as lime. 'Cockney' was given this work.

---

[45] Boiling was used to remove impurities such as water or dirt.

At night anchor watch had to be kept. 'Pincher' and Mr Mate had had another rumpus. 'Pincher' in future would keep to himself, would have his meals in his state cabin, and the two black servants would fare very little different to the crew. This, as before mentioned, was part of the programme to prevent a new officer to the coast getting a footing into the secrets of the trade. Among themselves the coast traders were very 'canny' with outsiders, and when all the trust was given out, their life became a round of pleasure. When in company with other ships, they met together for late dinner, cards and a sing-song. But if the 'scum' for'ard were to continue their sing-song beyond eight bells, there would be mutiny to pay. I felt very sorry for Mr Mate, for he became a very lone man. 'Old Shocker' would only grunt, and when off duty would turn in. Mr Mate could not, of course, chin wag with the men, but, with it all, he was a stoic. 'Well, Jerry', said Mr Mate, 'it can't last for ever'. His partiality for me I knew full well was noticed and my turn had yet to come.

We stayed at Grand Drewin about ten days, and our next trading place was Duke Walker's Town.[46] King Duke Walker was 'Koffee's' father. Almost the same scene will suffice at each place of call as that of Drewin. Our next call was Kromwell Town[47] and then Sassandrew River,[48] where the natives were the most overbearing I had seen on the coast, nearly always at war with the surrounding towns, theirs being well protected by the river, and the other people had very little chance to get at them. The Sassandrew men therefore had swollen heads, and they didn't omit to let other people know it. With a glow of pride they would point out the remains of a small ship lying on their beach, and say, 'Our fathers took that'. It appeared that a cute American some years ago had run down the coast and sold coal-dust for gunpowder. The next ship down belonged to an honest trader, and everybody except one boy were massacred. I little thought then that on another voyage my ship would get involved with these people. But that's another story.

Our next call was Trepoo,[49] where the land after leaving the river

[46] Untraced on modern maps, but clearly close to Sassandra in Côte d'Ivoire.

[47] Untraced but clearly close to Sassandra in Côte d'Ivoire.

[48] Sassandra in Côte d'Ivoire. Originally named São Andrea by the Portuguese, it was called St Andrews (or sometimes King George's Town) by the English. Its importance for maritime trade derived from the break in the surf that gave it a sheltered anchorage. Robertson in 1819 commented on the 'great trade' at this port, which he estimated as worth £4,000 pa; Robertson, *Notes*, pp. 75, 361. The reputation of its traders among visitors was however somewhat negative; an American supercargo in 1841 commented that 'St Andrews people are considered a treacherous set of scoundrels'; Brooks, *Kru Mariner*, p. 97.

[49] Untraced on modern maps but marked on the Madden report map between Sassandra and Fresco in Côte d'Ivoire; possibly modern Trepoint? In his 'Diary and

was low lying. Then we came to Kutrou[50] where we passed a cliff of iron stone, which affected our compass and also our Kroo boys, for they believed another 'grand debil' resided in those rocks. When passing they would turn their faces away from it, for one look might spell disaster for all time. I had no doubt a few cunning medicine men were doing good business with the iron ore. The 'grand debil' is only a gag. The ordinary native was so simple, he would believe anything either good or evil. I had acquired a few simple conjuring tricks, one being the swallowing of a knife. One day, while seated at dinner, I said to Booto and Dago, the two black servants, 'See me eat knife'. 'Quee, it fits kill you.' 'No kill me', I replied, 'I got witch'. 'Quee, Quee.' I so say wrapped the knife in paper, but it really fell into my lap, and pretended to swallow it, and made a few grimaces as if in pain. They were fearful that the knife was inside me and shouted to the other boys, 'Jerry eat knife, he die, he got witch, tell cappy quick'. 'Pincher' came to see what was up and found me laughing. 'Where's the knife?' he demanded. I showed it to him and explained. The boys really thought it had passed through me, and said 'He got witch'. 'Pincher' advised me to be careful or I would get peppered.

We next anchored at Frisco,[51] the King of which was named Dick Squire, and much trust was given out. Here it is that the lagoon country starts and the inland water made a pretty effect on the landscape. We stayed here for about fourteen days, and then made for Piccanny Hou,[52] a small trading town where we did our business in a short time, and then left for Cape Lahou.[53] During the night a mail boat[54] came up

notebook, 1883–84', 27 September 1883, Langdon places Trepoo as four miles from Sassandra.

[50] Untraced on modern maps but marked on the Madden report map between Sassandra and Fresco in Côte d'Ivoire; possibly modern Kotrohou?

[51] Fresco in Côte d'Ivoire.

[52] Untraced on modern maps but the Madden report map shows Piccanninny Lahou to the east of Fresco.

[53] Grand-Lahou in Côte d'Ivoire to the west of Abidjan, described by Babington in 1875 as 'a very large town'; 'Remarks on the general description of the trade', p. 248. Strictly speaking, Lahou-Plage is the old trading port. Adams, *Remarks*, p. 3, noted that 'the town of Cape Lahoo is built on a narrow peninsula of sand formed by the sea and river, and may consist of 150 houses, containing a population of seven or eight hundred souls. The Dutch, at a former period, carried on here a considerable trade in slaves and ivory, in which article the Lahoo people have always dealt largely'. Robertson remarked on the extent of its trade 'more business is done here than in the whole distance from Cape Mount to St Andrews; the quantity of gold and ivory sold annually, is greater than at any of the European settlements, Cape Coast and Accra excepted'; he estimated it as worth £16,500 pa; Robertson, *Notes*, pp. 82, 361.

[54] From 1852 a regular steamer service was operating between Britain and West Africa. This was generated by the government mail contract established from that year. Initially services were every month but by this period had become fortnightly. It had several consequences for trade on the coast and, not least, allowed passengers to travel between

the coast with the King of Lahou and his wives and slaves on board. Owing to the darkness they had missed the Cape, and to save going back the commander inquired if we would take his passengers and land them in due course. 'Pincher' was only too pleased to comply with his request, for the King of Cape Lahou was a great man. He was returning from a visit to another great man, William, King of Half Jack, who was educated at Bristol and christened at St Mary Redcliff Church.[55] He was now reputed to have several hundred wives. The big, fat, bleary eyed monster! If the stories I heard about him were true, and I believe they were, his cruelty to women and slaves was almost beyond comprehension.

Well, the King of Cape Lahou came on board and was received at the gangway by 'Pincher'. He had with him about fifteen wives and the same number of slaves. They were a sorry lot. Most of the women were sea-sick. The cabins were full to overflowing, some sat on the lockers, and the rest squatted on the floor. 'Pincher' decided to get away at once, and we were making good progress when suddenly the sails were 'all-a-back', and we were in a tornado. We had not seen it coming owing to the darkness, or the excitement of seeing so many ladies. Before the ship could be got before the wind, it was touch and go whether we turned turtle. Much water was shipped, and flooded the cabins. What a sight! The women who were on the lockers were pitched off, and they were all prostrate. Swish! Swish! The water rushed from one side to the other as the ship reeled. Vomit and filth! We had to hold our noses, for the stench was fearful. We had to set to and clean the cabins, and later when I opened the door of my berth to turn in, I stepped on something soft and greasy. Oh, horror! It was a black lady. We anchored at Cape Lahou, and were not sorry to see the last of our passengers, who were far from smelling sweet. Cape Lahou was the second largest trading town on what was called the 'weather coast'.[56] Half Jack was the first.

We stayed at Cape Lahou some eight weeks or more, at the end of which time all our trust had been given out, and the trade room was empty, except for cash sales and 'Dash'. My services would not be required much longer. The black boys would be able to manage, and besides, are they not 'much more trustworthy than a white boy?'

ports on the West African littoral; P.N. Davies, *The Trade Makers: Elder Dempster in West Africa, 1852–1972* (London, 1973).

[55] It was not uncommon in this period for British traders to arrange for children of African brokers to be educated in Britain during the nineteenth century, an arrangement that would be of mutual benefit. R. & W. King arranged for the education in Bristol of the son of King Bell of the Cameroons; FO 541/16, Dowell to Admiralty, 10 January 1869.

[56] i.e. Windward coast.

'Pincher' had had his eye on Mr Mate and myself, finding much fault – 'can't do things like the black boys'. This got my pepper up. I was fully aware that I was in the way, and 'Pincher' knew, much to his annoyance, that anything I saw or heard, I should tell Mr Mate. But I didn't care. 'If you are not careful', said 'Pincher', I will send you for'ard'. It was nag, nag, nag, day after day, and I was so fed up that one day when he said he would send me for'ard, I replied, 'I wish you would'. 'What! What! What!' said 'Pincher', 'you answer me? There was a time when I could have triced you up at the gangway and given you two round dozen. Get for'ard and I'll make you sorry for this'. I was glad to go and the men were pleased to have me, for I should keep their pots and pans, and the fo'c'sle clean, which was more than Cockney did. If I couldn't keep things cleaner than he did I should feel ashamed. I knew 'Pincher' was going to put me through the mill, but whatever work-up job he had in store for me, I was determined to put my best into it and keep smiling. Great Scot! To hear men talking freely among each other was like being in heaven. I turned in, thankful at last to be out of the cabin. Yes, but what of the next day? Would it be polishing the copper on the ship's side, or what?

The next morning I turned out with the men. 'Jerry', said Mr Mate, 'tar down all the standing rigging, back stays, fore and aft stays, and mind, lad (in a kindly way) you don't leave any holidays (parts not tarred), or you will have to shin up and put it right. From six to six'. 'Aye, aye, Sir', I replied. No doubt it would have been nuts to 'Pincher' to make me shin up a newly tarred back stay to cover up the holidays. But the men had warned me about this particular. The tarring took about two weeks – tar, tar from six in the morning till six at night. It meant that I had my supper an hour after the men, and then I had to do the fo'c'sle work, which, by the way, Cockney refused to help with. He said it was the work for the youngest hand to do, so I sparred up to him. The men insisted on his taking a share of the work. (White men again.) My next work-up job was to scrape and varnish the masts and yards, which took about three weeks, but was a much cleaner job, and as nothing was said of working from six till six, I had my supper when the men went below. I expected to have been called up again, but I was not, and I thought this is victory number one.

The barque *Watkins*[57] had arrived from home and we were all anxious, of course, for news. I heard that my elder brother, Harry, was aboard serving as cook and steward. He had sailed with 'Pincher' on a former voyage and was given permission to visit our ship. 'Pincher' had told him of my bad character, and one evening I was severely admonished by my brother for my evil ways. He said I was losing a

[57] 278 tons.

good chance in life by not staying aft, and if I was not careful in mixing
with the men for'ard I should become a blackguard. Brotherly advice
no doubt, but I hit back pretty strongly. The flunkey business would
not lead to quarter deck, and the men for'ard were real white men.
Harry was much concerned that he could not convert me to his own
views.

In due course we left Cape Lahou and beat to windward[58] to gather
in any cargo that might be ready at the towns where our trust had
been given out. But before doing so we had to deliver a number of
passengers (slaves) to William, King of Half Jack, and on our way down
some cash trade was done at Jack Lahou[59] and Three Towns.[60] At the
last named there was a tremendously large tree, the branches of which
extended each way for some half mile. I believe it was called a banian
tree. We discharged our passengers at Half Jack, and I saw that pot-
bellied bleary-eyed William, and from what I heard his Christian
training and education had not made him any better than his fellow
countrymen. We shipped from here our first consignment of palm oil
and palm kernels for home, per steamer, and I may state here that a
long and good trading voyage produced perhaps twice the amount of
our own cargo.

Our decks were now clear of accumulations of casks of oil, and we
started our beat to windward, which might take a few days or a few
weeks, as luck determined. We had to do battle with a very strong
current, head winds and calms. We sailed away from the coast close-
hauled almost due south for some days, and then put the ship about
and sailed in again for land. Sometimes it happened that we sighted
land again below where we started. But it was good to be at sea again
with all our wings spread.

'Pincher' had taught me how to steer, and from eight am till six pm
Jerry had to take the wheel. It was very tiring, standing some nine
hours a day under a tropical sun, or should it happen to be the rainy
season, in a deluge that would last several weeks. But it was warm rain,
and, wet or fine, I liked steering. I felt somewhat proud in steering a
fair sized ship under sail, for really I was almost in charge. Sometimes
when there was a good breeze and a choppy sea, 'Pincher' would say
for a joke, 'Luff her up quick, Jerry, and give those fellows for'ard a
good dousing'. I would then bring her up sharp against wind and sea,
and splash would come a wave over the weather bow and some one

[58] i.e. returning along the coast to the west, against the wind.

[59] Untraced on modern maps but the Madden report map places Jack Lahou (also
known as Trade Town) to the west of Half Jack and close to the position of modern
Abidjan.

[60] Untraced on modern maps; not placed on the Madden report map.

would get a wetting. 'Pincher' would chuckle and the Kroo boys would say 'Them Jerry no savey how to steer'. But he did.

After a run of some twelve days, we again made land at early dawn, and when we were able to distinguish we found it to be Berraby. As before stated 'Pincher' was wanted here for a peppering, and he became a bit jumpy, but fortunately the breeze held out and later the same day we anchored at Grand Drewin, our first trading town, and also the home of our Kroo boys. Our arrival caused some jubilation with their people.

Owing to the rainy season there was not much oil ready,[61] so we dropped down the coast again calling at our trading towns, picking up small quantities of oil, kernels, and perhaps a few passengers here and there, and, of course, if there was any ivory or gold-dust about, 'Pincher' was on it. He needed to be very smart in buying gold-dust, because it was nearly always adulterated with brass filings or sand, but after it had been tested with acid, washed and dried, and reduced to its correct proportion, the quantity of actual gold-dust which remained caused a look of blank astonishment on the faces of the natives. And by the time 'Pincher' had done with it it was still smaller, at least by weight. Ivorys were also bought by weight, generally short weight.

We came again to Cape Lahou, where we stayed eight weeks or more. The captains of the different ships to pass away the time organised sailing boat races. 'Pincher' rigged his gig with mast and sails, and it was jolly taking part in the races. We did not get a prize on that great day because 'Pincher' was disqualified for wetting the sails. Nevertheless, it was nuts for the others and myself.

The sides of the ship had to be painted, and Cockney and I are told off to do it with British paint (tar). We were working at it under the starboard counter, Cockney was sitting on the stage, and his legs, when the ship rolled, were well in the sea. I was on the deck pulling in the stage guy ropes or handing down things required when I spotted Mr ground shark coming up from under the keel and making for Cockney's legs. I saw his white belly, for he had turned on his back in an instant, and was about to bite when I shouted for all I was worth, 'Cockney, put your legs up!' He was just in time for the great shark's snout was then right under the stage. He is a great coward and noise will nearly always frighten him. It was now my turn to paint the port counter, with Cockney on deck attending to the guy ropes. I kept my feet well on the stage and told Cockney to keep a good look out. One should never show funk on a ship, however one might feel it.

---

[61] Harvesting of palm fruits usually began at the start of the rainy season; it would then be some weeks before the palm oil was ready for sale. In the centre of the oil trade, the rivers of the Niger Delta, the buying season began around March.

Needless to say, I was not sorry when this painting job was finished. The shark, without doubt, is the enemy of sailormen. But it is great fun capturing him, whether by hook or harpoon. Hook 'em in the top jaw, run a bowline down, hoist on deck, stand clear of tail, which would cause much injury if it gave you one of its lashings, get axe across the tail as soon as you can, but even then he is dangerous, for in his last kick will leap many feet above the deck. Dead. Post-mortem, see what his last meal was, cut out jaws for a curio, back-bone for a walking-stick, and skin for sand-paper. The rest dump overboard. No sailorman would eat shark at any price, although the natives consider it a delicacy.

On our ship during a previous voyage a Kroo boy had been nipped by a shark, when pulling the boat through the surf. The poor fellow was bitten across the buttocks. His own countrymen refused in any way to help him because, according to their superstition, he must have a witch, otherwise the shark would not have bitten him. When the surf boat came alongside us we placed the injured boy on a hatch and hoisted him on deck. His own people were afraid to come near him. He was dying, putting out his hands and talking in his own tongue. We asked to whom he was talking. 'He say he see big river, him mother be on tother side, who say come.' One might ask where did this so-called poor benighted heathen get the idea of a future life? Christianity had not yet reached his country. Nevertheless, they had some idea of God, for in my many conversations on that point, they would say something like this about the Creation. 'When the Great Grand Debil, who is above the other Grand Debils, first made the world, and then two men, one black and one white, he said I have two things to offer you, a box or a book. You, blackman, shall have first choice. He chose the box, because it would be useful to keep all his possessions in. A big, big, fool he was. White man, of course, had the book (knowledge) and savey all things. Never mind, "softly, softly catchee monkey", blackman will have book some day.' And I was sure they would, for they were all very eager to acquire knowledge. 'Jerry, Jerry, teach me book, and then I no let white man cheat me.' Talent was there, but as yet undeveloped. Many times, in my own way, when looking at a crowd of West Africans, I was struck by the vast amount of European crossings. An untrained eye could easily detect it. They were all shades of colour, from tawny white to dark brown, with straight hair, and probably a few reds. These were very treacherous and difficult to deal with, but the true negro, with his big head, flat nose, etc was generally a good fellow to get on with.

Booth[62] and Dago, our cabin boys, and Dabbery, the cook's mate,

[62] [sic], Booto in the rest of the text.

were negroes, and I tried to teach them what little 'book' I knew, and they in return taught me their lingo. But to converse all along the West Coast it would be necessary to know at least a dozen dialects. They had few verbs (if any), counted in tens, and measured time by the moon. They had but few synonyms. 'Light' and 'fire' would be the same word, 'kusha', so that if any one wanted a light for his pipe he would say, 'kusha-daddy', fire-pipe. They were highly superstitious. Food was taken every night to the graves of the departed, and without doubt the cunning medicine men 'saw to that'.

It was very interesting to talk to these boys about trials by ordeal. On the occurrence of any calamity, such as small-pox, fever, death, theft, some one was charged with witchcraft and was tried by fetish and medicine men. To prove his innocence the accused had to drink poison (saucy water). If death resulted, 'Well then, he did have witch', and members of his family would have to go under, or pay forfeit. If he should not die, however, then the accusers had to go through the mill. These trials sometimes took weeks to decide, and often held up trade. From what I gathered from the boys, the cunning medicine men pulled the strings for their own advantage. Power, power, all the world over, educated or otherwise.

The saddest event of the voyage was the passing of Captain Hunt of the brig *Dauntless*, after some days illness. 'Pincher' and his brother traders did all they could, but the ensign one morning was hoisted at half mast. He was to be buried at sea. At 2 pm each ship sent a boat's crew to pay their last respects. It was a very solemn procession, headed by the boat in which lay the mortal remains of Captain Hunt. When well out from land, the committal service was read, with bowed heads and all standing. The plank was gently tilted, and the body, well weighted and sewn up in canvas, glided into the sea, which at this spot was between twenty and thirty fathoms deep. The mourners then returned to the deceased captain's ship and were given refreshments, including much rum. The personal effects were sold by auction, and the bidders, being in a muddled rum-soaked state, paid some fancy prices. Later on I asked 'Old Joe' why they did not bury Captain Hunt on shore. 'Bury him on shore, lad? Why, if he had on only a shirt [...] [they] [...] would dig him up for it. No, lad, he was a sailorman, and his proper grave was in the deep.'

It is some time since I last mentioned Mr Mate. He was still a lone man. The breach with 'Pincher' would continue until we left the coast for home. Every evening 'Pincher' gave or attended parties of brother traders, but Mr Mate was never invited. Whatever time they or 'Pincher' arrived or left, Mr Mate had to be at the gangway to receive 'His Majesty', or see 'Their Majesties' off. The side most of these men assumed stuck fast to me as a boy, and it still sticks – to treat a gentleman in such a manner!

Boat-sailing with them had become flat. Big game hunting was then more in their line, so Mr Mate asked 'Pincher' for permission to use the gig and sails on Sundays. To the surprise of everybody leave was granted. He chose an AB[63] and myself to work the boat, and many happy Sundays spent in boat sailing with this gentleman, which he was, for I learnt much of his school life and family history, will always be remembered. We use to leave the ship soon after 9 am. Our provisions consisted of a keg of water, salt junk, biscuits, pipes and tobacco for the men (boys were not expected to smoke in those far off days), and fishing tackle. We beat miles and miles to windward, at times close in, at others well off shore, and selected a good spot for swimming and fishing. We would only swim, however, one at a time, the other two would keep a good look out for Mr Shark. The water was lovely and warm, and if it had not been for the man-eaters we could almost have lived in it.

Alas, these jolly days came to an abrupt end. One day we got well away to windward when the wind failed and it became a dead calm. The sea was almost like glass, and there was a thick West African mist. We had only two paddles and we did our utmost to get back before sunset. We watched the sun sink like a great ball of fire, and twenty minutes after it was pitch dark, for there was no moon. We had no compass, but we knew the set of the current and just let the boat drift in the hope of spotting our ship's lights. Black darkness – could almost cut it! Soon we heard the Kroo boys' boat chant, for 'Pincher' had sent them out to look for us. We hailed them and were soon taken in tow. Unfortunately, our Mr Mate would be in the soup, and he was, for when the boat was hoisted in, 'Pincher', in his best Yankee drawl, said, 'Waal, Mr Mate, I guess this will be the last time you have my boat'. So that was the end of many, many perfect days.

'Pincher' had bought a parrot in a cage and hung it near the wheel, and the wicked sailormen intended to get some fun out of it by teaching it to say what they themselves would like to say if they dared. It was agreed that everyone on passing the cage should repeat certain words. In due time Polly was shrieking out 'Pincher, Pincher, you mean ——'. (Let Polly say the last word.) When 'Pincher' realised what the bird was saying, our sky was black for a long time, and mean and petty work-up jobs were the result. But it did not matter for we had had our money's worth. Later on Polly was sold to another trader.

The crew of the barque *Burnswark*[64] sent us a very peculiar request,

[63] i.e. Able Seaman.
[64] 252 tons. The *Burnswark*, Capt. Venning, returned to Bristol from 'Lahon' with a

'Can you supply us with a consignment of cockroaches, we are swarmed out with bugs and fleas'. It was generally understood that if the first named predominated they would eat up all the latter. We had often grumbled about our cockroach pest, but thank goodness we were not in the same boat as our friends. A hunt was there and then organised, the result of which was that a bucket three parts full of cockroaches was collected in a very short time and sent to the *Burnswark*, who acknowledged it with thanks.

While dealing with this subject I may say that our pests were very troublesome at times. They were two or three inches long. Unless the smaller kind predominate the larger ones eat them up, for both kinds are cannibals. At night, before wet weather, they fly many yards, sometimes extinguishing our fo'c'sle-hole light. Look out if you get one in the face. Another annoying trick of theirs was to nibble the hard skin on the bottom of your feet while you were asleep, and, my word, you would know it next morning when washing the decks with salt water. Our men, who had been in those dreadful West African rivers, said that when a man was down with the fever, it was always a sure sign that his number was up when these pests commenced boldly to attack a few hours before death. Our pigs and fowls would snap them up with relish, and the hens in return would give us some decent eggs – at least we presumed they were.

Rats, too, were legion, and gave us much sport. In the early morning we would find many aloft drinking the dew in our furled sails, and we chased and shook them from rope to rope, whilst the men on deck were ready to do the mighty deed when Mr Rat lost his hold and fell.

Ants – these were almost too interesting to call pests (I had read a little about them, and here was a chance to see for myself.) Hour after hour I spent watching these tiny creatures at work. It was wonderful to watch the order and intelligence with which they removed some object, generally a cockroach turned over on its back. A scout would first spot the object and then chase off and tell the others, when column after column would appear, each lead by what were apparently officers, and the object would be carried to their nest. My only regret was that I could not see what happened there.

It was Christmas Day. 'Moses', the cook, had become very drunk the night before, one of those states of drunkenness which is first madness. Perhaps he had been doped with the drink he had obtained from the natives. Anyhow, he ran amok with a butcher's knife, and wanted to kill everybody. Poor, silly 'Moses' had to be lashed up. But what of the Christmas fare? It was all done for, even the plum duff.

cargo of palm oil, camwood and coconuts for R. & W. King in September 1882; *Customs Bills of Entry Bill A*, 16 September 1882.

The usual salt junk and biscuits would be the menu. But I was in luck's way, for 'Pincher', upon the request of my big brother, had given me permission to spend the day with him on board the barque *Watkins*, and the gig was placed at my disposal. The Kroo boys on this special day used oars, and, as I held the yoke lines, and gave the order to push off, I felt almost bursting with pride. How was I dressed? Why, in my best, of course – white calico shirt and pants and red sash, (swank, no doubt), and, thanks to dear 'Old Joe', they were all my own making. I was well received on board the *Watkins*, for my brother was a Somebody, being well up in his business of Cook and Steward. His ship was well rationed. 'Full and plenty, no waste' was his motto, and in the end it was cheaper than doling out the pound and pint. The men were much more contented, because they knew there would be something on their plates for every meal. Whereas with wretched 'Moses', one day's rations, badly cooked, were sent to the fo'c'sle at mid-day, with the result that after supper there would be nothing left for breakfast. The same applied to tea, sugar and coffee, which was served out weekly.

I had dinner with the men, which was my wish, and I noted well how nicely it was served. Soup, stuffed roast pork, and plum duff. Each had his own knife and fork and plates (no sheath knife or tin plates here.) The cook was a good one and the men knew and appreciated his services. Any food not eaten was returned to the galley and hashed up for the next meal. I had supper aft (there is no tea-time on board ship). At sundown I returned to my ship more than ever dissatisfied with the way in which our rations were cooked and served.

On the West Coast shoals of whales are often met with. The Gulf of Guinea, I believe, is a breeding ground, so that they are free from being hunted. I have seen them so close to the ship that I could have thrown a lump of coal into their blow hole. To see these huge monsters covered with barnacles is a sight not to be forgotten. On one particular day the men said there was a thrasher about, but whether he was fighting or at play, I could not say. He would leap right out of the water and his tail would flop the surface with the report of a cannon. I could quite understand what I read about small ships or boats getting a whack and it was all up.

Talking of barnacles reminds me that our ship, having been at sea a long time, would be covered with them on the sides and bottom, which impeded sailing and steering. At even tide our Kroo boys were organised to dive under and pick off what they could. Each boy had his own bucket which he placed on deck at the spot from which he was diving, and brought the barnacles up as he picked them off. The owner of the bucket which was filled first would get the best prize. But the wicked sailormen would take out some while the boys were diving, and they could not understand why the buckets would not fill up. 'Quee, quee, some witch bucket, no full.' This went on for several evenings, until one of the boys who had dived right under and came up on the other side spotted the last lot we had dumped sinking through the water. Needless to say, for the future a boy remained on deck to watch the buckets. Poor, silly boys – 'when the horse has bolted'. However, they were elated that they had 'catchee white man'.

'Cockney' was in disgrace. During his anchor watch he was caught red-handed by 'Pincher' stealing onions from the poop deck. It was a silly thing to do because 'Pincher's' berth was right underneath. All hands were mustered aft to receive a lecture on this terrible crime. The same old yarn – 'There was a time when I could have given a dozen lashes or more, but as I can't do that now, and to make you all remember that I'm captain of this ship, I will make him polish the copper swung in a bow-line'. This was most refined cruelty, for he had to sit in a loop of rope from 6 am till 6 pm day after day, and the rope would soon cut into his flesh. Moreover, every time the ship rolled he would be up to his neck in water, and water infested with sharks! Just think, if you can, what this job meant. The poor fellow's gruelling lasted a fortnight, and then he went sick, which was not to be wondered at. When the ship arrives home the people will probably say, 'How nice and bright her copper is!' They little know how and why!

For some time past I had had a nice job. 'Bung' had got very much behindhand in making casks, and oil was coming aboard very fast. So I was told off as an assistant. I liked the work very much, for using tools was my delight. I was also learning something useful, and in my spare time I made toy tubs and various articles in this line. 'Bung' gave me every encouragement to push on and learn, and my little smattering of geometry now came in very useful.

Our rations had lately been very bad. The salt beef and pork had turned green and rancid, the biscuits and flour mouldy and full of weevils, likewise the peas and rice, the sugar had turned into a liquid. The black stewards were to blame for all this except in the case of the meat, for they in their carelessness had often left off the covers of the lockers in the store room, and cockroaches, ants and other insects had caused havoc. All sorts of things not wanted would get served up with our food, and at last we could stand it no longer. Everybody agreed that we should go aft and complain, with 'Old Joe' as our spokesman. I had yet to learn how little to be trusted were the two who were most voluble in their praise of the proposition – 'Cockney' and 'Moses'. They did the most shouting, but when it came to going aft and complaining they were conspicuous by their absence. The sneaks backed out at the last moment by saying that as 'Pincher' was always down on them it would be better for all if they kept out of it. The real white men faced the music, and, each carrying some part of the rations, marched aft. 'Pincher' was walking the poop when we came up to him, and he expressed some surprise. 'What's up, men?' he inquired. 'Old Joe', respectfully taking off his cap (we all did likewise), said, 'Sorry, Captain, but our grub is not what it ought to be'. 'Oh, I was not aware that anything was wrong with it', replied 'Pincher'. He then examined our food, and said, 'Sorry men it is so bad, those two black scamps must have left the lockers open, and those nasty things got in. Men, I want you to remember that the food had been aboard over twelve months, and heaven only knows when the meat was first salted, or the other stuff made. However, the next ship out is bringing our second year's provisions. In the meantime try and put up with it, and I will do my best to buy what may be obtained on shore in the way of pigs (bosilla), but these are not over good for you, because they are the scavengers of the towns, eating up all the filth. I must be careful in this matter.' 'Old Joe' thanked him for giving us a hearing and hoped that all good feeling would continue fore and aft, and we returned to our quarters. Needless to say, the two skunks had a rough time.

We were now running down the coast for the last time, and where the trusts were not fully met, passengers were sometimes taken in lieu. Our last trading town, Cape Lahou, had completed its quota, and it only remained for us to sail to Half Jack, exchange our passengers, get three new hands from the other ships there, discharge our Kroo boys, and hop it for home, having had some fourteen months on the coast.

The Kroo boys were leaving to return to their country, and we to ours. Everybody was happy. They, especially, for they had been given our old unseaworthy surf-boat, which was loaded with the balance of wages due to them. There were twenty-eight of them, and they had a pull of some hundred miles or more against wind and strong current in an old leaky boat. Many were now rich and would be buying their first wife. 'Dabbery', the cook's mate, would be able to claim his lovely 'Buggery Isaiah' (this was a very general personal name on the coast.) Without any breach of confidence I well know his feelings towards her. Whites are not the only people who have love matches.

Good-byes were said – 'I you, I you, Ka' – and finger snapping with the whole twenty-eight of them. 'Booto', 'Dago' and 'Dabbery' were most affectionate. 'Jerry, you come next voyage and teach us book, we like you bery much.' Away they went, chanting a song to the rhythm of the paddles. Happy Kroo boys. They would have a pull of several days. But what odds? It was for home and loved ones.

We got our three new hands. Old ones, of course, were always transferred, because they were more likely to fall sick. From two of these men I learnt a great deal of the world and its peoples. Tom H——, an old naval man, had spent much time in Japan, and he told wonderful stories of the Japanese. He was in the ship that carried our first ambassadors in 1864.[65] The other, old Jerry B——, had sailed in the old packet ships, windjammers of the Western Ocean, prior to the great steamship lines. He was an old man now, for disease and the rough life had played havoc with him. His legs were black from frost-bite and scurvy. 'Old Joe' and he had been ship-mates before. Both had travelled the world over and its roads, and knew its wrong turnings, and I gleaned much from their experience.

We had on board thirty parrots, one or more to each man. Also, everybody had his West African curios, model canoes, paddles, monkeys' skins, native cloth and gold rings, besides a host of things made by themselves in their spare time, such as mats and rugs. A good sailorman is never idle.

On the morning of sailing 'Pincher' said, 'Jerry, get your kit, and resume duties in the cabin for the homeward passage, and tell Mr Mate I shall be dining with him in the fore cabin'. I saluted and said, 'Yes, sir'. I had expected this. The black servants were now gone and there would be no interference. I knew my work and intended to put my best into it. Mr Mate was not over pleased with my message. 'Well, Jerry', he said, 'I suppose I must dine with him, although he doesn't deserve it. But it will be somebody to talk to'.

The anchor came up with a flip, and 'Fare thee well, we're homeward bound for Bristol town'. 'Blow the man down' was sung by the men. Sails were set, ensign dipped, and the West Coast of Africa soon disappeared from view. Watches were set and soon everything was in ship-shape order. My duties in the cabin were light. 'Pincher' and Mr Mate were now settled down and it was a pleasure to listen to the conversation. 'Pincher' was far from well, but with me he was OK, often testing me on what knowledge I'd gained in the fo'c'sle of seamanship, knots and splices and things in general. I came well up to scratch in my work and in my answers and he said, 'Waal, Jerry, your brother is a splendid cook and steward, but you're cut out for a sailorman'. 'That's my intention, sir', I said.

Four weeks had passed since we had left the coast, and my only adventures were the capture of a few sharks and the hooking of pilot fish. They are about six inches long, and supposed to be great pals with Mr Shark, going before him to seek out his prey: hence the name pilot. In the water they look very pretty, striped black and yellow like a tiger. There were some swimming under our cutwater. I made a very small hook, baited it, and number one was soon in a bucket of salt

---

[65] This may refer to the bombardment in 1864 by a combined British, French, Dutch, and American fleet to reopen the Shimonoseki Straits. Alternatively Langdon may be referring to the arrival of Harry Parkes as British minister to Japan in 1865.

water. Number two soon followed, and I said to 'Pincher', 'I've two of those fish, sir'. He was very surprised, and said that he had never known them to take the hook before. 'You young beggar, you can catch anything'. In a few hours, however, these fish went west, and when dead they lost all their beautiful colouring.

Calm after calm succeeded, and we just drifted south. The men were kept painting the ship, for she must look spick and span for our home-coming (including the polished copper on the sides).

Wonder of wonders, there was a ship bearing down on us, the first ship we had seen since we had left the coast. It was a mail boat, SS *Roman*,[66] and it passed close to our stern. 'Pincher' hailed to get our bearings and Greenwich time, for our chronometers were rocky, at least I heard 'Pincher' say that they did not keep time.

I noted when holding the chart that we were four degrees south of the line.[67] 'Pincher' was always whistling for wind. A puff came from the SE. It freshened. It was the south-east trade wind, and every stitch of canvas was put on, and we were now really homeward bound. North by west was our course, and we soon re-crossed the line, and at about one degree north I saw the North Star just dipping on the horizon. Every night I used to watch this star rise higher, and the Southern Cross sink lower.

With the south-east trade we met with an immense school of albacore and benito, which must have numbered hundreds of thousands. The sea all around was just covered with these fish, and they followed us for some three weeks, the barnacles on the sides and bottom of our ship being no doubt the attraction, for it meant a good feed for them. I heard old Tom remark that if anyone fell overboard it would be all up. He had seen a similar lot when serving in HMS——. A messmate fell overboard, and before the ship hove to, the fish were at him. They could be seen clinging to his raised arms. His captain, since there was no hope of rescuing him in time, had him shot to end his misery. I heard also that a school of mackerel would attack anyone who was unfortunate enough to fall among them.

We got much sport from these fish, and several hooks and lines were lost when trying to hook twenty to thirty pounders. It was no easy matter to hold a large fish with the ship going through the water at eight or ten knots. Our lost lines could be seen for days dangling to the fish which had got away. We tried to re-hook them, but nothing done. Once bitten, twice shy. Then for sheer wantonness I

---

[66] Possibly the SS *Roman Empire*, 1,542 tons, of the Calcutta run.

[67] i.e. the Equator. It was usual for ships trading to West Africa to sail south of the line for their return, in order to catch the south-east trade winds, rather than attempt to return directly along the coast.

would catch one and tie pieces of tin or wood to it and throw it back into the sea and watch it swimming with the rest. Porpoises played havoc with them, but there was no apparent diminution in numbers. I here got the finest sport I should ever have. I was out on the jib-boom and was letting the fish chase the hook. When you won't let them take the hook they sort of get wild, and a good number would bunch themselves together and jump for it, when you could take your choice. I was doing this one day when a porpoise and family suddenly appeared and they made short work of the bunch. I hooked a benito, however, and dangled it before the porpoises, who chased it, and I played with them as I played with the others, until finally benito and hook disappeared inside the porpoise. It was rather a unique catch, but I couldn't hold the monster. It must have weighed one hundred and fifty pounds or more. How it digested my large fish-hook I cannot say.

We had fish fried, boiled or baked for every meal, and to give 'Moses' some little credit he made some delicious fish-soup by simmering the fish for several days. Even 'Pincher' praised it, and I think it did him good, for after his good fare on the coast our salt junk, which might have been some old cab-horse, did upset his digestion.

In due course we ran through the south-east trade wind and for a few days were in the Doldrums, with the usual thunder storms, calms, or wind boxing the compass almost every hour. We picked up the north-east trade wind and away we went towards the roaring forties, where we sighted a splendid four-masted barque. She was bearing towards us and passed close enough to read our message written on a large blackboard and to answer in a similar manner. This was found to be much quicker than flag-wagging. Her decks were well lined with men, women and children. She was an emigrant ship, eleven days out from Glasgow, bound for Melbourne. 'Pincher' again obtained our bearings and Greenwich time (it was almost like asking our way home). What a magnificent sight she looked. Somebody has said that a ship is the most beautiful thing man ever made. Yes, but she must be in full sail, with a good breeze, bowing to every swell. Then, indeed, she certainly becomes a thing of life and beauty. She carried a great spread of canvas, including sky-sails and studding sails. Our little cockle-shell of two hundred and ninety three tons seemed so small, and indeed, we all felt so little gazing at such a stately object.

We sighted and passed the two western islands of the Azores. 'Pincher' again got his bearings and the time, he seemed always worried about his chronometer. I would hear at table, 'They are not correct', 'Our longitude is out', 'On such and such a night the moon or a star will be eclipsed, must take a sight'. Jerry was very keen on this, and wanted to know much about the heavens. Of course, he was supposed not to hear what was said at table, but he did, and much of it was added to his store of knowledge.

There was much grousing among the crew. It appeared that 'Pincher' had promised to serve out grog after we had passed the western islands. Some time previously I had noticed, when down in the lazaretto, that the bung in the cask of rum had been withdrawn and the barrel was upside-down. I reported this to 'Pincher', who said, 'That's alright, Jerry, I did it, was going to give them grog, but changed my mind'. This almost cost him his job, for after our arrival home, somebody spread the yarn that he drank the rum himself, was drunk most of the time with it, and could not navigate properly. The owners held an inquiry, but I was able to corroborate his ill health, and the empty rum cask, by which, I hope, I did 'Pincher' at least one good turn.

For some days the wind had been dead ahead and we were tacking and putting ship about every four hours. I saw by the chart that we were just outside the Bay of Biscay. I also noted the bearings of Falmouth, whither we were bound for orders, but unless the wind changed we should be a long time reaching there.[68] 'Pincher', whose health had not improved, was much worried by the adverse wind, and spent most of his time on deck repeating to the helmsman, 'Keep her close, keep her close to the wind'. Many times I would hear through the skylight, 'Jerry, load another pipe, light it, see that it draws well, and bring it on deck'.

'Square the yards!' Hullo, what's up? We had sighted a strange object on the lee-bow, and bearing towards it discovered it to be a large telegraph buoy which had become adrift. 'Pincher' said that this must be entered in the official log and reported. A few days later we got another scare. It was on a lovely moonlight evening, with a stiff head wind blowing, when I heard through the sky-light (I was in the cabin), 'Jerry, the glasses, sharp!' I knew what the last word meant, and he had them in a tick. On our weather quarter, only a few yards away, was a fair sized ship bottom upwards. A close shave. Had we bumped her it might have been Davy Jones' locker for all of us. 'This also', said 'Pincher', 'must be logged and reported'.

We were nearing land and the colour of the sea had changed from deep blue to green. Orders were given for deep sea soundings (this was fresh to me). 'Pincher' had already given me good practice, when on the coast, with the hand lead line up to fifteen fathoms. This would be one hundred fathoms with a lead of thirty pounds. The bottom of this lead was hollowed out and filled with tallow, so that when it reached

[68] Ships returning from West Africa would return to Falmouth, Plymouth, or, as occurred on Langdon's second voyage, Cobh, for orders as to where they were to take their cargo for landing. This would usually depend on market prices.

the bottom of the sea the tallow or arming would pick up a sample of the soil from the sea-bed, by which 'Pincher' could get his bearings on refer-ring to the chart. Deep sea soundings cannot be taken while the ship is sailing. She has to be brought to a standstill, hove to, and then the lead is passed outside the ship from stern to jib-boom, each member of the crew at equal distances holding the line clear of obstacles. As the line pays out, each man calls to the next, 'Watch, there, watch', until it reaches the officer in charge at the stern, who watches the whole line pay out. 'Ninety fathoms, sir, and no bottom.' It was hard work for all hands to haul in this length with a thirty pounds weight on the end, the strain had been increased by the lee-way the ship had been making. After several attempts, at intervals of four hours, bottom at eighty fathoms was obtained, with the arming showing small brown pebbles. 'Pincher' had now his where-abouts and the course was set for the English channel.

The next day at supper, 5.30 pm, 'Pincher' said, 'Jerry, when you have washed up, take the glasses to the royal yard and have a good look round'. At sunset I reported land on the port bow, about twenty miles distant. When it became dark, and we were nearing the point sighted, we saw the reflection of flashes of light well up in the sky appear at regular intervals. It was the Lizard. 'Waal, Mr Mate', said 'Pincher', 'I guess we shan't make Falmouth with this wind by the morning. We shall fetch the Eddystone and put into Plymouth.'

In the early morning a Plymouth pilot took charge. There was very little wind, but my word, he knew how to handle a ship. He made good use of every catspaw or current, and we were soon so close to Eddystone that we could have knocked the old stump lighthouse with a biscuit shy. The sea here must be very deep. We drifted into the Sound, dropped anchor, and for the first time for over eighteen months the ship lay without a roll.

A medical officer from the Board of Health arrived. 'You are from the West Coast of Africa, any fever on board? No? Well, you are from the fever climate. Forty-eight hours quarantine.' The yellow flag 'Q' was then hoisted. Next came the Board of Trade officer for any reports, and to examine the official log. He saw the entry for the telegraph buoy adrift and for the ship bottom up, and said that it must be seen to at once. Within an hour a Trinity House[69] ship, whose commander had taken full particulars, was steaming out on the search.

'Pincher' had gone ashore to wire the owners for orders and another captain to take charge, for his health would not hold out any longer.

---

[69] Trinity House was the institution responsible, under the Board of Trade, for regulating the safety of British shipping, particularly with reference to maintaining lighthouses and navigation buoys and licensing pilots. It was also responsible for clearing wrecks.

This would cause some two days delay, but my time was very profitably spent, for old Tom H——, being an ex-naval man, knew Plymouth well, and he told me all about the building of the breakwater by convict labour, and of the training brigs.

We got a visit from the port missionary, but he was not asked if he would like a bass. Oh no, he was not out for that. He shook hands and said, 'How de do, lads, you've had a long voyage and been away from home a long time'. Gradually the temptations of shore life were brought up, and he gave us some very sound advice. His proposal to hold a service in the fo'c'sle hold was received with acclamation, and it will never be forgotten. It touched the hearts of everybody. But alas, his good work was soon marred by the foul work of the bum-boat men. Drink was obtained from them and when the men had no more money to pay for it they parted with their kit or valuable curios. Silly fellows, to let those rascals take advantage. I should just like to have put the punch on them.

Fresh vegetables were received, but 'Moses' was on the beer, and, as during his last bout at Christmas Eve, they were not properly cooked. The result of all this beer drinking was that their tummies were very much out of order, for they had been on salt tack and lime-juice for nearly three months.

Our new captain had arrived, a very young man, who had risen to a trader.[70] This was his first command, and he strutted about the poop like a bantam cock. Our orders were for Bristol, so up came the anchor, and down the English Channel we sailed and rounded Land's End clear of the Longships. When I made the close acquaintance of our new captain's boot, for answering 'Old Shocker' pertly, this was the first act of brutality during the voyage, and from a little wipper snapper not much bigger than myself, I should very much like to have returned the compliment by using some of the tricks I had learnt from the men in boxing. But I thought it best not to, since these men have great power behind them, and, knowing this, many of the skunks are always ready to use it.

We were becalmed off the west of Lundy Island. It was a glorious moonlight night, and the old tug *Refuge* came alongside and asked where we were bound for. 'Bristol', we replied. 'Tow you up for thirty pounds', they said, 'using our own tow rope'. After much haggling the price was dropped to twenty pounds with the use of our tow rope. Twice this rope was wilfully broken by sudden jerks from the tug, because they wished to use their own and so earn another fiver. Our bantam cock showed himself off at his best by saying, with several cuss-words interspersed for emphasis, 'I say, Mr Tug, if you part that rope again I shall cry off'. It did not happen again.

[70] Capt. Luke, *Bristol Presentments*, 14 September 1882.

We had a sixteen hours tow before us, so the sails were stowed in the best ship-shape fashion, and the ship looked spick and span to enter the dear old port of Bristol.

How beautiful and green England appeared after the yellow sands of Africa on that lovely autumn Sunday evening. All Bristol seemed to be at Cumberland Basin.[71] I could only get a glimpse, for I was kept busy with the customs officers, putting contrabands under seal.

The men were going ashore. 'Shake, Jerry, shake, you're a good lad', they said. With 'Old Shocker', dear 'Old Joe', and old Jerry B——, it was the last shake, for before I embarked on my second voyage their toes were turned up to the daisies. The beer and fresh vegetables did it.

At last I was ready to leave, and walked the plank ashore, feeling very bashful at seeing so many people in their Sunday best. 'Ain't he a brown 'un?' I heard somebody remark. [...] I was very shabby-looking for I had much outgrown my clothes, such as they were. Still, it did not matter for I'd a pay day coming.

I had confidence in myself, for years of experience had been rolled into eighteen months and ten days. I had rubbed shoulders with men and things, had gained much knowledge of things in general, but above all of the two sides of life, Good and Evil, and I felt within myself the will to hold fast to the first and reject the latter.

---

[71] The *Ceara*, Capt. Luke, returned to Bristol from the west coast of Africa with a cargo of 688 casks of palm oil and a quantity of coconuts for R. & W. King on 14 September, *Customs Bills of Entry, Bill A*, 16 September 1882.

SECOND VOYAGE

13 October 1882 to 25 March 1883

I've been home nearly a month, and funds are getting low. [...] I have two offers, as an ordinary seaman, thirty shillings a month, to the West African Rivers.[72] The first was made by that little Cock-Crow, with whose boot I had already made an acquaintance; the bruise has not yet disappeared. I turn it down. Lucky kick! Lucky Jerry! for that ship after leaving Bristol was never heard of. The second was on my old ship. Another captain and also a Trader from a competitive firm had been taken on.[73]

Our owners, I believe, always started their captains with a river voyage, and if they returned with a whole skin, were given a trading voyage. Even sailormen would fight shy of these pestilential rivers. I had heard 'Pincher' talk of his gruelling. Most of his men were down with fever, and three died. 'Never again, Mr Mate', he said, 'will I take command of a river ship'. This and other yarns had somewhat fired my imagination, so I decided to take my chance. Also I had heard that the wearing of flannels, if you could, would ward off fever, so I get a fair supply made up.

Signing-on day, and the usual crowd of pimps outside the shipping office. 'Join your ship at Bathurst Basin, on Saturday October 13th at 7 am Attwood.' I keep my ears and eyes open when signing on, and take note of my coming ship-mates. All save old Tom H—— are strangers, mostly Americans. There was a Jordie[74] (north-east coast man), and also a well-dressed Bristol boy, whose pay for the voyage was five pounds. The mate, Mr Mac—— looks hot stuff, red hair, pointed beard, an Irishman. The second mate, a big fellow, had a full grey beard, was cross-eyed, and he too was not nice looking. The cook and steward is my big brother, who had returned in the barque *Watkins* about a week ago, and was off again at once. He was saving to get

---

[72] i.e. the rivers of the Niger Delta and its neigbours in the Bights of Benin and Biafra.

[73] Capt. Gay, *Bristol Presentments*, 12 October 1882. For voyages to the Niger Delta and its neighbouring rivers in the early nineteenth century it was usual for there to be a supercargo, in addition to the master, on board the ship; the former would be responsible for the trading activities of the voyage. There were few remaining 'competitive firms' to Kings in Bristol in this period; the main one would have been Lucas Bros, owners of the *Watkins* that Langdon's brother served on.

[74] i.e. Geordie.

married, and has four pounds a month against my thirty shillings. I shall have to put in four years before the mast to get my AB ticket.

Mr Mac—— invited everyone to a drink. Rather unusual for an officer, I thought, to thus mix with the men. The reason was soon known. His father-in-law, an ex-convict, ex-pugilist, now a cab-driver, keeps on the quay, or rather his wife does, a pub and boarding house of very evil repute. Nearly all the crew are staying at this house, hence the free drinks. Poor beggars, there won't be much of their advance note left when these wretches have skinned them. They were very surprised at my taking only ginger beer. 'Why, you'll never be a sailorman on that stuff.' 'I'm going to try, sir', I said. I chink my glass with him, saying, 'Good health and voyage, sir'. 'H'm, he knows how to do it.' The pimps and parasites are now mingling with the crew, to get free drinks, and perchance rob them. I, too, have my advance note. Hop it, Jerry.

Sailing day arrives. [...] I am full of confidence, feel well grounded in my work, eager to start and show what I really know. Good-bye is said. 'Mind you keep your promise and always wear your flannels.'

On board, and away we go. The same old story; crew drunk, including the two mates, and the powder runners[75] work the ship. Ninety tons have to be taken aboard whilst slowly towing down channel. The jib-boom has to be got out, the back-stays, back-ropes and martin-gale have to be set up. Mr Mac stands at the ship's hand, or tries to, holding on to a rope for support. It is much past the bee season but a great number are buzzing around, he must have a nest inside his mouth. No matter, my aim is to show that I know my job. When everything is home and set taut I overhear him say, to the second, 'That young —— will be in my watch'.

Off Battery Point[76] the lighter with ninety tons of gunpowder hauls alongside, and fires are extinguished. This has to be handled without a break by passing from hand to hand and stowed in our fore peak. The position allotted to myself is between the two ships, a most uncomfortable one, a slip would land me in the soup, also I have to cry 'tally' up to ten. Hour after hour at this was hard and trying work, and when finished I am hoarse with calling 'tally', my muscles and back ache badly.

I then take my first turn at the wheel, steering after the tug-boat, and find it much easier than steering by the compass or by the wind. We are now well in sight of Lundy, and it is getting dark. The tug hauls alongside and takes off the runners and pilot, who, when leaving, gives the course and remarks, 'You'll have a dirty night, shouldn't get

---

[75] i.e. the seamen responsible for loading gunpowder.
[76] At the mouth of the Avon, by Portishead.

above the top-sails, if I were you, captain. Good-bye. Safe voyage.'

The crew assemble aft and watches are picked. Mr Mac places his hand on my shoulder and says to the second mate, 'This lad is mine'. Each officer gives his men a short homily, in rather profound language, what he expects of them. 'Aye, aye, sir', reply the men.

The first watch at sea is always taken by the first mate, eight till twelve midnight. We start with a fierce south-wester, and I have the first look-out. I thought of the last time I sailed this way, the sea-sickness and turps will never be forgotten. I inwardly chuckle for I've got my sea legs now, and am able to go aloft and watch the ship dip her nose into the heavy sea. Still, it gave one a creepy feeling to think of the jib or flying-jib being stowed, for it was so very dangerous on the jib-boom when it was blowing hard, and one has to stand sort of sideways on the foot-ropes. Chanty[77] songs out there are not of much use to guide the men, it is either hang on or get washed off. At midnight I turned in.

Up again next morning at four, eight bells, and, though it was Sunday, all hands are kept busy lashing down, coiling ropes towards getting ship in good sea trim.

By now everybody has realised that they were under the command of brutal officers. Save cuss words, I never received a blow from Mr Mac. A blackguard and a brute he was, but before the end of the voyage I learnt that even he possessed a soul, and he became my friend and protector. I cannot say the same for Mr Second Mate, but will sum him up as a big muscular bully.

I must now introduce a few of the ship's company, with their pet names and characteristics.

The captain. Well, on the whole, not a bad sort. No side, and so different from 'Pincher'. Never interferes with the mates, and rarely gives orders to the men direct, save on special occasions. Very fond of pea-soup, has it at table every meal. Perhaps he thinks that like the flannel it will ward off the fever. He loves to drive the ship for all she's worth, sits on the taff-rail and watches the ship put her nose into a big roller, and jokes with the helmsman, 'That's a good one', forgetting that it meant wet berths for us chaps for'ard. 'The soup or peas, I know not which', he says, 'become very tuneful'. A most jolly fellow.

'Uncle John', an AB, American (State of Maine), a six-footer, was in the American Civil War, and the *Kearsarge* of *Alabama* fame.[78] Was a well read man, also a splendid reader. Book after book he would read

---

[77] [*sic*] Shanty.

[78] The CSS *Alabama* was a warship built at a British dock for the confederate government during the American Civil War. Launched in 1862, it inflicted considerable damage on federal shipping until sunk by the USS *Kearsarge* near Cherbourg in 1864.

aloud, and to those who could not read it was a great delight. They would say, 'Uncle, give us some reading, will you, or spin us a yarn?' He was never aggressive, although I never met his equal in boxing, it was really beautiful to see him knock out a bully. I learnt much of his history. The same old story. Has now passed his prime. Sciatica has its grip on him.

'Chester', another AB, six-footer, American, had sailed much in the lake[79] schooners, a fresh water sailor. Pages could be written about this man. A born artist, and he looked it. Long lank hair with gaunt features. Reckless abandon. Only twenty-six years of age and has to pay the price of his folly already. Just left a certain hospital and his mind is affected. Won't turn in for sleep, but sits on his sea-chest, with his head in his hands, breathing out terrible vengeance on women of a certain class. Poor 'Chester', I won't say he was a bad man at heart, but I must say he was a foolish one. Sketching or painting were the only things that would take him out of himself. He was always daubing, and what beautiful shades he would make from the ship's paint pots. If he saw a lovely sky or sunset, he would say, 'I must paint that'. He did, but also, the evil side of nature was not left out, and this I must say was in most demand.

Another A.B., who calls himself an American, was a powerful bully. 'Uncle John' says he's a fraud, a German posing as a Yank. Name of Bill Smith. He can't read or write, I write and read his love letters. Tries to bully, and 'Uncle John' knocks him out in the first round. Oh, it was grand to see a lump of fourteen stone crying for quarter.

The next is a Jordie man, who served an apprenticeship in North Sea fishing, spent some time on the Grand Banks[80] in this line, and was a good shanty man. Decent fellow on the whole, but his one failing was that he thought the North Coast men were The Ones and only ones, and this sometimes caused fierce discussion and bitterness.

And lastly, the ship's boy. Poor kid, this was to be his first and last voyage. He had never fended for himself, and had been overcared for at home. To him it is truly a dog's life. Has a good number of starched shirts, frilled fronts, collars and ties, and on Sundays does the swank. Wore a watch and chain, but was told to stow that unless he wanted it pinched. Has no go in him, scared to go aloft, never did. All the odd jobs were given him, helped the cook. He is in the second mate's watch and is having a sorry time with that brute.

We are about two weeks out and the head winds and gales have driven us well into the Bay of Biscay. If we could only clear Cape Finsterre the way would be open to sail south. We've had a gruelling.

---

[79] Presumably the Great Lakes of North America.
[80] i.e. the Grand Banks fisheries off Newfoundland.

Tack and tack, and the ship is overstrained with such driving, the deck seams have opened and our fo'c'sle and berths are always wet. During every Watch the pumps are manned, but it takes some time before we hear the joyful cry, 'There she sucks'. We never had this in 'Pincher's' time, he would not carry on in bad weather.

The men are in a very bad mood, the mates have been rubbing it in, every night watch it was sweat up this or that, mostly unnecessary work. They are talking among themselves that when sweating up the braces all will simultaneously let go, and of course, the officer who always takes the lead will have his whole weight on the rope, and will just be flicked overboard. In fact, his number will be up. This was, I had heard, an old trick often done to get rid of brutal officers. Life to some of these dare-devils was so very cheap. I hear all but say nothing. It shan't come off. As the youngest seaman, the belaying-pin is mine, I have to take the turns off pin, haul in the slack, if any, and make fast. Thanks to 'Pincher' being a splendid teacher I never take off the last turn until the slack is in. Like the reef-knot, he always explained the danger to life by not doing the right thing on board a ship. The men, I feel sure, did, on several occasions, slacken their hold, but the turn was always on the pin.

We have cleared the Cape, the wind shifted a point or two, and we are now heading south. The weather continues rough. One morning I came on deck at 4 am and away to the east the sky appears to be on fire. With awe, wonder and amazement I gaze at the great comet of November 1882.[81] Its brilliant head is about 23 degrees above the horizon, and the tail appears to fall into the sea. A beautiful spectacle. Every morning I watch it rise. It becomes smaller and smaller until at Cameroon in December, it was overheard at 10 pm, but very faint. We had altered our position some thousands of miles, the 'comet' some millions. Oh, how I did wish I was clever enough to work out its course.

'Uncle John' has gone sick – sciatica. The poor fellow can't move. I take him in hand, for last voyage I had read and re-read *The Ship's Captain's Medical Guide*. In fact, I possess a copy. I used to help 'Pincher', who, when dosing the men, would say, 'Jerry, see that so and so gets a dose of Epsom Salts for a week', and I became fairly well acquainted with the Medicine Chest and its uses, even to the making of poultices. 'Uncle John' gets some rather hot salt-water bathing – hot flannels, hot salt bag over affected part. Someone, who had my welfare at heart, packed in my kit a large bottle of Enos' Fruit Salts, with orders 'to take

[81] The comet of 1882, sometimes termed the Great September comet, initially became visible to the naked eye on 1 September 1882 and remained so for 135 days; S.P. Maran (ed.), *The Astronomy and Astrophysics Encyclopedia* (Cambridge, 1992), p. 117.

a dose every morning, when in those dreadful rivers'. I dig it out, and 'Uncle' says, 'Why, Jerry, that's a godsend; it always did me good'. He is dosed with the whole of it, and in a week is back to duty. He was so grateful. 'Jerry, my lad, I shall never forget you.' I have made a good friend.

Madeira is sighted and passed. It was grand weather. We have a passenger, called 'Bob, the Carpenter', who has been home on leave, got married, and was going back to his job: he was under a contract for three years. He had with him a dog, and was looking forward to its companionship in the lonely life he would have to live. It is missing, and suspicion has fallen on the Second Mate, who had repeatedly kicked it, owing to the ropes getting messed up, and had threatened to dump it overboard. No one ever thought such a cruel threat could be carried out. It was sad to see how 'Bob' grieved – 'My all, my chum, who would have shared my solitude, when I may not see a white man for weeks. Later I shall learn no good has come to this ship.' The men are indignant; only a dirty skunk could do a dog in. 'Old Tom', who always has a parallel for every event, says, 'I don't like it, boys, that dog will bring bad luck to this ship. If this ship ever gets to the "Rivers", and I see her empty, then perhaps I'll tell something. I was in her afore. I'm looking for something.' 'What are you looking for?' 'Shan't say, until I'm sure; don't want to frighten anybody.' 'What's he looking for, Jerry, you was in her last voyage?' 'Bust if I know.'

A few days later we run into a severe thunder storm. It's our watch below. Fearful lightning flashes and thunder crashes. 'D'ye feel that? Pins and needles all over like. It's hit something!' All hands on deck! Yes, it has struck the yard-arm of the fore-yard, ran down the lower top-sail sheet to the deck, and knocked a man down. We find he is only stunned, and on revival says, 'What a whack it gave me'. The 'sheet', which was an iron chain, is fused. It is soon replaced by another and we fellows go below to talk. 'Old Tom' – 'What did I say? That dog would bring bad luck, shouldn't wonder if he ain't a-following us. What about the 90 tons of powder, only a few inches below a lightning flash?' 'Good Lor!' No one save Tom had thought of it.

The Cook and the Second Mate are having a royal battle of words. He who always overrides anyone below his own rating, it appeared, had entered the 'Cook's own Galley', without permission, and helped himself to hot water. They are calling each other names. It's nuts for myself to hear someone who is 'king of his own castle' talk freely to this bully. 'You call yourself a cook? I could make a better one out of putty. What about that burnt pea-soup? After dinner, I thought my last day had come.' 'You call your self a Mate? I could buy better ones for four a penny, you old boggle-cross-eyed cad. Can't take a sight without standing on your head. Can't see the side-lights. If the Board of Trade knew, you would lose your ticket.'[82] This last did it. The Mate loses his control (if he had any). The Cook is down, and the brute is putting his boot into him. My brother! I can't stand this. In a flash an iron belaying-pin is whipped out, and I let fly. 'Twas a good shot – across his shoulders and neck. His attention is now turned towards myself. My fighting instincts are well to the fore, every trick I know crowds into my mind. If only I had my boots on! I step in sideways, my foot on his instep, get a bunch of his whiskers – for a keepsake. Look out, Jerry, or he will be on yours. It was a most unequal scrap – 12 stone against seven and a half – but one could only say I did my best. The Cook, who in the meantime had got himself together, went to the cabin and informed the Captain. His damaged face told its own tale. 'Struck you, has he? And a man living aft? I shall have a say in this.' In quick time he is on the scene of action. 'Stop that, Mr Mate, and go aft.' 'But, Sir, he slung a belaying-pin at me.' 'Go aft, I say, at once, or there'll be mutiny on this ship, ere long.' 'I did throw a pin at him, Sir, couldn't help it. He was kicking a man when down, and my brother, too! Had he been as big as the mainmast, I couldn't have stopped myself.' 'Go and wash your face, Jerry.' Scientifically, 'Uncle John' repairs the damage. 'Jerry, I'm so sorry you got such a drubbing. It could not be expected otherwise, but, lad, if ever I get half a chance, I'll mark that skunk, and it shall be a square scrap.'

What happened in the cabin, we chaps for'ard are supposed not to know. Gleefully, the Cook told me all about it. Both Mates got a lecture and it ran something like this. 'Mind you, he had rough stuff to tackle, his shooting-iron was handy. Mr Mates, you know I've never interfered between you and the men in the working of this ship. When in the Bay, if either of you had gone overboard from off the Braces, I should not have been surprised. There's that dog business, too. A dastardly act, whoever did it. It has unsettled the men and also myself, because I once had a dog, and know what Bob's feelings must be. But when an Officer so far forgets himself as to strike a man living aft, and to enter his Galley without permission, I must tell him that it is a breach of discipline which I would not be guilty of myself. He's a good man, adds much to our comfort, and is one of ourselves. Therefore, you'll agree I'm only doing my duty in telling you these things.' 'Yes, Sir', says the Second Mate, 'I'm very sorry I lost my temper and struck the Cook. I couldn't stand what he said about my eyesight and the Board of Trade – that it would not stand a test. I have a wife and family to think of.' 'Yes, I know', says the captain, 'on that point I shall not let you down, but you must be careful, or you will let yourself down by

---

[82] The Board of Trade was responsible for issuing certificates of efficiency for ship's officers after examination; this examination included an eyesight requirement.

the way you are treating the men'. 'Thank you, Sir. But what are you going to do about that kid who slung a belaying-pin at me? Suppose you'll log him? He ought to be triced up and I give him a round dozen or two.' 'I shall do neither. With some Captains it would be a very serious offence, he would soon be clapped in irons, logged, and perhaps at end of voyage, sent to prison. To tell you the truth, I always admire pluck.' 'And so do I', chimes in Mr Mac. 'The days of round dozens are past, which you must know. I am one of the few who desires to uplift the lower deck men. It's up to you to lend a hand. Try it. Save for two slackers, we have a decent lower deck crowd. Do your best for them and we'll leave it at that. Good afternoon, Mr Mates.'

After the Captain's straight and reasonable talk to his mates the ship became comfortable and happy. Only once did the Second lose his temper and strike a man, and this was entirely our own fault. We had discovered his tender spot, and our chanty-man was most unmerciful.

'Our Bo'sn, a Boggle-eyed son of a Gun,
Blow, my Bully boys, blow,
Lights red or green, they are not seen,
Blow, my Bully boys, blow,
Belaying pins are flying about,
Blow, my Bully boys, blow,
Burnt pea-soup gives him the Blues,
Blow, my Bully boys, blow.
His Wife and Kids are sure to suffer,
Blow, my Bully boys, blow.'

The praises of Captain and Mate were not forgotten. Landsmen may ask what purpose does chanty singing serve. Much. They are often used to give vent to feelings. Point out the Bill of Fare:

'What d'ye think he gave for dinner?
Monkeys' tails and Bullocks' liver.'

The sails Chanties are, I consider, the most serviceable. They have on many occasions saved life. Supposing, say, the large mainsail has to be stowed. Blowing hard, a black pitch night, ship tossing like a cork, no lights, save in very bad weather 'St Elmo's Fire' may be seen on iron work. The men take their stations on main-yard, the 'bunt' (centre), yard-arm and foot-rope. The sail is gathered up towards 'bunt' and is under the yard, the men on the foot-rope are leaning well forward, feet pointing aft. The sail has to be rolled over to the top of the yard. The chanty-man at the 'bunt' sings:

'Oh now you Johnnie Boker,
Come roll and turn me over,
Do, my Johnnie Boker, do.'

At the last word 'do' every man pulls his best, up rolls the sail to the top of the yard, the men on the foot-rope are forced backwards, and their feet being reversed, it is easy to visualise what would happen to anyone who failed to act at the right moment. Hence the great value of chanty songs.

Rhyme, too, has a big place in seamanship. Most of the work is set to rhyme: 'the rule of the road', knots, splicing and a host of other things, which makes them very easy to remember.

Whilst dealing with this topic I must recount how the Second Mate lost his temper. After some weeks of sweet peace we have just entered the river. Sails have to be stowed, and 'Jordie' had composed a parody on 'Johnnie Boker', which was most offensive. 'It's too hot. I can't stand this any longer', and the Second put the punch on 'Jordie'. 'Uncle John' then takes a hand. 'You strike a man when on the main-yard, do you? Strike me!' 'No, "Uncle John", it's not your quarrel.' 'I shall make it mine', says 'Uncle John'. 'Oh', replies the Second, 'double-banked am I?' 'You are not.' The Second retreated down the main rigging, muttering, 'I don't know what ships and captains are coming to, now-a-day'. What can one think of 'Uncle John'? Nobility, if you wish. He dared to risk even his life to save a ship-mate from this powerful bully. I have no doubt my affair was at the back of it. 'Jerry, if I get half a chance I'll mark that skunk.'

We encounter another thunderstorm and for some half an hour we were in an inferno. Continuous lightning flashes of all sorts and from all points, many striking the sea, which had the appearance of boiling. Deafening thunder. Three fire-balls. One with a bang as it met the water was most uncomfortably close. 'Old Tom' must, of course, call our attention to the powder. 'If that had only hit us there would have been a bust-up, and it's on a Saturday, too.' Sulphurous fumes affect breathing. Someone aptly remarked, 'There's lumps of thunder drop-ping into the sea'. All were thankful when it passed, even our hard nuts admit they felt scared and wished never to see the like of it again.

The storm has set 'Old Tom' a-talking. 'I've told you boys before and again Saturday's the unlucky day for this ship.' 'Stow that. Friday is the day for sailors' bad luck.' ''Tain't for this ship. We left port on a Saturday, saw the comet, Bob's dog dumped overboard, struck by lightning, Jerry had that awful licking.' 'That was good luck for us', says someone. 'Wast thee married on a Saturday?' 'Oh, Lor', now I remember I was.' 'Then it's your unlucky day, Tom.' 'It ain't, that was the luckiest of my life. Missus keeps like a sort of shop out Bedminster way.[83] I shall soon stop going to sea.' 'And sail in steam-boats?' interrupted one of the boys. 'No, I shan't, I shall stay home and help her. Say what you like, Saturday puts nails in her coffin. Wait until I've seen her empty, then I'll talk.' 'You old Jonah, why don't you say what you are looking for?' 'Wait, don't ask questions.'

The following Friday, 'Land Ho on the starboard beam'. The high land of Fernando Island (10,000 feet).[84] Away on our port bow is seen the Peak of Cameroon Mountains (13,000 feet) – a beautiful sight, away looking up in the clear blue sky its snow-covered top sparkles in the sun. Next morning we are well in shore and can see the mountain base plainly. Does not appear very far inland. Difficult to say how far. Such a great mass upsets one's calculation. The lines of vegetation are plainly seen. Later the land becomes very flat, with watery patches.

Early evening we drop anchor, they say at the mouth of Cameroon River.[85] When aloft furling sails I well spy out the land. Cannot see any sign of a river for miles around save a few patches of mud or sand covered with trees, some of the tops of which only show above the water. How much I would like to have a good peep at the chart, pinned to the cabin table. The Captain and Mr Mac are well studying it; they have without a doubt a very difficult task to navigate with so few points of bearing.

Sunday, with tide and sea breeze the ship's head is pointed towards the river. My station is in the main chains heaving the lead. Chart and soundings are the most essential. I cry the various depths – 'By the mark 7, deep 6, by the mark 5, deep 4, by the mark 3. Great Scott! Six threes are 18. She's drawing 16 feet of water. The lead is not going over the ground and a soft bottom, Sir'. 'Aye, aye.' The ship has grounded on the bar.[86] The sails are well filled but no progress is made. Later I report that the lead is dragging over the ground. The bar is cleared and the water deepens in places to 6, 7 and 8 fathoms. As we proceed up, the land on the right slightly rises, which gives some semblance of a bank. The hulks are sighted (store ships).[87] Sails clewed

---

[83] To the south-west of Bristol.

[84] The island of Fernando Po (now Bioko), which the Spanish had claimed since 1778, was formally occupied by Spain in 1858. It had been briefly occupied by the British between 1827–1834 and acted thereafter as an important provisioning centre for ships in the trade of the Bight of Biafra. Its facilities included a rudimentary hospital. It was also used as a depot where Kru could be landed at the end of a trading voyage to await a ship returning to the Kru coast.

[85] Strictly, the Cameroons estuary of the Wouri river.

[86] Most of the rivers in the Bights of Benin and Biafra had submerged sand bars at their mouths. Navigating across these was extremely hazardous; the use of local pilots was usually required, though payment of these became an issue of some controversy between British traders and local authorities.

[87] Hulks, which were used as store ships by traders, became increasingly common in

up and stored. Are now proceeding with the tide, which is very fast, some six to seven knots. The Captain is giving Mr Mac orders, 'Take your station at the head, there's no room to swing her. Head on to tide, I shall let go running.' This is a very dangerous manoeuvre. Umteen things can happen. Say, a ship travelling five to six knots an hour, 100 fathoms of chain cable may pay out before the anchor takes the strain, sometimes cutting hawse pipe to water's edge, or if the ship failed to answer the helm quickly would run over cable and cause damage to bottom. All buckets are filled with water to dowse windlass and hawse pipe, some sparks will fly presently. The hulks are passed. 'Let go!' Crash! The windlass and hawse pipe are like a blacksmith's anvil. 'Old Tom' – – 'What about the powder stowed in the fore-peak'. 'Shut up, you old Jonah, this ain't Saturday, it's Sunday.' Ninety fathoms before the anchor takes the strain. The ship trembles from stem to stern as if in fear, then swings in her own length, head on to tide. The cable up to 15 fathoms is hove in, hawse pipe blocked, no ropes are to be left dangling over the side at night – water snakes may wish to pay a visit. Bob has already said that there are lots of funny things in this river.

How nice it is after a rather stormy outward voyage of some 48 days[88] to sit under the fore-deck awning and have a good quiz. I note the tide is out. The fairway of the river is narrow. For miles looking seaward are banks of mud or sand, with water channels. Flocks of birds, clouds of flies, seeking, I suppose, what the tide has left. It is most uncomfortably hot. Flannel shirts are very irritating with one's body covered with prickly heat. They have to be worn. That is the order. Can wash and dry one in about a quarter of an hour, there's plenty of water now. I look towards the town (King Bell's), or rather three towns, each is enclosed within its own stockade, only a few feet above high water.[89] I've heard much from Bob. In the rainy season they are often under water. The white-washed school-house and church; its minister, a West Indian (his father formerly a slave) married the daughter of the former white parson.[90] When Bob left for home they

West African rivers once the steamship services between Britain and West Africa began in 1852. They allowed traders to bulk their produce and despatch it on the steamer. However, firms like Kings who did not regularly use the steamers, found hulks useful in allowing them to cut down 'turn-around' time on the coast.

[88] This was relatively quick for a voyage from Britain.

[89] The Duala of the Cameroons estuary were divided into three main quarters or 'towns', named after their ruler, Akwa, Bell and Deido.

[90] The Baptist Missionary Society set up its mission in the Cameroons estuary in 1845; this mission was an offshoot of its work on Fernando Po. It was established in response to an initiative originating in the West Indies and a number of its staff were Jamaican. The missionary referred to in Langdon's account was Joseph Jackson Fuller, a Jamaican who began his ministry in 1859 and who in 1861 married the daughter of Joseph Diboll,

had at least eight piccaninnies.[91] Expect there are more by now. Away up the river, less than a quarter of a mile away, is moored the hospital ship, close to a mangrove swamp.[92] Silly place to have it – so many flies. Skill, attention and cleanliness are sadly lacking. 'Abandon hope ye who enter here.'

There are four hulks, each belonging to a different firm. Ours is the *Lord Raglan*. How often had I looked at this beautiful ship lovingly, which for years was laid up near the Drawbridge, a sort of ward in Chancery.[93] Sold very cheap to our owners on condition she was not to be used for sailing. A hulk now. Her splendid spars, save the lower masts, are taken away, and the deck thatched over. She will never sail again. How often we boys have watched for an opportunity to climb her rigging. The watchman, however, was always there, and besides, being so near the Bridge, many 'snouts' (policemen) were about, who wore belts and used them on boys. They hurt, but the laughs from the grown-ups hurt more.

It is getting dark, fires are kindling in the town. Sounds of revelry, the beating of tom-toms, weird chanting and dancing. I think of the many yarns told by Bob – the fabulous animal supposed to live at the back of the Cameroons, not yet seen, save its three-toed foot-prints. The danger of swimming in the river. What! Shan't I get a swim? It's risky, lots of funny things there. The natives use the creeks. The boys who had fallen overboard or upset canoes were never seen again. Are there any saw-fish? These, I know, the Sassandrew men on the weather coast would not use their river for this reason. No, not many. They say there is an under-current, sort of eddy, once in it you are done for. Then again one may be looking at the river. There's something out there, looks like the trunk or bough of a tree, not the least movement, throw in a stone, make a ripple, it moves quickly. Allos or crocs. Dead bodies are often seen drifting down stream, some bust-up or scrap higher up; may be an epidemic, always caused by the witch. Push 'em into the river with sticks, and the sticks as well for fear of contagion. Awful thing this witch-craft business.

It's time to turn in. The men already have their beds on deck. 'Jerry, you can't doss in the fo'c'sle, it's too blinking hot.' We have some good-

an English minister in the Baptist mission. The Baptist mission left the Cameroons estuary in 1886 following the German annexation. Fuller retired in 1888. J. van Slageren, *Les origines de l'église évangélique du Cameroun* (Yaoundé, 1972), pp. 29–35.

[91] i.e. children.

[92] In many of the rivers involved in the West African trade it was common for the traders to combine together to provide a hospital ship and a surgeon for the use of ships coming out.

[93] In this period the swivel bridge, commonly called the drawbridge, at the entrance to the floating harbour in Bristol.

humoured chaff, 'Won't be now all the hot stuff is on deck. Besides I
don't like the early morning African dews, and it's dangerous to the
eyes to sleep in the moonlight (moon blindness). They say it will draw
a fellow's mouth right round to his ear (facial paralysis). I must keep
my good looks because some day I hope to get married.' 'Jerry, if you
sleep below you'll be a dead man in the morning.' 'I'll tell thee, lad,
where a light won't burn it's no place to doss. Have your own way, go
and kill yourself and put us all to the trouble of attending your funeral.'
'Oh, thanks, mind you carry me steady, no jostlings mind. Good night.'
I turn into my bunk. Can't sleep, the air is so suffocating, am compelled
to take my 'donkey's breakfast' (straw bed) and sleep on deck. Count
the beautiful stars and listen to the strange cries of the African bush.

Next morning we warp ship[94] alongside the *Lord Raglan* and for the
first time see the few white clerks in charge – ghastly white, bloodless,
dressed in immaculate white, walking corpses, they are never exposed
to the sun, no manual work (above it), waited upon hand and foot by
their black servants.[95] Bob the carpenter said, 'I'm not one of them
because I have to work, and a good thing, too, in this country, it keeps
you out of yourself. When these chaps are walking and feel tired they
are carried, slung in a pole hammock, by the natives.' He was not far
wrong. These fellows never during our stay exchanged a salutation
with us common sailormen. Perhaps after all, they may have been only
the sons of poor men with just a school board education. How often
when a kiddie I've heard my people say that the School Board Act[96]
would create a class of black-coats above the dignity of work.

The *Lord Raglan* has a small army of Kroo-Boys. I know not their
lingo, they speak fair pigeon English.[97] I address a few with some wild
Drewin cuss-words – 'Hay-a-coo' (your mother die), 'Nay-a-to-co' (your
grandmother die). 'That be damn black nigger talk, we be free Liberia
men, savey some book.' Yes, yes, one thinks, swollen heads, some
knowledge above his fellows, how will the future generations turn out?

Work, work, from 6 till 5 on deck or in ship's hold in an almost
unbearable heat. I love work, always did, nice to feel at end of day
one has done more than his bit. Other fellows may not like it, that's
my business not theirs. Everybody without grousing worked well. Why?

[94] To warp a ship involved moving the vessel in an anchorage by use of a hawser and
a kedge anchor, hauled by the crew.

[95] Such resident agents, who would remain on the coast for the palm oil 'season',
buying produce, became increasingly common in the West African trade, and more
specifically the river trade, after the introduction of steamship services in 1852.

[96] Presumably a reference to Forster's Education Act of 1870 and the school boards it
established.

[97] Pidgin English was the lingua franca of the West African trade, though (as seen in
words like 'dash' and 'palaver') it borrowed from the Portuguese of the original maritime
traders to the coast.

Because our Captain was a very decent man and wanted to make his first voyage for the owners in record time.

The Right Reverend Somebody of the Cameroons is on board. I well size him up. True negro features, heavily built – a six-footer, dressed somewhat like a bishop (I'm not well up in church ratings), silk top-hat, black frock-coat, high waist-coat, all-round collar buttoned at the back, some sort of gaiters, with a leg many in his line of business would be proud of. He is shown over the ship, but never a word said he to us sailormen. 'Captain, I would very much like my wife and elder children to inspect your ship.' 'Very pleased to see them on board any time you like.' 'Oh, thank you, Captain, you are so very kind.' Stays to lunch.

Next day the 'inspection'. I likewise size up his wife, a white woman, daughter of the late clergyman, born at Cameroons, a little sick-looking four-and-a-half-foot-come-under-my-arm woman, and mother of some ten 'mulatto kids', many with wool and the rest with hair. She wore a Dolly Varden[98] hat, a princess robe dress, its train caught up with a dress-holder – the only bit of skirt I saw on the West Coast of Africa. They, too, said never a word to we common sailormen.

Almost every day His Reverence, under some pretence, would come on board. I ask Cook whether he talks much about his church. 'Not much, save to cadge, always short of everything. "Can you, good Captain, spare me this or that, it's not for myself, you know." Not much time to talk, he'll scoff and swallow all that's going. Fancy I, Cook and Steward of this 'ere ship and a white man, too, have, after my cooking, to don my best whites, lay table in best style, and with a napkin on my arm wait on the likes of that.' 'Serves you right, you always did like the flunkey business.' 'Yes, I know, but this part I don't like. "Oh, Captain, it's so nice to sit at a well-laid table, with a splendid waiter, it reminds me of my college days."' 'That's the stuff to give you, old Cookie.' The men's remarks about her Ladyship – 'Poor little dear, what she must have to put up with with such a hulk of a husband and big family'. What was said about his Lordship will not be written. Their varied experience came well to the fore. I agree with 'Old Tom', 'He was not like the good man of Plymouth, he sort of got right inside of a fellow'. Yes, had the Vicar General of the Cameroons held out a handshake, or said, 'Men I would like to see you at my church on Sunday, be he black or white', the cloth would have been respected. I myself was intensely disappointed at not attending at least one service.

---

[98] Dolly Varden hats, which were popular in the early 1870s, were named after the heroine in Charles Dickens's *Barnaby Rudge* (London, 1841). They were straw hats with a low crown and a wide brim and were sometimes referred to as shepherdess hats. I am grateful to Ms Lucy Pratt of the Victoria and Albert museum for this information.

On a Sunday morning to hear the bell calling to church and so far
away from home. The longing for these things is difficult to describe.
It created a poor impression, especially after Covally River. But, I've
only seen the worst, the best have yet to come. There are, and must
be, real missionaries.

After one has worked very hard all day in a baking temperature,
that irresistible longing for a swim is bound to come. 'The many funny
things in this river' are somewhat a set-back for a dip. I've taken
chances before. On the Weather Coast I always went over with the
Kroo boys. Booto or Dago would say, 'Jerry, one of us, he savey swim
much'. When a school-boy I took chances with Mr Policeman (no free
swimming-baths). These very noble men would pinch our clothes and
faithfully serve their Queen and country for two-and-a-tenner a day.
We poor kids would have to run home without a fig-leaf. The grown-
ups would laugh, aye and the women, too. The laugh did hurt. Our
mothers would go to the police station to get the clothes. Two-and-six
with costs for going through our streets minus a 'leaf'. Disgraceful,
disgusting, would cry the goody-goody; they ought to come to the West
Coast of Africa where every day they would see thousands without 'fig-
leaves'. Splash! I take another chance. The 'funny things' make one
sort of creep. 'Jerry', says 'Uncle John', 'we shall yet have to attend
your funeral'. 'No, you won't Uncle, I should only be a mouthful for
the crocs; they would save the trouble.' 'Very kind of them', replies
Uncle.

The main hold is empty of cargo. We start loading our return cargo
of palm kernels in bulk.[99] The ship is not properly equipped for such
cargo – we have no 'dunnage mats'[100] nor 'shifting boards'. Nothing to
cover the 'bilge holes' and the openings of her inside skin, save
makeshifts, and very little of that. The Bulkhead of 'Chain Lockers' is
rocky. The officers' attention is drawn to these things. Can't be helped,
must take its chance. Day after day the kernels are shot into the fore,
main and after holds; we lads are below trimming.

'Uncle John' goes sick – his old enemy sciatica. 'Uncle', says I, 'do
you remember the book you read to us about the three sailormen who
had rheumatism; their mess-mates buried them up to the neck in the
hot sand; then after such hot work left them for a while to get a drink
or something; and the crocs came along and pinched off their heads?'
'Yes, what about it?' 'I was thinking if we buried you in the palm
kernels – they are hot and oily – it may do you good.' 'That's a good

---

[99] Palm kernels were usually transported bulked together in 'mats' made of rope.

[100] Dunnage mats were stowed in the hold to prevent damage to freight and to stabilize
the cargo. The shifting of a cargo of kernels, as occurred on this voyage, was of
considerable hazard.

suggestion', says the boys. Every morning 'Uncle' is placed on a hatch, lowered into the hold and covered with the palm kernels. In less than a week he is back to duty, hopping about like a young two-year-old, and says, 'Boys, it was so kind of you, I feel better than I have for years'.

For some days a look-out has been kept for a barque belonging to our owners. She is sighted coming up the river from Rotterdam to Calabar and Cameroon with a cargo of gin.[101] We were looking forward to seeing fresh faces, but not yet, she has grounded on a sloping bank and at low water is careered well over. Sorry time for crew, who will have to get about like monkeys. She will have to be lightened. A small steamer (same firm) is coming from Calabar[102] to attend, and will, if we are ready, tow our ship out of the river. We also hear that some of the barque's crew are down with fever.

There's a commotion among the *Lord Raglan*'s Kroo boys. All are shouting and gesticulating. Two of their number have a grievance as to which is the best man at scrapping. They are going to fight it out. Each has his own backers. Ivory bracelets are worn. It must be understood the blackman has but few rules, if any, for their game. We use our fists; they close the fist with thumb pushed up between the first and second finger. The thumb nail is carefully trained to grow like a gouge, and at every blow a twist is given. Pieces of flesh are gouged out like cheese. The 'ivories' are used with pull down slanting blow, surprising how the square edge will chip lumps off. Their primary object is to gouge out the eyes. In a moment an eye is out. Sometimes it is replaced in the socket and the fight proceeds. This fight lasted over an hour. The furious savageness was most disgusting. Which was the victor I do not know, only blindness of each stopped the fight. Hence the phrase 'one-eyed nigger' may have some meaning, and there are many on the West Coast.

Christmas Day. The bell is calling to church. In my mind it seems to say, 'Not for you, Jerry, not for you'. This and other events will never be forgotten. It is fearfully hot – 110 degrees in the shade – strange we all feel the heat more than when at work; may be our sumptuous fare is the cause – turtle, African beef (tough), real plum-duff, yams (sweet potatoes), plantains and heaps of other fruit. We have a good cook and captain, too. He is giving his best in return for our best, 'Mr Mac, as much as I want the ship ready to sail in order to get a tow down the river, the men shan't work on Christmas Day'. The cook has much to

---

[101] Gin, or more strictly Dutch schnapps, was a staple of the West African trade.

[102] Calabar (usually termed Old Calabar in this period) was one of the major ports of the Bights for the West African trade. Kings had only entered its trade, however, in 1879.

do; others and myself lend a hand. The shell of turtle has to be taken off and a post-mortem held. Says cookie, 'It's a lady'. A bucket-full of eggs and entrails is given to the Kroo-boys, it will all go into their cooking pot – mix well with the palm oil – fish and monkey already there. The natives are not over choice. Chop (food) is usually scarce – cannibalism is not yet minus, at least so I had heard from those who had professed to have partaken, and of course I, nosey like, asked what it tasted like. 'Pig', was the reply.

Our feast is served, which is just IT. Healths are drank to everybody near and far – some chin-wag – sleep – then early supper, soft tack and cake.

'Say lads, that barque what got off the ground yesterday and came up, what d'ye say if we take our boat and pay a Christmas visit, some are down with fever, might cheer them up, maybe help them.' Right-ho, we will! I must be in this. Arrive at ship and not a soul is to be seen, make for the fo'c'sle and shout, 'Below there, a merry Christmas'. No answer. We look at each other. 'Old Tom' said, 'Can't help it boys, manners or no manners, I'm going down'. The rest follow. What a sight! Every man was in his bunk, and to make matters more difficult every man was a Dutchman, and those who could speak English were too ill to talk. In the thick, fetid atmosphere, with spluttering oil-lamp, cockroaches are swarming, you crunch them under foot, in the bunks, and worst of all crawling over the sick men. A bad sign this. To-morrow the worst of these men will be removed to the hospital ship. May heaven help them. We return to our ship, sorry we had done so little to help these poor fellows.

A few days after the river takes toll from us. 'Mr Mac', two seamen, the Cook and boy are ill. The hospital doctor attends. I lack words to describe the drunken, filthy, foul-mouthed blackguard. Three visits, each time drunk. Never have I heard such low-down talk. Sailormen will use cuss-words, but few talk filth. Perhaps, as 'Uncle John' said, he mistook us men for swine, and like an accommodating gentleman came to its level.

The ship is loaded to Plimsoll's mark. More and more is shot in. 'Are you going to sink her?' says someone to the officers. 'No, but we must get the kernels well up to deck, or they will shift when she rolls'. At last she can't take any more, there is only a few inches of free board, a bucket of water at gangway can be dipped up easily.

The eve of sailing. The Blue Peter[103] is hoisted at the fore. What for? I don't know, unless to inform a few white clerks, and by the way, one

[103] The Blue Peter flag is used to signal that the ship is about to sail and that all concerned should report on board.

of their number, who can't stand the climate – twelve months nearly cooked him – is returning with us, of course as first-class passenger. More work for old cookie. Bob, the carpenter, had to live for'ard. 'Bust it, why don't sailormen don a black coat and get the better things of life?'

There's a confab going on – 'Old Tom' a-talking. 'This 'ere ship is much overloaded for a northerly winter passage. When she gets in the roaring forties that there cargo is going to shift. She'll be on her beam-ends and down she goes like a stone. I've reasons for knowing, to-morrow is Saturday, her bad luck day. I've seen her empty and didn't find a-what I was looking for.' 'Shut up you silly old Jonah, why in the blazes don't you say what you wanted to find?' 'Oh, that's so easy now, don't get frightened.' 'Rats I was looking for, last voyage she was overrun. Ask Jerry.' This I confirm. 'You all know what it means when they desert a ship, her number is up. I tell 'ee again she ain't going to reach her next port, she's much below the Plimsoll mark. The law is on our side, we ought to chuck it.'

'Uncle John' takes a hand, 'There is much in what Tom says, the law is on our side, but who is there in this God-forsaken country to administer it? Cape Coast Castle is the nearest consul,[104] it would take weeks to get at him. If we were bound for an English port we might get a say, but Falmouth for orders means somewhere on the Continent, otherwise the ship would not be loaded so deeply. Say, if we did down tools, some of her stuffing taken out, and without shifting boards, the ship would be more dangerous than before. We should all get logged at end of voyage. There would be a big bill for delay and paid out of our wages.' The last did it. Take our chance and carry on.

Next day we start our homeward voyage, are towed out of the river.[105] Mr Second Mate is at the head, 'Mr Mac' too ill for duty. One can only hope he will soon get well. I have no particular wish to be in this bully's watch. His whiskers are so tempting. A good bunch would make a fine watch-chain if cross-pointed (round plait).

At sea again. So good at least to breathe pure air and occasionally get a breeze. All save 'Mr Mac' are getting better, is in a bad way. I broke the ice by just popping into his berth to say, 'How d'ye do?' I noted he could hardly help himself, so make him comfy and tidy up berth. 'So grateful, you'll come and see me again, Jerry?' 'Yes, I'll pop in every watch.' For weeks this continued, the very kind boys often during

---

[104] The trading castle at Cape Coast was the centre of British administration on the Gold Coast; the Gold Coast was annexed in 1874. The official commanding British administration was the governor, not the consul. However, from 1872 there was a British consul, with a consular court, based much closer to the Cameroons at Old Calabar.

[105] i.e. by the small steamer from Old Calabar referred to above.

the night watch would take my look-out, or turn at wheel, to enable
me to give him attention. He said much during that time. His early
life, wife and children, that hell of a pub and boarding house his father-
in-law kept, he would never see them again. 'Yes, you will, Mr Mac, I
got you in tow and will see you through.' 'Jerry, your kindness hurts,
you ought to be a woman. Only to think I was so unkind to you on
the outward voyage, I can't understand it.' 'That's nothing, Mr Mac,
you never landed me one.' 'No, I'm glad of that, because I took a
fancy for you when coming down the Bristol river. I hope that bully
will keep his hands off you. That talk which the captain gave us did
me much good.' 'Don't worry, Mr Mac, let bye-gones be bye-gones, if
the Second Mate was in your present boat he would get good attention.'
'I can't understand it, Jerry, I've never been used to it.' One night,
after some three weeks of illness, he is in a very weak state. 'Jerry, they
tell me sharks are following the ship.' 'Well, that's nothing, there's
plenty in these waters.' 'They are waiting for me, I shan't see the
morning.' 'Yes, you will. I've told you before, I've got you in tow.'
'Jerry, come closer. I've been a bad man, I once did a man in, and it
was not a fair scrap (particulars were given, but need not be written).
Since then I've never been happy. I changed my name. "He" had a
wife and family. Oh, what misery I have caused. Always before me,
even when drunk. Do you think God will forgive me?' 'Yes, I'm sure
He will because you are sorry, but it will be up to you when better to
make what amends you can.' 'Jerry, give me your hand.' He held it a
good time. He sleeps – the first for a long time. The crisis has passed.

We make slow progress. Drift past the island of Fernando.[106] Only
calms and cats-paws.[107] Three weeks after leaving [the] river are off
Prince's Island, further drift south-west of the line and meet the south-
east trade wind. Sails are squared and north we go. Later, the north-
east trade wind, pass the Western Islands, and here our troubles
commence, well in the roaring forties. One night are hove-to on the
port-tack; our middle watch has had a rough time, glad to get below
at 4 am; ship is pitching badly, at seven bells.[108] 'Now you jolly sleepers
below there, tumble out and have your breakfast.' 'Old Tom', to save
our getting a wetting, has brought the coffee and cracker ash from the
galley. He is in his oil-skins. 'We've had an awful time since 4 o'clock,
she put one over that almost put her on her beam-ends, I never
expected her to rise again. When she did, most of the starboard
bulwarks had gone. See what a list to starboard there is; those blessed

---

[106] As on the windward on Langdon's first voyage, because of the prevailing winds and
currents in the Gulf of Guinea, it was the practice of traders to this region to drift south
in order to catch the south-east trade winds for the return to Britain.

[107] Light breezes marked by slight ripples on the surface of the sea.

[108] i.e. 7.30 am.

palm kernels have busted the chain locker bulkhead into the pump wells, and they are choked with them kernels. I told you before what would happen, and it's Saturday, too.' Things are not rosy, the list is most uncomfortable. One has to eat sitting on the fo'c'sle deck, with feet against some thing solid to avoid slipping to leeward. Our turn on deck. 'Jerry, there's a gasket adrift on the main upper topsail yard.' I mount aloft; the wind is terrific; try to face it; can't, takes away one's breath. Not very far away to leeward a fine barque is hove-to. When we dip into a valley of water neither ship is visible to the other, and when on top of a wave one is looking down on the other. My work done I return to deck. 'Get the flag-bag, Jerry, going to signal the barque.' Our ensign upside-down (distress signal) is hoisted. In a few minutes the French flag is flying on the barque which is manoeuvring for a favourable position. Her stay-sails are set; she's dancing towards us — a thing of life. Splendid seamanship. Beautiful sight to see how skilfully she was handled. This iron barque of Bordeaux, with black and white chequered sides, looked like a bird as she sailed past our lee quarter.[109] Written on our signal-board, 'Our cargo has shifted to starboard, pumps choked, making water, going to ware, will you stand by?' Up go her flags, 'I'll stand by, ware ship'.[110]

To ware a heavily listed ship in a roaring gale and heavy seas is a most difficult and dangerous manoeuvre. The ship has to be turned right-about-face; then the wind and waves will beat upon our best side. Three great risks have to be taken, twice the ship will get into the trough of sea, and once before the wind and sea. In the trough there's every chance of capsizing. Before the wind and sea, if ship pooped a sea, she would go down steer first.[111] As we are almost on our beam-ends these risks must be taken, or turn turtle.

We take our stations, squaring the yards as ship pays off before the wind. I am at the main port braces. We know the danger. There is no fear. We are cracking jokes. The ship is now before the wind, with yards squared, like a log, no steerage way, a fearful big sea is rolling up aft. (Picture looking up to Brandon Hill,[112] and you've got it.) 'Say your prayers, boys', says 'Uncle John', 'that will finish us'. Inwardly mine were said. This mountain of water reaches the stern, the ship rises with it, we are just sliding down a huge wave, much broken water is shipped, but this doesn't count. 'Hurrah! She's moving, has steering

---

[109] Bordeaux and Marseilles were the main French ports involved in the West African trade.

[110] More usually spelt 'wear'. This involved turning the ship from port tack to starboard, or vice versa, by allowing the wind to pass around the stern.

[111] [sic]; presumably stern first.

[112] In the centre of Bristol close to College Green; site of a fort and part of the city's defensive walls.

way, the yards are braced up, wind is now on our best side and will safely outride the gale.' I look in to see how 'Mr Mac' had fared during the last few hours. Much water I know had entered the cabin; am anxious because he is now convalescent, but he must not come on deck, it's too cold. I see the affrighted face of our 'passenger'. 'Jerry, it grieves me to be locked here with this when you boys are in the thick of it.' The other, it appears, had given way to scare. Even for 'Mr Mac' it was not a relish, and he was a fearless man. It had been said he feared neither God, man nor the devil – a changed man now. 'Jerry, we were very near it, but something within me, what, I cannot explain, said it would be alright.'

When the gale abated, the ship was sailed close-hauled on the starboard tack for all she was worth, to re-shift the cargo; and it was done. With patched canvas bulwarks, like a wounded bird, we limp north and sight the Scillies. A Falmouth pilot comes aboard, 'I have your orders, an easy fiver this time. Harburg, 13 miles above Hamburg.'[113] You have a fair wind up Channel. Good-bye, quick passage.' All are intensely disappointed, are most done in. Salt-water boils are in abundance – I have a beauty on my wrist (sugar and soap will draw anything). Others have bruises, owing to slimy decks. Another reason – we wanted to test the new Plimsoll Act about overloading. 'Uncle John' had it already, 'No', says he, 'the owners are too artful to let ship touch an English port'. The result is our two slackers again go sick; only the grub will ferret them out of their bunks.

The fair wind takes us to the Start, its back's right in our teeth.[114] For days are tacking from English to French coast. Our mainsail gets busted. 'Come, lads, with me', says our Captain, 'and save the bits'. Good stuff, this man; has taken his watch since our leaving the river, owing to 'Mr Mac's' illness. All man the main yard. Flop! Bash! The ribbons are flying over our heads, more than one gets a black eye. Wind again changes to our favour. Creep up to Deal. A North Sea pilot boards, 'Take you across for £25, Captain?' 'I'll give £20.' 'It's too cheap, but as it's a fair wind, I'll take it.' Our good man can now take a well-earned rest. The pilot drives for all she's worth, pass those dreaded Goodwins. The Galloper Lightship is just lighting up. At night are sailing in the North Sea. Lane after lane of fishing boats' lights.

[113] Hamburg was the main port for the palm kernel trade from West Africa, the kernels then being transported to the German and Dutch markets for processing. The sharp increase in Hamburg's African trade only began in the late 1870s and was due to the development of the margarine industry in this period, for which palm kernel oil was a vital ingredient. Kings' involvement in the Hamburg trade was a sign of considerable enterprise; L. Harding, 'Hamburg's West Africa trade in the nineteenth century', in Liesegang, Pasch and Jones, *Figuring African Trade*, pp. 363–391.
[114] Presumably Start Point, South Devon.

Marvel how Mr Pilot can twist in and out. Only another couple of days, and then in port. But not yet. We yet have to take our worst gruelling. Next day wind changed dead ahead, with fierce blizzards for a week. Another man goes sick (genuine, we think). Rigging and ropes are covered with icicles. The few hands have to tack ship every watch. Pass a great number of packing cases; some ship must have gone down. 'Keep a good look-out.' One afternoon, my two hours at wheel is almost up. Mr Pilot comes on deck, looks away to windward, a-sort of sniffs like, says it's going to blow. 'Oh Lor', thinks I, 'it is a-blowing now'. Take in the upper topsails, another half-an-hour at wheel. I had been numbed, but now I feel nothing of it. The relief man at last! Go forward, take off mittens, can't straighten out fingers. Flop my arms to warm up like. Pins and needles, can't stand the pain, it makes one yell. 'What's the matter, Jerry?' 'Don't know, it's awful.' 'I do', says he, after looking at my fingers, 'you've got frost-bite. Icy cold water, put 'em in and rub well and keep away from the galley fire.' Mine was only a touch, what the pain of real frost-bite must be, one dare not think. That night it blew a raging gale. Next day (Good Friday)[115] it died down, and towards evening it became a dead calm with sunshine. My pen cannot describe the sunset – all colours, those angry greens, chariots and horses a-racing; what heaps of things can be seen when looking at a gorgeous sunset. 'Chester, do come on deck and look at it, sure you would sketch it.' 'I'm too ill, regret I cannot.' Then he must be ill, yet – strange – always ready for grub. It is so pleasant to have dry decks and feet. Never again will I take another voyage without sea-boots. Those flannels did it, yet the somebody meant well.

Midnight – just a puff from the west – with fine snow flakes. At last a fair wind. Square the yards. At 4 am our watch below; at 8 am our next watch on deck. It is blowing a gale and ship is covered with snow. Heligoland looms on our port bow. Mr Pilot has his bearings. Crowd on all sails, I'll give her beans. Are making a good ten knots, ship creaking and groaning as if in pain. Two Hamburg pilot boats are sighted. 'We want a Hamburg pilot', is signalled. Get in reply, 'Can't board you, sea running too high'. 'No matter', says our North Sea pilot, 'my ticket goes well up the Elbe. Shall expect that extra fiver'.

Sniffing round the galley, say, 'Cookie, there's something good for dinner'. 'Yes, fore and aft will get a good bust, am using my last tins of meat and soup.' 'Kind old Cookie, you've fed the wild animals well, why don't you apply for a job at the Zoological Gardens?' My expectations for dinner are great. Mr Second Mate is in the fo'c'sle, asking the sick men to show a leg on deck. 'Come, lads, I won't ask you to work, we want a clean bill of health.' The Germans are so very

[115] 23 March 1883.

strict with ships coming from a fever country. What about 'Mr Mac'?
Oh, he's on duty for the first time this morning. 'Now, my good lads,
do start, if only to oblige me and a good captain. If you don't we shall
be clapped in quarantine for a long time.' Only the last sick man
responded. The other two were old hands, they knew the German
medical officer would order them to hospital. For weeks would have a
lazy time, well treated, and later a passage to England at the owners'
expense. These are the fellows who always enjoy bad health.

Eight bells, am just going below. 'Clew the royals up.'[116] Up you go,
Jerry', says that bully, the Second Mate. I think of my nice dinner, it
will get cold. When a little up rigging and clear of his boot, I hold
forth – it just ripped out. 'You old cross-eyed...'. I feel better after this.
At the royal the sail is well covered with snow, and bellied out. Get it
almost in, blown out again by heavy gust of wind. Finger nails started
and bleeding. At last the gasket is around it and I return to deck. My
weather eye is kept on Mr Second Mate, he will give me a sly one.
Nothing was said. I think he feared the captain and 'Mr Mac' who
were on deck.

I get below and have dinner alone. The boys have turned in to sleep.
Bump! She's aground! The two sick men in a tick are out of their
bunks. All hands on deck. They are first up. Bumps and bumps. Look
out! The top-masts are falling. At each bump we are thrown off our
feet. Mr Second Mate, axe in hand, asks for instructions. 'Shall I cut
the masts out of her, Sir?' 'No, it won't be of any use, the tide is past
flood.' Mr Pilot is ringing his hands and with tears in his eyes says,
'For twenty years I've been a North Sea pilot, and never sprung a
rope-yarn. This old tub will be my ruin.' Green rollers are dashing
over the stern. Decks are awash. 'Get out the boat!' As usual it's lashed
on main hatch and full of lumber. Nasty remarks are passing. The two
sick men are trying to save their own skin. In this quarter things look
ugly. Somebody will walk into the two if they give much lip. Bump!
Bash! Bang!! Like a cannon report, the deck lifts and splits right across
amidships. She's done for, her back is broken. The water rushed in
with a gurgling sound. Yes, she had passed over. Not a movement.
Dead. The sea had claimed her.

The boat is now cleared of rubbish. To remove from main hatch
the fore topsail halliard are hooked on and lifted to rail of ship. It has
to be launched broadside to sea. 'Watch your chance, boys. On the
third roller heave.' Out she goes, fills with water on the next roller. In
our haste only one painter (bow rope) was on her, and of course is
broadside to sea without a stern rope to haul her round. 'Down you
go, Jerry, and haul her round', says the Second Mate. I slip over the

---

[116] i.e. draw up the sails to the yard on the mast in preparation for furling.

side and enter boat. The icy water up to my waist gives a sort of shiver, am making my way towards stern of boat, a big roller is looming up. 'Look out!' someone cries. Too late! The boat is turned bottom up. As it turns I slip over the gun-wale. The green water covers me. My eyes are open. Wonderful what one can think and see (home scenes) in a few seconds. I am rising, can feel the keel of the boat between my legs. I'm going to get some damage – rupture perhaps. To my great surprise am lifted gently like one would lift a baby, a rope coil is thrown. Good old 'Uncle John', a splendid shot, it lands over my head. I grab, the slack is hauled in, the receding wave leaves me for a few seconds out of the water. My wet clothes feel like a ton weight, am too numbed for any effort. 'Haul me up.' A lad drops over side on a rope, grabs hold of my coat collar, am soon on deck. 'Jerry, Jerry', says 'Mr Mac', I thought you were gone. Come in the cabin and get fixed up.' I hear his orders, 'No more of this foolhardy game, get the topsail halliards on her nose (bow of boat), lift her high and drop her quick again. That is a better way to empty her of water. It ought to have been done in the first place and not risk the lad's life.'

After getting fixed up, mostly by wringing out my wet clothes, am again on duty. A change has overtaken the weather, it has cleared, a lightship can be seen some miles away. Her flags and ours are a-wagging, 'Stand by your ship if you can, a life-boat from Cuxhaven will assist.' Good. In our own boat would have had a poor chance among so many sandbanks. Towards evening the life-boat, under sail, is bearing towards us. I note she has a small crew – sail being much used. We leave the wreck; each two men are given an oar; we are only too pleased to pull, it keeps us warm. After several hours we enter Cuxhaven Harbour. Many folk are watching as we step ashore on that frosty moonlight night, with crisp snow under-foot. A gentleman gave a short address in good English on the 'Providence of God', with prayer of thanks. Stimulants are served out; I'm not taking any – have my own reasons for refusing; a promise to one over the border is not easily broken. What! An English sailor not taking grog? As I walk through the streets of this quaint town, with its snow-covered buildings glistening in the moonlight, my companion, who speaks fluent English, is plying heaps of questions about the voyage, ship and crew. 'Old Tom's' voice is hard, 'Didn't I say Saturday was her unlucky day, and she would never reach port?' 'Yes, Tom, but we have.'

After our experience the comfort of an inn, warmth and security gives a feeling difficult to describe. An old-fashioned place with low ceiling and heavy beams. Lager and other drinks flow freely. Glasses clink – our lads are being treated. I am the odd dry number – refusal upon refusal, no thanks, no matter. I can and shall live it down; my will is my own and not other peoples'. Rattling tunes are played at the piano. Mine host, with spectacles and briar pipe, together with his sons, is serving us and laying the good things for our supper. Oh, my! What a take-in for us famished lads. By way of grace, 'The Fatherland' and 'God Save the Queen' are played – all standing. White soup – looks like water. One spoonful – it's nice and spicy. More please. German sausage by the yard. Help yourself. And heaps of other things. Then to bed.

My brother and I have a room to ourselves, very clean and comfortable. 'Say, Harry, d'ye think the bedclothes are enough, it's only a sheet and thin covering.' 'It's all feathers. Try it.' We tumble in – like falling into the warm sea. Soon asleep. I awake before daylight, am wet with perspiration, aches and pains all over like. Later when the others wake, say, how bad I feel. 'It must be those wet togs you kept on.' 'Or,' says I, 'the sausage'. 'Lay on a bit, kid, I'll go to the cook-house and get a strong cup of tea.' He did and it put me right, save for a cough and hoarseness. But I had my suspicion something stronger than tea was put in.

After a spanking breakfast mine host says, 'Gentlemen, if you will allow I vill read you the newspaper account of your wreck'. Newspapers on a Sunday, I think, are wicked; only last night I thought the Germans very religious. Mine host, almost without an error, translated the long account with many details through the voyage, into good English. Now I know who my nice companion was last night – the newspaper man!

Harry and I are out to see the sights. Easter Sunday morning – everybody looks so happy; most are going to church. Salutations from many are given in English. We wander round the harbour, spot the quaintly built Dutch ships, then round the dykes. 'Say, Harry, ain't this like our New Passage on a large scale? Remember our Sunday School treat there?' Enter the forts; not a soul about; all spick and span. 'Say, these guns are different to ours on Brandon Hill.' 'Rather! These are breach-loading.'[117] Get back to a jolly dinner and sight-see for the rest of the day.

On Monday have to attend the British Consul re our shipment to England and draw some cash. But before doing so we all raid the barber's for a trim up – and it's wanted, too, for some of us looked like Robinson Crusoe. In the afternoon are driven in by a snow-storm. 'Have a drink with me', says Bully Smith. With some lip – No thanks! 'Let's make the young —— have some.' In an instant my arms are pinioned and I am lifted off my feet. 'Now, Chester, pour it down his throat.' The heels of my boots are driven into his shins, and his hold is released, but before he could land me one, 'Mr Mac' had given him one behind the ear. The old spirit had returned. With eyes flashing he

[117] [sic]; breech-loading.

says, 'Anyone who touches that lad touches me. Come on' (to Smith). He, to his shame, was ready. 'No, you don't', says 'Uncle John', 'he's a sick man. I'll take his place. And all of you let Jerry alone. If he don't want to drink, there's not a man's son here that shall make him.' The bully climbed down, he already knew who was the better man.

On Tuesday our orders are to ship for London on Wednesday morning. I get in all the sight-seeing I can. In the evening I attend a concert and dance – splendid music; at least I thought so. On returning to the inn I find the boys fuddled and quarrelsome. 'Bully Smith' is still chewing how 'Uncle John' took him down yesterday. They sleep in the same room. When turning in, Smith is still nagging. 'Take that', says 'Uncle John', lifting a wash-basin high above his head. Bash! It's on the other fellow's head; the bottom is knocked out and the rim is resting on his shoulders. The scene is so ludicrous that everyone save Smith laughs. It's a red rag. The fellow is just furious; and hits out at anyone. Mine host appears, 'I will call the police, I never had such men in mine house before'. The rim has to be broken. 'Uncle John' is given another bed and peace is restored.

Next day, after a long pull well out in the Elbe, we board the SS *Martin*, from Hamburg to London, as fore-cabin passengers. There is already one lady passenger, and the affrighted look on this woman's face will never be forgotten when our rough lot of sailormen entered the cabin. I am glad to say the Captain found her a berth aft. Worse luck, there is a bar on board and our fellows have money. They have tasted blood with so much treating by the good people of Cuxhaven – a silly way I think of showing kindness. I take a good look around. Between decks cattle are penned, also there is a deck crowd of Polish Jews, who must not, as per order, enter our cabin. The men, women and children are the most motley lot I've ever seen.

We pass near our wreck. Dear old ship; for over two years it had been my home – my first love; met her doom only by a fluke; she was not very far off her course. If only that buoy had not been washed away. Just like life – so many 'ifs'. Glad it was not the old pilot's fault. Good-bye, old thing, I shall always remember you with pride.

Our rations are good and well served, so for a couple of days it will be eat and sleep. At night it blew great guns, and the ship is putting her nose into a very heavy sea. I am snug in my bunk. Lucky Jerry, no watch this night! But what about those poor people with a deck passage, who just now were hammering on our door, even praying for shelter? Those cruel orders; it hurts one, it does.

The frightful spectacle next morning – the men, women and children and babies had been battened down with the cattle! Awful sight! Human beings and cattle sea sick – all are laying in filth and muck! Mothers in last stage of collapse suckling their babies. Sick at heart I return to deck, having seen enough misery and wretchedness to last a lifetime.

Another sight, different from the last. Passing through a fishing fleet, the small steamers collecting from one boat to another; the Bethel-ship chasing round, too.[118] One wonders how her parson would act after seeing what I had just seen. I never felt so helpless.

Laying in my bunk am watching the silly antics of the now boisterous crowd. Mr Second Mate is smoking a cigar, and for a joke (so he said) puts its lighted end on my cheek. I yell out with the pain. 'Mr Mac' is again my champion and protector. He is going to walk into him. 'No, no, you don't', says 'Uncle John', 'you're a sick man; I want a turn at this. He was always down on Jerry'. A ring is formed and each commences to spar for an opening. Remember, each knew the game. The Captain appears, 'Men, I'll have no fighting on my ship. The drink will be stopped, if you don't desist. Don't forget I have a shooting iron and know how to use it'. Peace is again restored.

Have entered the Thames. Must take in every outline. Gravesend, Woolwich, Greenwich and the 'Pool'.[119] Turn in, and next morning are alongside St Katherine's Wharf. Have to pass the customs. My lady, the passenger, must, I think, be a governess – lots of books and much fine lingerie are on exhibition; those officers show but scant mercy. Our destination is Bristol. Up Tower Hill, turn to right and take underground to Paddington. I may mention I had drawn two pounds in German money, and after buying presents retained one-half gold mark, one silver pfenning and some bronze. The fare to Bristol is eleven and threepence. I change my money and get only nine and sixpence for the lot, so that I am short. What shall I do? 'Haven't you anything to sell?' I pull out an African gold ring. 'I'll give you the two bob for it.' In my anxiety I part with it. Jerry, you've got to pay for experience among the land sharks. At Paddington have to wait for train. Shipwrecked sailors – someone points. Toffs want to know all about it. 'Come and have a drink. Have what you fancy.' Silly stupid custom, will spend much in this way, but if one was to ask for the loan of a couple of bob, which I could not, even to save my ring, may get run in for begging.

Bristol at last! We shake. 'Mr Mac' – 'Jerry, I'm awfully sorry to see that scar on your face; you and I must sail again together. Don't forget to come and see me; I want to do you well'. We part, he to that hell of a boarding-house, and I to homely digs. And here ended my second voyage – a short one, but full of ripe experience and adventure.

Within a fortnight I heard that 'Mr Mac' had been taken to Bristol

---

[118] Presumably a mission boat of some kind. 'Bethel' was commonly used among sailors to refer to a place of worship.

[119] The Pool of London; Langdon's ship would berth in the Lower Pool.

Royal Infirmary and has expressed a wish to see me. I go. He was so delighted. Against orders he sits up to greet me. 'Nurse, nurse, this is Jerry.' 'Young man, your ears must often burn, he just raves about you.' 'Jerry, we must sail together, I'm going back to the West India Trade, never ought to have made that river trip, but I wanted to sample it. My former Captain will give you a berth, and I shall join her on the next voyage. I must pay for your schooling, and someday see you aft.'

Before I took my next voyage he had passed over, and it can only be hoped that his soul rests in peace.

THIRD VOYAGE

17 May 1883 to 19 November 1884

A few days after home arrival Harry and I are in town, and we run across 'Pincher'. 'Hully, you lads, I am so pleased to meet you.'[120] Our old ship got piled up.' 'Tell me about it.' An account is given. Then says 'Pincher', 'I want you both to sail with me. The owners are buying another ship for my command – a barquentine named the *Edmund Richardson*.[121] "She" is to be re-fitted with a six-foot false keel, new copper, and thoroughly overhauled, and I guess "she" will be the smartest craft on the coast. Also the fo'c'sle is a house on deck. The ship will be most comfortable.' 'Thank you, sir', says I, 'but I want to get away south, to Rio, round the Horn, and 'Frisco'. 'Yes, Jerry, I well know your ambition. Come with me another voyage; it will make a man of you. As I cannot yet ship you as an AB, I will give you five shillings per month less than the men, and further, as the ship has to be re-rigged, you shall have employment thereon.' The last did it. I could not let such an opportunity slip; it would mean much experience for the future. The visions of work-up jobs, including 'copper-polishing', which had already crowded into my mind, vanished like a mist at such a splendid offer. We sailormen, as a rule, have very short memories about the indignity of the work we are so often compelled to do.

For several weeks I am working on the ship and gaining much experience. In the 'Lime-kiln Dock' (Hotwell Road), the ship is lifted off the stocks by means of wedges; the false keel is added, and fastened with long copper bolts. It was here that I nearly lost the number of my mess. The old copper sheeting was being hoisted out of dock when off flies the winch handle and I am precipitated well over the edge of the dock. I am thankful I did not loose myself. My hands are dug well into the dock sides, and with sailor-like promptitude a shipmate has plumped himself across my legs. My word! I thought they were cracked; but save for some damage to my knuckles all is OK, and work is resumed.

I find 'Pincher' has engaged some of our last crowd to help re-rig the ship, with the promise to sign them on for the voyage; of course, it was much cheaper than employing professional 'riggers'. 'Uncle John'

[120] Langdon has clearly left out quotation marks here, since it would be himself reporting that the *Ceara* had sunk.
[121] 291 tons, Capt. Swan, R. & W. King, owners, *Bristol Presentments*, 17 May 1883.

and 'Chester' are very decent fellows, but the bully, Smith, and the cross-eyed Second Mate, whose whiskers are so tempting, I did not like. Our new First Mate, who will be called 'David', was an elderly man, holding a Master's Ticket. Owing to the passing of the old packet ship, he, like many others, had fallen on evil times. He was just the man 'Pincher' required – new to the coast and too old to become a Trader. 'David', in his younger days, was hot stuff, but had become a changed man. Occasionally, however, he did forget his changed nature, and let it rip. In the middle of a string of strong adjectives he would suddenly stop and say, 'Men, I'm sorry; I forget myself'. It was really genuine, for often a tear would glisten on his eyelid. In danger he was as brave as a lion. My great hope is to get selected for his watch.

I revel in the work of rigging a ship. Taking down, and sending up masts and yards, wire-splicing 'dead eyes', 'worm and parcel with the lay, turn and serve the other way', blankets round the masts to take the chafe of 'shrouds', setting up backstays and shrouds, 'rattling' down, 'bending' sails, and much more very interesting work. When all is finished my ship, I think, looks rakish, save the bowsprit and jib-boom; cocks up too much, but this cannot be altered owing to 'her' build. I am very proud of our deck, and to myself, 'she' has become a thing of real beauty.

Signing-on day. The usual crowd of parasites outside of shipping office. Fifty shillings a month are the AB's wages. 'What are you paying this young fellow?' asks the shipping master (Attwood). 'Pincher' in reply said, 'Forty-five shillings'. Upon which Attwood says, 'Captain, that's ten shillings above the rate; I suppose you know what you are doing'. 'Yes, yes', replied 'Pincher', 'he's worth it'. I do some mental arithmetic, and says to myself, 'That's another fiver for the voyage', simply by just speaking at the right moment.

'Join your ship at Cumberland Basin on May 17th 1883 at 2.30 pm' (Attwood). My sea chest and kit, including sea boots, are sent aboard. During this voyage I intend to keep a journal[122] so as to avoid, if possible, some of the fierce controversies arising out of events. Sailormen are very much prone to argument, and fellows like 'Bully Smith', if one did not agree with all they said, would soon start a row. [...] 'Uncle John' will be there, so that neither this bully nor the Second Mate will have their say always.

Sailing day. Glorious weather. [...] My ship looks spick and span. Many people are there to see a Guineaman depart. The crew are arriving,

---

[122] Held in Bristol City Library, 'Diary and Notebook of John Chandler Langdon, 1883–84'.

some just able to stagger aboard, while others are carried. 'What shall we do with a drunken sailor?' 'Put him in the long boat until he's sober.' Someone is calling, 'Jerry'. In an open carriage sits Mrs Pincher who, holding out her hand, says, 'Good-bye, Jerry, be a good lad and the Captain will make you a splendid sailorman'. I am just fit to bust. A Captain's wife condescending to speak to an ordinary seaman! All are aboard, save Smith, whose boarding-house master – ex-pugilist 'ticket-of-leave man' and now a cab-owner, has charged him ten shillings for driving him and his kit from the Broad Quay to Cumberland Basin. Smith won't pay and the other fellow won't part with his kit, so there's a row. The 'Bully' shows his mean spirit by challenging the 'ticket-of-leave man' to fight, well knowing that he dare not fight through his being on leave for manslaughter. Thus the skunk, Smith, was ever ready to take advantage of another fellow's helplessness. Without doubt, the ex-pugilist could have put Smith to sleep in a very short time.

Our pilot won't wait any longer. 'Can't help it, Captain, you must leave that fellow ashore, or we shall miss the tide.' 'Let go for'ard and aft' and away we go. I am secretly delighted that the cad had been left behind. 'I must get another man', says 'Pincher', 'or the Board of Trade will be on my track'. Among our powder runners are many able seamen – another case of taking advantage of a man's helplessness. 'Yes, at more than double wages, six pounds per month, with an early transfer to the first homeward-bounder.' One must be engaged. Articles are signed. As we proceed down the river, I am assisting David to get out the jib-boom and set up stays and back-ropes. At Pill 'Pincher' sings out, 'Jerry, take the wheel'. 'Aye, aye, Sir.' I relieve the pilot's steersman. 'Now Jerry', says 'Pincher', 'this is a quick steering ship, not like our last one, where you had to grind water before she would answer her helm'. Sure our ship was a beauty for steering. Save when boomed out, one spoke of the wheel would do the trick.

We are slowly towing down the Bristol Channel. Runners take from lighter and stow in our magazine sixty tons of gunpowder. 'Captain', says the Pilot, 'that tug-boat is signalling to come alongside'. 'Yes, I wonder what he's after?' replied 'Pincher', 'I hope it's not that fellow Smith, 'cos it will be a mix-up now that I've signed on another man'. This turned out to be correct and my delight had been very short-lived. 'Pincher' had to square the man signed on and Smith had to pay part out of his wages and also the tug-boat charges, so that in the end the miserable row with the boarding-house master cost him several pounds. Didn't we lads have many a chuckle over the affair!

Darkness is setting in and I am still at the wheel, drinking in the yarns 'Pincher' and the Pilot are spinning. Says the latter in a kind way, 'Captain, don't you think it was time this lad was relieved, he's been at the wheel over seven hours, and without grub?' 'Yes, I do', was his reply. 'I've told the mates to turn in for the night as the weather is so beautifully fine. I'll go for'ard and roust someone out.' 'Uncle John' was the only hand able to answer. 'Who's got the wheel, Captain?' 'Jerry, he's been at it a long spell without grub.' 'Oh, Jerry is my lad, I'll relieve him, Captain.' I hand over the wheel to 'Uncle John', giving the course 'follow the tug'. He can scarcely repeat the words, but I know 'Uncle' is doing his utmost to carry on. I just had time to get a snack where there came from the tug, 'What in the —— are you doing aboard there? D'ye want to go back to Bristol? Who have you got steering? Almost carried away your martingale'.[123] 'Uncle John' had fallen asleep over the wheel and the ship had got broadside to the tug. 'Jerry, come aft and take the wheel again.' 'Aye, aye, Sir.' And there I remain until well after midnight. Again 'Pincher' goes for'ard to ascertain if the fumes of drink had worn off. 'Uncle John' is again to the fore, his sleep had sobered him. Very soon he was on duty and I hand over the wheel to him, giving the course, which 'Uncle' can now repeat. 'Pincher' then says, 'Jerry, you turn in and don't turn out till six o'clock for anyone. Say that is my order'. 'Thank you, Sir.'

At six am I turn out. We have come abreast of Rat Island (Lundy), sea like a mill-pond. How different from my last two voyages in winter time with howling gales! The crew are now sober, but very thirsty. Oh, what would they not give for a livener, but it cannot be obtained so they are forced on the tea-pot or water-cask. The tug hauls alongside and takes off Pilot and runners. Sails are shaken out, the course set south and now begins the task of getting the ship into ship-shape order, with the crew suffering from fearful headache and thirst. David gives his commands in a decent way, with a sort of moral lesson on drink and the evils of life. The Second Mate, with his whiskers flopping about, is trying to bully the men to get a move on. I particularly note the absence of his usual vile cuss words. One can only presume that neither 'Pincher' nor David will allow it.

'Pincher', who is walking the poop-deck looking on, says, 'Jerry, come aft and take the wheel. You had a long spell at it yesterday, have another to-day while those fellows are hard at work getting the ship fixed up'. I stay at the wheel until late afternoon. Lundy fades from sight. 'Pincher', who is taking a good look at it, says, 'We shan't see Lundy again for a long time, Jerry'. 'No, Sir, the sailors do say "good-bye Lundy, good-bye Sunday".' 'What, you young beggar, do you mean to say I make you work on Sundays?' 'No, Sir, only when necessary, shipping oil to mail-boat or getting under weigh.' 'Ah, that's better. Some captains do make their men work on Sundays when on the coast, but I don't.'

---

[123] A martingale was a rope for guying down the jib-boom.

The mates select their men for watches. David lays his hand on my shoulder and says, 'This lad is mine'. I am so glad, feel sure from what I already know of him all will be well. He was without any doubt a splendid navigator and seaman and would save 'Pincher' much worry, and David was ever grateful to him for a berth at six pounds per month, while other unfortunate men holding Master's Tickets had to sail before the mast at fifty shillings. Why? Because of steamships. One would often hear, 'This will be my last voyage at sea, I shall give it up and go in steamboats'.

Save for a few incidents the outward voyage was almost a picnic. A few days out 'Pincher' shot a very large sun-fish of a size too great to haul aboard. On June 1st we passed Madeira and off Cape Verd[124] had an unusual squall. On June 8th it was my turn at wheel during afternoon watch. There was just a bit of black cloud to windward, which looked nothing, but there was something in it. All sail is set with yards braced and we bowled along at some eight to nine knots. The bit of black cloud developed into a terrific hailstorm and hurricane. It strikes the ship suddenly. All hands on deck! The various orders are fast and furious. Bang! Our mizzen gaff topsail, spanker and mizzen stay have parted. The loss of our aft sails causes the ship to pay off before the wind. In a tick, before the order was given, the helm was down so as to keep the ship up to the wind. The pitiless hail cuts one's face, yet only a few moments ago the hot sun was showering down its burning rays. Now it's like the North Sea blizzard of last voyage. It lasted only a few minutes, however, but quite long enough to capsize many a ship. I was relieved to put on dry clothes and attend to hail cuts. 'Pincher', I was told, was pleased that the helmsman did not lose himself when certain sails were carried away.

To recount the preparation for West Coast trade would be a repetition of my first voyage. The building up of trade-room and the watering of rum were duly carried out, and on June 25th land is sighted on the port-bow. In a few hours we are anchored at Grand Drewin, our first trading town. David, who did the navigation, had made landfall almost in a bee line – no asking other ships the time or bearings, he knew his work and did it.

We had not anchored very long ere a number of canoes put off from the shore. This time there is not any singing or showing off. I am somewhat perplexed about this for only recently one had been telling our lads, who are all new hands to the coast, what a reception we would get on the coast when we arrived. It seemed so strange and unusual, something certainly must have happened to these people. The canoes are alongside and 'Pincher' is at the gangway. King Quee and

[124] i.e. Cape Verde in modern Senegal.

his son 'Atto' are the first aboard and the rest follow, among them my
pals 'Booto', 'Dago' and 'Dabbery'. The salutation, I-U-Ka, with
snapping of fingers, is freely used. The last named is almost caressing.
'Our good Jerry come again to our country, he fita talk – teach – more
book.' 'Booto,' I say, 'what's the matter with your people, he no sing,
no make noise when white man come again your country?' 'Jerry,
Jerry, much trouble come our country since you went home over twelve
moons. Dem bad Sassandrew man make war, we finish all our powder,
some blow up dem bad men kill plenty our men, thief our women and
piccaninies. There must be witch somewhere. We talk you Jerry when
you keep anchor watch to-night.'

My first anchor watch was at 10 pm and in the meantime I had
gathered from conversation that on the following morning on board
our ship there was to be a great palaver concerning the question of
supplying only the Grand Drewin men with guns and powder, and
then giving the Sassandrew men the go by. A few minutes after
commencing my watch 'Booto' and his friends gather. 'Jerry', says he,
'we talk, tell us all you have done since we said good-bye at Half Jack,
also how the old ship was wrecked in the white rain (snow)'. That
glorious moonlight night almost skin to daylight, when my black friends
squatted around, their white sheets well tucked in for to them the night
was cold, will not readily be forgotten. I tell my story; they tell theirs,
about the war, and how the medicine and fetish men would attend the
coming palaver. 'Jerry,' says 'Booto', 'when we get big-men (rich) we
fita make you our blood-brother, then you be one of us'. Great Scott!
When I looked at the cabin clock I found that our chin-wag had taken
some four hours. The next watch was called and I turned in.

Soon after breakfast there was much commotion on the beach. A
good number of canoes were being hauled to the water's edge, ready
for launching. This great palaver was a big event for a number of
towns were involved in the war with the Sassandrew, and all of them
our trading towns, so big men from each, including the medicine and
fetish men, were attending and would have much to say at the palaver.
The canoes have cleared the surf and are now making toward our ship,
which they encircle three times, singing, chanting and showing off
really far better than on my first voyage. There is more fierceness in it
and at times their gestures with paddles are pointed toward the
Sassandrew country. One can easily visualise that they hope to make
mince-meat of their enemies; evidently the rum and gin taken ashore
yesterday must have gingered them up. I am glad of this because my
prestige with our lads had dropped owing to this matter. I heard
someone remark that that kid Jerry was right after all.

In the leading canoe sat King Quee and his son Atto under a canopy
in company with the medicine and fetish men. The latter are in their

best make-up, painted with different coloured pigments and smothered with charms, crowie shells[125] and palaver marks, i.e., small diamond cuts into their flesh which when healed leave deep indentations of various designs, thereby indicating how many palavers the wearer has attended. Some have their hair or wool plaited upwards, which give a semblance of horns – impressive and grand without doubt to their own fellows, but to us lads, most grotesque.

All this big crowd is on board and they are in a festive mood. I-U-Kas and snapping of fingers take place by the score. 'White man be our big friend, we bring plenty palm-wine, fruits and koker-nuts for him.' Yes, they did, but in drinking palm-wine our lads were beaten hands down. To them palavers are always boosey matches.

The big men are assembled on the poop-deck with King Quee as president and his son Atto acting as interpreter. A harangue lasting some hours follows in which everybody has much to say both in voice and gesture which would hurt many a Welsh orator. The essence of this long conflab, when boiled down, was that 'Pincher' was to supply the Grand Drewin people with the sinews of war at enhanced prices, but he must not under any pretence trade with Sassandrew (boycott). 'Pincher' refused this request saying that the last named had always been good tradesmen prompt in payment, and he would be asking for a peppering if he refused their trade. The Beraby men were already on his track for this punishment and he did not wish to create another enemy. His reply sets up a chorus of dissent. It was then very forcibly pointed out that he was already a blood-brother to them and to refuse would mean a worse punishment than peppering. In the end they may or would help themselves. Poor 'Pincher' was between the devil and the deep sea. But as he had become one of them there was no option so he had to do what his black brothers wished. To sign and seal the contract King Quee, who guaranteed safe payment, produced a manilla which was broken in the usual way, each retaining his respective half.

The way is now open for trade or trust and my brother and I have charge of the trade-room. Orders for guns and powder, gin, rum and tobacco top the lot. Day after day our decks are just like pandemonium, with the big-pots and little-pots buying or getting on trust the sinews of war.

---

[125] [sic]; cowrie shells. These were shells of *cypraea moneta* and *cypraea annulus* that were imported from the Indian Ocean and that had been used as a currency in West Africa for many centuries. These became particularly associated with the development of the palm oil trade, because of their use in paying for small quantities, and became increasingly prevalent in parts of West Africa (though less so the Windward Coast) during the nineteenth century in what came to be called the great cowrie inflation. M. Johnson, 'The cowrie currencies of West Africa, Part I', *Journal of African History*, 9 (1970), pp. 17–49 and 'Part II', *idem*, pp. 331–353; J. Hogendorn and M. Johnson, *The Shell Money of the Slave Trade* (Cambridge, 1986).

We finish our trading at Grand Drewin and then sail down the coast to our next two trading towns, Duke Walker and Kromwell, where almost the same scenes are enacted. The next two towns in our ordinary trade would be Sassandrew River and Treepo. The first named 'Pincher' has to give the go-by; the second is just outside the war zone, but 'Pincher' is afraid that being so near we may get a visit from the Sassandrew people, therefore he decides to pass by both towns. All is ready to slip past, we have the afternoon sea breeze, when almost ahead is sighted a number of large canoes that have put out from Sassandrew to intercept our passage. We head away from shore and I have charge of the wheel. The canoes are now astern and the men are paddling hard to overtake our ship. Bang! Bang! They are trying to pot up. 'Pincher', who is near, says, 'Jerry, don't be scared, I guess they can't catch this ship, she's the smartest sailor on the coast'. After a few parting shots they give up the chase and a few hours later we anchor at Kutrou, another trading town, then Frisco, Piccaninny Ho and Cape Lahou, our last trading town for trust.

Our stay at Cape Lahou lasted some eight weeks, during which time 'Chester' and another AB are transferred to a homeward-bounder. Poor 'Chester', the artist, 'reckless abandon', was ill most of the time, and the other fellow was a bully, but thanks to 'Uncle John' he and Smith were kept in their proper places. My log has already served some useful purpose in settling many a fierce argument caused by these two men. 'Good-bye, Chester' (a good man at heart). It was the last shake. The other fellow was given a post of Bos'un for the homeward voyage, and we heard later that he so ill-treated poor 'Chester' that soon after his arrival home he 'went west' at our Bristol Royal Infirmary. His, without a doubt, was a wasted life, and he was only twenty-seven years of age. But what of the other fellow! How often does one see and hear of those taken out of fo'c'sle becoming greater tyrants than those who have never lived for'ard.

We leave Cape Lahou for Half Jack. Cargo and provisions have to be delivered to ships belonging to our firm. There are a number of 'passengers' to be accounted for. I again catch sight of that big bleary-eyed monster William King who has some interest in our 'passengers'. Poor beggars, one can only guess what will happen to the girls of small stature. In carrying these poor wretched creatures we saw they were mostly boys and girls captured in bush raids, or girls who, perhaps through no fault of their own, had taken the wrong turning, and their value as wives would be nil, so were sold into slavery. Hence the splendid morals of the blacks, so often quoted as an example to we whites, became more a matter of cash than morals. They may be on board a week or more, and one can easily see that they are starving. I have on several occasions got scraps of food myself, making pretence of eating to show them it was not poisoned, but they would always with fear refuse to accept by gesture. Some Kroo-boy would remark, 'Him be damn bush nigger, him no eat white man's chop (food), him bery much fear witch (poison)'. Really their intelligence was far below the animal and in the event of a British gun-boat asking questions the reply would be that these people are passengers and were being carried for King or Headman So-and-So. During the voyage a grand palaver was held at Frisco by natives from Cape Coast Castle re this matter of bush raids and coast slavery, Dick Squire being in the Chair.

Our business here is soon completed and once again we are beating to windward[126] in due time arriving at Grand Drewin, where we get one of the greatest ovations I ever saw on the coast. Their joy was akin to madness, for during our absence they had, with our ammunition, just walked into the Sassandrew people and cut them up – from some of their yarns some were boiled or roasted – and having to pay so much attention to war, there is no oil ready, which makes 'Pincher' look very glum. Before we again left this town a deputation of headmen came up the coast from Treepo to inquire why 'Pincher' was not trading with them this voyage. He told them that their town was too near Sassandrew, to which they replied that the Sassandrew men dare not enter their territory, for if they did, it would mean war, which they – the Treepo people – would greatly welcome, if only just to wipe them off the map, and it would be an easy task in their now weak state. 'Pincher' swallowed all that was said, thinking perhaps that if the other fellows were wiped out there would be some balance of power on this part of the coast, and it would stabilise trade. So 'Pincher' promised to trade with them. He had made another silly mistake, for in the end it was found that these folk were simply acting on behalf of Sassandrew.

In due course we anchor at Treepo where a rousing welcome is accorded us. Manillas are broken and many orders are given for 'trust' – mostly guns and powder, which looks fishy. The reason given was that they wanted them in case the Sassandrew men cut up rough, but there was no doubt that they would be sold at enhanced value to Sassandrew. Towards late afternoon a canoe was sighted coming from the last named place and all our Kroo-boys, belonging as they did to Grand Drewin, are so agog with excitement and fear that they want to hop it at once. The Treepo men calm them, however, by saying, 'No fear, he no bite while we are aboard'. The canoe arrives and the occupants clamber up the side of the ship. At the sight of our Kroo-boys their knives are whipped out with fierce gestures, showing what they would like to do. Their headman holds them in hand and marching up to

---

[126] i.e. returning westwards along the coast, against the wind.

'Pincher' in an arrogant way says, 'What for Cappy you no trade with Sassandrew man?' 'Pincher', equally arrogant, says, 'That's my business; I suppose I can trade with whom I please without asking the likes of you'. 'No, Cappy, you can't; you always traded with us, and the Sassandrew man paid proper fit time. We know, Cappy, you be blood-brother to [...] Grand Drewin man, you let him have plenty guns and powder, he kill our people and now we want the same, we will fita pay you proper.' 'Get off my ship [...]', shouted 'Pincher'. 'Bery well Cappy, softly softly catchee monkey, we come again and then we make you sell.' They depart, telling our Kroo-boys that they would soon come again and cut their throats. This threat gets the wind up with the Kroo-boys who won't stay on the ship and request 'Pincher' to loan them the surf boat so that they could paddle to Kutrou and await our arrival. He does his best to calm them, 'Don't be cowards, they dare not touch you on an English ship, Sassandrew man only talk, me no fear him'. 'No, no, Cappy, we no stay on ship, we much savey Sassandrew man, him like big cat in bush, him jump when you no look.' So with several days' rations they depart, leaving only Dabbery the Cook's mate aboard.

That night, 27th September 1883, and the next day, 'Pincher' had treated the threats with ridicule, and supper being over, I hoisted the anchor lamp.[127] There is no moon, but a thick African mist. The lads in the fo'c'sle are playing cards and I am seated on the main hatch trying to play a concertina, while Dabbery, near by, is trying to make me talk 'book'. Suddenly, some fifty or more dark objects are seen standing on the starboard rail, with huge knives held between their teeth. For a moment they are all poised, then three fierce yells are given and, with the precision of training, they all simultaneously land on deck, one section making for the cabin and another for our fo'c'sle. Their gun muzzles are already pointed through the skylight and port-holes – in fact we are covered at all points. Dabbery, who spotted more quickly than I what was happening, makes a dash for the fo'c'sle and I follow. The poor kid has turned very pale, is cold and violently trembling. He is stowed under a bunk at once and some of the invaders entered and pinched our oilskins. As all our lads are new to the coast they cannot palaver (talk), but I could, however, and I addressed them thus, 'Now, now, you Sassandrew man, what for you come sailorman's house? He no say come (come in), spose he come you house, you no say come, you say clear out, I give you fum-fum (fight). It no be our palaver, go aft and see Cappy about it'. 'We want dem [...] Grand Drewin man, we fita proper cut him throat like bosilla' (pig). I get the

---

[127] A longer description of this incident was given by Langdon in 'Our bust up with the Nigger of Sassandrew River, West Coast of Africa, 1883–84'; typescript in Bristol City Library.

idea (Dabbery had not been spotted) and say, 'Oh, dem [...] bery much fear Sassandrew man, him run away in boat, say you much savey, like big cat in bush jump when you no look, and I (Jerry) think the same, you jump ship when we no look'. This sort of flattery pleased them and after more palaver our clothes which had been snatched from the doorway were returned.

But what is happening aft? They too are cornered at every point and 'Pincher', who is well armed, is holding a conflab through the cabin scuttle hatchway. Later the headmen are admitted and 'Pincher' is told that if he would sell they would pay, if not, they would take the ship, at the same time reminding him how their fathers took the schooner, mentioned in my first voyage. Again 'Pincher' was forced to knuckle under and manillas are broken for good faith and contracts made.

I receive orders to get an anchor lamp and open the trade-room. My brother has the many written orders which have to be made up at once, guns, powder, rum, gin and tobacco in the main. In the powder magazine, owing to want of air, it is difficult to keep our light burning, and several times it had to be taken out and snuffed. At last I discarded the lantern and choked the naked light between some kegs of gunpowder. 'Have a care', says Harry, 'this ship is a very bad roller'. 'Don't worry, old chappie', says I, 'we are not out of the wood yet. If the ship was blown up you and I and some fifty or sixty black niggers would go up too.' I make the suggestion of getting some loose powder, wetting it into paste and firing it right under the hatchway. It would make a good fizz and much smoke. Then I should rush on deck and say that the ship was going to blow up. Those black niggers would make a dash for their canoes and 'Pincher' could slip the cable and hop it. I wanted Harry to put the proposition to 'Pincher'. 'Not I', says he, 'he would call me a fool'. After several hours work in a stuffy atmosphere, for we were not allowed to uncover the hatch until all was ready for sending up, their wants are satisfied pro tem. Each tradesman has his goods, which he guards lest his pals steal a part, but they are not going to depart until daylight.

I was glad to be in the fresh air again. It is well past midnight and David has the deck. 'Jerry', says he, 'those fellows for'ard won't turn out for anchor watch. What shall we do?' 'Alright, Sir, you turn in and I'll keep the deck until morn. Our lads, like yourself, are not used to these black gentry.' So armed with a small hatchet under my coat I keep deck watch until 5.30 am. I take a squint around and all the fowls and a small pig have been killed. These fellows must have blood on their knives to spin a yarn at home, for they are such fearful liars and thieves. A cask of rice has been stoved in and the Sassandrew men are squatting about it in groups eating raw flesh and uncooked rice and washing it down with rum and water. The last named, I fear, will do the trick, and at times I chin-wag with them – they are on the war-path. After the feed they drop off to sleep, but Oh my! when the uncooked rice began to swell in their tummies many were downright ill. It must be remembered that chop (food) is always scarce with these people, and perhaps they had not had food for some time.

At daybreak they commence to pack their plunder (for such it was) into two large canoes and later take themselves off. With feelings of relief we watch them round a point of land, less than a quarter of a mile distant, and Dabbery, who had now left his hiding place, is watching too, when suddenly he uttered an exclamation of surprise, 'Quee, quee, look, look, mona (four) big canoes are coming. Dem Sassandrew man much savey. He hide him men all night'. Sure enough, four canoes have rounded the point and are making good speed towards our ship. Dabbery was right, they were hidden reserves held in readiness for a given signal. He was at once rushed off to another hiding place, the fore peak, and is given a supply of food and water. The black fellows are soon aboard and by some manoeuvre they seem to land on deck all together. With yells and curses (which need not be written) they shout, 'We want dem damn black nigger Drewin man'. Cut-throat gestures are made towards us and I have a feeling of cold water running down my back as a burly nigger has caught hold of David, who was sitting on the taffrail, and was shaking him, and to all appearances is about to plunge his knife into his heart. David did not turn a hair, but calmly looked the ruffian in the face till he loosened his hold, and the nigger said, 'Old white man no savey fear'. It was easy to see what their gag was, they wanted us to draw first blood. Well, if we had, I feel sure my story would not have been written. Their leaders are shouting to 'Pincher', 'We want trust, we fita pay you proper'. He has again to capitulate and the trade-room is opened, where orders are made up until sunset. More men arrive from Sassandrew, the Treepo men are fraternising with them, and all are clamouring to get their orders in for trust. In the late afternoon they depart, the unsuccessful ones hoping to place their orders on the following day, but 'Pincher' had had enough (and so had we), so that when it was dark, orders were given to hoist the anchor quietly (muffled wind-lass) and later during the night we drop it again at our next trading town, Kutrou, where orders are given to keep a sharp look-out for any suspicious canoes coming down the coast.

I heard that 'Pincher' had written a letter asking for protection to the Governor of Cape Coast Castle,[128] which would have to wait for

---

[128] The Governor in question would have been Sir Samuel Rowe, Governor of the Gold Coast and Lagos, 1881–1884. It was a belief among traders that Bristol ships in

posting until a mail-boat passed down. It must be understood that this part of the West Coast of Africa was at this period (1883) under no jurisdiction. Prior to the War of 1870 the French had claimed it and almost had it on their map, but after their defeat the English traders had a look in, and many of the older natives could even then 'parlez-vous'.[129] Only this year, for the first time since the War, several French schooners were trying to pick up the threads of their former trade.[130] It had put the wind up the English traders because they were so often told that the French-a-man gave much better value.

Next morning our Kroo-boys come aboard and are all agog with excitement. What they and Dabbery's people are going to do for us sailormen for stowing him away is to be great, but when they had heard the full story, of how the Sassandrew men had obtained a good supply of guns and powder, they are much concerned with regard to the danger, and say, 'Him will again chop our people up'. 'Cappy, too, our blood-brother, has broken his trust and promise. What will our people say?'

In due course we call at all our trading towns and beat to windward and make our third visit to Grand Drewin, where we let go the anchor just after sunrise. There is something in the air, for [...] many hours no notice was taken of our ship from the shore. Near mid-day there is a stir and bustle on the beach and several large canoes are launched, which are paddled many times round the ship, the occupants making a great noise, firing guns and making fearful gestures with their knives. All our men save the cooper and myself are given jobs aloft. They come aboard. King Quee, his son Atto and others make aft for 'Pincher' and another lot, brandishing knives, rush for'ard, where one tries the same trick on the cooper that was used on David. The poor fellow, much wanting in courage, just crumpled up; in fact, it took several

West Africa 'avoid the British colonies and settlements, preferring to trade with native states', allegedly because of a desire to avoid British regulations. The presence of pawns or 'passengers' on Langdon's voyages might confirm this; A. Swanzy, 'On trade in Western Africa with and without British protection', *Journal of the Society of Arts*, 22 (1874), pp. 48–87.

[129] This would refer to the Franco-Prussian war of 1870–1871. The French had been very active on the Ivory Coast in the 1830s and 1840s with the work of the naval officer Edouard Bouët-Willaumez. French garrisons had been established on the Ivory Coast in 1843; they were withdrawn following the Franco-Prussian war; E. Bouët-Willaumez, *Description nautique des côtes de l'Afrique Occidentale* (Paris, 1849).

[130] French traders had been prominent at Assinie and elsewhere on the Ivory Coast in the early part of the century and Robertson described their 'extensive trade' in 1819; Robertson, *Notes*, p. 96. Contrary to Langdon, Babington noted their presence in Grand Bassam and Assinie in the 1870s, 'Remarks on the general description of the trade', p. 249. The most prominent French firms in West Africa by the 1880s were Victor Régis of Victor et Louis Régis of Marseilles (taken over by Mantes Frères), and Cyprien Fabre of Augustin Fabre et fils of Marseilles.

hours before he regained consciousness. Aft a noisy palaver is taking place, in which 'Pincher' is told that he has broken his promise by selling guns and powder to the enemy, who had walked into them and sent a number of Drewin men west. The upshot was that a good big discount would have to be taken off the original contract. To this 'Pincher' had to consent and friendly relations are at once resumed. Atto makes a great speech with regard to our protection of Dabbery, and asks 'Pincher' to allow his men to be his guests the following Sunday. He ('Pincher') is on the horns of a dilemma, for to refuse would give offence, but what was the motive? Was it a trick to get at the ship? He stammered out a sort of excuse that perhaps his men would not like to go. 'Oh', replied Atto, 'I will ask them myself'. So coming for'ard says, 'Sailormen, I want to talk you. Sorry my men very much frighten the cooper, we only play. I ask Cabby to let you come my house next Sunday. He say you fear to come, we want to do you fit (well) for what you done for our Dabbery'. Needless to say we thanked him for the invitation. He then marched aft and says to 'Pincher', 'You men much glad to come my house. I do them proper fit'.

On Sunday, December 9th 1883, the Kroo-boys are dressed in their best, with bodies well greased so that they shone like a well polished boot. They have the surf-boat ready soon after breakfast and all save 'Uncle John' are going ashore; he, poor fellow, has had another attack of his old malady and can't move out of his bunk, but he is left quite comfy. We get a few words from 'Pincher', 'Men, I want you to be most careful not to give any offence. At 5 o'clock our flags will be hauled down and I shall expect you aboard at six. If they want you to stay later say you must obey my orders'. 'Aye, aye, Sir.'

Away we go, the Kroo-boys paddling with song through the surf up the top roller and in a tick they are overboard and the boat is pulled high and dry. All the world is there – big girls, little girls with skin well greased and painted – I-you, I-you-Kas, with finger snapping by the score. I have on a white jacket and trousers and I show Booto and Dabbery how we walk with our girls at home arm in arm, for which purpose two are selected, one on each side of me. Oh horror! The grease and paint have spoilt my nice white jacket, and we had to be presented to Royalty ere the day was out.

We arrive at Atto's house, or rather hut – bamboo, plastered over with mud. During the day I had a peculiar experience with this mud plaster. It was at Dabbery's Father's house where I saw a large beetle about the size of one's palm crawling up the wall, and with an umbrella I make a lunge at it. Great Scott! The umbrella went right through and to make up for the damage I promised the owner 'bora-bar-semmer' (one bar of soap). Palm wine and other refreshments are served by Atto's

wives. He then lent each of us an umbrella and appointed guides to
show us the sights. The first was the palm trees being felled down a
slope where about one quart of the wine would percolate into the
calabash in twenty-four hours. Our next visit was to some small bush
villages where I note that each has a very strong stockade and outside
of it all the filth is dumped, the bosilla (pigs) acting as scavengers. It is
fearfully hot and the sun is right overhead − no shade save that caused
by our very useful umbrellas.

We have dinner at Atto's house where each is given a mat about
the size of a tea-saucer to squat on. The viands were placed on the
ground and consisted of two large pots, one containing rice and the
other rather a mixture of fish, fowl and monkey stewed in palm oil.
The flesh of monkeys is considered a delicacy and is served to honoured
guests. Each guest is provided with a spoon only. The feast commenced
by Atto's taking the first spoonful, then all follow until the pots are
empty. I had often watched our Kroo-boys at meals and noted that
they used their hands only − and woe to him who took more than his
share! I must say that in this particular they were most fair − some
whites could learn a lesson from them. 'Bill and I do like duff-ends', so
the duff is cut in half. Our feast was washed down with palm wine
and the next adventure was our presentation to his great majesty
King Quee.

'I-you-Ka, I-you-Ka, old king live for ever' is the usual salutation at
these functions. The wizened old man is seated in state on piled packing
cases covered with leopard skins and his many wives are lined up on
each side, the youngest aged about 10, and the eldest I can't say what
age. I learnt during the ceremony that the head wife gave the younger
one a rough time with her tongue. The presentation consisted of
walking this lane of women and taking from the hand of King Quee a
tot of rum, he first taking a sip therefrom and in a peculiar way
squirting it through his teeth, a custom that the giver and receiver must
carry out, to omit which would be tantamount to saying that the stuff
was poisonous. If through health or fetish one does not want to drink,
the difficulty is overcome by just sipping, etc. I take my tot of rum
from the king, sip and squirt it through my teeth and say, 'I-you Ka,
old king live for ever'.

Our ship's flags are hauled down so we must soon get away, but one
of our number is out of action − Bill wants to stay ashore and marry
a black lady. 'Alright we will talk about it to-morrow, now get into the
boat.' 'Yes, when I've gone up the beach and kissed my girl', says Bill.
But into the boat was our orders and in he went and we get through
the heavy surf quite safely. Our watch on Bill being relaxed he is
overboard in a tick saying he was going to marry his black lady. We
must proceed for to get backwards into the surf would spell disaster.

We arrive at the ship and report Bill's amour. A message is sent ashore to the effect that he was to be sent off at once, even if he had to be triced up. But silly Billy, who became sobered by being dashed about in the surf, returned later in a very small canoe and it cost him out of his wages (via dash) fifteen shillings.

It was Christmas Day, and to amuse the Kroo-boys (and also myself) I make a large kite. 'What for you make', they ask. 'I make big bird go (pointing upwards) up, up.' A kite was much beyond their knowledge and they watch intently, asking many questions. The tassels and tail were a puzzle to them and they said, 'Him tassel be ears and monkey no go up tree with such a tail'. The kite is a great success and it flies splendidly. 'Quee, quee!' they exclaim, 'Dem Jerry got witch'. Such was their ignorance. Our cook has done us well, full and plenty with no waste. We sing carols, spin yarns, and talk about our last Christmas at the Cameroons, wondering how those poor Dutchmen fared in hospital. We then turn in and think of home and what sort of weather they are having. With us it is just roasting.

January 4th, 1884 has arrived. A homeward-bound mail-boat is near by. 'Pincher' has brought on the doctor to see 'Uncle John', and the verdict is that he must go home, for he wouldn't get better in this hot clime. We are so sorry to lose him, it's like going to our own funeral. Tenderly we place him on a hatch and take him aboard the mail-boat. 'Good-bye, you lads', says 'Uncle', 'you have been ever so kind to me'. With 'Uncle John's' absence our fo'c'sle will not be the same. He possessed a wonderful range of reason and, as before stated, when reason failed to settle a dispute his fists did the rest. He was a master at fisticuffs and used his fists, too, without malice, for after a scrap he would soon chum again with his late opponent. To me he was a councillor [sic] and a guide. How many laughs had we had with him. Even when the laugh was against him he would not get angry. Two such episodes are worth mentioning. 'Uncle John' was always the first out of his bunk when the kittle of coffee was served at 5.30 am. One particular morning 'Uncle' was spluttering with his coffee, 'Drat it, I forgot to wash the tea-leaves from my hook-pot'. Again and again we heard, 'Drat it' (for 'Uncle' was not a swearer), accompanied by the splutterings, and presently another fellow turns out, who, wanting a smoke, gets a light from the galley. Then 'Uncle John' discovers that he had left the cover off his hook-pot, and the pest of small cockroaches, which we had in abundance, had got in. So cockroach stew was a gag for many a day. Another incident was when 'Uncle John' and I are painting the outside of the cabin, which is a half-deck house with alley-ways each side. 'Pincher' is inside and I can hear from the haggle with the natives that he is buying gold and is about to test it with acid. To avoid the fumes and smell in the cabin he passes at arm's length through the port-hole the gold in the acid, at the same time well shaking it. 'Uncle' leaves his work, takes the vessel out of 'Pincher's' hand, and says, 'Throw it overboard, Sir?' 'No, no, you ——!' I was just in time to save the precious contents from being dumped overboard.

One Saturday evening we are having a sing-song, which continues after eight bells (8 pm). The whiskered Second Mate, in a very bullying way, gives orders for us to shut up and turn in, 'There's no singing on this ship after time', says he. 'Go to Jericho', was our reply. The next order came from 'Pincher' himself. 'Let go the second anchor.' 'What for?' we inquired, 'it's a moonlight night and the ship is not in danger'. 'Because you are singing after time and won't obey the Second Mate's orders, and I'll make you heave it up again Sunday morning.' 'Then, Sir', was our reply, 'if that's the case, we shan't do either'. 'What, what! You refuse duty! It's rank mutiny. I'll log the lot of you and bring it before the Board of Trade when we get to port.' That long whiskered bully, the Second Mate, is in his element and dancing around like a Red Indian and flourishing a hand-spike, says, 'Shall I make 'em do it, Sir?' 'No, no', replied 'Pincher', 'none of that on my ship'. After a parley 'Pincher' was told that those aft often carry on till past midnight with their sing-song and we never complained at being kept awake just because others were enjoying themselves, yet he refused us one hour, until two bells (9 o'clock).[131] I never knew 'Pincher' to be so diplomatic, he must have gauged the temper of his men. 'Oh', says he, 'if it's only an hour you want. You know, men, I must look after your health and see you get proper rest. You'll turn in at two bells.' 'Yes, Sir, we will.' 'Then have it', he says, 'and say no more about it'. 'Thank you, Sir', we replied.

Again we are beating to windward and are carrying several big men, Dick Squire of Frisco and other headmen are going to Sassandrew to adjudicate the boundary of the last-named and Grand Drewin. A truce has been arranged and this is to be some affair. The grand palaver will take three days. 'Pincher' has to attend to give evidence and Dick Squire will act as umpire. This very interesting man is well worth an introduction. When I served in the cabin I gathered much from his well balanced conversations, and for sagacity and fair dealing he was one of the best on the coast. In his appearance a streak of white blood could be traced. He was fully aware of the many shortcomings of his countrymen, the domination of fetish and medicine men and wiles of witchcraft and he also knew that if he attempted to introduce reform his life would be forfeit. His English was very good – how he acquired his good manners and breeding, I know not. He was, I may say, a blackman with the true instinct of a gentleman. For palavers or disputes

---

[131] i.e. 9 pm.

his services were much in demand, even by the officials at Cape Coast Castle. Such was the man whose help and knowledge 'Pincher' had solicited to get himself out of the fearful hash that he had already made with the Grand Drewin and Sassandrew people.

In due course we arrive at Sassandrew. Our Kroo-boys knew that if the palaver failed their number would be up, so they take themselves off in the surf-boat, this time Dabbery going with them. It's a joy day for the Sassandrew folk. 'Pincher', with the delegation, left the ship in royal state, with a fanfare of shouts and firing of flint-locks (guns). David is in charge and all day our decks are crowded with bare-backed savages coming and going, bringing palm-wine, rum, fruits and small presents for 'sailorman'. They over fraternise with us, with the result that at the end of the day the mixed drinks of palm wine and rum, and maybe some other drug as well, was too much for our lads. All save David and myself are drunk and very quarrelsome and all of us become involved in a scrap with each other. It was here that I saw the prowess of old David. 'Bully Smith' went for him and in a flash with one blow (an upper-cut), Smith was down and out. I thought what David must have been in his prime when on the packet-ships, or before he became a changed man. A moment after his knock-out blow, he is bending over Smith, saying, 'I am so sorry I forgot myself, but you made me do it'.

In the evening David says, 'Jerry, the men won't keep anchor watch to-night. I'll keep the deck until four bells (10 o'clock), then you take it until morning, and don't turn out to-morrow'. 'Aye, aye, Sir.' I keep my long night watch while most of my ship-mates, Smith is one of them, are lying about 'dead-ho', and to prevent the ill effects of moonshine and the early morning dews, which are almost as dangerous to health as the sun, I cover them over with sacks, and when they came to their senses they did indeed look a sorry lot. Smith had to keep his chin tied up for several days.

'Pincher' returned and said that the palaver was set, i.e., that justice had been done. I heard much about this conference from a native who was there. 'Pincher' did not talk much about it. I was told that after two days palavering or jabbering the boundary-line was fixed, and a broken manilla not being a sufficient pawn of good faith in this very big affair, a slave (human being) was placed on the boundary-line, severed in twain and the medicine men of each side taking a half. It is horrible to relate, but I was assured by my black boy's friends that it was true. They further said that the medicine men would make much money from this for years to come, for they would sell parts of the body for charms, etc.

A new shipmate has come aboard, transferred from another ship just arrived from home, and we call him Tom, for such was his name.

He was a well-known character on the coast. His mother, when alive, held a very responsible post in the family of our owners,[132] and I believe many a little 'king' had cause to bless her. His brother had risen from ship's boy to Captain and Trader, had offended the natives, got peppered and died. Tom's failing was drink. He would sell his very skin for it, but when he was sober one could not wish for a better fellow. One day he got an overdose – doped, I think – and was just mad-like. 'Put that fellow in irons', came the order from 'Pincher'. 'We can't do that to a shipmate', was our reply. But again the command was given, 'I will have that fellow placed in irons, and if you won't do it, I shall order the Kroo-boys to do so'. To avoid this deep insult, which would probably have ended in bloodshed, for without doubt we men were just full of indignation at such an un-white man's order, with strong imprecations directed towards 'Pincher', we overpower our shipmate and the hand-cuffs and anklets are on. Poor Tom is lashed to a stanchion, which makes him the more mad, and his fearful struggles to free himself will cause injury to himself. Even 'Pincher' had the 'wind-up', for Tom, whatever he may have been, was well known to our owners and some enquiry would sure to be made. 'What can I do with him?', asks 'Pincher'. 'Release him, and let his shipmates (whitemen) take care of him', was our reply. 'Do so', says 'Pincher', 'and I wish the fellow had never come aboard my ship'. Tom is therefore taken into the fo'c'sle and, with strong language, is told to turn in and keep quiet. I, Jerry, has to watch until he slumbers, and when I thought he was asleep I resumed duty on deck. Later I visit the fo'c'sle to see if all is OK and Great Scott! Tom is sitting on his sea chest, laughing and pointing to a fair sized pickle jar, says, 'I always had my eye on that. Thee thought I was asleep, but I wasn't'. The jar belonged to a curio hunter and contained a baby alligator, some small snakes and other funny things, covered with rum. We are in the soup for Tom is now very ill and has turned a peculiar colour. 'Pincher' must be told, but our difficulty lay in the fact that the rum in the jar had been pinched. He would be sure to ask questions. 'Jerry', asks someone, 'you're a good lad at explaining things, and the old man (the captain) must be told, so you go aft and spin him a yarn, but don't you let us down about that rum'. I wondered how the late George Washington would have felt, but I report to 'Pincher', and to my great surprise no questions were asked. I rather think that he, too, had the wind-up and said that Tom must be dosed at once, so from the medicine chest he pours out a stiff emetic. It had the desired effect, but it was a fortnight before Tom was back to duty.

It is now February 20th 1884, and we are again at Grand Drewin.

[132] i.e. R. & W. King.

HMS *Electro*, a small wooden clinker, built for a gun-boat, has come down the coast and anchored close to our ship. An officer comes aboard and says, 'Captain, I've been looking for your ship for some eight weeks or more, and have been in and out of the rivers and creeks from Cape Coast Castle to Cape Palmas'. 'Sorry', replied 'Pincher', 'you must have missed us when we were beating to windward for we got well south of the line on that journey'. 'Quite so', replied the officer, 'now according to your communication to the Governor, you have had some trouble with the natives'. 'Pincher' thereupon gives an account. 'Captain', says the officer, 'I can do nothing. This part of the coast is under no jurisdiction and the French have eyes on it. With that fact alone we have to be very careful what we do. If only one British subject had been killed by the Sassandrew people, there would have been justification for bombarding their town. But even if that were done, the beggars would not have suffered much, save the loss of some mud-huts, which they would re-build in a few days. They would hop off to the bush and have a good laugh at us. However, I will steam down to Sassandrew, get the headmen aboard if I can, and give them a reprimand and show them how our "dogs" (guns) can bark.' Later during the day we heard gun-firing from this direction, and the next time we were at this place the Sassandrew men had much to say, 'Dem big guns, him bite big rock, big tree, him be devil'.

We are working down the coast and owing to the unsettled state of the natives trade is very poor indeed. At Frisco the brig '*Agnes*' is anchored, and she looks smart and trim. The next time we were at this town this fair ship was on the beach, a wreck, for one night in swinging to the current, she fouled her anchor. This danger has to be closely watched by the man keeping anchor watch. The wreck is soon looted by thousands of natives. They say that everything that is washed up on their shore is theirs. I have a little yarn about this, and it happened at the same place. There was a small ten-ton cutter working close in shore, doing petty cash trade and natives, without canoes, will often swim the surf to do some small trade. The cutter belonged to the barque *Jane Lamb* (Captain S——).[133] Her size enables her to enter rivers and creeks where a big ship could not go. In fact, much small trade is often done by ships' boats during daylight – but, back to the ship at night! This cutter, with one white man in charge, proceeded

---

[133] It was common in the West African trade for larger ships to use a smaller cutter to collect small quanitities of produce from several different ports. This was particularly so in the river trade of the Niger Delta region, where a shallow bar at the river entrance could make access dangerous. The *Jane Lamb*, 303 tons, Capt. Rawlinson, arrived in Bristol from Antwerp in July 1883 with a cargo of coconuts for Cummins & Co. It is likely it would have unloaded a cargo of African produce at Antwerp before sailing for Bristol; *Customs Bills of Entry, Bill A*, 6 July 1883.

down the coast and the *Jane Lamb* would follow in a week or more to unload and reload the cutter with merchandise. A few days after the cutter had passed and was forgotten, toward sunset a small canoe approached out ship and in it were two natives and a nude white man. The natives are soon aboard. 'Dash, dash, cabby (pay, pay), we bring white man your ship'. It appears that the cutter had fouled her anchor the previous night, got into the surf and became a wreck. She was soon looted, and the man too robbed of his clothes. That evening he told us that he had that day walked sixteen miles of beach, and those —— black niggers would not give him a bite of food or a drop of water for fear of witchcraft. The dash to bring him from the shore was about fifteen shillings in goods. Needless to say we made him very welcome until his own ship arrived, and we lads rigged him out with clothes.

No mention has yet been made about work-up jobs (punishment). Bill, a young AB, for wanting to marry a black lady, was given the task of holystoning the jib-guys, seated in a bowline. I, for some petty offence, was put to scraping down the mizzenmast, standing on the gauntlings (a small wire rope from rigging to rigging) bare-footed. I had to hold on with one hand and scrape with the other. 'Pincher' took a delight in ordering these dangerous jobs to be done. I ask David if I might use a bos'un chair or a bowline. 'No, Jerry', said he, 'my orders are "from the gauntlings"'. 'Alright, Sir, I'll do it, but it's very dangerous, this ship is such a quick roller.' 'Yes, I know', he replied, 'but, lad, take care you don't come a cropper'. I was dealing with a humane man, who, like myself, had to obey orders. David and I were fairly chummy, so far as our rating would allow, and many a soft job he would give me. I would hear something like this. 'Jerry, there's not much doing to-day, get into a quiet corner and do some mending for me. I can't thread needles like I used to.' The dear old fellow, his wardrobe was very scant, he had fallen on evil times, and was for so long out of a berth, and besides there were some little birds in the nest at home. It was a delight to me to work for him, therefore I gave of my very best in mending, patching and making his clothes.

By accident I am in the soup. I had purchased some herrings for breakfast from some fisher boys returning at sunset, and, on my haunches, was cleaning them alongside a big up-turned cask. There were pigs aboard and Mr Pig snaps up one herring, so that's my breakfast gone. And methinks the pig from the opposite direction had the other one, and my paddy is up. Knife in hand I make a lunge at the pig and the ship, taking a heavy lurch, the point of the knife entered the hind part of the pig. Pig-like, he had much to say about it and yell followed yell. Silly, pig, for it cost him his life. 'Pincher', 'Pincher', what was he not going to do to me? 'There was a time, etc., yes, and there was a time when you would have swung from the yard-arm for that.

Mr Mate make this fellow, from six to six, polish the copper from stem to stern, swung in a bowline.' In vain I plead that it was an accident. The pig, to have a respectable death, was there and then killed, and orders were given that I was not to partake of any.

That night I have much to think about – the sharks, and 'Cockney's' feet on a former voyage. Somebody had to have this job and it was my wretched luck. It was jolly hard, seeing that I was hoping to give the boys a surprise for breakfast. When keeping watch, I look toward the shore. If only the people there were civilised I would dump a hatch overboard, chancing the sharks, drift ashore and then hop it. No, those black fellows would pinch my clothes and bring me back to the ship and demand a big dash. So I tell myself that 'Pincher' won't get all his own way. I've had my thinking cap on. I will not refuse to polish the copper, but I will refuse to sit in a bowline.

The next morning at six o'clock I had to turn to. My orders from David are to polish the copper. Nothing was said about using a bowline, so with an 'Aye, aye, Sir', I start the work slung in a bos'un chair. Very soon I am wet right up to my neck and when 'Pincher' makes his appearance on deck and sees me at work he's just boiling with rage. 'Mr Mate, didn't I tell you that that fellow was to sit in a bowline?' 'Yes, sir, but I didn't think you meant it.' 'Pincher' then tells his same old story. 'I'm captain of this ship and you, Mr Mate, must carry out my orders or there will be trouble.' David then looks over the ship's side and says, 'Jerry, you must sit in a bowline'. 'No, sir, I will not, and you may tell the captain.' The die is cast and I feel ever so much better. I will face the music, and do what he may, I will not sit in a bowline. I enter the fo'c'sle. 'Pincher' comes in with hand-cuffs. 'Are you going to polish the copper?' 'Yes, sir, but not in a bowline.' 'Then you refuse duty?' 'No, sir, I do not refuse to do my duty.' 'Hold out your hands!' 'I shan't, if you want to put those things on me, do it yourself, I shan't help you.' Then 'Pincher' suddenly tripped me over with his foot. I had kept my head so far but now it is the reverse and I go for him. Soon our shirts are in a very tattered state, and my head gets a bump on a sea chest, and I am winded. The darbies[134] are on and I am taken aft and chained to the wheel with anklets.

I feel my position very keenly and all through that wretched pig. Besides I was getting on so well. I had cut out and made a royal sail all on my own, and was rattling down the topmast rigging when this affair happened. Now I am being treated like a felon – biscuit and water for breakfast, and that sent by a blackman so that it makes me more defiant, and it hurts. 'Pincher' lays down the law relating to the terrible crime of my refusing duty. He always got the same answer.

---

[134] i.e. handcuffs.

'I've not refused duty, but I will not sit in a bowline. If Mr Shark came along I would have no chance.' 'Sharks or no sharks', says 'Pincher', 'if you won't obey my orders I will send you to the Consul[135] at Cape Coast Castle, and he will clap you in prison, and remember, Jerry, very few white men ever come out alive from a fever-stricken African prison'.

The Second Mate, too, had a try at persuasion, 'Don't be a fool, some captains would have had you keel-hauled (hauling a man under the ship's keel) for what you did'. David has nothing to say – at least not to me. I am in the open sun until dinner-time and 'Pincher's' temper has cooled a bit, and he now asks me round-a-bout questions. 'I didn't say how long I should keep you in a bowline', he said. I saw the point at once and said, 'If, sir, it's not your intention to keep me in a bowline all the time, I am ready to start the work'. In a tick he unlocks my shackles and I then make ready with bucket, sand and canvas, with bowline over the side. 'Pincher' stood watching and, holding up his hand says, 'Jerry, that will do, get about your other work, and say no more about it'. I am flabbergasted. Can it be true? It is. David, I believe, had a hand in it, although he never said so, but someone heard him telling 'Pincher' that it was risky for the man who had to do the work, and it was also risky to him who gave the order, and if anything happened he, 'Pincher', might lose his ticket. This, we all thought, did the trick, and I enter the fo'c'sle saying, 'Lads, I've a clean sheet. You have roast pork for dinner, and I too'.

Many incidents will occur on a long voyage which cannot be tabulated in general order, for instance, the sport of fishing. Most evenings, with the Kroo-boys, I would be fishing, with a line and several baited hooks. The fish at six or seven fathoms were most varied and plentiful and, like the natives, always seemed to be hungry. One would get a bite or two on the ground and more bites when hauling up. To haul up only one fish would be considered poor sport. Only two kinds of fish did the natives reject for food, but they are far from being fastidious, seeing that snakes, lizards and other funny things are eaten. But the devil fish, as they name it, is without scales, has a black and yellow colouring and scissor-shaped teeth which bite off the hook if not landed properly. With imprecations the native would inflate to a great size saying, 'Him devil, eat hook', and dumps it overboard, 'now go tell your brudder what blackman do you'. The other rejected fish was a sucker. Its under part was grooved like an India rubber mat and woe betide the fisherman if it caught the ship's side, for there it would suck, putting his line out of action. In daylight a native would dive down and pull off Mr Sucker, for the loss of hooks and line to them meant much. My strangest catch was a ribbon fish, two inches wide

---

[135] [sic], Governor.

and six feet in length. Shark hauls were many. One in particular I must mention. He was a ten-footer, and we had him well hooked in the upper jaw and he lashed the water furiously. We got a bowline on him and hoisted him on deck. 'Look out, lads, keep your distance.' It flopped and reared almost upright, lashing its tail about and pounding the deck. 'Pincher' was going to pot it with a shot to avoid injury to his men, but a Kroo-boy got in with a cut from a long-handled axe, near its tail. It was the most fierce I ever saw, and after the post-mortem the reason was apparent for a brood of little sharks was inside.

Two Kroo-boys had another tough fight with a young alligator which had got over the bar of a river and into the salt water. They chased it in a small canoe and with unerring aim plunged the harpoon home. Their next difficulty is to get it into the canoe. It lashed its tail and snapped its jaws. At the first chance given its eyes are gouged out and its throat cut. It measured six feet − a big feed for Kroo-boys. I was asked to partake, but declined; I also shied at eating alligator's eggs.

We once captured another man-eating fish, the great barracuda, the tiger of the sea. This monster is feared more than the shark and grows to a great size. It has the long jaw and similar teeth to the alligator. Amid the usual babble of noise the fish is sighted, and at once there is silence, the natives speaking only by gesture. It is difficult and dangerous to catch this monster because it is very wary and sometimes it will attack. The best harpooner, with another to paddle, creeps silently towards its tail end and a harpoon, some fifteen feet long without a line, finds its mark. For a moment it remains upright, then with a tremendous cheer from the natives the fish dives and reappears several times, the shaft of the harpoon showing its whereabouts. After a great fight it is hauled aboard and another big feast is partaken of. The flesh, when cooked, looks rather tempting, but I could not at any price relish a man-eater.

Endurance and apparent indifference to pain among the natives are very marked. It was not unusual to see them lance their own abcesses (and large ones too), in the groin, or amputate a toe when suffering from Jiggher worm. One would ask how's your bad toe and the reply would be, 'Him better, I cut him off myself'. It may be stated that prior to the operation they would dose themselves with kola nut[136] and many were addicted to its use. Another malady is the guinea worm, taken, I believe, in the drinking water.[137] This worm, they say, works its way through the body causing withered limbs, so that when it appears on the surface it is trained to continue its journey through a

---

[136] Kola nuts (the nuts of *cola acuminata* and *cola nitide*, both native to Africa) contain caffeine and are prized as a mild stimulant.

[137] Guinea worm, a common parasite in tropical regions, is transmitted by water and causes *dracunculis* in humans.

hollow reed or pipe stem and a cure may thus be effected. Undoubtedly the drinking water must contain the larva of many funny things. This fact was easily proved, for coast water, after being casked a few days or even months, when broached mosquitoes by the score would make for the open air through the bung hole. One is apt to ask the question with regard to the dreadful malaria whether or not Mr or Mrs Mosquito is not just as dangerous from within as from without.[138]

To show the immense trade carried on by Bristol ships on a strip of coast of about 200 miles, I have culled from my log the names of 27 vessels, from the largest of 500 tons to the smallest (the cutter *Auspicious*) of 50–60 tons.[139] This last small ship has just completed the voyage from home and it must have been a very jumpy trip, for when at anchor she bobs up and down like a cork. How the large casks of oil are hoisted inboard, I know not, but one must admire the crew's pluck to sail such a small vessel over thousands of ocean miles. Whether she ever made the tortuous voyage home or not, I don't know. Perhaps she became a wreck, like the small schooner *Cyprus* which recently fouled her anchor at Frisco. 'That's mine', said the natives. They were doing well – two shipwrecks in one year. These small ships carry only one or two white hands, the Kroo-boys make the casks and work the ship, therefore efficiency is much lacking.

List of Bristol ships

Barques	*Mohican, Sir Humphry Davy, Cerea, La Zingara, Watkins, Jane Lamb, Avonside, Echo, Beatrice, Mervyn, Ibis, Gift, Celoria, Laughing Water, Burnswark, Alanso, Bolivia, Valdivia.*
Barquentines	*Edmund Richardson, Elvira Camino, Flora de la Plata, Zizine.*
Brigs	*Agnes, Dauntless.*
Schooners	*Cyprus, Vanguard,* and
Cutter	*Auspicious.*

To the above must be added the well known names of the Captain Traders: Hampton, Cook, Swan, Pollyblank, Budd, Salmond, Jeffries, Golding, Venning, Tresise, Johnson, Hunt and Lawton.

[138] The connection between malaria and the mosquito by Sir Ronald Ross was not made until 1896–1897.

[139] Although these were typically-sized ships for the sailing ships of the West African trade in the first part of the nineteenth century, they were relatively small for this period, following the introduction of steamers into the trade in the 1850s. By 1880, the average ship in the West African trade was some 800 tons.

It had been my pleasure, when serving in the cabin, to listen to the yarns of most of these men, watch their carousals, and serve the liquid refreshment.

Much could be written with regard to the mannerisms of the Captain Trader – a class to themselves, and often spoken of as counter-jumpers. Say, is not our trade room a draper's shop, minus the shop-walker? We have muslins, calicoe, brocades, in name only, and heaps of other haberdashery on sale. I hear the men say, and I believe it, that some of these Captain Traders only knew enough navigation and seamanship to bring a ship to the coast, when they would complete their trade and return home by the mail-boat to buy cargo for the next voyage. Their own ships will return sometimes with only one navigator aboard holding a master mate's ticket. Hence the value of old David who had a master's ticket. These Captain Traders were very affected and used jaw-breaking words, which of course the common sailorman was supposed not to understand. One command to illustrate this is worth mentioning, because of its originality. 'Mr Mate, will you kindly see that the ship is systematically arranged and the men duly organised in their respective stations preparatory to putting the ship about.' Someone remarked that he must be barmy. Such pomposity towards sailormen was nauseous!

On June 23rd we were at Cape Lahou. HMS *Starling* (gunboat) had steamed up the coast and anchored for a few hours near our ship. The commander wanted to know if we had any more trouble with the natives, and he also discussed the question of the French traders creeping in, and the attitude of the natives towards them. Further, the annexation of this part of the coast by the French nation was almost sure to follow.[140] This, with the present bad trade and the expected loss on the voyage, has put 'Pincher' in a very bad way.

Again we are at Grand Drewin and are running down the coast for the last time, having been some fifteen months from home. Much trust has to go by default owing to the late war and the Frenchmen. Passengers (slaves) in lieu thereof are likewise scarce, they having already been sold for war expenses. It is going to be a very lean voyage and 'Pincher', I hear, is going to send the ship home under the command of David, while he himself will stay aboard another ship belonging to our owners. Once more he will run down the coast to collect, if possible, any further balance of trust overdue, and then return home by a mail-boat. But it is a question whether he will have any success. The Frenchy-a-man, says the native, gives better value and stronger rum.

[140] In 1886 the French re-asserted their presence on the Ivory Coast and commenced a piece-meal occupation of the territory, a process that culminated in the declaration of a French colony in 1893.

Our last trip down is completed and even after disposing of our few passengers at Half Jack the ship is not fully loaded. Awnings are taken down, boats got in board and our merry Kroo-boys have said I-You-Ka, which answers for good-bye or how d'ye do. 'Jerry', they said, 'you come again our country we fita work for you. When you be trader you talk us boys plenty book, we much thank you.' Booto is coming to see the white man's country, so that the cook will have a very soft job. David will be captain, the Second Mate with the whiskers will be First Mate, and bully Smith will live aft and become Bos'un. With the last two named we expect a warm time, unless of course David puts his foot down, but he can't always be on deck.

On September 5th 'Pincher' takes his quarters on another ship and two fresh hands are transferred to ours. With one real navigator aboard we dip our ensign to the ships at Half Jack bound for Queenstown[141] for orders. Some little mention may be given of the two new men. One was a Bristol lad, Charlie by name, who had just got his AB ticket, and was the son of a well known Bristol gentleman. Charlie had been apprenticed to a reputed firm of silk mercers in College Green and didn't like it so he hopped off to sea. He and I are at once great chums. The other lad came from the one and only town in the world – Birmingham, and would, if he could, have been a bully and also a prig. Watches are set and I am in the Whiskered Mate's watch. Some asking for information from other ships on our way home, the routine was similar to that of my first homeward voyage. David who was navigating could, so to speak, take a much better sight of the sun with a ham-bone than could the other so-called mate with a sextant, and we soon ran into the roaring forties. My afternoon watches below were spent aft, where David was teaching me my ABC in navigation.

As we sail further north Booto, who has not yet discarded his native costume, feels the cold and he must be attended to. 'Pincher' had left his spare wardrobe behind which had to be extended to fit the lad. I was successful with the clothes but when it came to the boots I was properly boxed up. Booto had some feet. So I made him a pair of half wellington canvas topped clogs, painted black. 'Oh, Jerry', says he, 'I so warm, and I thank you very much'. It was amusing to see the lad trying to dress himself in European clothes. The buttons gave him much trouble and I had to impress upon him the importance of having everything proper fast (secure).

We ran through the trades[142] and there have been a few rows between the Mates and men, generally during the night watches. One morning at four o'clock I took my turn at the wheel and the ship was running

141 i.e. Cobh, Co. Cork.
142 i.e. the south-east trade winds.

before a stiff breeze with a jumpy sea. The main and mizzen sails are boomed out and the compass card is very unsteady owing to the quick movement of the ship. Mr Whiskers quizzes his squinty eye into the binnacle and with a vile oath says, 'She's two points off her course'. 'No she's not', says I. 'What, you contradict me, a mate of this 'ere ship?' 'I do', was my reply, at the same time thinking that I was king of the castle by being in charge of the wheel and that he would not dare to strike, so I felt free to tell him off with some lip. His vile oaths still smarted and his whiskers were so tempting that I let rip. 'You, mate of this ship? You never were and never will be. You're more fit for a coal barge. The ship is not half a point off her course. The compass card is jumping and you know that your eyesight is so bad that you can't see the lubber point.' The mention of his eyesight did it. Bash! All the stars and planets are crowded into my eyes at once, and danger to the ship or not, I leave my hold of the wheel, jump on his foot and grab a good bunch of his whiskers with one hand, while with the other I punch somewhat blindly at his face. Again, it is an unequal scrap, for he is very heavy and muscular, while I am a lightweight stripling of eighteen. We clinch and I still retain my hold on his whiskers, but I am forced to release owing to intense pain for the brute had got his teeth into my hand and held on like a bull-dog. David, who was in his bunk, rushed on deck in his sleeping bags, he must have been roused by the whirl of an unattended wheel and the rattle of tiller chains and the peculiar motion of the ship when about to broach-to. His first act is to seize the fast revolving wheel and get the ship before the wind. Then he called the watch aft to separate the combatants, and with all my hurts, it was good to hear how David slated Mr Whiskers. 'You, an officer', said David, 'strike the helmsman with the ship boomed out? In another moment, if I had not caught the wheel, she would have broached-to, and it would have taken the masts out of her in a breeze like this.' 'But, sir', said Whiskers, 'he was so cheeky, said my eyesight was so bad that I could not see. And that I could not stand.' 'I don't care what he said', replied David, 'you, Mr Mate, have endangered the ship by striking the man at the wheel, and by doing so you have broken a hard and fast sea law. It would be my duty to log you for it, but, like myself, you have little ones at home. You may hear more of it yet, however.'

My injuries are dressed and I resume duties at daylight. I am ordered to paint the main truck and all the iron work on the main top mast, a most unusual command and very dangerous when fore and aft sails are boomed out. I see the gag. Perhaps he hopes I shall refuse and he will then get a set-off for the recent scrape. 'Aye, aye', says I, and up the rigging I go with a paint pot slung on my left wrist. Above the cross trees I have to shin up to the royal mast head, above which is five feet of bare mast pole, then the truck and above that the sky. I feel groggy – one of my eyes is bandaged and also one hand. I am almost blind for the other eye was also damaged. I shall skip the truck and paint downward. At eight bells I return to the deck, and am asked by Whiskers if I painted the main truck. I say to him that that was a funny question to ask when he saw me up there doing it. Really his sight was so bad that it was questionable if he could see the truck.

The men are very angry at the brute's biting my hand, for they too have had some hard cracks during the night watches with brutal officers. Dump him overboard from the braces, was their wish. 'No, no', says Charlie, 'Jerry has got a good case. I'll write out an account of the affair to be signed by Jerry and myself and he will hand it to the shipping master when we are paid off, and I will ask my people to take the matter in hand.'

Copy

Schooner *Edmund Richardson*

I, John Langdon, make this statement that whilst serving on-board the above named Schooner as ordinary seaman on a passage from Half Jaques W. C. Africa, to the United Kingdom was assaulted by the Chief-Officer Mr Parslow on the 2nd of October whilst at the ship's wheel during an altercation concerning the ship's course. He struck me a severe blow in the face and in attempting to protect myself he maliciously and wilfully bite me through the palm of hand in my catching hold of his hand to prevent myself from being thrown over the spindle of wheel. He called out for the Captain which brought to the scene H. Langdon my brother and Charles Bridgeman who took charge of the wheel.

This I can on my oath swear is a true statement.

Signed John Langdon
Witness Charles Bridgeman

Soon after this affair the Mate's manner entirely changed, and he was nice to everybody. He even enquired about my future, when was I going to start school for navigation and a host of other things. I knew he had wind of my intentions. Charlie's father may have a say. David, too, for obvious reasons, would much rather that no fuss was made about it, so that when it was my wheel during the night Mr Mate says, 'Jerry, I am sorry about that bust-up we had. If my sight was tested by the Board of Trade I should lose my ticket, and besides I have a wife and kids at home to work for.' The last did it. They would have to suffer if I tried to get him punished, so I told him that I would let bygones be bygones. 'Do you mean it, Jerry?' 'I do', I replied. 'Then', says he, 'give me your hand on it'. Which I did.

Every night when it is clear I note by the altitude of the North Star that we are getting more north, and calculate that we are forty-six degrees north. On November 5th I get two unforgettable experiences. It was in the early morn at wheel in fair weather when suddenly the whole of the horizon for a few seconds was illuminated with a reddish yellow glow. There was an explosion and then a fizz like a red-hot iron in water. An aerolite had fallen! Very appropriate on that day. The next experience happened on our first night watch below. We were so comfy when we heard, 'All hands on deck!' and the ship had to be heaved-to with only the fore-lower topsail and storm-stay sail. A north-wester is on us, and, just my luck, I am the one who has to stow the jib, the most dangerous sail on a ship. Every time she puts her nose into the sea we fellows out on the jibboom get a ducking, and when, after stowing, we were getting inboard, a sea completely covered me. Needless I held on to the forestay like – yes, you know ――, and holding my breath until the ship lifted on the next wave, took a jump aboard. It was four o'clock next morning before we again went below.

Land ho! Queenstown. David the navigator had made land-fall almost in a bee-line, and not once had we sighted land nor asked our bearings, neither did he take a deep sea sounding. So different from 'Pincher' who kept the men swinging the deep sea lead day after day. Bum-boats and the main deck has become a slop-shop. Free drinks are given and when it has done its foul work, fancy prices are charged for the rubbish sold. Silly sailormen. David, who will have to write the docket therefore, will get a good commission, so the silly fellows are done at each end.

Someone has to go ashore for orders and for obvious reasons David must not. He had fallen on evil times at Queenstown. The acting Mate cannot be trusted, for he may get on the beer, and the Bos'un can neither read nor write, so the Cook has to go in a shore-boat. After some hours he returned saying that our orders were for Bristol. The bum-boats are therefore cleared from the ship. They in the meantime had smuggled beer aboard, our lads paying for it with curios. Free drinks at beginning, fancy price at end.

Sails are set for home. Bally-Cotten[143] is passed. The wind heads us and we beat for Lundy, pick up a Bristol pilot later and at early morning anchor off Barry Island. Save getting the anchor up the tug did the rest.[144] The last turn at the wheel fell to myself. At Pill I hand

---

[143] i.e. Ballycotton, Co. Cork.

[144] The *Edmund Richardson*, 291 tons, Capt. Cummins, arrived in Bristol from 'Cape Lahore' on 24 November, with a cargo of 551 casks of palm oil and 10,000 coconuts for R. & W. King, *Customs Bills of Entry, Bill A*, 25 November 1884.

over the wheel to the pilot's river steersman, who says, 'Old chappie, you've been at this wheel a long time, I gave her over to you when she started the voyage, now you hand her back to me'. 'Yes', I replied, 'I've had a good many months standing on these wheel gratings'. It was my last turn at steering a ship, and, like my last day at school, I did not know it. My intention was to apply for my AB's ticket, get away south before winter, then work up for a Mate's ticket. But the fates willed it otherwise. [...] It was all for the best. My coming pay-day was a good one and from the same I apprenticed myself to a craft.[145] Thus ended the seafaring of Jerry.

One day, a few years after I had settled down to shore life, I met 'Pincher' and our conversation turned to this particular voyage. 'Did you', I ask, 'ever get in the whole of the trust?' 'No', he replied, 'the French soon after annexed that part of the coast, which helped the natives to repudiate their English debts.[146] That voyage was a loss to the owners of some two thousand pounds. Now our trade from ship-board is gone for ever. I haven't a ship now, but I have a shack and store at Grand Drewin. At present I am home buying goods. How nice it would have been if you, Jerry, had stuck with me and become a trader. I could have spent much more time at home, by having someone I myself had trained able to take charge out there.'

It was the last time I saw him. A few months later I read his obituary, 'At Grand Drewin, West Coast of Africa, aged 42'. It was said that he was poisoned. Probably he was.

Fifty years are nearly past since these happenings. Kind folk then said I was very foolish to give up such a promising career. It was putting the clock back, shore life would be irksome. So it was at first, and so different from the life I had left behind. Get on or get off was now more intense than ever. At the same time I was careful not to get the other fellow off. My few years at sea had given me good physical health and an energy much above my fellows. The foundations of healthy manhood were well laid. I was years behind my fellow craftsmen, for they had already served their seven years of apprenticeship, and I was to serve only three years. Within me was the will to be a first-class journeyman at the end of my time. I did it, although obstacles were sometimes placed across my path. I had learnt to hold my own on a fair basis, to do my bit, and a bit more if required, taking no notice whatever of what the other fellows may say. I and only I had to steer my own ship [...].

---

[145] i.e. bookbinding.
[146] 1886–1893.

INDEX